6/23/98

Money, Credit, and Capital

BOOKS BY JAMES TOBIN

(With Seymour E. Harris, Carl Kaysen, and Francis X. Sutton) *The American Business Creed,* Cambridge, MA: Harvard University Press, 1956.

National Economic Policy (essays), New Haven: Yale University Press, May 1966.

Ed. (with D. Hester), *Risk Aversion and Portfolio Choice,* Cowles Foundation Monograph No. 19, New York: J. Wiley & Sons, 1967.

Ed. (with D. Hester), *Studies of Portfolio Behavior,* Cowles Foundation Monograph No. 20, New York: J. Wiley & Sons, 1967.

Ed. (with D. Hester), *Financial Markets and Economic Activity,* Cowles Foundation Monograph No. 21, New York: J. Wiley & Sons, 1967.

(With W. Allen Wallis), *Welfare Programs: An Economic Appraisal,* Washington, DC: American Enterprise Institute for Public Policy Research, 1968.

Essays in Economics: Vol. 1. Macroeconomics, Chicago: Markham Publishing Company, 1971. Republished, Cambridge, MA: MIT Press, 1987.

The New Economics One Decade Older, Princeton: Princeton University Press, 1974.

Essays in Economics: Vol. 2. Consumption and Econometrics, Amsterdam: North-Holland Publishing Company, 1975. Republished, Cambridge MA: MIT Press, 1987.

Asset Accumulation and Economic Activity, Oxford: Basil Blackwell, and Chicago: University of Chicago Press, 1980.

Essays in Economics: Vol. 3. Theory and Policy, Cambridge, MA: MIT Press, 1982.

Ed., *Macroeconomics Prices & Quantities* (Essays in Memory of Arthur M. Okun), Washington, DC: The Brookings Institution, 1983.

Policies for Prosperity: Essays in a Keynesian Mode, Brighton, Sussex, England: Wheatsheaf Books, and Cambridge, MA: MIT Press, 1987.

Ed. (with Murray Weidenbaum), *Two Revolutions in Economic Theory: The First Economic Reports of Presidents Kennedy and Reagan,* Cambridge, MA: MIT Press, 1988.

Essays In Economics: Vol. 4. National and International, Cambridge, MA: MIT Press, 1996.

Full Employment and Growth; Further Keynesian Essays on Policy, Cheltenham, UK: Edward Elgar, 1996.

Money, Credit, and Capital

James Tobin
Yale University

with the collaboration of
Stephen S. Golub
Swarthmore College

Irwin
McGraw-Hill

Boston, Massachusetts   Burr Ridge, Illinois   Dubuque, Iowa
Madison, Wisconsin   New York, New York   San Francisco, California
St. Louis, Missouri

Irwin/McGraw-Hill

A Division of The **McGraw-Hill** Companies

MONEY, CREDIT, AND CAPITAL

This book is printed on acid-free paper.

1 2 3 4 5 6 7 8 9 FGR FGR 9 0 0 9 8 7

ISBN 0-07-065336-4

This book was set in Times Roman by Publication Services.
The editors were Lucille Sutton and Curt Berkowitz;
the production supervisor was Richard A. Ausburn.
The cover was designed by Carla Bauer.
Cover painting: Quentin Metsys, The Money-Lender and His Wife, *Louvre, Paris, France (Courtesy of Eric Lessing / Art Resources, NY).*
Project supervision was done by Publication Services.
Quebecor Printing / Fairfield was printer and binder.

Library of Congress Cataloging-in-Publication Data

Tobin, James
    Money, credit, and capital / James Tobin with the collaboration of
Stephen S. Golub.
        p.   cm. – (McGraw-Hill advanced series in economics)
    Includes bibliographical references and index.
    ISBN 0-07-065336-4
    1. Money.   2. Capital.   3. Credit.   I. Golub, Stephen S.
II. Title.   III. Series.
HG221.T594 1998
332.4–dc21   97-3766

http://www.mhhe.com

ABOUT THE AUTHORS

JAMES TOBIN is Sterling Professor of Economics Emeritus at Yale University. He joined the Yale faculty in 1950 and formally retired in 1988.

Tobin was born in Champaign, Illinois, and attended the University High School in Urbana. He was graduated from Harvard College summa cum laude in 1939. His economics graduate study was interrupted by World War II; he served in the U.S. Navy as a destroyer officer in 1942–1946. He received his Ph.D. in economics from Harvard in 1947 and studied on a postdoctoral fellowship at Harvard and Cambridge England the next three years. In 1961–1962, on leave from Yale, he was a Member of the Council of Economic Advisers to President Kennedy in Washington, D. C.

In 1955, the American Economic Association awarded him the John Bates Clark medal for an economist under 40 years of age. He was elected to the National Academy of Sciences in 1972. In 1981 he received the Prize in Economic Science established by the Bank of Sweden in Memory of Alfred Nobel. He is author or editor of sixteen books and more than four hundred articles. His main subjects have been macroeconomics; monetary theory and policy; fiscal policy and public finance; consumption, saving, and investment; unemployment and inflation; portfolio choice and asset markets; econometrics; inequality and poverty. He has written for the general public as well as for professional readers.

He and his wife Betty celebrated their fiftieth wedding anniversary in 1996 in northern Wisconsin, where they were married and spend their summers. They have four children and three grandchildren. The family likes tennis, chess, sailing, fishing, canoeing, skiing, and seeing the world.

STEPHEN S. GOLUB was born in Chicago in 1953, and, as the son of two artists, grew up in Paris and New York. He graduated from Williams College in 1974 and obtained his Ph.D. from Yale in 1983, under the supervision of James Tobin. He first became acquainted with an early draft of *Money, Credit, and Capital* in Tobin's graduate course, Money and Banking, in 1976.

He has taught at Swarthmore College since 1981, where he is currently professor and chairman of the Economics Department. He previously worked at the U. S. Department of the Treasury and the Federal Reserve Board. He has held visiting positions at Columbia, Yale, and the University of California at Berkeley, and consulted for several organizations, including the International Monetary Fund and the Organization for Economic Cooperation and Development. He has written a number of articles in the area of international trade and finance on such topics as exchange-rate determination, international portfolio diversification, trade balances, and the effects of international differences in labor costs on trade patterns.

Steve is married to Kit Raven, a martial arts teacher and recreation director, and they have two daughters, Zoe and Celeste, ages 4 and 5. In addition to playing with his daughters, Steve's hobbies are playing soccer and swimming.

To
Our wives, Betty and Kit,
with love and appreciation.

CONTENTS IN BRIEF

1   National Wealth and Individual Wealth   1

2   Properties of Assets   9

3   Portfolio Selection with Predictable Assets, with Application to the Demand for Money   31

4   Portfolio Selection with Imperfectly Predictable Assets   60

5   Portfolio Balance: Currency, Capital, and Loans   101

6   Financial Markets and Asset Prices   146

7   The Banking Firm: A Simple Model   170

8   The Monetary and Banking System of the United States: History and Institutions   205

9   The Monetary and Banking System of the United States: Analytic Description   232

10   Money and Government Debt in a General Equilibrium Framework   263

References   293

Name Index   301

Index   305

TABLE OF CONTENTS

Preface   xxiii

Introduction   xxv

1   National Wealth and Individual Wealth   1

2   Properties of Assets   9

  2.1   Asset Properties and Investor Attitudes   9

  2.2   Liquidity   12

  2.3   Reversibility   14

  2.4   Divisibility   15

  2.5   Predictability   16

  2.6   Yield and Return   20

  2.7   Predictability of Real Values and Real Returns   23

  2.8   Acceptability in Exchange   26

  Appendix 2A: Asset Prices, Yields, and Returns   28

3   Portfolio Selection with Predictable Assets, with Application to the Demand for Money   31

  3.1   The Role of Liquidity in Portfolio Choice   31

    3.1.1   Perfect Asset Markets   31

    3.1.2   Imperfect Asset Markets   32

      3.1.2.1 The frequency of portfolio shifts and investment decisions / 3.1.2.2 Effects of timing of accumulation goals / 3.1.2.3 Liquidity preference: Diversification for mixed and uncertain target dates

  3.2   The Demand for Money   39

    3.2.1   Transactions and Cash Requirements   39

      3.2.1.1 Transactions on income account and asset exchanges / 3.2.1.2 The working balance 3.2.1.3 The demand for working balances

    3.2.2   The Share of Cash in Working Balances   46

      3.2.2.1 A model of the transactions demand for money / 3.2.2.2 Digression applying the model to the currency versus deposits choice / 3.2.2.3 Uncertainty and precautionary demand / 3.2.2.4 The quantity theory of money

3.2.3   Working Balances and Cash in the Permanent Portfolio   54
3.2.3.1 The transactions motive / 3.2.3.2 The investment motive

3.2.4   Financial Innovation and Liberalization   58

4   Portfolio Selection with Imperfectly Predictable Assets   60

4.1   The Ranking of Uncertain Prospects   61
4.1.1   Preferences Concerning Risks and Expectations of Return   61
4.1.2   Maximization of Expected Utility   62
4.1.3   Characterizing Risk Aversion   67

4.2   Mean-Variance Analysis   69
4.2.1   The Measurement of Risk as Standard Deviation of Return   69
4.2.2   Indifference Curves and Budget Constraints   71
4.2.2.1 Risk-expectation indifference curves—loci of constant expected utility / 4.2.2.2 Opportunities for expectation and risk / 4.2.2.3 Optimal portfolio choices

4.3   The Separation Theorem   89
4.4   Multiperiod Investment   91
4.4.1   Portfolio Choice with a Single Future Consumption Date   91
4.4.2   Modeling Multiperiod Portfolio Choice   94
4.4.3   Sequential Portfolio Decisions   96
4.4.4   Multiperiod Consumption and Portfolio Choice   97

Appendix 4A: Measures of Risk Aversion   98

5   Portfolio Balance: Currency, Capital, and Loans   101

5.1   Portfolio Balance in a Two-Asset Economy   102
5.2   Capital Market Equilibrium with Two Assets   105
5.3   The Loan Market   107
5.4   Analysis of the Loan Market: First Approximation   109
5.4.1   Borrowers   109
5.4.2   Lenders   113
5.4.3   Market Equilibrium: Return on Capital as Equilibrator   114
5.4.4   Market Equilibrium: Financial Market Value of Capital as Equilibrator   116

5.5   The Loan Market: Second Approximation, a Model with No Currency   117
5.5.1   Default Risk and Credit Limits   118

5.5.2 Lenders 119

5.5.3 Borrowers 122

5.5.4 Market Equilibrium with No Currency 124

5.6 Market Equilibrium with Currency, Loans, and Capital: Second Approximation 126

5.7 The Monetization of Capital 129

Appendix 5A: Algebra of Lenders' and Borrowers' Portfolios 130

Appendix 5B: Marketwide Constraints 133

Appendix 5C: Asset Market Equations 133

Appendix 5D: Asset Statistics 134

Sources of Data for Tables 5.1 and 5.2 and Figures 5.14, 5.15, 5.16, and 5.17 141

6 Financial Markets and Asset Prices 146

6.1 Valuations of Capital Assets and the q Ratio 147

6.1.1 New and Used Goods 147

6.1.2 Business and Corporate Capital 147

6.1.3 A Stock-Flow Model of Investment and q 153

6.1.4 The Saving-Investment Nexus 155

6.2 Capital Asset Pricing 156

6.2.1 The Capital Asset Pricing Model 156

6.2.2 Extensions of the CAPM 157

6.2.3 Critical Assessment of CAPM and Its Extensions 157

6.3 A "Fundamentals" Approach to Asset Values 159

6.4 Financial Markets in Practice 161

6.4.1 Fundamentals and Bubbles 161

6.4.2 The Asset Menu 164

Conclusion 165

Appendix 6A

6A.1 The Separation Theorem Again 166

6A.2 Market Clearing and the CAPM 168

7 The Banking Firm: A Simple Model 170

7.1 The Portfolio Choices of a Bank 171

7.2 The Bank's Deposits 172

7.3 Bank Portfolios and Profits 174

7.3.1 Penalties for Negative Defensive Position 176

7.3.2 The Value and Cost of Equity 179

7.3.3 The Value and Cost of Deposits 179

7.3.4 Unrestricted Competition for Deposits 180

7.4 Uncertainty about Deposits   181
    7.4.1 The Function of Reserves and Defensive Assets   181
    7.4.2 The Portfolio that Maximizes Expected Profit   182
    7.4.3 Effects of Uncertainty   185
    7.4.4 Value and Cost of Deposits   189

7.5 The Bank's Response to External Changes   191
    7.5.1 Exogenous Changes in Expected Deposits   191
    7.5.2 Other Changes in Available Funds   193
    7.5.3 The Yield of Defensive Assets   193
    7.5.4 Penalties for Negative Defensive Position   193
    7.5.5 Required Reserve Ratio   194

7.6 Retention of Deposits   195

7.7 Risk Neutrality or Risk Aversion?   196

7.8 Concluding Remarks   197

Appendix 7A: Certainty about Deposits   198
    7A.1 Deposits Exogenous and Costless   198
    7A.2 Deposits Exogenous at a Given Cost   200
    7A.3 Deposits Endogenous   200

Appendix 7B: Uncertainty about Deposits   202
    7B.1 Deposits Exogenous but Random   202
    7B.2 Deposits Endogenous and Stochastic   203

8   The Monetary and Banking System of the United States: History and Institutions   205

    8.1 Banking in the United States Today   206

    8.2 A Quick History of U.S. Banking   206

    8.3 Banking Panics   208

    8.4 The Federal Reserve Act of 1913   210

    8.5 The Great Depression and the Banking Crisis of 1932–1933   211

    8.6 The Banking and Financial Reforms of the 1930s   212

    8.7 Gold and Silver in the U.S. Monetary System   213

    8.8 The Bretton Woods System, 1945–1971   216

    8.9 Federal Debt, Banks, and Money   217

    8.10 Monetary Control and Debt Management   221

    8.11 The Supply of Bank Reserves   222

    8.12 Sources of Changes in Supplies of Banks' Total Reserves   225

    8.13 Monetary Policy Operations and Targets   229

9   The Monetary and Banking System of the United States: Analytic Description   232

   9.1 The Money Multiplier   232

       9.1.1 Currency versus Deposits   233

       9.1.2 Relation of Deposits to the Reserve Base   234

   9.2 Secondary Reserves   239

   9.3 Composition of Banks' Defensive Position: No Federal Funds Market   244

   9.4 The Federal Funds Market   249

   9.5 The Banking System's Defensive Position   256

   9.6 The Demand for Bank Deposits   258

   9.7 Equilibrium in the Money Market   260

10   Money and Government Debt in a General Equilibrium Framework   263

   Introduction   263

   10.1 Does Government Financial Policy Matter?   265

       10.1.1 Monetary Policy   265

       10.1.2 Deficit Finance   266

   10.2 General Equilibrium Models of the Capital Account   269

       10.2.1 Two Interpretations of a Money-Capital Economy   271

       10.2.2 Accounting Framework   276

       10.2.3 The Analytical Framework   276

            10.2.3.1 A money-securities-capital economy

            10.2.3.2 An extended model

   10.3 Monetary Policies and the Economy   284

       10.3.1 Open-Market Operations   284

       10.3.2 Foreign Exchange Market Intervention   286

       10.3.3 The Central Bank Discount Rate   287

       10.3.4 Changes in Required Reserve Ratios   289

   10.4 Summary   290

References   293

Name Index   301

Index   305

FIGURES

Figure 2.1	Liquidity—perfect and imperfect.	12
Figure 2.2	Predictability illustrated.	18
Figure 2.3	Yield and appreciation.	22
Figure 2.4	Real stock prices and the purchasing power of money 1950–1992.	25
Figure 3.1	Two-period investment opportunities.	36
Figure 3.2	Investment and consumption choices: Two special cases.	37
Figure 3.3	Prospective receipts, expenditures, wealth determination of working balance.	42
Figure 3.4	Time path of working balance, cash, and time deposits.	48
Figure 3.5	Precautionary demand for liquidity.	52
Figure 3.6	Precautionary balance decreases with variance.	53
Figure 3.7	Precautionary balance increases with variance.	53
Figure 4.1	Alternative schedules of utility of return.	66
Figure 4.2	Indifference curves in expected return (μ) and standard deviation (σ).	72
Figure 4.3	Return and risk for various assets and portfolios.	76
Figure 4.4	Efficiency locus in a currency-capital economy.	77
Figure 4.5	Opportunity loci for alternative assumptions about correlation.	79
Figure 4.6	Efficiency locus with three assets.	80
Figure 4.7	Portfolio shares and efficiency locus for a three-asset economy.	82
Figure 4.8	U.S. private holdings of foreign assets, in percent of U.S. domestic asset supplies.	84
Figure 4.9	Foreign private holdings of U.S. assets, in percent of U.S. domestic asset supplies.	85
Figure 4.10	Choices of extreme points.	87
Figure 4.11	Choices of intermediate points.	88
Figure 4.12	Income and substitution effects of a shift in the efficiency locus.	89
Figure 4.13	Efficiency locus with a riskless asset.	90

Figure 4.14   Efficiency locus when borrowing and lending rates are different.   91

Figure 5.1   Portfolio balance with two assets.   105

Figure 5.2   Equilibrium for a risk-averse borrower.   110

Figure 5.3   Risk-seeking borrower; nonzero risk on currency.   112

Figure 5.4   Different borrowing and lending rates.   114

Figure 5.5   Portfolio balance with currency, capital, and loans.   115

Figure 5.6   Effects of an endogenous loan interest rate.   117

Figure 5.7   Portfolio return with endogenous loan default risk.   120

Figure 5.8   Lenders' portfolio choice as function of credit limit and interest rate.   122

Figure 5.9   Returns to borrowers.   123

Figure 5.10   Derivation of the loan supply curve.   124

Figure 5.11   Equilibrium loan rates and credit lines.   125

Figure 5.12   Portfolio return with three assets and endogenous default risk.   127

Figure 5.13   Separating equilibrium with three assets.   128

Figure 5.14   Net monetary assets and monetized capital as shares of gross monetary assets.   136

Figure 5.15   Monetary assets and private wealth.   138

Figure 5.16   Monetized capital relative to private wealth.   139

Figure 5.17   M2/GMA.   140

Figure 6.1 q ratio, 1900–1995.   152

Figure 6.2   The stock demand for capital and the flow supply of new capital.   153

Figure 6.3   Adjustment to a rise in the stock demand for capital.   155

Figure 7.1   Schematic representation of bank balance sheet.   173

Figure 7.2   Loans, required reserves, and disposable assets in relation to deposits.   175

Figure 7.3   Maximizing net revenue from loans and defensive position.   176

Figure 7.4   (*a*) Maximizing net revenue, given penalty interest for borrowing; (*b*) Maximizing net revenue, given penalty interest and fixed cost; (*c*) Maximizing net revenue, corner solution.   177–178

Figure 7.5   Balance sheet outcomes depending on deposits
realized after loans decided.   183

Figure 7.6   Cumulative probability distribution of deposits.   184

Figure 7.7   Maximizing expected net revenue with deposits
uncertain: (*a*) Penalty rate and no fixed cost;
(*b*) Penalty rate and small fixed cost; (*c*) Penalty
rate and large fixed cost.   185–187

Figure 7.8   Full equilibrium of a bank.   190

Figure 9.1   Reserves supplied and required, the constant-
multiple case.   236

Figure 9.2   (*a*) Reserves supplied and required, general
case; (*b*) bill rate in relation to reserve supplies.   237

Figure 9.3   (*a*) Net free reserves relative to required
reserves, $nfr(t)/rr(t-1)$, monthly 1959–1994;
(*b*) monthly change in $nfr(t)/rr(t-1)$,
1959–1994; (*c*) frequency distribution of
$nfr(t)/rr(t-1)$, monthly 1959–1994; (*d*) frequency
distribution of change in $nfr(t)/rr(t-1)$,
monthly 1959–1994.   240–242

Figure 9.4   Bank cash preference curve.   246

Figure 9.5   Bank cash preference at alternative discount
rates.   248

Figure 9.6   Change in banks' cash preference function due
to federal funds market.   250

Figure 9.7   Determination of the federal funds rate: (*a*) bill
rate low relative to discount rate; (*b*) bill rate
high relative to discount rate.   252–253

Figure 9.8   Relationship of bill rate and federal funds rate.   254

Figure 9.9   Relationship of federal funds rate to the bill
rate.   255

Figure 9.10   Relationship of banks' portfolio choice to loan
rate.   257

Figure 9.11   Public portfolio preferences and asset supplies.   259

Figure 9.12   Bank portfolio preferences and asset supplies.   261

TABLES

Table 1.1	National wealth of the United States, trillions of current dollars, 1994	2
Table 4.1		61
Table 4.2	Utility of return; Expected utility of portfolio, rank in parentheses	65
Table 4.3	Outcomes of mixed portfolio assuming independence	75
Table 5.1	Assets in U.S. economy (in units of $ billion)	134
Table 5.2	Shares of monetized capital (MC) in private capital (PC) and in private wealth (PC + NMA)	135
Table 7.1	Effect of uncertainty about deposits on volume of loans and investments and expected defensive position	189
Table 7.2	Bank balance sheets and deposit losses	192
Table 7.3	Balance sheets with losses of expected deposits	192
Table 7.4	Balance sheets and increased reserve requirements	194
Table 8.1	Estimated composition and distribution of federal debt (billions of dollars)	218
Table 8.2	Estimated supply and holdings of federal debt demand debt, end of December (billions of dollars)	220
Table 8.3A	Reserve requirements, Federal Reserve member banks January 30, 1967 (percent of deposits)	222
Table 8.3B	Reserve requirements, all depository institutions June 30, 1994 (percent of deposits)	223
Table 8.4	Reserve accounting identities for Anybank and for all banks	224
Table 8.5	Aggregate reserve accounts of banks: two hypothetical examples (billions of dollars)	225
Table 10.1	Asset/sector matrix for two countries	277
Table 10.2	Effects on endogenous variables of increase in specified variables, with all others held constant	281

PREFACE

Money, Credit, and Capital has been a long time in the making. I started writing it in 1958 while on a sabbatical year in Geneva. When I returned to Yale, I taught the several chapters in my graduate money course and added others. Initial drafts of most of the chapters were completed by the end of 1960. Mimeographed chapters were used for many years in graduate courses at Yale, and also at MIT and elsewhere. Copies circulated widely.

In the early 1960s I was distracted from the book by my sojourn in Washington and my continued involvement in public policy. I was also writing a series of monetary and macroeconomic journal articles with a focus related to but somewhat different from the book chapters. The book required revisions to keep up with the profession and with the world of affairs. I found them to be a daunting task, mounting with the passage of time and never finished to my satisfaction.

I did not give up the objective of completing and publishing the book. My good fortune was that Stephen Golub made it possible. He had studied the mimeo chapters as a graduate student at Yale and admired them. He spontaneously volunteered to help me put the book in publishable form. That he has done, these past years ever since 1990. He has contributed knowledge, wisdom, clarity, and judgment; he has believed in the book, and he has often saved me from myself. He has related our work to relevant modern literature and brought it closer to being up to date. The book has been inestimably improved by his participation.

Yet the approach, the thematic ideas, the shortcomings are my own for better or worse, dating back to 1958. Steve is not responsible for the idiosyncratic and perhaps anachronistic aspects of my approach.

In these final laps I have also been lucky to have the help of Joseph Boyer, now an advanced graduate student at Yale. He has read everything critically; checked mathematics, charts, and notations; warned against errors, inconsistencies, and obscurities; dug up statistics and facts of history, institutions, and literature. My debt to him is enormous. (He has also been an excellent teaching assistant for me in undergraduate macroeconomics.)

Some of the chapters of this book found their way into journals or edited volumes. In particular, much of Chapters 3 and 4 was published in Tobin (1965) and Chapter 7 was published in Tobin (1982b) virtually as it had been circulating in draft and as it now appears here. Likewise, as noted throughout the book, ideas and materials from my journal articles have been used, adapted, and referred to. This book is not at all, however, a collection of essays. The book has its own integrated theme and development, in some ways narrower and in some ways broader than my other works.

This project was originally commissioned by Seymour Harris, a professor, mentor, collaborator, and dear friend of mine at Harvard. My friendship with him and my debt to him are expressed in my tribute at the memorial service for him in 1975 (Tobin, 1996). Seymour was an entrepreneur, always organizing forums, editing books and journals, writing and getting others to write on important current topics of theory and policy. He was editor of a series of economics handbooks for McGraw-Hill. My book was to be the handbook on money. I felt bad for disappointing Seymour Harris, and I still do. When this book was finally approaching submission for publication, I thought I owed McGraw-Hill the right to publish it as originally agreed if they wished to do so after so long a delay, though they surely had no obligation. I was pleased that Lucille Sutton did want the book, and I am grateful for her interest, encouragement, and patience.

Over the years, a sequence of student research assistants and others have helped me with the project, doubtless to their frustration. Their contributions are embodied in this final version; often they may still be quite recognizable. My first research assistant was Donald Hester. Don was a sophomore in Yale College in 1954 when I found him. He began working on the book chapters in 1959. As he became a Yale graduate student and faculty member, I continued to rely on him. Don has been a distinguished scholar and writer in monetary economics in his own right; he has spent most of his career at the University of Wisconsin. During those same years another loyal graduate student, Leroy S. Wehrle, contributed painstaking research and many ideas.

I am indebted to many other students and colleagues at Yale for help at various stages of the manuscript: among them, Roger Grawe, the late Koen Suryatmodo, and Gary Smith.

Ever since William C. Brainard came to Yale as a new graduate student in 1957, I have been running up intellectual debts to him, many of them on the subjects of this book. Arthur Okun, tragically cut off in the prime of life, was always an inspiration. I was fortunate to have as a faculty colleague the late Raymond Goldsmith, the world's leading authority on worldwide financial institutions and national balance sheets throughout history. Experts who critically examined chapters for my benefit included Ralph Young and Stephen Axilrod at the Board of Governors of the Federal Reserve System, Jerome Stein, Henry Wallich, and Karen Johnson. Emilio Barone called my attention to a subtle error in (Tobin, 1982b), corrected in Chapter 7 herein.

I honor the memories of Althea Strauss and Laura Harrison, who long before the days of word processing accurately typed one draft chapter after another. Recently Glena Ames has been my trouble-shooting technical word processor. Emre Deliveli, a talented undergraduate, has quickly solved a variety of last-minute troubles with tables and figures. In the transition from our manuscript to a printed product, Kris Engberg and her colleagues at Publication Services saved us from errors and improved our book.

At various stages, the Rockefeller, Sloan, and National Science foundations have supported research related to this book. McGraw-Hill paid for a research assistant one summer. Above all, the Cowles Foundation for Research in Economics at Yale University, my professional home since its coming in 1955, has always supported my work with funds, service, friendship, and inspiration.

James Tobin

New Haven
March 5, 1997

INTRODUCTION

The vision of the financial system portrayed in this book has several characteristic themes:

1. The actors in the economy are wealth owners (not necessarily wealthy) who are managing their portfolios, their balance sheets. They face menus of assets and debts with various properties, differing, for example, in liquidity, risk, and return. The menus offer assets that run the gamut from hand-to-hand currency to reproducible capital goods. These assets and debts are substitutes for one another, but generally imperfect substitutes. The microeconomic foundations here tell how these actors, who differ from each other in circumstances and preferences, go about making these portfolio decisions.

2. Financial markets and institutions enable agents to buy and sell assets and in the process generate asset prices and interest rates, a whole structure of them. Banks are important intermediaries, largely because they are the fulcrum for central bank monetary policies. They and similar institutions are, like the general public, portfolio managers. They "monetize" capital in the sense that their monetary liabilities correspond to nonmonetary assets like loans to businesses to finance real investments. But the macroeconomic interface between financial markets and the real economy is much broader than the direct activities of banks. The book pays particular attention to the relation between the valuations of claims on real capital assets and the replacement cost of the capital itself. This "q" ratio is in principle an influence on new real investment activity.

3. The mechanisms of Federal Reserve monetary policies are analyzed in detail. They relate to federal debt in its various forms, and they depend upon legal institutions and on the central bank's operating procedures. The point is to link Federal Reserve policy moves to real investment activity via q and via the interest rates and credit lines offered private borrowers.

Money, Credit, and Capital

CHAPTER 1

National Wealth and Individual Wealth

The national wealth of the United States at the end of 1994 has been estimated at $19.1 trillion or about $75,000 per capita.[1] This figure is the inventory of the tangible assets in the country plus the net foreign asset position of the United States. The components of national wealth are shown in Table 1.1.

Tangible assets represent provision by the American people for satisfying some of their future needs and desires. They do so in a variety of ways. Some of them, for example, the inventories on the shelves of retail stores, can be directly consumed. Others, durable goods like houses and cars, will yield services to consumers over useful lifetimes of years or decades. Consumer goods, nondurable or durable, require relatively little human labor to yield their value. But a large proportion of national wealth consists either of tools that magnify the power of human labor or of natural resources, whose potential for satisfying human wants can be exploited only by the application of human effort and intelligence.

The inventory of tangible assets includes a staggering diversity of objects, incommensurable in their physical dimensions. It is not possible to add together acres of land, tons of ore, numbers of computers, and cubic feet of warehouse space. To be summarized in a single number, so that national wealth at December 31, 1994, can be compared to national wealth at some other date, the inventory must reckon assets using a common measure. In a market economy, in which assets are bought and sold at observable prices, or produced at calculable money costs, dollar value provides

---

[1] This is the estimate reported by the Federal Reserve Board in *Balance Sheets for the U.S. Economy, 1945–94*, publication C.9, Flow of Funds Section, June 1995. The estimates of the U.S. national balance sheets are extensions of the monumental work of Raymond Goldsmith (1962, 1982). For a comparative study of national balance sheets see Goldsmith (1985). Lipsey and Tice (1989) survey a variety of issues relating to the measurement of saving, investment, and wealth.

TABLE 1.1

National wealth of the United States, trillions of current dollars, 1994[a]

Tangible assets[b]	20.00
Reproducible assets	15.63
Residential structures	5.86
Nonresidential plant and equipment	6.06
Inventories	1.22
Consumer durables	2.49
Land	4.36
U.S. monetary gold and SDRs	0.02
Net foreign assets	−0.89
+ U.S. holdings of foreign assets	1.59
− Foreign holdings of U.S. assets	2.48
National wealth	19.13

[a] Reproducibles assets are valued at current cost, land at market value, and foreign assets at a mix of market values (financial assets) and book values (direct investment).
[b] Excludes government-owned tangible assets.
Source: Board of Governors of the Federal Reserve System, *Balance Sheets for the U.S. Economy,* 1945–94, publication C.9, Flow of Funds section, June 1995.

a common measure. Reproducible assets are valued at depreciated replacement cost. For example, the value of structures on December 31, 1994, is the cost—in labor and materials on that date—of replacing the existing structures, after deducting an allowance for their age. Some assets, in particular land, are not reproducible: for these, the values are market prices.

The asset prices and values employed in estimating the national wealth assume a considerable continuity in society's tastes and technology. Should the public suddenly abandon tobacco because of its reported hazards to health, cigarette-making machinery would no longer be worth its replacement cost and the value of tobacco land would be reduced. The advent of the atomic age greatly increased the value of uranium-bearing land; concerns about the safety of nuclear power have had the opposite effect.

The wealth of the American nation does not consist entirely of tangible assets within the one country. United States citizens own property abroad and other claims on foreigners, which can be used to obtain goods and services in the future. Foreigners, of course, own similar claims on the United States economy. Until the mid-1980s, the balance had long been modestly in favor of the United States. But the current-account external deficits of the 1980s turned the United States into a net debtor. The *net* claims of the United States against the world were estimated as −$886 billion on December 31, 1994. This net debtor position does not take account of $21 billion in U.S. international monetary reserves: gold, foreign currencies, and claims on the International Monetary Fund.

Tangible assets and international purchasing power are not the only ways a people can make provision for their economic future. This measure of wealth and Table 1.1 exclude human capital, the value of the future earning power of the labor force, which is very large relative to tangible wealth.[2] The human capital embodied in a given population can be augmented by education and health care.

Economic welfare is only one dimension, and probably not the most important one, of a people's well-being. The character, initiative, and mutual trust of the society may be as important as countable national wealth in determining levels of production and consumption attainable in the future. These attributes of the population are, in any case, important in their own right. The views from mountaintops, the Constitution, the cultural and scientific tradition, the bonds of family, friendship, and community—these can hardly be reckoned in terms of replacement cost or market value, but they no doubt contribute more to the happiness of generations than things which can be so reckoned.

Both its advocates and its opponents refer to the American economic system as "capitalism." The nation's capital is its wealth—its stocks of tangible assets and claims against the rest of the world. A similar inventory of capital could be taken in China and other economies generally regarded as noncapitalist.[3] These inventories would be quite similar in the kinds of things counted, although the valuation of the components might be quite different. It is, of course, not the existence of capital but its ownership that distinguishes the United States economy from that of the former Soviet Union. According to Boskin, Robinson, and Huber (1989, p. 306), in the United States the share of governments in the ownership of reproducible capital was 21 percent in 1985; the remaining 79 percent was privately owned. In the former Soviet Union, the share privately owned was much smaller, though by no means zero. Privatization is occurring rapidly in former communist countries and even in communist China.

Virtually all American national wealth is owned by private citizens. Yet an individual may be wealthy without owning any of the assets counted in the above enumeration of national wealth. Although many American households own houses, cars, refrigerators, and computers, few are direct owners of machine tools, office buildings, and inventories of raw cotton. An individual's inventory of her own wealth might include as assets many items that were not listed at all: dollar bills, bank deposits, savings bonds, government or corporate bonds, insurance policies, shares of corporate stock. These are paper assets representing claims of various kinds against other individuals, institutions, or governments. In reckoning her *net worth*, each individual would deduct from her total assets the claims of others against her. If the net worths of all economic units in the nation—households, corporations, institutions, governments—are added up, these paper claims and obligations will cancel each other. All that will remain will be the tangible assets and net foreign assets of the nation, both publicly and privately owned, the items in the estimate of national wealth in Table 1.1.[4]

---

[2]See Jorgenson and Fraumeni (1989) for estimates of the magnitude of human capital accumulation in the United States. In 1984, they estimated U.S. total wealth at $209.5 trillion, of which 92.5 percent was human wealth and 7.5 percent nonhuman wealth.

[3]See Goldsmith (1985, pp. 273–278) for historical estimates of the former Soviet Union's balance sheet.

[4]These calculations are shown explicitly in the Federal Reserve *Balance Sheets for the U.S. Economy,* cited above.

If the central government is excepted from this process of aggregation, the net worth of private individuals and institutions and subordinate governments will include not only the tangible assets they own but also their net claims against the central government. These claims include interest-bearing obligations: federal bonds, certificates of indebtedness, notes, and bills. They also include obligations that bear no interest: coin and currency issued by the United States Treasury and the Federal Reserve Banks. Thus aggregate "private" net worth—as calculated by individuals, business firms, and subordinate governments—generally exceeds the total value of privately owned tangible assets plus net foreign assets. Indeed, aggregate private net worth may exceed total national wealth, because there is no necessary correspondence between the size of the central government's debts and the value of the assets it owns.

One principal objective of monetary economics is to analyze the economic consequences of the size and form of government debt—to analyze, in other words, the implications of the fact that the total apparent wealth of private citizens exceeds net national wealth. (For convenience, the word "private" will generally be stretched to include governments other than the central government.)

Some politicians and economists like to point out that babies born in the United States come into the world with a national debt averaging $20,000 per capita around their necks. This "national debt" is the debt of the federal government and must not be confused with the debt of the American nation as a whole—including private households and businesses as well as governments—to foreigners. As shown in Table 1.1, in 1994 this was about $2.5 trillion gross, $10,000 per capita, and less than $0.9 trillion, $3600 per capita, when American-owned foreign assets are netted out. Some of our gross external debt happens to take the form of federal obligations, about $1 trillion, a fifth of the federal debt. For the most part, however, babies are born with silver spoons in their mouths, government bonds in their parents' safe deposit boxes equivalent to their shares of the federal debt.

The accounting excess of private wealth over national wealth representing the federal debt could be eliminated by entering in private balance sheets a debit item for the present value of the future taxes they might rationally expect to pay to cover interest on the federal debt.[5] Liabilities for future taxes, however, are conjectural and inchoate. They depend mainly on future incomes. Since these are mainly wage incomes, expectations of taxes would be largely reflected in lower estimates of personal human capital. People are likely to discount future incomes heavily in estimating their present net worth. If so, they will not estimate their expected income tax payments to be as large as the equivalent interest-bearing government securities.[6]

---

[5]There is, of course, no interest on the part of the debt that takes the form of currency and coin, or their equivalent. But it can be argued that monetary issues impose other costs on the community equivalent to taxes to pay interest.

[6]Robert Barro (1974) revived the argument of David Ricardo (1817) that government debt does not constitute net private wealth. The accounting issue is not as important as the operational question: Is the spending and saving behavior of the private sector any different when government expenditures are financed by issuing debt or printing money than when they are met by taxes? Barro's "Ricardian equivalence" answer is no. Tobin (1952) briefly considered this issue. It is also discussed in more detail in Tobin (1980, Ch. 3) and Haliassos and Tobin (1990), and is considered again in Chapter 10 of this book.

Private net worth, then, consists of three parts: privately owned tangible assets, private claims on foreigners net of private debts to foreigners, and government obligations. But these ultimate constituents of private net worth are owned by private citizens not directly but through the intermediation of a complex network of debts and claims. For the purpose of aggregative accounting, the network washes out. One person's asset is another person's debt. But for the functioning of the economy, this network is of the greatest importance. A second major objective of monetary theory in this book is to analyze the workings of the financial institutions and arrangements for private ownership of wealth in a capitalist economy, the United States in particular. These institutions are the central and distinctive features of the capitalist organization of economic life.[7]

A preliminary indication of their importance may be gained by considering certain striking differences between national assets and private assets. The main components of national wealth are durable tangible assets of a highly specific kind: a house in a given location and style, a machine designed to cut a certain material in a given pattern, a railroad serving a particular territory. For the nation as a whole, it is not easy to change the form of capital without destroying some of its value. Capital can be withdrawn, without loss, from a railroad no more rapidly than the railroad will wear out in the absence of replacement. It can be put into equipment for air transportation no more rapidly than planes and terminals can be built. To change the form of national wealth by reducing the share of railroad equipment in favor of air transport equipment is a time-consuming process. In contrast, an individual investor can shift from owning shares in railroad companies to owning shares in airlines as quickly as she can call a broker and the broker can execute the order.

Indeed, an individual investor can hold her wealth in a much more generalized form than shares of stock; currency and bank deposits, as media of exchange, represent not title to specific assets but the power to purchase any species of physical goods. The only comparable component of national wealth is the nation's stock of generalized international purchasing power. For the United States, this component is small relative to national wealth, as indicated in Table 1.1.

Just as an individual can change the form of her wealth quickly without loss of value while a whole nation cannot, so an individual can consume wealth much more rapidly than a nation can. Most individual wealth is held in assets whose value can be fairly quickly realized. The proceeds of selling assets, or of pledging them as collateral for loans, can increase the individual's consumption whether she wishes to consume at a rapid rate for a short period or at a slow rate for a long period. A nation, in contrast, would encounter great difficulties in consuming its wealth, and these difficulties would be greater the more rapidly the nation tried to consume it. For the most part, durable tangible assets will yield their value in consumption only if they are employed in specific ways with the cooperation of labor and other productive resources. Trucks are worthless without drivers and fuel. The society can consume these assets, without destroying their value, only in an indirect and slow manner, that is, by using the labor and other resources needed to maintain and replace

---

[7]The approach of Gurley and Shaw (1955) is in the same spirit.

them to produce consumers' goods. Even durable assets whose services are directly consumed can scarcely be hurried to give up their value. The valuation of a house is predicated on its potential for being lived in for forty or fifty years, or more. There is no way of living in it more intensively for one or two or five years and realizing its value right away.

Thus, if an individual with $50,000 a year wage or salary income is worth $150,000, it is quite conceivable that in any one year she could spend $100,000, twice her income, on consumption. Indeed, she could cease to work and still consume $50,000 for three years. But if the United States has an annual national income of $5 trillion and a national wealth of $15 trillion, this does not mean that the nation can consume as much as it likes of that wealth in any one year.

True, the nation can—temporarily at least—raise consumption by borrowing from other countries to import more goods and services than it exports. The United States has been doing that since 1980, running up the negative position in net foreign assets shown in Table 1.1. Although financial assets are increasingly mobile worldwide, the net volume of international capital flows remains surprisingly small relative to domestic saving and investment, as Feldstein and Horioka (1980) demonstrated. Their finding has been corroborated by many subsequent studies. Although the Japanese current account surpluses of the 1980s were very controversial, they averaged only about 2 percent of Japan's GDP. Thus nations, even wealthy ones, are much more circumscribed than wealthy individuals in their ability to consume more than they produce, either by selling assets to foreigners or by borrowing.

The monetary and financial institutions of capitalism permit a "division of labor" among wealth owners' different requirements. Assets can be tailor-made to the circumstances (age, health, family responsibilities, income, wealth, occupation), tastes (attitudes towards risks), and opinions (estimates of economic outlook) of the individual. Those whose main concern is for funds to be immediately and assuredly available for unusual expenditures can hold bank deposits or easily marketable securities. Those whose interest is in long-run capital appreciation, even at some risk, can be the owners of specific tangible assets.

By enabling individuals to hold wealth in fluid, flexible, and generalized forms and to consume wealth at will, our monetary and financial institutions create an illusion. The tangible assets that are ultimately the chief constituents of private net worth do not possess these characteristics. One individual's wealth is both consumable in total and fluid in form without loss of value, but only so long as most other wealth owners refrain from exploiting these same characteristics. The analogy to banking is instructive. Each individual depositor of a bank can convert her deposit into currency on demand, provided most other depositors refrain from exercising this privilege. But if all depositors try to cash in their deposits at once, the bank will fall far short of the currency to meet its obligations. Similarly, it is quite impossible for all individuals in the nation to consume their wealth at the same time.

Just as there are differences between the individual and society in ability to consume wealth, there are also differences, though less striking ones, in accumulation of wealth. The principal process through which national wealth grows is national saving. The inventory of tangible assets grows when new buildings, new machines, new computers, new aircraft, and so forth are produced in greater quantities than old ones are wearing out or becoming obsolete. To accomplish such accumulation, the nation must consume less than it produces and devote some of its labor and other productive resources to turning out capital goods in excess of the requirements of replacement and maintenance. Accumulation by saving takes time, of course. A low rate of saving persisting over a long time will add a great deal to wealth. A high rate of saving for only a short period will accumulate very little.

National wealth may, it is true, sometimes increase in more dramatic and less time-consuming ways, without corresponding saving by the community. Examples of national "capital gains" are accidental new discoveries or acquisitions of mineral or land resources, changes in tastes or technology that increase the usefulness of existing resources, and increases in the import-purchasing power of international claims. Of these, the first two are more important in a geographically incompletely explored country, like the nineteenth-century United States, than in a mature economy. The third is more important in a small country highly dependent on international trade than in a more nearly self-contained economy like the United States. For the contemporary American economy, saving is almost the only available process for increasing wealth. Of course, the productivity of capital will increase with technological progress, and it is admittedly hard to decide in many particular cases whether a technological improvement that enhances the utility of some existing resource should be regarded as increasing the size or the productivity of wealth.

One prominent omission from the list of ways in which the national wealth can increase is a general increase in prices. Inflation will increase the money value of tangible assets without changing their real value. Inflation increases the costs of food and clothing, the wages of labor, as well as the values of real estate and machinery. The nominal value of wealth will be increased, but its usefulness in providing for the future needs of the population remains unchanged. For the same reasons, a general deflation does not alter the real value of the national wealth, although its value reckoned in money is lower.

Saving—consuming less than income—is also the principal process involved in individual accumulation of wealth, although the alternative ways in which wealth grows are more important at the individual than at the social level. Individual saving can take the form of acquiring a wide variety of types of assets. Some are claims against other individuals; in this case one person's saving is another's dissaving, and neither aggregate private net worth nor national wealth is altered. Similarly, individuals may buy from other individuals claims against government or equities in tangible assets; these transfers do not change aggregate private net worth or national wealth. If the supply of claims against government increases, private net worth may grow (depending on expectations of taxes), though national wealth remains unchanged, unless government investment increases as well. If equities in new tangible assets are acquired by individuals, there will be corresponding saving on the national level, and national wealth, as well as private net worth, will grow.

There are several ways in which an individual's wealth may increase without saving: capital gifts or bequests from other individuals, capital gains due to price increases. For the individual as for the nation, it is important to distinguish money capital gains from real capital gains. If all asset prices rise proportionately, and the cost of living goes up in the same proportion, an individual's wealth has risen in nominal value but not in real value. The owner's command of consumption goods has not changed. But if an individual owns shares that rise 50 percent while the cost of living goes up 25 percent, she enjoys a real capital gain of 20 percent $((1.50 - 1.25)/1.25)$. The owner of a dollar bill suffers a $33\frac{1}{3}$ percent capital loss if the price level increases 50 percent; she receives a real capital gain if the price level falls.

Somehow the money and capital markets and institutions must reconcile the consumability of individual wealth to the limited consumability of the tangible components of social wealth, the generality of individual wealth to the specificity of national wealth, and the flexibility of composition of individual wealth to the rigidity of composition of national wealth. The desires of individuals to save in a variety of assets must be reconciled to the fact that social saving can occur only through the accumulation of tangible assets. A principal purpose of monetary theory is to analyze how, and how well, our monetary, fiscal, and financial institutions perform these reconciliations. How well the job is done determines whether our potential for economic growth is achieved fully and smoothly or whether the economic process is punctuated by setbacks involving depression and unemployment and bursts of excess demand and inflation.

CHAPTER 2

Properties of Assets

2.1
ASSET PROPERTIES AND INVESTOR ATTITUDES

The institutions and markets of an advanced capitalistic economy offer an immense variety of assets as vehicles for holding wealth. Some are direct or indirect claims to real property. Some represent claims against the central government. Still others are the debts of private individuals or corporations. The same institutions and markets provide numerous ways to incur debt. Almost all of these assets can be bought and sold, or otherwise exchanged for each other. The relative values of assets—how much a unit of asset A is worth in terms of asset B, or how much each of them is worth in terms of currency—are established in these exchanges. The purpose of the present chapter is to examine the characteristics of assets most important in determining these relative values. In subsequent chapters attention will be focused on the circumstances and attitudes of investors in relation to these characteristics of assets.

Like commodity prices, asset prices reflect supply and demand, that is, the quantities of various assets that individuals or institutions wish to acquire or to provide. These quantities depend on prices, and prices tend to those levels that clear markets. Behind supply and demand in asset markets are preferences among assets, attributable to the objective properties of the assets themselves and to the circumstances, expectations, and tastes of individuals and institutions.

Examination of the relevant objective properties of assets—attributes independent of their owners or potential owners—can contribute substantially to understanding the structure of asset values. Assets, or combinations of assets, with identical properties will have the same value, as surely as a ten-dollar bill is equal to 2 fives or 10 ones.[1] But it is by no means always possible to construct the complete

---

[1]This is the basic idea of the *arbitrage pricing theory* (Chen, Roll, and Ross, 1986).

equivalent of one asset in terms of other assets simply from their objective properties. The equivalence must be sought in the minds of actual and potential investors and borrowers, given their present economic circumstances, the state of their information about asset markets, their estimates of their future needs and tastes, their views of the prospects of alternative investments, their attitudes toward risks of various kinds and degrees. A reading of the print, gross and fine, on an IBM stock certificate, even supplemented by access to the books of the corporation, cannot reveal how many dollars a share is worth. In this respect shares of stocks and other marketable securities contrast sharply with ten-dollar bills or time deposits, whose value in dollar bills can be ascertained merely by reading the documents.

The theory of asset values must appeal ultimately to subjective preferences of individuals; these preferences, however, do not concern specific assets per se but rather the prospects and risks attributed to them. IBM common stock and AT&T bonds are not valued for themselves but for the prospects of income, capital gain, and loss associated with them. These prospects have values quite independent of the specific securities that carry them. Should investors alter their estimates of the prospects and risks of IBM common stock and AT&T bonds, they would also alter their valuations of the two securities.

Some assets, to be sure, are purely speculative. They have no source of value in today's market except the expectation of the market prices they will command in the future. A work of art commands high prices in auctions today because buyers think it will command still higher prices next year. Unless the price rises enough to earn the owner as much return as he could get from a savings bank or a government bond, such an investment is not likely to be worthwhile.[2] Objets d'art, old stamps, coins, and baseball cards pay no interest or dividends. They may be beautiful or interesting to look at or show off, but these pay-offs could generally be obtained in copies or in museums. Certainly, direct enjoyment is not sufficient basis for the auction prices. These assets are not replicable or reproducible. Their supply is fixed forever. Their prices, therefore, have nothing to do with costs of production. Asset prices detached from fundamentals, from yields in use and from costs of replacement, are bubbles. They are fully speculative. That is, prices depend on future prices, which in turn depend on further future prices, and so on.

Assets of economic interest are generally not floating freely without anchors. Some of them are claims to payments of interest or repayments of principal. Some of them entitle the owners to dividend shares of business profits. Some of them yield services of value in consumption or production. They may be contingent claims on real estate or other properties. They or close substitutes for them—for example, cars, houses, machines—may be reproducible at calculable costs.

An interesting but unresolved question is the role of bubbles and speculation in the prices of these assets. The theory of efficient financial markets, which became

---

[2]Such assets might also be attractive if their prices are expected to be weakly or even negatively correlated with those of other assets, allowing an investor to reduce portfolio risk. Chapter 4 discusses these matters in detail.

popular in the 1970s and 1980s, has it that these prices consistently and accurately reflect all available information about the objective prospects and risks of the respective assets, that is, their "fundamentals." An alternative view is that speculative behavior often leads to divergences, at least in the short run, between fundamental values and market values. Stock market quotations, exchange rates, and other asset prices are often extremely volatile, day to day and even hour to hour. It is usually hard to identify objective causes for such frequent and large revisions of the relevant expectations of the future.[3] Keynes's famous description of equity markets as casinos where assessments of long-term investment prospects are overwhelmed by frantic short-term guesses about what average opinion will think average opinion will think—and so on, to the nth degree—rings as true today as when he wrote it.[4] In recent years, the recognition that asset prices often do not seem to reflect fundamental factors has led to formal models of speculation.[5]

One dimension of the difference between speculators and fundamentalists is that speculators often extrapolate price changes, betting on further movements in the same direction. Their purchases or sales are destabilizing. Fundamentalists, on the other hand, have regressive price expectations, and their actions tend to stabilize the markets. In Chapter 6 this difference is explored further.

The remainder of this chapter analyzes the fundamental properties of assets, as determined by their intrinsic natures and by the markets in which they are traded. Most of the relevant properties can be classified under the headings *liquidity, reversibility, divisibility, predictability of value,* and *yield and return.* By the *value* of an asset at a given time is meant the maximum amount of cash that could be obtained by selling or otherwise liquidating the asset at that time, under the most favorable conditions and with all useful prior preparation for the disposal. The *liquidity* of an asset concerns the ease and speed with which its value can be realized. The *reversibility* of an asset concerns the discrepancy between the value an owner can realize, if any, and the contemporaneous cost of acquisition of the asset. An asset's *predictability of value* refers to the certainty with which its value at various future dates can be anticipated by informed investors. The *yield* of an asset over an interval of time consists of all the receipts and costs entailed by ownership of the asset over the interval. These receipts and costs may take a variety of forms; both the composition and the predictability of the yield are important to the valuation of the asset. The *return* to ownership over an interval is the algebraic sum of its increment in value and the value of its yield. See the appendix to this chapter for further discussion.

---

[3]Robert Shiller has provided a precise interpretation of excessive volatility of asset prices and marshalled evidence demonstrating excessive volatility. See Shiller (1989) for a comprehensive presentation of this evidence and a rebuttal to critics of his earlier work.

[4]Keynes (1936, Ch. 12, especially pp. 156–160).

[5]This literature emphasizes the role of irrational speculators who disregard fundamentals, called noise traders because their activity distorts the signal registered in market prices of assets. See, for example, Shiller (1989, ch. 1); Cutler, Poterba, and Summers (1990); Black (1986); and Delong, Shleifer, Summers, and Waldmann (1990). These models, however, do not quite capture Keynes's idea, that fashions and bandwagon effects cause speculative fluctuations.

2.2
LIQUIDITY

At a given moment of time an asset has a certain full *value*. But the percentage of
this value that can actually be realized will generally depend on how long ago the
decision to sell the asset was reached. This relationship, between the realized price
of the asset and the length of time the decision to sell preceded the actual sale, can be
shown graphically, as in Fig. 2.1. The horizontal axis measures, right to left, the time
between the decision and the sale; the vertical axis measures the percentage of full
market value realized. A perfectly liquid asset is represented by a horizontal line at
100 percent, meaning that no matter how recently the decision to sell was reached,
the full value of the asset can be realized. By definition, perfect liquidity characterizes *cash*—currency and other assets generally acceptable as means of payment.
Indeed realization of the value of an asset means realization in cash.

No other asset is literally perfectly liquid, for there is always some delay in
turning it into cash, if only hours or minutes or seconds. Some assets can be realized
at full value as soon as they can be sold, or otherwise liquidated. Their liquidity
would be depicted by cutting off the 100 percent liquidity line before it reaches 0
(time of sale), as at *d* in Fig. 2.1; for times shorter than *d* realization would be 0
percent, as the asset cannot be sold at all on such short notice. The delay time *d*
may be shorter or longer depending on the asset and on the time and place of the
owner's decision to sell. Savings deposits are examples of this kind of asset; they
can be turned into their full cash value as soon as the depositor can get to the bank
or savings institution. Likewise, any listed security can be sold at its current value
as quickly as the owner can communicate with a broker and the broker with his
representative on the exchange. For most purposes assets of this kind with a delay of

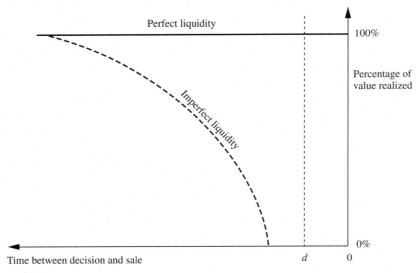

FIGURE 2.1
Liquidity—perfect and imperfect.

at most two or three days may be regarded as perfectly liquid. In contrast, the delay time for certain types of U.S. savings bonds may be several weeks.

The curve marked "imperfect liquidity" in Fig. 2.1 depicts a different kind of asset. Its full value can be realized only if sufficient time is allowed to find a buyer. With shorter notice, up to a limit, the asset can be sold, but less will be realized the later the decision was reached. A house is an instructive example of this kind of imperfect liquidity. To obtain the value of a house, the seller must have it on the market long enough for buyers attracted to its particular location and design to appear. The imperfect liquidity of a house, in contrast to the near perfect liquidity of a listed security, is the consequence of several factors. Whereas one share of IBM stock is exactly like every other share, no one house is exactly like any other. Each particular house is only occasionally on the market; some shares of IBM stock are always for sale. While the price of IBM stock is being established hour by hour in actual exchanges, the market price of a particular house is not continuously available. Its value must be learned from experience with potential buyers once the house has been put up for sale. Nor will the potential buyers appear at once. The spread of information is imperfect and slow. The events that put a family into the housing market—changes in family size, economic circumstances, job location, tastes—occur infrequently. It may be necessary to wait quite a while—longer in a small community than in a large one—for such an event to occur to a family that values highly the design and location of the particular house up for sale.

Differentiation of particular assets from each other, infrequency of trading of any one item, scarcity of buyers at short notice, unorganized and slow communication— one or more of these attributes characterize the markets for imperfectly liquid assets. Not only houses but other real estate and most consumers' and producers' durable goods provide examples of markets where all these attributes are present. In other cases imperfect liquidity may be due to no more than one of these characteristics. The would-be seller of a large block of a well-known security traded on an organized exchange must face the fact that the price of the security on a given day is not independent of the amount he is trying to sell. The longer the interval he is willing to wait until the entire block has been sold, the greater will be his percentage realization for the block. Like the seller of a house, the seller of a business or of a substantial share of a business will generally gain by being able to sell to the buyers who appear over an interval of time rather than being confined to the buyers of a single day.

On these definitions of liquidity and value there is no complete illiquidity to place at the opposite pole from perfect liquidity. If nothing can be realized from the disposition of an asset at a given moment no matter how careful and how long the preparation, the definitions say that it has no value at this time; its liquidity therefore is indeterminate, although such an asset is illiquid in the everyday usage of this term. An asset may have zero value today but positive value in the future, anticipated with more or less certainty; and an asset of zero value to its owner today may cost much more than zero to acquire. Both points are illustrated by the rights of a participant in a retirement program before he is eligible for its benefits. Such assets will be termed completely *irreversible* rather than *illiquid*.

The value of an asset has been defined as the maximum cash that the holder can realize by its disposition. Value is reckoned net of the costs of sale—fees, commissions, taxes, communication costs, the time and effort of the owner himself. A sale prepared as long in advance as contributes to the cash realized will still face some of these costs. The value of an asset, therefore, is generally less than its cost to a buyer. For an imperfectly liquid asset, costs and waiting are frequently substitutes. Market imperfections may be overcome by more vigorous canvassing and more extensive advertising. Delays may be shortened by extraordinary means of communication. But all such measures have their cost. For any given length of delay on the horizontal axis of Fig. 2.1, there are a variety of possible selling prices corresponding to different procedures and costs of selling. Any point on the liquidity relationship represents the optimal choice among these alternatives, that is, the one that yields the maximum proceeds net of costs of selling.

The discussion of liquidity, and most of the examples, have run in terms of marketable assets liquidated by sale, and it is mainly for such cases that the concept is useful. However, it applies also to nonmarketable assets and to other means of converting assets into cash, as the example of time deposits illustrates. In these cases the method of disposition is to exercise rights to payment by the debtor. In other cases pledging the asset as security for a loan may be the most convenient way or the only way of turning it into cash; consider, for example, the life insurance policy of a person who has become an uninsurable risk.

Since the liquidity of an asset is a property described by a functional relationship between delay time and percentage realization, and not by a single number, there may be no simple ordering of assets according to liquidity. Conceivably the curves for two imperfectly liquid assets can cross, so that for certain delay times one has the greater realization while for other delay times the position is reversed. But such difficulties of ranking will not obscure the important and broad differences between imperfectly liquid assets and those of perfect or near perfect liquidity.

2.3
REVERSIBILITY

By the *reversibility* of an asset is meant the value of the asset to its holder expressed as a percentage of its contemporaneous cost to a buyer. For a perfectly reversible asset, this percentage would be 100, indicating that a seller could realize in cash all that it costs a buyer to acquire the asset. (The concept, like that of liquidity, applies not only to market exchanges but also to assets liquidated and acquired by means other than market sales and purchases. "Seller" and "buyer" should be broadly interpreted.) Strictly perfect reversibility is difficult to conceive. Any exchange of assets is bound to occasion some costs: actual cash outlays for fees, commissions, insurance, and the like; the personal time and energies of the seller and buyer. Although both liquidity and reversibility are related to the degree of perfection and organization of the markets where assets are traded, they are distinct properties. Exchange costs occur even for assets of perfect or near perfect liquidity; indeed, there are sometimes costs, even cash costs, for converting one form of cash into another, charges for depositing currency into a checking account or for "cashing" a check.

Some assets are completely irreversible. They cost something to acquire; but the holder, once he has acquired them, cannot turn them into cash in any way. The rights to retirement and death benefits purchased by contributions to certain retirement programs have already been cited as an example; these rights cannot be sold or assigned to anyone else, or surrendered for cash, or used as security for a loan. A different kind of irreversibility occurs when the asset has a value to its owner but cannot be purchased at any price. Consider, for example, a nonmarketable 10-year government savings bond with only one year left until maturity. The owner can convert it into cash at a stated value. But no one can purchase a 9-year-old savings bond; the Treasury offers only brand new ones. The measure of reversibility can be set at 0 percent in this case, as in the preceding one, by the convention of regarding the purchase cost as infinite when the asset cannot be bought at all. A certificate of deposit obligates the bank to pay a defined amount, say $1000, on or after a particular date, and nothing before. If it has no secondary market, if it is not transferable from one holder to another, then it is completely irreversible and it has no value before maturity.

Most assets are imperfectly reversible. Exchange costs are of two general kinds, which frequently occur in combination. Some of the costs of a given exchange are independent of the size of the transaction, while others are proportionate to the value exchanged. Examples of the first type are bank service charges for deposits or checks; the personal inconvenience involved in making a withdrawal from a savings account; the design, accounting, and administrative costs of a firm ordering new machinery. Examples of the second type are the difference between buying and selling prices, or "bid" and "asked" prices, quoted in many organized markets; the real estate agent's commission; the tax payable in the United States on realized capital gains; the handling and delivery costs of an order of materials or equipment.

2.4
DIVISIBILITY

The size of the smallest unit in which dealings in an asset can occur is important in determining the costs, and often the very possibility, of certain transactions in the asset. Currency and bank deposits, both time and demand accounts, are for all practical purposes completely divisible. Any holder can dispose of any fraction of his holdings, however small; or the asset can be acquired in any quantity desired. Fractions of a penny are unattainable, it is true, but they are of no practical significance. Other assets—bonds, stocks, commodities, durable goods—come in units of significant value relative to the wealth of many actual or potential investors, and it is either impossible or costly to sell or to buy fractions. Many corporations endeavor, by stock splitting when necessary, to keep the unit share low in value. Mutual funds and many individual corporations allow shareowners to purchase fractional shares, permitting smaller investors to obtain greater diversification than the indivisibilities of securities would otherwise allow.

2.5
PREDICTABILITY

If the cash value of an asset at every future date can be predicted with complete certainty, the asset is *perfectly predictable.* (This is not to say that its purchasing power in commodities is perfectly predictable. That matter will be discussed later, in Section 2.7.) The predictable value may be the same for every future date, as exemplified by cash assets themselves and savings accounts. Or the predictable value may be different for different future dates; the redemption values of government savings bonds depend, in a perfectly foreseeable way, on the length of time they have been held.

If the value of an asset can be predicted with certainty for some future dates but not for others, the asset is *partially predictable.* Marketable bonds provide the principal example. For dates before its maturity, the price of a bond cannot be predicted with certainty. Issued as, say, a 3 percent bond, it will rise above or fall below par—the promised return of principal at maturity—as interest rates on competing maturities go below or above 3 percent. Another source of partial unpredictability is the option the debtor sometimes reserves to repay the full principal early, without paying remaining interest coupons. For dates at or beyond the assured latest date of maturity, the value of a bond depends only on the certainty that the debtor will fulfill the contract. For a bond of the federal government, there is, almost by definition, no risk of default; after all, the currency in which the bonds are payable is simply a different kind of obligation of the same government. Bonds and other obligations of private debtors are not of completely predictable value even at maturity, because there is always some possibility, although frequently almost negligible probability, of default.

The remaining category, *imperfectly predictable* assets, includes those whose value cannot be certainly known for any future date. Within this category assets vary tremendously in degree of unpredictability. On the one hand are short-term debts of well-established private debtors or subordinate governments, almost certain to be safe at maturity and to deviate very little from maturity value in the interim. At the other extreme are speculative common stocks of, for example, "wildcat" oil companies or unknown high-technology ventures; these shares may double in value or lose all value within a week, and their prospects for more distant future dates are even more unpredictable.

For bonds and other finite contractual debts, predictable upper limits to value can be specified for every future date, though there are generally no lower limits other than zero. A contract for future payments can never command a price greater than the sum of all the remaining payments of interest and principal to which a holder may be entitled. At a price equal to that sum, the holder could obtain at once all the payments to which the contract would ever entitle him. To put the same point in other language, interest rates applicable to obligations to pay currency can conceivably rise without limit but cannot fall below zero, because currency itself bears a zero rate of return. (Strictly speaking, the yield on currency for most holders is of negative rather than zero value because of the costs of protection against loss. Conceivably, therefore, creditors would be willing to pay something—negative interest—for the safekeeping of their wealth. But they would not pay more for safekeeping in bonds than for safekeeping in bank deposits payable on demand.)

The zero rate of return on currency is an institutional fact, determined by the government in its discretion, rather than a necessity of nature. Interest-bearing currency is conceivable—periodically the government would give every applicant a certain additional amount of currency per dollar of proved currency holdings. If this rate of return were predictable, it would set a positive floor to other rates of interest. Accordingly, the ceiling on the price of bonds and other payments contracts would be lower than the sum of all future payments. Likewise, negative interest on currency is entirely within the bounds of imagination. Silvio Gesell (1929) proposed "stamped money" as a depression remedy. To retain its legal validity, currency would have to be stamped periodically at an established cost per dollar to the holder. Under this regime, negative interest rates could also arise for obligations to pay currency; that is, their current value might exceed the sum of obligated future payments.

Some obligations to make future payments of currency continue indefinitely and have no finite sum. The *consol,* issued by treasuries in the British Commonwealth to consolidate debts of short maturities, obligates the government to make a certain annual cash payment in perpetuity. When the interest rate floor is zero, there is no upper limit to the value of a consol.

Differences in predictability may be illustrated diagrammatically, as in Fig. 2.2. The horizontal axes measure time, looking forward from the present; the vertical axes measure the value of an asset as a percentage of its value today. For each asset a band of possible values at each future date is shown: (i) the absolute upper limit, if any; (ii) the value which has, in the investor's view, only a 10 percent probability of being exceeded; (iii) the investor's estimate of the median value, which has a 50 percent probability of being exceeded; (iv) the value which, by his estimate, has a 90 percent probability of being exceeded; (v) the absolute lower limit, if any.

Perfectly predictable assets are illustrated in Figs. 2.2a and 2.2b, where all the estimates (i) to (v) coincide for every future date; the band is simply a single curve. For cash, Fig. 2.2a, this curve is a horizontal line at 100 percent of today's value. But for an asset such as a nonmarketable time deposit, Fig. 2.2b, the curve is not a simple horizontal line but reflects the fact that the deposit may be withdrawn before maturity only at a progressively smaller penalty. Figure 2.2c illustrates a possible estimate of the band of predictability for a marketable government bond of definite maturity. From the maturity date on, the bond will be like cash. In the interim, however, it may fluctuate in value as market interest rates vary. The upper limit, curve (i), represents the simple sum of future payments of interest and principal to which the bond entitles the holder. Curve (iii) is shown as a horizontal line, meaning that the bond is now selling at maturity value and that on balance the investor expects it to continue to do so. His expectations need not be so simple, of course; curve (iii) might have any shape, for example, the configuration of (iii) in Fig. 2.2d. The convergence of (ii), (iii), and (iv) in Figs. 2.2c and 2.2d reflects a view that the shorter the term of a security, the smaller its range of probable value; a given change in the interest rate will produce a smaller change in the value of a fixed-dollar obligation the shorter its term. Their convergence at the other end illustrates a belief in some inertia in securities markets—large changes in security prices and interest rates generally take

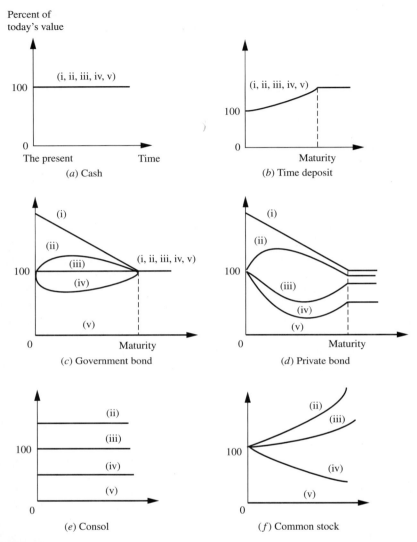

FIGURE 2.2
Predictability illustrated.

a longer time than small changes. Figure 2.2*d* differs from Fig. 2.2*c* in depicting a bond with some possibility of complete or partial default. For this reason, the curves do not completely converge at the maturity date.

The last two parts of Fig. 2.2 illustrate assets that never mature. In the case of a consol, the obligated payments never come to an end. As interest rates on competing obligations rise and fall, the value of a given consol will fall and rise. There is no upper limit, and there is no maturity to pull the various curves together. Figure 2.2*e* depicts a possible, but not necessarily typical, set of beliefs about a consol. The investor believes that, on balance, the interest rate applicable to perpetuities will always remain the same as today, and that the chance of the rate's being a specific percentage higher or lower is the same no matter how near or distant the future date. In the case of corporate common stock, Fig. 2.2f, there are no obligated payments at all. To uncertainty about the rate at which future payments will be discounted is added uncertainty of the amount of the payments themselves. The spread of probable values is shown becoming larger and larger as the future becomes more distant and less foreseeable. At the same time the general upward tilt of the band describes an investor's belief in the appreciation of the stock. Like the other examples, Fig. 2.2f is meant to be illustrative of the meaning of predictability as an attribute of an asset. Fig. 2.2 is, even in its entirety, far from an exhaustive catalog of possible asset properties and investor expectations.

The main sources of unpredictability of asset values have been illustrated in the discussion of Fig. 2.2 and can be briefly recapitulated. First there is uncertainty about the rates of interest by which the market will discount future payments of currency to arrive at their present value. Bonds, consols, stocks, and other prospects for future payments will fluctuate in price as the applicable interest rates vary. This source of uncertainty applies even when the amounts of future payments are known for certain. Second, for debtors other than the central government, there is a risk of default, temporary or permanent, of obligated payments of interest or principal. These two sources of uncertainty apply to assets that are essentially promises to pay currency. Additional uncertainties apply to assets that are not anchored to cash but represent instead equities in physical capital or claims to goods and services. Third, general price levels of consumers' goods and capital equities fluctuate. Fourth, superimposed on variations of the currency value of goods and services in general are changes in relative prices and in the relative fortunes of particular enterprises, which can make any individual real investment more or less valuable in terms of other goods and services.

In general, bands of predictability will vary for different investors as well as for different assets. For some assets, for example, those illustrated in Figs. 2.2a and 2.2b, the properties of the asset itself determine completely its value for all future dates; it is not possible to conceive of differences of opinion among informed and rational investors. For other assets, like the marketable government bond of Fig. 2.2c, differences of opinion are inconceivable for certain future dates, at maturity and beyond, but quite likely for others. For most assets, there can be differences among investors for all future dates. Common observation suggests a correlation between the degrees of unpredictability of the value of an asset on a certain date (the widths of the bands) and the variation among individuals in estimates of the asset's median value (the heights of the bands). But this correlation is empirical, not essential. One can imagine an asset whose value on a given date is far from perfectly predictable but is subject to objectively known probabilities. A government lottery bond provides an example. On a certain date the Treasury draws several numbers at random, and the holder of a bond with a lucky number receives a large prize. Knowing the odds, investors will all agree as to the band of predictability, although it may be a very wide band. In fact, however, assets of this nature are rare. Agreement among investors is generally confined to assets with little or no possible spread in value. Wide bands usually arise not because of known objective probabilities but because of unknown probabilities that each investor must guess for himself. Unlike lottery drawings, the main sources of uncertainty listed above—interest rates, default risks, price levels, relative prices—are not governed by objectively calculable odds.

2.6
YIELD AND RETURN

The *yield* of an asset over an interval of time consists of all the receipts and costs occasioned by its ownership throughout the interval. Both receipts and costs may take a variety of forms. Even the receipts due to financial assets are not always cash payments of interest and dividends but sometimes take the form of securities, for example, dividends paid in stock, rights to purchase stocks or bonds. Moreover, even financial assets involve carrying costs of various kinds: insurance against loss, safe deposit vault rental, record keeping, taxes. The variety of forms of receipts and costs is, of course, more striking for physical assets. The major receipt of the individual who owns his home is its use, and this is typical of consumers' durable goods. On the cost side, ownership of a durable good entails both cash outlay for insurance, repairs, and taxes, and personal effort in management, operation, and maintenance. Yields of producers' durable goods are, in general, still more complex. Their services are not directly consumed but contribute to the production of other goods and services. Their use involves a host of interrelated costs, mainly materials and labor for operating, housing, and maintaining the equipment.

In this usage, then, *yield* cannot be represented in a single dimension. To describe the yield of an asset requires as many numbers as there are kinds of receipts and costs: so much cash, so many man-hours of personal effort by the owner, so many hours of maintenance labor, so many hours of service of a machine, and so on. If all these receipts and costs can be valued in cash, the *value of the yield* can be reckoned.

Since the yield of an asset may take a variety of forms, the liquidity and reversibility of these forms are relevant properties of the asset. An asset with a positive cash yield is quite different from a consumers' durable good, like an automobile or washing machine, whose yield takes the form of services of little value except as directly consumed by the owner, and from a producers' durable good, like the tools and dies for automobile bodies of a particular design, whose positive yield consists of specialized parts soon obsolete.

Assets differ in the predictability of their yields, and a fortiori in the value of their yields. The miser holding currency in a safe deposit box knows for sure that it will be barren of receipts; he can also predict, for a year or so ahead at least, the carrying costs. Similarly the owner of a bond with fixed-interest coupons and no risk of default can foresee the yield of the asset and the value of the yield with complete certainty. In these cases the predictable receipts and costs are in cash form, but this is not essential. A well-controlled technological process may be virtually predictable in respect to its physical inputs and outputs. If the yields of simple goods of high durability, like jewelry or furniture, are reckoned in terms of time available for enjoyment by the owner, then they too are predictable.

The yields of most assets are far from completely predictable. The size and, often, the form of dividends; the ability and willingness of a debtor to meet interest obligations on time; the magnitudes of insurance, storage, taxes, and other carrying costs—all these are in some degree subject to uncertainty. The outputs and inputs associated with consumers' and producers' durable goods are not wholly foreseeable or controllable. To the extent that some of the components, positive or negative, of an asset's yield take forms other than cash, the valuation of these components is an additional source of uncertainty for the value of the yield. Even if the yield is perfectly predictable in terms of goods, services, or financial assets other than cash, the value of the yield will be uncertain unless the cash prices of these noncash items are known for sure in advance.

The value of the yield of an asset over an interval of time is, of course, not the sole fruit of owning it for that period. The asset itself may appreciate or depreciate in value over the interval. The total *return* to the owner is the algebraic sum of the value of the yield and the appreciation. Expressing the return as a percentage of the value of the asset at the beginning of the interval gives the *rate of return* for the period. The return and, therefore, the rate of return will generally be greater the longer the interval. To standardize returns for periods of different length, each rate of return is conventionally multiplied by (one year)/(length of period in years) to obtain the approximate equivalent rate of return per annum (ignoring compounding). Thus a rate of 1 percent over one quarter is equivalent to 4 percent a year, and a rate of 10 percent for a period of two years is the equivalent of 5 percent per annum.

Just as the form of the yield of an asset may be a relevant concern of the investor, so the proportions in which a given return is divided between yield and appreciation may be of importance to him. If both the asset and its yield were perfectly liquid, perfectly reversible, and finely divisible relative to the holdings of the investor, he would not care how the return was split between yield and appreciation. Should a corporation shareholder care whether he obtains the profits of the corporation as dividends or as appreciation in the value of the shares? If he is a big holder relative to the size of the shares, he will be able to convert cash dividends into larger holdings of the same stock or to convert into cash capital gains due to retained earnings. And if the exchange costs of these conversions are negligible and taxes are the same either way, the dividend policy of the corporation will be a matter of indifference to the shareholder. But the indivisibility of shares may be a problem to any investor to whom the return is smaller than the value of one share. If he would like to increase his equity in the corporation, he will not welcome cash dividends; if he would like to maintain his present equity and receive cash income, he will not be pleased by a plowing-back policy. Moreover, exchange costs are seldom negligible even for large holders. Exchange costs include trading, accounting, and handling costs for shares and dividend checks; and, much more important for many investors, they include income taxes on dividends and capital gains taxes on realized appreciations. These costs of share-to-cash and cash-to-shares conversions make the corporation's dividend policy very relevant to the investor.

In the case of most financial assets, the individual investor—unless he is a very large factor in the market—is powerless to influence the division of the return between yield and appreciation. This division is determined by the issuer—a government, a corporation, or a financial institution; and on the basis of the terms offered him the investor decides how much of the asset to hold. The situation is different for almost all physical assets: real estate and both producers' and consumers' durable goods. The owner has a range of choice as to the proportions in which his return is divided between yield and appreciation, or depreciation; and as a byproduct of this choice, he frequently determines also the size of his total return.

Figure 2.3 illustrates the nature of the choice. The horizontal axis measures the value of the yield over a given time interval; this can be either positive or negative, depending on whether the cash receipts and use of the asset outweigh in value the costs of operating, maintaining, and owning the asset. The vertical axis measures the appreciation in value over the interval; this also can be either positive or negative, because it is a compound of price changes and physical depreciation, depletion, and obsolescence. The yield-appreciation possibility locus shows for every attainable value of yield the maximum feasible appreciation, or minimum feasible depreciation. LL' is an example of such a locus, for a durable good. If a net yield of Y' is taken, the minimum depreciation that can occur is A'. Smaller yield—less use and more maintenance—will be accompanied by less depreciation; for example, at zero yield there would be depreciation of only A. The generally downward slope of the locus is a reflection of technological fact; the more current use demanded of an asset, the less useful it will be for the future. But there will frequently be upward-sloping ranges of the locus, as in the illustration. There is a point below which a car, for example, will deteriorate more the less it is used.

The return on the asset is the sum of the value of the yield, the abscissa, and the appreciation, the ordinate, where this sum is a maximum. On the illustrative locus in Fig. 2.3, the largest attainable return is at point M, where the slope of LL'

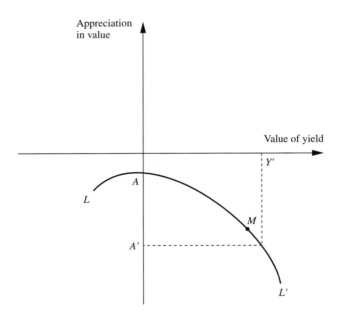

FIGURE 2.3
Yield and appreciation.

is −1. But the owner will not necessarily choose the maximum return. He may prefer to sacrifice total return either for a higher yield or for slower depreciation, unless the asset and its yield are perfectly liquid and reversible. Suppose that the total return on an automobile would be maximized by driving at a rate of 7500 miles per year. If the markets for cars and car services were perfect, no rational owner would drive more or less than 7500 miles a year. An owner desiring more mileage would rent the additional service in another car. But in an imperfect market for car services, the costs of renting mileage exceed the value of mileage to an owner. In consequence the owner has an incentive to use his own car even at some sacrifice of total return. On the other hand, an owner may wish to preserve his automobile investment above the level to which use at a rate of 7500 miles a year would reduce the value of his car. In a perfect market he would let to others any of the 7500 miles he did not himself desire and use the resulting cash, along with his depreciated car, to build up his automobile investment to the desired level. But since cars are imperfectly reversible—it costs more to buy one than the owner can obtain by selling it—there is some incentive to avoid the loss involved in exchanging one car for another.

2.7
PREDICTABILITY OF REAL VALUES AND REAL RETURNS

Value has been defined in terms of currency. But only misers desire currency for its own sake rather than for what it can buy. Rational individuals save to provide, either from yield or from capital, for their own or others' future needs and desires for goods and services. Future consumption requirements may be anticipated with considerable uncertainty and imprecision, but ultimately they are the raison d'être for holding and accumulating wealth. Therefore the real values of assets and of asset yields and returns—their purchasing power over goods and services—are more relevant than the cash values. Of course consumption patterns vary with individual circumstance and taste, and there is a different "real value" for every variation. Vegetarians do not care what happens to the price of meat; congenital aristocrats worry more about the costs of domestic service than of appliances; bachelors do not feel the rising costs of diapers. But for most practical purposes a single index of prices, in the United States the Consumers' Price Index (CPI) of the Bureau of Labor Statistics, can be used to measure changes in the purchasing power of the dollar. The weights given various items in such an index are based on average consumption patterns as revealed in family budget surveys. Actual families deviate in greater or smaller degree from the standard market basket represented by these weights.

The appropriateness of the index is enhanced by the fact that, because major inflationary and deflationary movements of prices tend to be pervasive, the index is not sensitive to small changes in relative weights. But market baskets change, weights become out of date, and the index must be re-based periodically. A less tractable problem is adjustment for changes in the quality of existing goods and services— medical services, personal computers, automobiles—and, even more difficult, for the introduction of entirely new products such as compact disks, televisions, fax machines. Many experts suspect that the CPI exaggerates inflation rates by from one-half to two percentage points per year.[6]

By the *real value* of a unit of currency is meant its purchasing power, expressed relative to its purchasing power at an arbitrary base period, in terms of the standard consumption pattern used in weighting the CPI. Thus, for example, if the three-year period 1982–84 is the base, an index of 150 means that the real value of currency is $\frac{2}{3}$ or $66\frac{2}{3}$ percent of what it was in 1982–84. By the *real value* of an asset on a particular date is meant simply its value in currency multiplied by the real value of currency at that date. The real value of the yield of an asset is similarly reckoned. Some caution is needed in converting money return to real return. The *real return* over an interval of time is the change in the real value of the asset plus the real value of the yield. Suppose that at the beginning of an interval the consumers' price index stood at 120 and that it rose to 160 by the end of the period. Consider an asset valued at $120 at the beginning and $140 at the end, with a net yield of $20 becoming available at the end of the period. In terms of currency, or current dollars, there was a capital gain of $20, a total return of $40, a rate of return of $33\frac{1}{3}$ percent. But in terms of base period dollars, the value of the asset declined from 100 at the beginning of the period to 87.5 ($= \frac{140}{160}$) at the end, a capital loss of 12.5. This was just offset by the real value of the yield, 12.5 ($= \frac{20}{160}$). The real return was therefore zero. Note that it would not be correct to compute, in place of the *change in real value,* the *real value of the change in money value.* In the example, there was a capital gain, in terms of cash, of $20, which had a real value of 12.5. But this does not allow for the 25 percent loss of purchasing power of the $120 representing the initial value of the asset.

If values are reckoned in real terms rather than money terms, assets rank very differently in predictability of value and of yield. Few assets available in the United States are perfectly predictable in real value. Cash assets themselves are quite unpredictable in real value, as a glance at the history of any general price index will show. They would have to be described by diagrams like Figs. 2.2e and 2.2f rather than 2.2a. For the same reason, bonds and other obligations to pay currency lose, in the realm of real values, the predictability (see Figs. 2.2b–2.2c) they have in the world of money values. Indeed, equities in nonfinancial corporations and other titles to physical goods may well be more predictable than obligations expressed in money terms. If the important fluctuations in price level are all-pervasive, even a single good may have more stability of general purchasing power than currency or claims to currency. But the investor can do better than confine himself to a single good. He can buy shares in a diversified corporation or in an equity mutual fund, or he can diversify his own portfolio. In these ways he can protect himself in the long run against erratic changes in the relative price structure and erratic events in the fortunes of particular firms and yet at the same time follow the significant movements of the general price level. Figure 2.4 shows the purchasing power of the dollar and the purchasing power of an index of industrial stocks, each related to the three-year average 1982–84 as 100. For short periods of time, say a year or less, the dollar is generally more predictable in real value. However, in the long run, although stock

---

[6]In December 1996 a federal commission chaired by Michael Boskin, chairman of the Council of Economic Advisers to President Bush, estimated the upward bias as 1.1 percentage points.

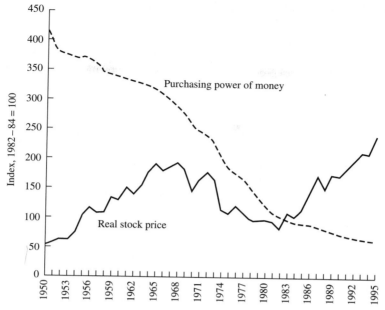

FIGURE 2.4
Real stock prices and the purchasing power of money 1950–1992. The
real equity price is the Standard & Poor 500 stock index divided by the
consumer price index. The real purchasing power of money is 1/CPI.
(*Source:* Council of Economic Advisors, *Annual Report,* 1996.)

prices are quite volatile, broad stock averages are more stable than the dollar in real
value.

The traditions of financial institutions and the public regulations that govern
them are strongly wedded to the convention that the dollar bill is the standard
of value. Considerable private and governmental initiative has been devoted to
providing the public with assets predictable in money value, tailored to a wide variety of circumstances, tastes, and degrees of financial sophistication—government
and corporate obligations of all forms, bank deposits and savings-and-loan shares,
innumerable kinds of life insurance contracts, and various retirement and pension
schemes.

Aside from home ownership, life insurance and participation in retirement programs are the most convenient and important assets for the great mass of savers of
modest means. While they do not offer CPI-indexed annuities, they often permit the
holder to increase coverage automatically as the CPI rises. Private retirement funds
are generally fairly good investment hedges insofar as they are invested in equities
and short-term interest-bearing assets. Variable annuities explicitly reflect equity
investments. Social Security payments are indexed to the CPI, and both Medicare
and most private health insurance keep up with medical costs. Over the long run,
the purchasing power of equities is independent of commodity prices, as indicated

in Fig. 2.4. The *Fisher effect*[7] of inflationary expectations on short-term interest rates makes short-term securities quite stable in real purchasing power. Long-term bonds, however, are much more vulnerable to purchasing-power risk.

Little effort has been directed toward offering the public assets predictable in real value. The United States Treasury never issued bonds with value and yield tied to the CPI.[8] *Purchasing power bonds* would fill the gap in the present spectrum of available assets; they would be, at least for certain future dates, predictable in real value. In determining other features, the Treasury would have the same range of choice as its conventional offerings provide. Purchasing power bonds could be made marketable, highly liquid, and highly reversible. If financial institutions were eligible to hold them, they could serve as the basis for variable life insurance and pension contracts from which both the unavoidable residual risks and the social stigma of stock market speculation would be removed. One can even imagine banks' investing in these bonds and in turn offering savings deposits of fixed purchasing power to savers desiring a divisible asset free of risks of change of value due to interest rate fluctuations. As an alternative or a supplement to marketable issues, the Treasury could offer nonmarketable bonds, eligible only for individuals, on the general pattern of its present savings bonds. These could be made more or less liquid, as desired; indeed, the price of the purchasing power guarantee might be the holding of the bond until maturity.

2.8
ACCEPTABILITY IN EXCHANGE

Goods and services are purchased, and obligations are settled, in many different ways. Barter transactions, ranging from housework performed in exchange for board and room to swaps of entire industrial plants, are common even in advanced economies. Goods and services are purchased not only by currency or by check but also by credit card charges, debits to automatic teller machine cards, installment loans, open book credit, and other promises to pay cash later. Even obligations to pay cash are sometimes settled by securities or goods of equivalent value.

The use of the dollar as the unit of account in transactions is to be distinguished from the transfer of dollar currency. Dollar values are convenient for reckoning the equivalence of the two sides of an exchange, even if it is entirely a barter involving neither currency nor promises to pay currency. Indeed, it is entirely conceivable to have a unit of account without any physical counterpart ever used as a medium of exchange. The present arrangements in the United States may be thus interpreted. After all, what is a dollar? Bills that formerly circulated as currency said that they were promises to pay one, or five, or ten, or x "dollars." But anyone who asked the Treasury or the Federal Reserve Banks, who had issued these bills, for "dollars"

---

[7] According to Irving Fisher (1930), nominal interest rates set in financial markets compensate for expected inflation, at least in long runs. Short maturities are more reliable inflation hedges than long maturities, which lose capital value when inflation and interest rates rise.

[8] In 1996 the U.S. Treasury announced that it will issue indexed securities. See Shiller (1995) for proposals to offer savers not only CPI-indexed bonds but other assets tailored to hedge their risks.

in redemption of currency would just receive different currency bearing the same promise. Now the fiction has been abandoned, and the currently issued Federal Reserve note defines itself on its face as dollars of legal tender.

In a formal legal sense the dollar is still a prescribed weight of gold, 0.0231 ounces, implying a gold price of $43.22 per ounce, about one-eighth of the free market price. Before 1933 gold coins of the then prescribed weight—corresponding to a gold price of $20.67—were in circulation. Since 1933 no gold coins have been in circulation, and the Treasury has not been willing to convert paper dollars held by private individuals into gold at the theoretical parity. Indeed between 1933 and 1975, U.S. citizens could not legally own gold except for numismatic, ornamental, or industrial purposes. Since 1971 the U.S. Treasury has not been willing to redeem in gold even those dollars held by foreign central banks and governments or international monetary institutions. See Chapter 8 and Tobin (1992).

The acceptability of an asset as payment for goods and services or as settlement of contractual obligations is another relevant asset characteristic. Clearly assets vary tremendously in the likelihood that they will be accepted at value in transactions. Some assets are generally acceptable within a national jurisdiction. In the United States and most other advanced economies the generally acceptable media are currency issues of the government or central bank and the demand obligations of other banks. (Personal checks are not generally acceptable media of exchange. It is the liability of the bank, which a personal check transfers from the payor depositor to a payee, that is generally acceptable. The check is accepted in payment only when the payee is confident that the drawer of the check is able to transfer the bank's liability.)

Why are some assets selected by a society as generally acceptable media of exchange while others are not? This is not an easy question, because the selection is self-justifying. If my creditors will take marbles in settlement of my debts to them, why should not I in turn take marbles from my debtors? Marbles—or stones, or cigarettes, or precious metals—may have little or no intrinsic value; their value will arise from the willingness of others to give things of utility in exchange for them. Anthropology testifies to the variety of assets that various peoples around the world through the ages have chosen as media of exchange.[9]

In advanced societies the central government is in a strong position to make certain assets generally acceptable media. By its willingness to accept a designated asset in settlement of taxes and other obligations, the government makes that asset acceptable to any who have such obligations, and in turn to others who have obligations to them, and so on. In addition, the government is the ultimate reliance for enforcement of private contracts; whatever assets the government designates as legal tender are bound to be accepted by creditors.

In addition to those assets designated by the government as legal tender or acceptable in payment of obligation to the government, others may become generally acceptable media. To be a good candidate for this status, an asset should possess certain obvious characteristics: stability and predictability of value, high liquidity and reversibility, divisibility, a yield comparable in value to that of currency. But a listing

---

[9]See Einzig (1966) for a catalogue of various types of assets used as money in other cultures.

of this kind is not a satisfactory explanation. A new asset endowed with all these properties would no doubt become a generally acceptable medium of exchange. On the other hand, general acceptability itself would bestow many of these properties and render irrelevant the absence of others. Ninety-day U.S. Treasury bills, payable to bearer, are not generally acceptable, and this fact can be rationalized in a number of ways. Bills can vary in price, and it takes ordinary folks a little time and some cost to sell them. They come only in large denominations. The trouble with the rationalization is that if Treasury bills were a medium of exchange they would not vary in price, and selling them would be quick and cheap—and also unnecessary. Even their indivisibility could be put up with, given that there are other media available for making change. The principal reason, then, that Treasury bills are not media of exchange is that they are not generally acceptable. This unsatisfactory circular conclusion underlines the essential point that general acceptability in exchange is one of those phenomena—like language, rules of the road, fashion in dress—where the fact of social consensus is much more important and much more predictable than the content. Whether or not an asset is a generally acceptable means of payment will have to be taken as a datum determined by legal institutions and social conventions, rather than as something to be explained by economic theory.

APPENDIX 2A: ASSET PRICES, YIELDS, AND RETURNS

As noted in the text, asset returns consist of two components, yield and appreciation. Let $r(t)$, $y(t)$, and $V(t)$ be the rate of return, value of yield, and value of asset, respectively, of an asset at time t. They can usually be written without misunderstanding simply as r, y, V. Let $\dot{V}$ be dV/dt. Time is taken to be continuous. The three variables are related as follows:

$$r = y/V + \dot{V}/V. \tag{2A.1}$$

Thus a share of stock currently valued at \$100 that is appreciating at 5 percent per year and paying a \$2 dividend would be returning 7 percent per year. (This kind of calculation can be made in either real or nominal terms.)

The same relationship can be written as (2A.2), which can be interpreted as the basic differential equation for asset valuation V. Given the time paths of r, y, the equation tells the time path of V. Here the rate of return r can be regarded as the rate holders require of this asset because it can be earned by competitive assets available to them in the market. That opportunity-cost market rate serves as the rate of discount of the future yields y of the asset being evaluated.

$$\dot{V} = rV - y \tag{2A.2}$$

A solution to (2A.2) is $V^*(t)$, the familiar formula for discounted present value:

$$V^*(t) = \int_t^\infty y(s)e^{-\int_t^s r(\tau)d\tau}\,ds. \tag{2A.3}$$

If r is constant at $\bar{r}$, this solution reduces to

$$V^*(t) = \int_t^\infty y(s)e^{-(s-t)\bar{r}}\,ds. \tag{2A.4}$$

Here it is assumed that the future paths of y and r are foreseen with certainty, or that their expected values can be used as certainty equivalents. Asset valuations with uncertainty are discussed in subsequent chapters. If y is growing at a constant rate g, so that $y(s) = y(t)e^{g(s-t)}$, then

$$V^*(t) = \int_t^\infty y(s)e^{-(s-t)\bar{r}}\,ds = y(t)\int_t^\infty e^{-(s-t)(\bar{r}-g)}\,ds. \tag{2A.5}$$

Examples

For illustration, consider some special cases, with stationary discount rates $\bar{r}$.

Bill. A bill is title to a single nonrecurrent payment $y(T)$ at time T (or any time thereafter). For $t \geq T$, $V^*(t) = y(T)$. That is, after maturity, an unexercised claim is simply worth $y(T)$.

$$V^*(t) = y(T)e^{-(T-t)\bar{r}} \qquad (0 \leq t \leq T) \tag{2A.6}$$

Bond. A bond combines a sequence of coupons $y(s)$ with a bill, a single final payment at maturity T of $y(T)$. The coupons are usually a fixed amount $\bar{y}$ paid at regular intervals, conventionally twice a year. Here they are approximated as a steady continuous flow:

$$V^*(t) = y(T)e^{-(T-t)\bar{r}} + \bar{y}\int_t^T e^{-(s-t)\bar{r}}\,ds$$

$$= y(T)e^{-(T-t)\bar{r}} + (\bar{y}/\bar{r})(1 - e^{-(T-t)\bar{r}}) \qquad (0 \leq t \leq T). \tag{2A.7}$$

Consol. A consol is a bond which promises a perpetual constant stream of income of $\bar{y}$ per year, without any bill-like final payment. In that case,

$$V^*(t) = \bar{y}\int_t^\infty e^{-(s-t)\bar{r}}\,ds = \bar{y}/\bar{r}. \tag{2A.8}$$

Equity stock. Like a consol, a share of stock has no maturity. Its dividends y are not constant. As a special case, consider a stock whose dividends are expected to grow forever at an exponential rate g from time t onwards. Thus $y(s) = y(t)e^{g(s-t)}$. In that case,

$$V^*(t) = \frac{y(t)}{\bar{r} - g},$$

provided that $\bar{r} > g$. Of course, in reality, yields on stocks are uncertain and cannot be described by such a simple process.

Bubbles. Equation (2A.3), of which (2A.4) is a special case, is not the only possible solution of the differential equation (2A.2). The general solution contains a self-fulfilling speculative component, in which V is expected to grow and does grow at the rate of return r.

$$V(t) = Ae^{\int_0^t r(s)\,ds} + V^*(t) \tag{2A.9}$$

where A is an arbitrary constant. Readers can satisfy themselves that this is a solution by differentiating it with respect to t and obtaining (2A.2). One can regard the second term of (2A.9) as the fundamental value of the asset and the first term as the speculative bubble component. From (2A.9) at some arbitrary time zero,

$$V(0) = A + V^*(0) \qquad \text{and} \qquad A = V(0) - V^*(0) \tag{2A.10}$$

$$V(t) = [V(0) - V^*(0)]e^{\int_0^t r(s)\,ds} + V^*(t).$$

This indicates that once a speculative component arises ($A \neq 0$), it eventually dominates V^* and if not unexpectedly reversed takes V to plus or minus infinity as time approaches infinity. A rational expectations theorist would say that market participants, knowing that this cannot happen, will value the asset at V^*.

Some assets are purely speculative, that is, $y(t) = 0$ for all t, and $V^*(t) = 0$. As noted in the text, their value is based solely on the value that future speculators' markets will place on them.

CHAPTER 3

Portfolio Selection with Predictable Assets, with Application to the Demand for Money

This and the following chapter analyze portfolio choice. This chapter begins with perfectly predictable assets, as defined in the previous chapter, and concentrates on the role of liquidity. The analysis is applied in some detail to the demand for money. Chapter 4 turns to portfolio selection with imperfectly predictable assets, developing and making use of mean-variance analysis both for a single period and for a multi-period investment decision. These chapters provide foundations for understanding asset demands. Subsequent chapters will introduce asset supplies and endogenous determination of asset prices.

3.1
THE ROLE OF LIQUIDITY IN PORTFOLIO CHOICE

3.1.1 Perfect Asset Markets

The complex of considerations involved in selection of an investment portfolio can be approached by commencing with a set of fully liquid, perfectly reversible, and completely divisible assets and with an investor who is completely certain of the future of every asset. The investor's decision is then extremely simple. Of the portfolios available to her at any moment, she will select one with at least as high a current rate of return as any other. If there is one asset that in her judgment promises a higher rate of return than any other, she will put her entire wealth into that asset and nothing into any other. (Indeed, to the extent that she can borrow at a rate lower than the return on the most lucrative asset, she will invest in it more than her net worth.) Should the rate of return on several, or all, assets be identical, there is no unique optimum portfolio.

    This description of portfolio selection applies in principle no matter how short the period ahead over which rates of return are calculated. Given the assumed perfection of assets and asset markets, returns for longer periods do not matter. The portfolio can always be changed without cost whenever a different selection of assets offers a higher current return. For example, suppose that over month one the rate of return on portfolio A is expected to be .01 and that on portfolio B .02. But over the next two months together the rate of return on A is expected to be .04 while that on B remains .02. This implies that in month two the rate of return on A is expected to be .03/1.01, nearly .03, while that on B is expected to be zero. The superiority of A in month two, even though it gives A an overall edge for the full two months, is irrelevant to the selection of a portfolio today. The thing to do is to hold B the first month, then sell B and buy A. This gives a rate of return over the two months of 1.02(1.04/1.01) − 1.00, a little better than .05, which is better than can be earned by holding either A or B for the entire two months. There is no reason why the months in this argument cannot be weeks, or days, or hours, or minutes. However short the period, it is only returns over the period immediately ahead that are relevant to portfolio selection. This is true no matter how near or distant the dates when the investor intends to consume her wealth and its earnings. In the example, whether the investor wants to consume her wealth after one month or not until the end of the two months, her best initial investment is B.

3.1.2 Imperfect Asset Markets

3.1.2.1 The frequency of portfolio shifts and investment decisions

Asset exchange costs, illiquidities, and irreversibilities impart some inertia and stability to portfolio choices, keeping the planned period for holding any portfolio from being infinitesimally short. Some shifts are just not possible, and any portfolio shift involves some costs in time, effort, and money. Any new portfolio must promise enough advantage in return over the old to compensate for these costs. Suppose that an investor is seeking to maximize the value of her wealth on a definite and unique target date—the day she plans to retire, the summer she is going to travel around the world, or the September her daughter enters college. She knows, or at least believes she knows, the future of all assets from today until the target date. She can estimate the possibilities and costs of portfolio shifts at any time during the relevant period. Innumerable portfolio sequences are available to her. Each sequence specifies the quantities of all the assets to be held on every date. Sequences vary in the frequency and cost of asset transactions they imply. At one extreme are portfolio sequences involving no shifts and no exchange costs; even current yields are left in whatever asset form they occur, cash dividends in cash, stock dividends in stock, deposit interest on deposit, and so forth. At the other extreme are sequences involving daily or hourly shifts in response to small or temporary differences in asset prospects. For each possible sequence it is in principle possible to compute the overall return that may be expected, net of shifting costs, for the period from today until the target date. The investor will choose the sequence of maximum net return, and today's portfolio will be her first step in the chosen sequence. If tomorrow or next month her expectations or circumstances change, she will make this decision anew, unconstrained by her previous choice of sequence except by the fact that her existing portfolio has the advantage, over other possible initial steps in a new sequence, of costing nothing to shift into.

The impact of shifting costs on portfolio sequence choices depends on, among other things, the relation of the costs to (a) the number of portfolio shifts, (b) the number of assets involved in a shift, and (c) the total value of the transactions. Costs that depend on (a) encourage infrequent but thorough portfolio revisions. Costs that depend on (b) are an incentive to minimize the number of assets involved in any portfolio shift and to concentrate on particular occasions the dealings in any one asset. To save costs that depend on (c), the investor will seek to keep the total value of transactions down, but in the absence of the other two relationships she would not care whether shifts were frequent and small or infrequent and large. A specific example of the impact of costs of types (a) and (c) on portfolio strategy is given in Section 3.2 in the discussion of the transactions demand for cash.

Shifting costs and decision-making costs should be distinguished. The decision is the choice of a portfolio sequence. Once a decision is made, it implies certain portfolio switches and asset transactions. These involve costs, but they do not involve new decisions. Executing the scheduled shifts is a mechanical matter, which might be left to the investor's assistants or agents, properly instructed. Reconsideration of the sequence itself, in the light of new evaluations of asset prospects, may occur either more or less frequently than shifting within a given chosen sequence. Reconsideration may be almost continuous, but the decision typically resulting may be to stick with a chosen sequence involving little or no shifting. Or the investor may conceivably go in for complex portfolio strategies reconsidered only rarely. Frequency of decision making depends on some calculus of the average estimated gains from basing holdings on up-to-date information and expectations against the costs and troubles of the decision process. The professional expert who has the knowledge and point of vantage to turn this morning's market quotations into profit will strike this balance differently from the amateur who has little reason to think her appraisals of the future today are any better than her guesses, implicit or explicit, of the same future a year ago. Although portfolio shifting and decision making are different in principle, their timing no doubt coincides in practice for many investors.

3.1.2.2 Effects of timing of accumulation goals

Besides limiting the frequency of portfolio shifts, imperfections of assets and asset markets make the timing of the investor's accumulation objectives relevant to her portfolio decision. In the example used above, suppose that the costs of switching from B to A at the end of the first month exceeded 1 percent of the value of the portfolio. This could be true for several reasons: for example, asset exchange costs, or imperfect liquidity, depriving both A and B, or A alone, of some value if held for less than two months. Greater appreciation over the two months would be obtained by holding A the entire time. For an investor concerned only with the value of her wealth a month hence, the best bet is B. For an investor concerned only with her wealth after two months, regardless of what may happen to its value meanwhile, the choice is A. An investor with mixed accumulation objectives—some wealth destined for expenditure after a month and the rest after two months—will hold a mixture of A and B.

The simple example makes the point: One reason for portfolio diversification is diversity in the timing of the objectives of accumulating wealth. Given imperfect liquidities, irreversibilities, and costs of asset exchanges, the portfolio sequence or strategy that promises the highest return for one date is not the same one that promises the highest return for another date. A retirement fund is not a sensible or even a possible way to save up for next year's new car. A savings account, useful for short-run objectives because of its liquidity and reversibility, offers insufficient return to serve as a vehicle for retirement savings. An individual may well hold both.

There are two senses in which an investor may have mixed accumulation objectives. First, she may be certain of the timing of her consumption requirements and preferences and of her income from sources other than wealth holdings, as well as of the returns she can expect until every date from possible portfolio sequences. Within the possibilities open to her, she chooses the planned pattern of consumption she likes the best. She plans to distribute consumption of her wealth over time so that it fills in most effectively the gaps between consumption requirements and expected income, always taking account of the fact that the later she consumes, the more she can consume. Second, she may anticipate a consumption-income gap due to an emergency that increases consumption requirements or reduces earning power, but she may be quite uncertain when it will occur. If the function of her wealth is to meet such a gap, she must choose a portfolio that will do so whenever the emergency occurs.

3.1.2.3 Liquidity preference: Diversification for mixed and uncertain target dates

The nature of the asset choices facing an individual with mixed accumulation objectives—in either or both of the two senses just defined—may be illustrated in a simple example involving only two assets and two dates.[1] Asset X is the illiquid asset. Over two periods a dollar invested in X will increase in value to $(1 + r_x)^2$. But X simply cannot be sold at any price until it has been held two periods. In contrast, investment in a dollar's worth of Z, the liquid asset, can be realized at the end of one period at $1 + r_z$ or at the end of two periods at $(1 + r_z)^2$. At the end of the first investment period, the individual expects to receive an income y_1 from sources other than her wealth, and at the end of the second period, y_2. Following the end of the first investment period, she will engage in consumption expenditure c_1, within limits permitted by her disposable wealth at that time and her other income y_1. Borrowing is ruled out, although this is not essential, for reasons given below. Following the second investment period, she will engage in consumption expenditure c_2, using up the remainder of her wealth and her other income y_2. Let consumption and income, the c_i and y_i, be expressed for convenience as proportions of initial wealth. The problem is to divide initial wealth into a fraction x invested in X and $z = 1 - x$ invested in Z so as to obtain the optimal combination of consumptions (c_1, c_2). It is

---

[1] This example also illustrates the intertemporal dimension of portfolio selection, an aspect which has been strongly emphasized in the recent literature in finance. See, for example, the surveys by Breeden (1989), Hakansson (1989), and Merton (1989). Chapter 4 discusses intertemporal aspects of portfolio selection.

assumed that r_x exceeds r_z, as otherwise asset X would clearly have no claim for consideration.

The decision depends, of course, on the relative sizes of y_1 and y_2; the function of wealth is to iron out fluctuations of income relative to consumption requirements. If y_2 is low, investment in X to increase c_2 is indicated, whereas if y_1 is low, investment in Z is required to support c_1. The objective of the consumer-investor, to achieve the optimal combination of first-period consumption and second-period consumption, may be expressed by saying that she wishes to maximize a utility or satisfaction level $U(c_1, c_2)$. This utility function is assumed to have the standard properties that guarantee diminishing marginal rates of substitution between first- and second-period consumption. A high consumption requirement in one period has the same effects on investment planning as an abnormally low income in that period, and the argument to follow will apply equally to fluctuations in consumption requirements. An abnormal consumption requirement in period 1, for example, can be interpreted as a constant increase in the level of total first-period consumption required to produce a given level of utility. Thus an abnormal requirement of amount C would mean that the utility function is replaced by a new utility function V such that $V(c_1, c_2) = U(c_1 - C, c_2)$.

Consider first the combinations of first- and second-period consumption that are attainable by the investor, given her initial wealth, her incomes in the two periods, and the rates of return on the two assets. The maximum possible first-period consumption c_1, conditional on portfolio choice of z and x, is first-period income y_1 plus the value, after one period, of the investment in Z:

$$c_1 \leq z(1 + r_z) + y_1. \tag{3.1}$$

If c_1 is less than this maximum, the remainder can be invested in Z for the second period. Second-period consumption will consist of three parts—the proceeds of this one-period investment in Z, the proceeds of the two-period investment in X, and income y_2.

$$c_2 = [z(1 + r_z) + y_1 - c_1](1 + r_z) + x(1 + r_x)^2 + y_2. \tag{3.2}$$

The maximum possible c_1 occurs when x, the fraction invested in X, is set at zero; the corresponding c_2 is y_2. From this point there are two ways to increase c_2 at the expense of c_1. One way is to hold x constant at zero but to save for later consumption some of the first-period proceeds of investment in Z. A dollar less c_1 will thus produce $1 + r_z$ more c_2. The other way is to vary x; shifting $1/(1 + r_z)$ from initial investment in Z to X will reduce c_1 by 1 and increase c_2 by $(1 + r_x)^2/(1 + r_z)$. Given that r_x exceeds r_z, the second way is clearly the more efficient. It can proceed until $x = 1$, where $c_1 = y_1$ and $c_2 = (1 + r_x)^2 + y_2$. Further substitution of c_2 for c_1 can occur only by investing some of y_1 in Z, increasing c_2 by $1 + r_z$ for every unit reduction of c_1. The situation is pictured in Fig. 3.1. The kinked line ABC represents the efficient set of possible consumption combinations (c_1, c_2), constructed, as just described, to depict the maximum possible c_2 compatible with each obtainable level of c_1.

The curves convex to the origin in Fig. 3.1 are indifference loci—along any curve are combinations of consumption (c_1, c_2) representing equal levels of utility.

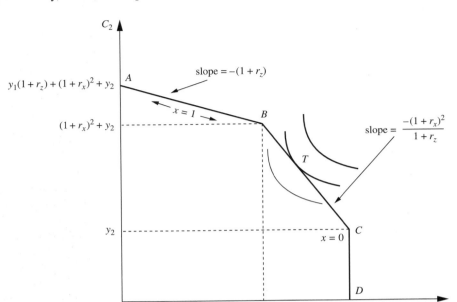

FIGURE 3.1
Two-period investment opportunities.

Higher curves are, of course, preferred to lower ones. In the figure, T, the point of tangency of an indifference curve and the line BC, is the most satisfactory of the attainable consumption combinations. To obtain T, the investor must choose an initial investment mixture of roughly three-fifths X and two-fifths Z.

The optimal initial portfolio will, in general, be sensitive to the excess of r_x over r_z. An increase of r_x will lift points A and B vertically by equal amounts, while C and D remain fixed; thus BC becomes steeper. The new tangency, on a higher indifference curve, may be either to the left or to the right of the old, or directly above it; correspondingly x may be increased or decreased or the same. The outcome depends on the familiar war of substitution and income effects. The increase in r_x is an incentive to substitute later consumption for earlier; the rewards of waiting are increased. But the increase in r_x constitutes also an increment in the overall resources at the disposition of the investor, part of which she would normally allocate to early consumption.

The central point of the example can be made most clearly by considering the two extreme cases where income is zero in one period and equal to 1 in the other. Figures 3.2*a* and 3.2*b* show the opportunity locus of Fig. 3.1 in these two special cases. The indifference loci have been deliberately drawn so that the investor's choice is 100 percent Z ($x = 0$) in Fig. 3.2*a*, where income is concentrated in the second period, and 100 percent X ($x = 1$) in Fig. 3.2*b*, where income is concentrated in the first period.

Now suppose that the investor is sure that an income of 1 will occur in one of the two periods, but she is not sure which. (Or—what amounts analytically to the same

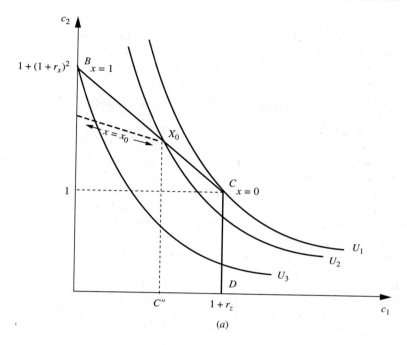

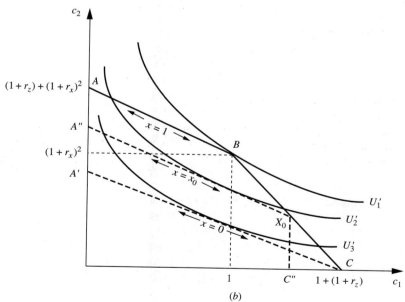

FIGURE 3.2
Investment and consumption choices: Two special cases. (a) $y_1 = 0$, $y_2 = 1$;
(b) $y_1 = 1$, $y_2 = 0$.

thing—although her income is known in advance to be evenly divided between the two periods, she anticipates an extraordinary consumption requirement but does not know in which period.) If she sets x at 1—100 percent investment in X—and it turns out that her income is delayed until the second period, she will be unable to consume anything in the first period. She will wind up at point B in Fig. 3.2a, at a utility level U_3. If she sets x at 0—100 percent investment in Z—and it turns out that the whole income occurs in the first period, she will likewise have cause for regret. But she is not so badly off as in the case of the opposite error. She can still provide for some consumption in the second period by refraining from consuming all her wealth and income at once. The amount that she saves for later consumption will earn only r_z, the interest on Z. Once she lets the chance to invest in X go by, the terms on which she can substitute c_2 for c_1 are given in Fig. 3.2b by $A'C$, with a slope of $-(1 + r_z)$. This will enable her to reach utility level U_3'. Rather than take the chance of being reduced in utility level either to U_3 or to U_3', the investor may prefer a mixed portfolio, say x_0 in X and $1 - x_0$ in Z. Once x_0 is fixed, c_1 is limited to $(1 - x_0)(1 + r_z) + y_1$, indicated by points C'' in Figs. 3.2a and 3.2b. Further increase in c_2 at the expense of c_1 can be obtained by investment in Z for the second period, on the terms indicated by the lines $A''X_0$, which have the same slope $-(1 + r_z)$ as AB and $A'C$ in Fig. 3.2b. A portfolio x_0 would give the investor a utility level U_2 if y_1 turns out to be zero and U_2' if y_1 turns out to be 1. Conceivably x_0 could be chosen so that U_2 and U_2' are equal. In any case, the worse outcome from a mixed portfolio is a happier result than either U_3 or U_3', the worse outcomes of the two pure portfolios. The decision problem may be summarized as follows:

Investor utility as a function of portfolio choice

	$x = 0$	$x = 1$	$x = x_0$
If $y_1 = 0, y_2 = 1$	U_1	U_3	U_2
If $y_1 = 1, y_2 = 0$	U_3'	U_1'	U_2'

The actual mixture x_0 chosen would depend on the investor's estimate of the probabilities of the two income patterns. The greater the probability of the second pattern, the closer x_0 will be to 1. But if the indifference loci are strongly curved, indicating that the investor resists departures from rough equality between the two consumption levels, the asymmetry of the situation favors the liquid asset.

This asymmetry could be removed, without affecting the essential point of the example, by permitting the investor to increase her first-period consumption either by selling X or by borrowing against X or y_2. There must, of course, be a penalty for incorrect foresight; the terms on which c_1 can be expanded at the expense of c_2 at the end of the first period must be less favorable than the terms on which this could have been done initially. That is, the discount in selling X or borrowing at the end of the first period must be such that for each unit of original investment in X, representing potential second-period consumption of $(1 + r_x)^2$, the investor obtains less than $1 + r_x$ in first-period consumption.

3.2
THE DEMAND FOR MONEY

Among the assets that may play a part in the portfolio decisions discussed in the preceding section are means of payment, and the purpose of the present section is to apply the theory of portfolio choice to the classical question of the determinants of the demand for money. In this book money means generally acceptable means of payment, unless otherwise specified. Basically there are two possible motives for holding money, the *transactions motive* and the *investment motive*. Money held for the transactions motive may be divided into two parts: money's share in the *working balances* held in connection with transactions on income account, and transient cash holdings incident to the management of portfolios. In addition, in some financial systems money may be held for the second motive, as a long-run investment.

The *transactions motive* arises most obviously in systems wherein money is unique among assets in being a generally acceptable means of payment. Anyone expecting to make a payment must have the required amount of money in her possession in advance; a snapshot inventory taken during that advance period, which may indeed be very short, would show her holding a certain cash balance. Analogously, anyone expecting to ride a New York subway must provide herself with the necessary turnstile token at least a few seconds in advance. A snapshot taken during those few seconds would show the prospective rider to have a transactions balance of one token, perhaps more if she is a habitual rider and wishes to avoid the delays and inconveniences of frequent token purchases. At any moment there is a considerable aggregate transactions balance of tokens, in the hands of riders at that moment approaching the turnstiles and of riders elsewhere who have anticipated future needs. The *investment motive* is connected with money's property as a store of value, a characteristic money shares with all other assets available for the portfolios of wealth owners. To pursue the subway-token analogy, it is conceivable, if far-fetched, to imagine an individual to hold subway tokens as an investment or speculation, without any particular intention of using them to ride the subway. She might be led to do so if she thought it possible that the subway authority would raise the price of tokens without canceling the validity of those outstanding. In certain circumstances a portfolio manager might hold cash balances not because she anticipated need for means of payment but because she regarded the prospects of appreciation in real value as favorable relative to the prospects of other available assets.

3.2.1 Transactions and Cash Requirements

3.2.1.1 Transactions on income account and asset exchanges

The temptation is strong to point out the obvious fact that the economy's transactions requirements for means of payment depend on the rate at which transactions occur, perhaps to postulate a relation of proportionality between volume of transactions per year and stock of money (the transactions velocity of money), and to leave the matter there. Unfortunately this approach is as defective as it is simple. It leaves unexplored the fundamental determinants of transactions velocity. What determines how long in advance of an expected payment a transactor provides herself with the necessary cash, and how long the payee retains the cash she receives? To what extent are these practices the reflection of institutions and habits slow to change, and to what extent are they sensitive to current economic and financial conditions? A fatal logical defect of the simple transactions velocity approach is that a global concept of transactions encompasses exchanges between money and other assets that are undertaken by economic units precisely to adjust their cash balances to desired levels. If a corporation purchases a Treasury bill to reduce its cash holding, it is scarcely helpful to attribute the corporation's holding of cash to the prospect of this transaction. It is more accurate to attribute the Treasury bill purchase to its excess cash holding. Thus the volume of transactions, both for an individual unit and for the economy as a whole, is far from independent of the demand for money and cannot be used to explain the demand for money. The explanation of both the volume of financial transactions and the levels of desired money holdings must be sought in more basic determinants of portfolio choice.

To extract the kernel of truth from the transactions velocity approach, it is essential to distinguish between transactions on income account, arising from current production of goods and services, and transactions on capital account, exchanges of assets. The volume of transactions on income account is a legitimate determinant of the demand for cash; these transactions do not, at least in the short run, arise from the process of adjustment of cash holdings itself. In this fundamental respect, the concept of income velocity of money makes more sense than the global transactions velocity. But it does not tell the whole story. As shown in Section 3.2.2.4, there is a demand for cash unrelated to transactions on income account.

3.2.1.2 The working balance

To isolate income-account transactions as a principal source of demand for money holdings, it is convenient to regard an individual (or other economic unit) as splitting her present net worth into two parts, her *working balance* and her *permanent wealth,* as follows. Over the year ahead, her total net worth—calculated, in a first approximation, without regard to investment earnings—will fluctuate according to the expected pattern of receipts and outlays on income account. If these receipts and outlays were perfectly synchronized, seasonal fluctuations in net worth would not occur. Her wealth would grow gradually, stay constant, or decline evenly over the year, depending on whether she was saving, breaking even, or dissaving. But if certain days, or weeks, or months, are relatively heavy with receipts, while others are relatively heavy with expenditures, there will be seasonal fluctuations of net worth. Consider, for the year ahead, the lowest value the individual's net worth will reach. This may, by chance, be her present net worth; more likely, the lowest point is reached at some future date. The low point may be positive or negative. This minimum net worth may be regarded as the individual's permanent wealth, which she can invest solely with regard for long-run appreciation, taking advantage of the long-run prospects of assets that cannot be liquidated within a year, except perhaps at great cost or risk. The remainder of her current net worth—the excess, if any, of her present wealth over the minimum she expects her net worth to reach during the year ahead—is her working balance. This she cannot invest solely for long-run appreciation. She must take account of the possibilities and costs of converting the working balance into means of payment to meet anticipated excesses of expenditures over receipts. The distinction between working balance and permanent wealth, and the accompanying distinction between appropriate categories of assets, is an application of the principles of liquidity preference set forth earlier in this chapter.

The concepts are illustrated in Fig. 3.3. Time is measured horizontally from the present to a year ahead. Expected receipts and expenditures cumulated from the present (time 0) are shown in Fig. 3.3a. The slopes of these curves are the expected rates of receipts and expenditures; these are shown in Fig. 3.3b. Present net worth is OW in Fig. 3.3c, and the curve is the subsequent time path of net worth implied by the anticipated receipts and expenditures. The minimum of this curve, OP, is permanent wealth. The remainder PW of present net worth is the working balance.

Permanent wealth might be negative, indicating that the individual will need to be permanently in debt to provide herself with the working balance she needs. Working balances may be as low as zero; if future receipts will provide for future payments, no special provision for them need be made from current net worth.

The size of the working balance fluctuates seasonally. Suppose, in Fig. 3.3, that time moves forward from O to O'. Suppose also that during the period OO' net worth developed as anticipated and that the expectations held at O for the remainder of the year still hold at O'. In addition, expectations for a subsequent period of length equal to OO' now become relevant; these are shown in the extensions of the figures beyond one year. At O', present net worth is OW'; permanent wealth is, as it happens, unchanged at OP; the working balance has increased to PW'. Figure 3.3 pictures an individual who is doing net saving over the year. In consequence, if the same seasonal pattern of expenditures and receipts is expected in the subsequent year, the general level of wealth will be higher. After time O'' is past, permanent wealth will increase.

The distinction between investment and working balance is somewhat less straightforward if account is taken of increases in net worth due to earnings and appreciations of investments during the year. The amount and timing of these expected returns may affect the partition of current net worth between the two balances. In turn, since the investment balance presumably earns a higher rate of return, the partition of current net worth has a reciprocal influence on the prospective appreciation of wealth over the year. Of the alternative ways of splitting current net worth, an investor certain of future receipts, outlays, and investment returns will select the one that gives her the highest rate of appreciation, generally the one with the lowest working balance.

The "year" in the foregoing exposition is arbitrary. The period the portfolio manager uses to define her working balance is a policy choice. It depends on the rate-of-return advantages of investment assets over short-term assets (the greater, the shorter the period covered by the working balance) and on the costs of moving in and out of investment balances (the greater, the more conservative the working-balance coverage).

Uncertainties about needs for funds and about asset returns may lead to caution. What Keynes called the precautionary motive will lead to larger working balances

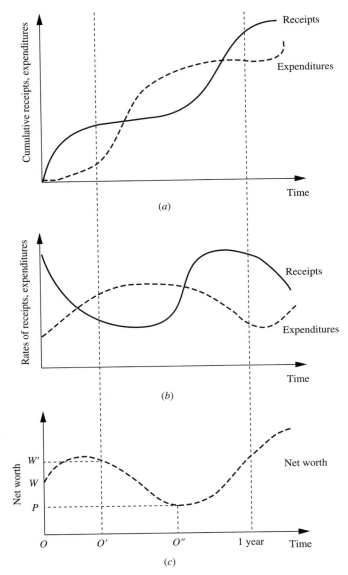

FIGURE 3.3
Prospective receipts, expenditures, wealth determination of
working balance.

against the twin contingencies of unexpectedly great needs for funds and disappointing returns on investments. Of course, caution has its cost in income sacrificed. The greater the prospects of return on the investment balance in comparison with the earnings to be expected on the working balance, the greater are the incentives to take the risks involved in keeping the working balance low. Section 3.2.2.3 presents a simple model of precautionary demand.

The time paths in Fig. 3.3 could be regarded as midpoints of zones of uncertainty that become wider the more distant the future date. The investor will not necessarily behave in the same way in the face of such uncertainty as she would if she were sure of the central path. She faces penalties for either too low or too high a working balance. But they are not symmetrical. The penalty for too high a working balance is simply the loss of the higher returns available in the investment balance. The penalty for too low a working balance is forced liquidation of part of the investment balance. The investor must sell an illiquid asset at less than full value; or she must sell an imperfectly reversible asset before she has held it long enough to recoup the transactions costs; or she must sell assets of variable price at a time when the price is low; or she must borrow on unfavorable terms. Alternatively she may, like the consumer of Section 3.1.2.3, squeeze her consumption when her working balance vanishes. To limit the probability of having to incur such penalties, the investor will hold a larger working balance than she would if she were sure of the future pattern of receipts and outlays. This is the explanation, offered in detail in Chapter 7, for the reserve demands of commercial banks. The analysis of Chapter 7 and Section 3.2.2.3 of this chapter can be applied generally to the precautionary behavior of individuals and firms. Asymmetry in costs will lead to precautionary behavior even if the investor is risk-neutral. A risk-averse investor will take similar precautions even if the costs are symmetrical; the asymmetry of losses of utility to her have the same effect.

Economies of scale mitigate the need for additional working balances as a precaution against unfavorable contingencies. In Fig. 3.3c, an individual or firm with larger-scale operations may face a relatively narrower band of probable net worth developments. If so, the need for working balances will increase in less than proportion to the income and wealth of the unit. This economy of scale arises when the larger scale results from a larger number of independent transactions, either receipts or outlays. It does not arise when the larger scale reflects merely an increase in the size of the same number of transactions, with no change in their degree of interdependence. For example, a bank will need proportionately less liquid assets if it grows by attracting new depositors whose probabilities of making deposits and withdrawals are in some degree independent of the behavior of the old depositors. It will need the same proportion of liquid assets to deposits if it grows simply because inflation causes its existing depositors to raise the dollar entries both on their deposit slips and on their checks. Similarly, a grocery store that is large because its clientele is numerous and diverse can be more confident of meeting its weekly payroll from its sales receipts than a small store where chance loss of a few customers could make a big difference. The small store could reduce the size of its working balance relative to its average receipts and payroll if it grew by diversifying its customers, but not if it grew simply because its old customers became more affluent.

3.2.1.3 The demand for working balances

The working balance, to give a summary definition, is that part of the individual's wealth that will have to be liquidated within the year to meet with reasonable probability expected seasonal excesses of outlays over receipts on income account. The need for working balances arises from the failure of receipts and outlays to be perfectly synchronized. The degree of synchronization is related in turn to social institutions and customs regarding the frequency and timing of payments and settlements of accounts. The family shops for groceries every weekend. Some employees are paid at the end of every week; in higher echelons salaries are paid at the end of every month. Rents are payable at the beginning of the month. Utility companies charge their customers monthly or quarterly, and expect payment by the middle of the month. Taxes are due on specified dates quarterly, semiannually, or annually. And so on.

Given the degree of synchronization, the economy's need for working balances will depend on the volume of income-account transactions. The volume of these transactions clearly depends on the rate of national output in money value. Whether a given national output entails few or many transactions is related to such factors as the complexity of interindustry relations, the extent of vertical integration of industry, and the prevalence of bilateral and multilateral clearing arrangements. Since these institutional factors, like those determining the degree of synchronization, change slowly, the demand for working balances can be regarded as a fairly stable proportion of money national income, a measure of the economy's total volume of transactions on income account.

This is only step one, however, in relating money balances to the volume of transactions on income account. The argument so far is a theory of the demand for working balances, but it leaves open the question of the asset composition—in particular, money's share—of these balances. Step two is to explain why part of working balances is held in cash and what determines how large this part is.

It used to be that in traditional explanations of the income velocity of money, step two was omitted and the amount of cash holdings needed for a given volume of transactions on income account was taken as determined by the institutions and conventions governing the degree of synchronization of receipts and expenditures. To take a simple example, suppose that an individual receives $100 the first of each month but distributes a monthly total outlay of $100 evenly through the month. Her cash balance would vary between $100 on the first of each month and zero at the end of the month. On the average her cash holdings would equal $50, or $\frac{1}{24}$ of her annual receipts and expenditures. If she were paid once a year this ratio would be $\frac{1}{2}$ instead of $\frac{1}{24}$; and if she were paid once a week it would be $\frac{1}{104}$.

The failure of receipts and expenditures to be perfectly synchronized certainly creates the need for working balances. But it is not obvious that these balances must be cash. Why not hold working balances in assets with higher yields than cash, shifting into cash only at the time an outlay must be made? The individual in the preceding example could buy $100 of higher-yielding assets at the beginning of the month and gradually sell these for cash as she needs to make disbursements. On the average her cash holdings would be zero, and her holdings of other assets $50. The advantage of this procedure is, of course, the yield. The disadvantage is the cost, pecuniary and nonpecuniary, of such frequent and small exchanges between cash and other assets. There are intermediate possibilities, for example, dividing the $50 average balance between cash and other assets. The greater the individual sets her average cash holding, the lower will be both the yield of her working balance and the costs of her asset exchanges. When the yield disadvantage of cash is slight, the costs of frequent exchanges will deter the holding of other assets, and average cash holdings will be large. When the yield disadvantage of cash is great, it is worthwhile to incur large exchange costs and keep average cash holdings low. Thus, it seems plausible that the share of cash in working balances will be related inversely to the interest rate on other assets. Section 3.2.3 is a rigorous proof of this possibility.[2]

The omission of step two from traditional monetary theory and recent cash-in-advance models is a curious fact, which seems to be closely related to the vagueness and confusion in the theory of velocity concerning the scope of the relevant concept of money. If the explanation of the demand for working balances is regarded as an explanation of demand for money, then money is synonymous with the whole class of assets, whether means of payment or not, in which working balances might be invested. There is evidence that the early velocity theorists, both Irving Fisher (1911) and the Cambridge school (Lavington [1941], Pigou [1917]), did in fact intend this identification. They were thinking, more or less explicitly, of an economy with a sharp gulf between means of payment and assets too illiquid or unpredictable for working balances. They did not envisage a twilight zone of assets that can compete both with money for place in working balances and with capital equity for place in permanent portfolios. (But the monetary theorists of this tradition did not adequately recognize that, in the absence of such intermediate assets, money itself would have some role among investments of permanent wealth; the institutional determinants of velocity, as Keynes ultimately saw, would be only part of the story of the demand for cash.)

Given a twilight zone of near moneys and other intermediate assets, income-velocity theory does not tell the whole story about the demand for money narrowly defined as means of payment. Instead it tells a *part* of the story about the demand for a whole class of assets, difficult in practice to delimit. Those monetary economists who, in seeking to apply the theory of velocity statistically, have included time as well as demand deposits in the money whose velocity they are measuring, have in this respect followed sound instincts. But they have probably not been inclusive enough. The velocity of means of payment is not an institutional constant or even a unique function of the volume of income-account transactions. It is sensitive to the rates of return that can be earned on the substitutes for money in working balances. The obvious substitutes in practice are time deposits, savings accounts, short-term government securities, money market mutual funds, and other high-quality short-term paper; and it is to the rates on these assets (rather than to long-run interest rates or equity yields) that the demand for money for transactions purposes should be related.

---

[2]These observations about the distinction between cash and working balances have somehow been forgotten in currently fashionable cash-in-advance models, for example, Lucas (1980).

3.2.2 The Share of Cash in Working Balances

This section models the choice of a transactor between money proper and the near moneys and other liquid assets available to be held as working balances. The distinguishing feature of money is that it is a generally acceptable means of payment. This property is shared by currency and checkable demand deposits, and for most purposes they can be considered equivalent ways of satisfying the transactions demands for money of private agents.

Households and businesses do face another choice, namely how to divide their transactions balances between the two media of payments. The model of transactions demand for money versus nonmoney liquid assets about to be set forth in Section 3.2.2.1 can also be applied to the demand for currency versus checkable deposits. This is done in Section 3.2.2.2, but throughout the remainder of this chapter money is discussed as a single homogeneous means of payment. The currency/deposits choice comes up again in Chapter 9, Section 9.1.1.

3.2.2.1 A model of the transactions demand for money[3]

Let time deposits represent the alternative asset in which working balances might be held. Time deposits and cash are the same except in two respects. One difference is that time deposits are not a means of payment. The other is that time deposits bear an interest rate. Cash's own-rate of interest, that is the cash yield of cash, is assumed zero; if cash bore a fixed non-zero interest, the argument would be essentially the same. By the interest rate on time deposits is really meant the difference between the yield on time deposits and the fixed yield on cash. If cash bears an endogenous market-determined interest rate, however, the theory requires important modifications, as discussed in Section 3.2.4. There is no risk of default on time deposits nor any risk of a change in the rate of interest within the relevant period.

Cost per transaction is assumed to be fixed at a; that is, it does not vary with the size of the transaction. For a more general treatment in which this cost has both fixed and variable components, see Tobin (1956). The fixed cost consists primarily of the time and effort devoted to making a trip to a bank or automatic teller machine. Automatic teller machines and other innovations have undoubtedly lowered transactions costs, as discussed further below.

At the first of each time period ($t = 0$), the individual receives $\$Y$. She disburses this at a uniform rate throughout the period, and at the end of the period ($t = 1$) she has disbursed it all. Thus her total working balance, $B(t)$, whatever its composition, is

$$B(t) = (1 - t)Y \qquad (0 \le t \le 1). \tag{3.3}$$

[3]The model presented here is a simplified version of Tobin (1956). A similar model had been independently developed by Baumol (1952). Maurice Allais also earlier published in French a similar analysis (see Baumol and Tobin [1989]). Because the model is by now very well known, the exposition here stresses how the model fits into the larger framework of portfolio theory rather than the technical details.

Her average working balance is

$$\overline{B} = \int_0^1 Y(1 - t)\,dt = Y/2. \tag{3.4}$$

$B(t)$ is divided between cash $C(t)$ and time deposits $D(t)$:

$$B(t) = D(t) + C(t), \qquad 0 \le D(t), C(t). \tag{3.5}$$

Let $\overline{D}$ and $\overline{C}$ be average time deposit holding and cash holding, respectively:

$$\overline{D} = \int_0^1 D(t)\,dt$$

$$\overline{C} = \int_0^1 C(t)\,dt \tag{3.6}$$

with $\overline{D} + \overline{C} = \overline{B} = Y/2$.

The interest rate per time period is r. (If the unit period—the interval between receipts—is one month, the relevant interest rate is the interest earned by holding a dollar of time deposits one month, that is, approximately $\frac{1}{12}$ of the usually quoted per annum interest rate.) Time deposits earn interest in proportion to the length of time they are held, no matter how short.

The argument would not be essentially changed by considering instead an individual or business firm who receives cash at a uniform rate and must make a single periodic disbursement. It may not be too far-fetched to claim that, at a given season, almost every transactor in the economy can be approximated by one of these two models. Either the transactor is accumulating a series of small receipts toward the day when large disbursements must be made, or she is gradually disbursing in small payments a prior large receipt. At different seasons of the year, or month, or week, the same transactor may sometimes be of one type and sometimes of the other. Of course actual transactions balances $B(t)$ need not decline or grow linearly, as assumed in this simple model.

Suppose the individual chooses $D(t)$ and $C(t)$ so as to maximize her interest earnings, net of exchange costs. Let the interest rate r vary, and suppose her to recalculate the most profitable $D(t)$ and $C(t)$. What is the relationship between $\overline{D}$ (and hence $\overline{C}$) and the interest rate? The relationship may be found in three steps:

1. Suppose that the number of asset exchanges during the period were fixed at n. Given r, what would be the optimal times $(t_1, t_2, \ldots, t_n)$ and amounts of these n exchanges? What would be the revenue R_n from this optimal plan? What are the corresponding values of $\overline{D}$ and $\overline{C}$?
2. Given r, but now considering n variable, what would be the value of n—call it n^*—for which R_n is a maximum?
3. How does n^*, the optimal number of exchanges, depend on r? As n^* varies with r, so will $\overline{D}$ and $\overline{C}$. Also, how do n^*, $\overline{D}$, and $\overline{C}$ depend on Y, the volume of transactions?

The first problem is the optimal timing and amounts of a given number of exchanges. If there is an initial exchange, from cash into time deposits, there must be at least a second transaction, from time deposits back into cash. Time deposits cannot be used for payments, and the entire initial working balance must be paid out by the end of the period. Two principles guide the optimal scheduling of these two transactions.

1. All conversion from cash into time deposits should occur at time zero. Whatever the size of an exchange in this direction, to postpone it is only to lose interest.
2. An exchange from time deposits into cash should not occur until the cash balance is zero. To make this exchange before it is necessary only loses interest that would be earned by holding time deposits a longer time.

These two principles together indicate that if only two transactions are allowed, an initial deposit D_1 is made at time zero, and the time of the second transaction t_2, the time at which initial cash $Y - D_1$ is exhausted, will be $(Y - D_1)/Y$. Total revenue will be $rD_1t_2 = rY(1 - t_2)t_2$. It is easy to verify that revenue is maximized when $t_2 = \frac{1}{2}$ and hence when $D_1 = Y/2$.

Figure 3.4a illustrates the time path of the working balance, cash, and time deposits.

If three exchanges are allowed, it is not necessary to sell all the time deposits at one time. Some may be sold at time t_2 and the remainder at time t_3. This makes it possible to buy more time deposits initially. Figure 3.4b shows the optimal schedule.

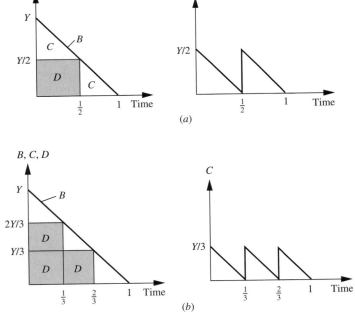

FIGURE 3.4
Time path of working balance, cash, and time deposits. (a) Two transactions; (b) Three transactions.

In general, for n exchanges, the optimal schedule is to acquire at time zero $Y(n-1)/n$ time deposits and to cash them in equal installments of Y/n at times $t_2 = 1/n$, $t_3 = 2/n$, $\ldots$, $t_i = (i-1)/n$, $\ldots$, $t_n = (n-1)/n$. Cash holdings fall repeatedly from Y/n to 0; their average, $\overline{C}$, is $Y/2n$. Since average time deposit holding, $\overline{D}$, is $\overline{B} - \overline{C}$ or $Y/2 - \overline{C}$, average time deposits for n exchanges are

$$\overline{D}_n = Y/2 - Y/2n = Y(n-1)/2n, \qquad n \ge 2. \tag{3.7}$$

Revenue is $r\overline{D}_n$, or

$$R_n = Yr(n-1)/2n, \qquad n \ge 2. \tag{3.8}$$

Exchange costs are equal to na, so that net return is

$$\pi_n = Yr(n-1)/2n - na, \qquad n \ge 2. \tag{3.9}$$

The next step is to determine the number of exchanges, n, which maximizes π_n. The change in profit due to making one more exchange is

$$\Delta\pi_n = \pi_n - \pi_{n-1} = Yr/2n(n-1) - a. \tag{3.10}$$

Profits will be maximized at that value of n for which $\Delta\pi_n$ exceeds zero while $\Delta\pi_{n+1}$ is less than zero. If the discrete nature of the problem were ignored and Eq. (3.9) maximized as if it were a continuous differentiable function of n, condition (3.10) could be written

$$\partial\pi_n/\partial n = Yr/2n^2 - a = 0, \qquad n^* = \sqrt{Yr/2a}. \tag{3.11}$$

Therefore the optimal average cash holding is

$$\overline{C}^* = Y/2n^* = \sqrt{2aY/r}. \tag{3.12}$$

This indicates that the demand for cash increases with the square root of the level of transactions Y, and inversely with the square root of the interest rate. This square root rule is a famous elementary finding of the theory of inventories, and it is not surprising that it applies to the inventory of cash. The square root formula need not be taken literally. The important point, which the rule illustrates, is that economies of scale in the management of inventories of cash, or other materials, result from costs that are as large for hundred-dollar transactions as for million-dollar transactions.

In the short run, with population and technology constant, the effect of a rise in money national income on velocity depends on how it is divided between increase of real output and increase of prices. A rise in real output, with prices and wages stable, does permit economy of cash. The model suggests that velocity will increase even if the interest rate is constant. This may be one reason why velocity is higher in prosperity than in depression. In pure price inflation, however, money income and transactions costs will rise in the same proportion. In this case the model suggests that velocity will be unchanged.

Thus, caution is necessary in drawing economy-wide inferences about the income velocity of money from the inventory model just presented. The model does *not* imply that every increase of national income will, by permitting economies of scale in the management of transactions, cause velocity to increase. Consider, for example, growth in the number of transactors—the population of households and business firms—without any increase in the average scale of their operations. At given interest rates and transactions costs, the demand for money will increase in proportion to the volume of income-account transactions.

The square-root rule ignores the role of integer constraints in deriving the optimal number of asset exchanges. The existence of agents with corner solutions means that the income and interest-rate elasticities may be different from what the square root rule implies. Many agents with low incomes, for example, may not find it worthwhile to undertake any transactions between cash and time deposits. For such individuals, increases in income will be held entirely in cash, implying that the income elasticity of demand for money is greater than $\frac{1}{2}$ and the interest elasticity is smaller than $\frac{1}{2}$ in absolute value.

As remarked earlier, financial innovation may alter the demand for money. For example, the development of credit cards allows individuals to shift their money holdings to the credit card companies. Given the economies of scale in transactions management, this shifting is likely to lower the overall demand for money. New technology lowers the cost of asset exchanges. For instance, automatic teller machines surely have reduced the need to carry currency outside banking hours.

The model discussed in this section has provided the theoretical foundation for much empirical research into the demand for money. Goldfeld's well-known (1973) money-demand equation consisted of Eq. (3.12) combined with a partial adjustment of desired to actual money balances. Goldfeld (1973) found strong support for the inventory theory and concluded that "the money demand functions does not exhibit marked short-run instability" (p. 590) and "on balance, then, the evidence does not seem to suggest any need to estimate the money demand equation over separate subsamples of the postwar period" (p. 592). Shortly after the Goldfeld (1973) results were published, however, marked instability in the demand for money function appeared, as documented in Goldfeld (1976). One of the main reasons for this instability has been the financial innovation and deregulation that has taken place since the early 1970s, which is briefly discussed in Section 3.2.4.

3.2.2.2 Digression applying the model to the currency versus deposits choice

The inventory model of the previous section can be applied to the division of the cash balance between currency and checkable deposits. Currency holdings entail carrying costs in rough proportion to the size of the holdings; these are due to risks of loss and theft and to inconveniences of storage. In contrast to this negative rate of return on currency, the rate on checking accounts is at worst zero and may be positive. Even in the past in the United States, when net payment of interest to checking account customers was legally forbidden, a small positive interest rate on demand deposits was allowed as a credit against bank service charges. Banks' service charges, when they exist, are based on the number, not the amount, of account transactions: deposits, deposit items, withdrawals, checks, wire transfers. In addition, the costs and inconveniences to the customer of bank transactions, in comparison with currency transactions, are relevant.

Two situations can be distinguished. First, economic units with cash balances large enough to avoid all service charges will not hold currency beyond minimal immediate needs. Since payments into and out of checking accounts are costless, it is advantageous to deposit all receipts at once, whether they are in the form of currency or checks—to use checks whenever possible to make payments—and to withdraw currency at the last possible moment before transactions requiring currency. For some units, the incentive of freedom from bank service charges may result in an increase in the share of wealth held in means of payment. Second, economic units with smaller working balances will be subject to some incentive to minimize bank transaction costs. When a series of payments can be made in currency at a cost per transaction less than the cost of drawing a check, bank transaction costs can be reduced by making a single consolidated withdrawal of currency sufficient for the whole series, or by withholding currency receipts from deposit to make such payments. However, these expedients reduce the bank balance on which interest is earned and add to currency holdings and their carrying costs. A compromise must be struck, in the manner of Section 3.2.2, between economy of transactions costs and economy of carrying costs. Applied in the present context, the conclusions of Section 3.2.2 are as follows: The higher the bank's interest rate and the carrying costs of currency, the more the compromise will favor demand deposits. The higher the costs of bank transactions and the lower the costs of currency payments, the more the compromise will favor currency. Individuals with large balances of means of payment will have a higher deposit proportion than those with small balances. If total cash balances fall below a certain level, it will not pay to have a checking account at all, especially if receipts come in currency or in checks that are at least as costly to deposit as to cash.

3.2.2.3 Uncertainty and precautionary demand

As noted above, uncertainty about the future course of receipts and outlays may lead investors to take the precaution of holding higher working balances. Indirectly this may lead to a higher demand for money, as well as for other liquid assets. Does uncertainty also lead to a greater preference for cash within the working balance? There seems to be no obvious reason why it should, so long as the noncash assets of the working balance—time deposits in the model—are perfectly liquid and predictable. The interest gained if a deposit can be left intact for an exceptionally long time is the same as the interest lost if it has to be withdrawn exceptionally early. The exchange costs are the same either way.

This issue can be investigated further by extending the model of the previous section to include uncertainty about the timing of expenditures and receipts. The model could also be applied to the division of wealth between working balances and permanent wealth, as discussed previously. During the month (or quarter or week) ahead, the individual's cash receipts, net of outlays, are denoted by X. X is uncertain, but its probability distribution is assumed known: $F(x)$ is the probability that X will be smaller than or equal to x, that is, $F(x) = \Pr(X \leq x)$. $F(x)$ goes from 0 to 1 as x goes from the lowest to the highest possible value of X. The derivative $F'(x)$, always nonnegative, is the probability density function. Figure 3.5 presents an example. The area under the curve $F'(x)$ is 1. In the figure the expected value of X is zero, but this need not be the case.

At the beginning of the period, the individual decides how much to hold in cash C instead of interest-bearing time deposits. As in the previous section, the interest

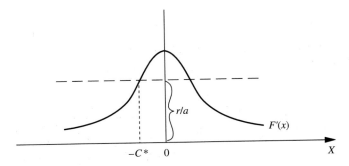

FIGURE 3.5
Precautionary demand for liquidity.

forgone is rC. The fixed cost of converting time deposits to cash is again denoted a. A conversion will be required if net receipts X are negative and greater in absolute value than initial cash holdings. That is, the fixed cost is incurred during a period if $C + X < 0$, that is, $X < -C$.

Total cost (TC) is summarized as follows:

$$TC = rC + a \qquad \text{if } X < -C \qquad (3.13)$$
$$TC = rC \qquad \text{if } X \geq -C.$$

The expected cost $E(TC)$ is

$$E(TC) = rC + aF(-C). \qquad (3.14)$$

Minimizing $E(TC)$ with respect to C yields the first-order condition $F'(-C) = r/a$, subject to the second-order condition $aF''(-C) > 0$. That is, the optimal C^* is where $F'(-C) = r/a$ on an upward-sloping part of $F'(x)$. The solution is illustrated in Fig. 3.5. It is easily seen that C^* depends negatively on r and positively on a. C^* also depends on the shape of $F'(x)$.

Here, unlike the Miller–Orr (1966) model of precautionary demand, cash holdings do not necessarily increase with the variance of X. It is not always true that a more spread-out (flatter) distribution will lead to a higher C^*. Consider Figs. 3.6 and 3.7. In both, $F_1'(x)$ is a flatter distribution (higher variance) than $F_2'(x)$. Figure 3.6 depicts a case where $C_1^* < C_2^*$, while in Fig. 3.7 $C_1^* > C_2^*$.

It may seem paradoxical that an increase in exogenous risk should lead a portfolio manager to shift to a riskier portfolio. The reason is that her decision depends on the *marginal* risk effect of holding more or less cash. Extra risk due to the adverse shift from the flattening of the probability distribution, from F_2' to F_1', is unavoidable. Flattening of F' also means that the reduction in risk achieved by increasing C^* is smaller per dollar of C^* and rC^*. In Fig. 3.6 this effect is big enough to lead the portfolio manager to a less liquid portfolio rather than a more liquid one.

As presented, the model assumes the disutility of TC to be proportional to TC itself. Risk aversion would make disutility an increasing function of total cost. Qualitatively minimization of disutility would be like increasing a relative to r and would increase C^*, the precautionary balance.

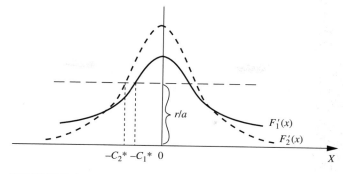

FIGURE 3.6
Precautionary balance decreases with variance.

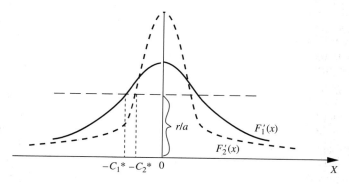

FIGURE 3.7
Precautionary balance increases with variance.

This model of precautionary demand for money probably applies better to a choice where C represents a broader class of liquid assets and the alternative assets X are illiquid or unpredictable or irreversible, or all three.

3.2.2.4 The quantity theory of money

The quantity theory goes back to David Hume, and probably further, but its major and most effective protagonists have been Irving Fisher (1911) and Milton Friedman (1956).

In its crudest form, the quantity theory is a mechanistic proposition strangely alien to the assumptions of rational maximizing behavior on which classical and neoclassical economic theories generally rely, as J. R. Hicks eloquently pointed out in a famous article (1935). Specifically, it ignores the effects of the returns to holding money on the amounts economic agents choose to hold, effects that were stressed in the models of transactions and precautionary demand just discussed. According to the quantity theory, the technology of monetary circulation fixes the annual turnover of a unit of money. Suppose that every dollar "sitting" supports just V dollars per year "on the wing," to use D. H. Robertson's famous terms (1959, p. 30). Suppose, further, that the economy is assumed to be in real equilibrium and the supply of money is doubled. The public will not wish to hold the additional money until the dollar value of transactions is doubled, and this requires prices to double.

Surely the demand for money to hold is not so mechanical. The velocity of money can be speeded up if people put up with more inconvenience and risk more illiquidity in managing their transactions. Money holdings depend, therefore, on the opportunity costs, the expected changes in the value of money, and the real yields of other assets in the working balance. At least in principle, Fisher and Friedman would agree.

Quantity theorists often argue that an increase in the quantity of money is equivalent to a change in the monetary unit. A hundredfold increase in the stock of French francs would be—would it not?—the same as De Gaulle's decree changing the unit of account to a new franc equivalent to 100 old francs. Since the units change could make no real difference, no other way of multiplying the money stock could either.

These analogies fail for several related reasons. In most economies money is by no means the only asset denominated in the monetary unit. There are many promises to pay base money on demand or at specified dates. If there is a thorough units change, like De Gaulle's, all these assets are automatically converted to the new unit of account. Roosevelt's devaluation of the dollar relative to gold was not a pure units change. He did not scale up the dollar values of outstanding currency or even of Treasury bonds, or make any provisions for such revaluation. Naturally, private assets and debts expressed in dollars were not scaled up either. Likewise, when the quantity of money is changed by normal operations of governments or central banks or by other events, the outstanding amounts of other nominally denominated assets are not scaled up or down in the same proportion. They may remain constant, as when money is printed to finance government expenditures. They may move in the opposite direction, as when central banks engage in open-market operations, which typically increase the amount of base money outstanding by buying bills or bonds, thus reducing the quantities of bills and bonds in the hands of the public.

3.2.3 Working Balances and Cash in the Permanent Portfolio

3.2.3.1 The transactions motive

The management of portfolios inevitably occasions a certain demand for means of payment as a share of investment balances. Basically this demand is, like the share of cash in working balances, a function of the costs and possibilities of asset exchanges in imperfect markets in relation to available rates of return. As remarked in Section 3.1.2.1, the costs of investment decisions and asset exchanges give some inertia to portfolio selection; there is always economy in sticking to the status quo, whatever it is. The portfolio status quo frequently turns out to include means of payment, and the inertia principle means that there will be some delay in converting money into assets of higher return.

Working balances tend to creep into portfolios in the following ways: First, wealth to be invested or reinvested generally appears initially in cash form. It may represent additions to net worth due to saving from earned income or from the yields of previous investments, or repayments of principal of bonds and other loans. The decisions and asset exchanges necessary to invest these funds involve costs, costs that include a substantial component independent of the dollar amounts of funds to be invested. Consequently some economy is obtained by permitting funds to accumulate until a single sizable investment decision and transaction can occur. The indivisibilities of certain remunerative assets give a further incentive to prefer relatively less frequent and larger investments. Second, cash awaiting investment may represent the proceeds of sales of assets as the result of a deliberate decision to shift portfolios. The general considerations determining the frequency of portfolio shifts have been discussed in Section 3.1.2.1. The point relevant here is that these shifts may create a temporary demand for cash holdings. The investor's market appraisals may lead her to make a sale before she is ready to undergo the costs of new purchases, or even perhaps the trouble of making new decisions.

Certain financial institutions operate to minimize the average cash holdings incident to portfolio management. For example, the investor may be content to hold claims against her broker instead of cash. The broker in turn lends to other investors who desire to hold more than 100 percent of their net worth in securities. The broker's cash holdings will be only a fraction of his liabilities. His intermediary function is like that of other financial intermediaries. The broker's liabilities are not a generally acceptable medium of exchange, but they are a means of payment for the specific purpose of buying securities. For persons sure of the future nature of their needs for means of payment, specific means of payment are a full substitute for general money.

Marshall (1923) was correct in relating the demand for money not only to the level of income but also to the level of wealth. He recognized that transactions incident to the management of wealth, like transactions accompanying the production and distribution of current output, give rise to demand for money holdings. It is unfortunate that his insight dropped out of the Cambridge (U.K.) monetary tradition he founded. But the share of money in permanent wealth is no more a constant than the share of money in the working balance. It depends on the rates of return on investment assets, as well as on asset exchange costs, indivisibilities, and a host of complex institutional arrangements. It also depends on the rate of growth of investment balances. The lag in investing new saving, which in the first instance takes the form of cash, means that money will be a larger proportion of growing wealth than of stable wealth.

When the cash income of an individual rises unexpectedly fast, her good luck will be reflected at first in her cash balance. Two things are happening. First, she is saving, building up her wealth, at an extraordinary rate. When she has had time to adjust her spending to her income, she will not accumulate either cash balances or any other assets so rapidly. Second, she is holding abnormally large amounts of cash, simply because that is the form in which her new wealth initially arrives. When she has time to react, and sufficient buildup of cash to make acquisition of income-earning assets worthwhile, she will reduce her cash holdings to a normal transactions balance. For this reason, the demand for cash balances relative to income will be abnormally high when income is rising unexpectedly fast, and abnormally low when income is falling or rising more slowly than anticipated.

As Keynes pointed out in his celebrated discussion of the relation of finance to the demand for cash, business firms undertaking an increase in investment in inventories or plants and equipment need to mobilize cash in advance of spending it (Keynes 1937). In a frictionless world, they would not do so; instead they would continuously borrow, or float or liquidate securities, in just the amounts they need to disburse. Given indivisibilities, transactions costs, and other imperfections, firms will consolidate and anticipate their needs and hold cash. In principle, this finance need seems to be no more than an example of the wealth-related transactions requirements for cash already discussed. But it is also another reason for expecting the demand for cash relative to wealth and income to be exceptionally large when wealth and income are rising exceptionally fast. Keynes argues that this is due to an essential asymmetry in the process of financing an increase in investment and income, even when it is correctly anticipated. The savers who will in the end lend to the investors, or buy their securities, have no reason to reduce their holdings of cash just at the time the investors need to mobilize it.

3.2.3.2 The investment motive

Is there any further investment demand for money, any reason for it to play a role in permanent portfolios that is independent of its means-of-payment property and of the imperfections of other assets and asset markets? If there were no reasons for inertia in portfolio choices, would money have any place in portfolios? The answer depends on the economy's repertory of assets, in particular on whether the repertory includes any assets (or portfolio sequences) that *dominate* money. An asset or sequence of asset holdings dominates money if in every eventuality it will have at least as high a rate of return as money, while in eventualities of nonzero probability it will have a higher return. In the absence of risks of default, thanks to government guarantees or general confidence, a time deposit in a bank dominates both demand deposits and currency. Time deposits are equally subject to the vicissitudes of changes in purchasing power; they cannot bear a lower rate of return than cash and in all probability will earn a higher rate. Sequences involving government savings bonds or, abstracting from indivisibilities, Treasury bills, likewise dominate cash. For investors with known distant target dates of accumulation, money is dominated also by long-term bonds of appropriate maturity. Moreover, professional portfolio managers, for whom the costs of asset exchanges between cash and noncash working balances are very low, will hold very little cash. When these managers speak of their cash positions they do not mean cash literally, but these dominating liquid assets. The turnover of demand deposits of New York City banks, where professional financial managers account for an unusually large part of financial transactions, was in excess of 4000 in 1992, ten times that of other banks (*Federal Reserve Bulletin*, Table A17, January 1994).

Thus the asset menus of the United States and other developed economies include assets that dominate money and exclude it from any place in permanent portfolios beyond the share it merits for reasons of inertia. At various points in the book, hypothetical situations are discussed where money is not so dominated. For example, in Sections 4.2.2.2 and 5.1, a mythical economy is discussed where only two assets—currency and capital—are available for portfolios. Currency is not dominated by the alternative asset, and consequently there is a portfolio demand for currency quite distinct from its role as means of payment. The undominated currency of that model must not be identified with dominated means of payment in actual economies. The broad principles of portfolio balance illustrated by the currency-capital model are to be applied rather to choices between two broad categories of assets—currency plus direct or indirect obligations to pay currency on the one hand, and claims to goods and services on the other. Like currency and capital in the two-asset world, these two asset categories differ strikingly in the impact upon their real values of changes in price levels and price structures. The first category includes a great deal more than means of payment.

Traditionally a central concern of monetary theory has been to explain the value of money, that is, the quantity of goods purchasable with a unit of money. Traditionally also, economic theory explains the value of a commodity by looking at determinants of the supply of the commodity and the demand for it. It was natural, therefore, to seek the explanation of the value of money in the factors determining the quantity of money supplied and demanded. But except in economies with very primitive financial systems, this approach involves a vast mistake of identification, a "fallacy of misplaced concreteness," to use Alfred North Whitehead's concept. The value of money is the value of a unit of account, for example, the dollar, in terms of which all kinds of private and public contracts, assets, and debts are denominated. Money in the sense of means of payment—currency and demand deposits—is far from the only asset that changes in value when the index of consumer prices rises or falls. There is no obvious presumption that the value of the dollar is determined by the supply of and demand for means of payment, to the exclusion of all the other assets also denominated in dollars. In some commodity markets, wheat for example, various grades, qualities, or varieties move together in price because their price differentials are held within narrow limits by substitutability in production or in use. The price of a standard grade of wheat can be used to measure the value of wheat, but no one would think that it could be analyzed by literally looking at the supply of and demand for the standard grade alone. Yet this is what is often done in analyzing the value of money, perhaps because of the semantic confusion between money as a unit of account and money as a means of payment.

Keynes's speculative motive for holding money attributes a demand for money to investors who expect bond prices to fall enough to cancel bond interest earnings. For the unwary, this could be another example of mistaken or confused identity of the asset money whose demand is being explained. The speculative motive is a reason for holding time deposits or other short-term obligations that dominate means of payment; it is not a reason for holding means of payment. Perhaps Keynes was either ignoring these intermediate assets or lumping them all together with means of payment as money. In any event, Hicks (1935) and Kaldor (1939) improved the relevance of the theory of the speculative motive by relating it to choices between short- and long-term securities and regarding the choice between means of payment and short-term securities as a matter of transactions requirements rather than speculation.

3.2.4 Financial Innovation and Liberalization

Financial innovation. Porter, Simpson, and Mauskopf (1979) show that financial liberalization and innovation were important factors accounting for the instability of money demand in the 1970s. New financial technologies have decreased the demand for transactions balances by both individuals and businesses. On the consumer side, the introduction of such financial services as automatic transfers between savings and checking accounts and automatic teller machines have reduced the individual and household demand for money. Porter, Simpson, and Mauskopf estimate that these new financial services explain up to one-fourth of the forecast errors in money demand in the 1970s from using the standard Goldfeld (1973) equation. The other three-fourths of the fall in money demand in the 1970s, however, was concentrated in the deposit holdings of nonfinancial corporations. Porter, Simpson, and Mauskopf point out that improved attention to and development of cash-management techniques have greatly reduced firms' holdings of non-interest-bearing deposits. The techniques used by firms to reduce cash holdings include control disbursement, lock boxes, and cash concentration accounts. These devices increase information about cash holdings and take advantage of economies of scale by centralizing cash holdings. These advances in cash-management technologies reflect general improvements in communications and computing as well as the incentive provided by the high interest rates in the 1970s. Although these developments have greatly increased the instability of the demand for money, they "can be readily interpreted within the established inventory theory of the demand for money" as Porter, Simpson, and Mauskopf point out (p. 217). The demand for money shifted down because the new financial technologies lowered the transactions cost (a in the model). Unfortunately for empirical analyses of money demand, the precise magnitude of this effect is very difficult to quantify, as Goldfeld (1989, p. 139) emphasizes.

Interest payments on checking accounts. Although financial innovation tended to decrease the demand for transactions balances by reducing transactions costs, the legalization of interest payment on checking accounts in the 1980s reduced the opportunity costs of holding money and had the reverse effect. Furthermore, to the extent that checkable accounts now pay a market-determined interest rate, the elasticity of the demand for money with respect to market interest rates has probably decreased.

The Depository Institutions Deregulation and Monetary Control Act of 1980 and the Garn–St. Germain Depository Institutions Act of 1982 included provisions for a gradual removal of all interest rate ceilings on savings and checking accounts. By 1986 all interest ceilings on checking accounts held by individuals and unincorporated businesses had been abolished, although incorporated business demand deposits still must pay zero interest.[4]

---

[4]Two exceptions to the prohibition on interest payments on corporate demand deposits are made for (1) sole proprietorships and (2) law firms holding the accounts on behalf of clients who would legally be able to own the accounts themselves.

The consequence of these reforms is that most means of payment now yield competitively determined interest rates. Although interest rates on checkable accounts are likely to remain below those on other liquid assets in the working balance, the differential between them will fluctuate much less. The differential reflects the depositories' marginal costs of intermediation, which have to be covered by the difference between returns on loans and securities and payments to depositors. If these costs are constant, the opportunity cost of holding checking accounts will be independent of the general level of interest rates. The opportunity cost of holding cash is therefore much more weakly related to the overall level of nominal interest rates than it was in the past.

There are still some reasons, however, to expect the traditional negative relationship. Not all deposits earn market-determined interest rates, and banks may not find it competitively necessary to raise deposit rates enough to maintain the differential when market interest rates rise, or competitively possible to reduce them when market rates fall. Of course, currency, which is about 25 percent of transactions money M1, continues to bear zero nominal interest.[5] However, currency demand does not appear to be sensitive to interest rates, especially when they are already very high. Interest-induced substitutions for or against currency are likely to be almost wholly with transactions deposits. Consequently, when deposits bear market-determined interest rates it may not be a bad approximation in modeling money demand decisions to regard those rates as applying to the whole transactions money supply.[6]

---

[5]Although the zero rate on currency seems universal and inevitable, interest payment on currency is imaginable. The government or an issuing bank might redeem a dollar note on specified dates with a dollar and change. Even a negative rate is conceivable, by requiring purchases of stamps periodically to affix to bills to maintain their validity—the Gesell proposal mentioned in Chapter 2. Electronic currency is now feasible, in the shape of debit cards issued for any desired amount, which the holder can draw down as convenient. It would be easy to program into the card any interest rate, plus or minus.

[6]For further analysis of the effects of the deregulation of interest rates on checking accounts, see Tobin (1983).

CHAPTER 4

Portfolio Selection with Imperfectly Predictable Assets

Chapter 3's discussion of portfolio selection assumed that the investor is perfectly certain of the future of every portfolio, or succession of portfolios, available to him. If all assets are fully liquid and reversible, the investor's optimal strategy is very simple: He always chooses the portfolio with the greatest current rate of return. This strategy is optimal no matter whether the future dates for which he is accumulating wealth are near or distant. However, the timing of the investor's accumulation objectives becomes relevant as soon as illiquidities, exchange costs, and other imperfections in asset markets are taken into account. The best portfolio for funds destined for a child's college education is not necessarily the best portfolio for retirement or bequest, or for next year's vacation trip. One reason for diversification, as Chapter 3 explained, is the interaction of imperfections in asset markets with an assortment of differently timed accumulation objectives.

It is now time to drop the assumption that asset yields and values are in the investor's view wholly predictable. Even if asset markets are perfect, even if there are no conflicts of dating of accumulation objectives, uncertainty about asset returns leads a cautious investor to diversify. To demonstrate this reason for diversification and to examine in general the effects of unpredictability on portfolio choices is the task of this chapter. Assets will be assumed to be fully liquid, reversible, and divisible. At first it will simply be assumed that the accumulation objectives of the investor are immediate; later the focus on the current rate of return will be justified by showing how in some circumstances it can bear also the weight of more distant accumulation objectives.

4.1
THE RANKING OF UNCERTAIN PROSPECTS

4.1.1 Preferences Concerning Risks and Expectations of Return

For each portfolio available to him, the investor may be imagined to estimate the various possible rates of return and the probability of each outcome. In general there will be a whole continuum of available portfolios, and for each one an infinity of possible outcomes. But it will simplify the exposition of the nature of portfolio choice under uncertainty to begin with an example in which there are only a few possible portfolios and for each portfolio a limited number of possible rates of return. These portfolios and returns are listed in Table 4.1. The portfolios are lettered for identification. For each one are listed the possible rates of return and the corresponding probabilities. The final two columns will be explained presently.

How will an investor rank these portfolios? The only ranking that is certain is a preference for C over B. The investor must be presumed to prefer higher returns to lower returns. The least favorable outcome of C is the same as the least favorable outcome of B and has no greater probability, while the other outcomes of C are better than those of B. Is D also better than B? So far as the top two outcomes are concerned, the answer seems to be yes. But D's worst outcome is more disastrous than B's, and

TABLE 4.1

Portfolio	Outcomes		Expectation of return	Risk (standard deviation)
	Rate of return	Estimated probability		
A	.05	1.00	.05	.00
B	.10	.33		
	.05	.33	.05	.041
	.00	.33		
C	.20	.33		
	.10	.33	.10	.082
	.00	.33		
D	.30	.083		
	.10	.833	.10	.082
	−.10	.083		
E	.30	.50		
	.00	.05	.105	.195
	−.10	.45		
F	.0605	.99		
	−1.00	.01	.05	.105
G	1.10	.01		
	.0395	.99	.05	.105

even though it has a low probability, the issue is left in doubt. One might be tempted to suggest that G is surely better than B. G's worst outcome is better than B's, and G offers a long shot at a spectacular gain. But G dooms the investor with near certainty to a return under .04, while B offers him with 2/1 odds a return not less than .05. Is A to be preferred to B? A offers certainty of .05. But certainty of .05 means no chance of any greater return as well as no chance of any smaller return. The investor may not wish to give up the chance of .10. What about A and F? With F there is a probability, though a very small one, that the investor will lose his entire net worth. Does this offset the fact that F offers at the same time a near certainty of a higher return than A?

One ranking principle is the *mathematical expectation of return,* given for each portfolio in the fourth column of Table 4.1. The concept of mathematical expectation was developed in connection with games of chance. The expectation of a game is the average amount per game one would win by playing the game a very large number— in principle an infinite number—of times. It represents in a sense the fair value of the game, for if the operator of a casino charged his clients fees equal to the expectations of games, he would in the long run pay out to winners exactly what he collects. The way to compute the mathematical expectation is to take a weighted average of the outcomes (col. 2), using as weights the probabilities (col. 3). Thus in case F in 100 plays of the game one would expect to earn .0605 ninety-nine times and −1.00 the other time, giving an average earning of .05. An investor who ranks portfolios solely in terms of mathematical expectation will be termed *neutral* in regard to risk. He regards B as equal to A, though A offers .05 for certain and B includes chances of both higher and lower returns. Similarly he values the asymmetrical prospects offered by E or F simply in terms of their averages.

Most people are not risk neutral. An investor may prefer B to A because the prospect of a return of .10 is more important to him than the offsetting prospect of .00. A similar evaluation of gains above expectation relative to returns below expectation would lead an investor to prefer D to C, E to A, F to E. Investors with preferences of this kind will be termed *risk lovers.* In choosing between portfolios with the same expectation of return, risk lovers prefer those with greater chances of above-average gain, portfolios which inevitably carry also greater chances of exceptional loss.

The opposite kind of investor, a *risk averter,* is more worried about below-average returns than attracted by above-average gains. In choosing between portfolios with the same expectation, he prefers those with smaller chances of exceptional loss and gain. In this usage, *risk* is a two-edged concept: Greater risk means greater opportunity for both exceeding and falling short of expectation. The concept of risk will be given more precision below.

4.1.2 Maximization of Expected Utility

The attitudes toward gains and losses, relative to expectation, that determine an investor's evaluation of risk may be summarized in a schedule of *utility of return or wealth,* giving for every outcome a number measuring its subjective value to the investor. To explain choices involving risk, a utility schedule must have certain properties. Naturally the utility number must be higher—or at least no lower—for a larger return than for a smaller one. Beyond that, the utility numbers must make possible comparisons of differences in return. Is the preference for .10 over .05 stronger or weaker than the preference for .05 over .00? That is, which is greater, the difference between the utility of .10 and the utility of .05 or the difference between the utilities of .05 and .00? The utility schedule must make it possible to rank returns themselves and also to rank differences between returns. These same rankings can be obtained from a whole family of utility schedules, just as heat and cold can be measured by a whole family of temperature scales, of which Fahrenheit and Celsius are two members. For utility, as for temperature, the location of zero and the size of the unit of measurement are arbitrary. A utility schedule of this type, which ranks not only the objects of choice but the intensity of preferences among pairs, is called a *cardinal* utility schedule.

The intellectual need for the concept of cardinal utility was felt early in the development of the theory of probability in connection with games of chance, in the seventeenth century. It is not difficult to construct a game of chance with an infinitely large mathematical expectation: Let a coin be tossed until the first head appears, and let the payoff be 2^n dollars, where n is the number of tosses. Though the expectation of gain is infinite, it is a rare gambler who would pay his entire finite fortune to play such a game. Bernoulli's solution to the St. Petersburg paradox, as this problem came to be known, was to invoke a concept of moral expectation, which would be finite for the game even though the mathematical expectation is infinite. Moral expectation is finite, according to Bernoulli, because equal additions to financial gain are of ever decreasing psychological significance. In the terminology of modern economics, the marginal utility of wealth is declining. (It can also be shown that to avoid similar paradoxes, one must postulate an upper bound on utility that cannot be exceeded no matter how large the gain.)

In economic theory the concept of utility originated in the second half of the nineteenth century in quite a different context—the theory of value, that is, the explanation of the relative prices of different commodities and resources. Previously the emphasis has been on physical costs of production, as in the labor theory of value of classical economists and Karl Marx. The role of utility was to focus attention on the subjective preferences of individuals as ultimate sources of economic value. Although the first utility theorists (Jevons, Walras, Menger) postulated cardinal utility, it turned out that their purpose required no more than ordinal utility, a mere ranking of the objects of choice. Since ordinal utility demands considerably less in the way of assumptions about human psychology or family sociology, cardinal utility went out of fashion.

The revival of cardinal utility after World War II coincided with a revival of interest in strategies for games involving chance and in the general problem of decision making in situations with uncertain outcomes. Anyone who confronts these questions is, like Bernouilli, instinctively and inevitably led to a concept of utility that permits ranking of the strengths of preferences as well as of the objects of choice themselves. In the modern renaissance of cardinal utility, much attention has been given to reducing the logically necessary axioms to a minimum number of psychologically plausible assumptions about human behavior. If these axioms are satisfied, the decision of an individual in a situation requiring choice among alternatives with uncertain outcomes can be described as selection of the alternative with the highest *expectation of utility,* or in Bernouilli's term, the highest moral expectation.[1]

Utility is usually assumed to be a function of wealth rather than of return on wealth. The two are not interchangeable except under special circumstances, as discussed below. It is not clear a priori whether it is correct to assume that utility depends on the level of wealth rather than its rate of change, or on both levels and rates of change. The view that utility depends on the change in wealth seems consistent with some aspects of investor behavior. For example, individuals with very different levels of wealth both buy insurance and gamble. It appears that people care about large changes in their wealth regardless of its initial level.[2] If utility is a function of the change in wealth rather than its level, it is appropriate to discuss the utility of return rather than the utility of wealth. Nevertheless, in the next section the implications of relating utility to wealth itself are examined.

For an illustration of the principle of expected utility maximization, consider again the problem of choices among the portfolios listed in Table 4.1. Table 4.2 presents four alternative utility schedules. Now consider the utility of return on a given level of initial wealth W_0. As explained above, the choices of zero and of the unit of measurement are arbitrary; for convenience, the utility of zero return is set at zero in each schedule, and a unit of utility is taken as the difference in utility between a return of .00 and a return of -1.00. In Fig. 4.1, these alternative utility schedules are shown graphically as smooth curves defined for intermediate values as well as for the returns listed in Table 4.2.

Utility schedule I is a straight line, implying everywhere constant marginal utility of return. Such a utility schedule characterizes a risk-neutral investor, who chooses a portfolio on the basis of expectation of return alone, without regard for other aspects of the probability distribution of outcomes. (This would be true of any straight-line utility function. It is only the arbitrary choices of zero point and unit of measurement that make the expectations of utility of schedule I numerically the same as the expectations of return.) Schedule II has, throughout the range shown, diminishing marginal utility of return, characteristic of a thorough-going risk averter. (Actually schedule II is the parabola $.8r - 2r^2$, where r is return. This parabola cannot serve as utility schedule beyond $r = 2$, where its slope turns negative.) Schedule III shows increasing marginal utility of return throughout, characteristic of a thorough-going risk lover. (Schedule III is the parabola $2r + r^2$, which cannot serve as a utility schedule for $r < -1$, if such values are conceivable, as its slope becomes negative

[1]This approach was developed by Ramsey (1931) and Von Neumann and Morgenstern (1944). See also Luce and Raiffa (1966) for an exposition. Recently, evidence has accumulated that the expected utility approach is inconsistent with actual behavior in a number of respects and has led economists to alternative approaches to decision making under uncertainty. See Machina (1987) for a survey. However, no alternative consensus model has yet replaced the expected utility approach, and Machina points out that some of the alternative formulations possess many of the features of Von Neumann-Morgenstern utility.
[2]Markowitz (1952b) argued that utility should be a function of changes in wealth rather than the level of wealth.

TABLE 4.2

| Return | | Utility of return | | |
	Schedule I	Schedule II	Schedule III	Schedule IV
−1.00	−1.00	−1.00	−1.00	−1.00
−.10	−.10	−.082	−.19	−.082
.00	.00	.00	.00	.00
.0395	.0395	.0313	.0806	.0313
.05	.05	.0395	.1025	.0395
.0605	.0605	.0477	.1246	.0477
.10	.10	.078	.21	.078
.20	.20	.152	.44	.152
.30	.30	.222	.69	.280
1.10	1.10	.640	3.41	1.20

| Portfolio | Expected utility of portfolio, rank in parentheses | | | |
	Schedule I	Schedule II	Schedule III	Schedule IV
A	.05 (4–7)	.0395 (4)	.1025 (7)	.0395 (5)
B	.05 (4–7)	.0392 (5)	.0142 (6)	.0392 (6)
C	.10 (2–3)	.077 (1–2)	.217 (2–3)	.077 (3)
D	.10 (2–3)	.077 (1–2)	.217 (2–3)	.078 (2)
E	.105 (1)	.074 (3)	.259 (1)	.103 (1)
F	.05 (4–7)	.0373 (6–7)	.1136 (4–5)	.0373 (7)
G	.05 (4–7)	.0373 (6–7)	.1136 (4–5)	.0421 (4)

at that point.) In schedule IV, there is a change from decreasing marginal utility of return to increasing marginal utility between .20 and .30. Such a schedule is characteristic of individuals who are cautious with respect to losses in relation to small improvements on their present position but are willing to take chances at least of small losses to obtain substantial gains. The success of lotteries and sweepstakes testifies to the willingness of many individuals to pay a small but actuarially unfair (i.e., greater than the expectation of gain) price for a small chance of a very large prize. The same individuals may hold a savings account rather than common stocks and insure themselves, again at actuarially unfair rates, against unlikely but heavy losses from fire or accident. This combination of behavior, inexplicable by any of the first three kinds of utility schedules, can be explained by a schedule of the general shape of IV.[3]

At the bottom of Table 4.2, expectations of utility are shown for each of the portfolios of Table 4.1 for each utility schedule, and the ranks of the portfolios are indicated for each schedule. An expectation of utility is a weighted average of the utilities of the various possible return outcomes for a portfolio, with the probabilities

---

[3]Friedman and Savage (1948) advanced a utility function of this form to explain simultaneous risk-loving and risk-averting behavior.

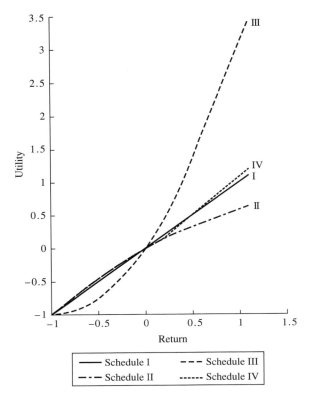

FIGURE 4.1

Alternative schedules of utility of return.

of the outcomes as weights. For example, the expected utility of portfolio B under schedule II is $(.33)(.00) + (.33)(.0395) + (.33)(.078) = .0392$. A risk averter, guided by schedule II, prefers the certainty of .05 to equal chances of .00, .05, and .10. The gambles involved in F and G appeal to him even less. He ranks E, which has the highest mathematical expectation of return, behind C and D. The rankings of the risk lover, schedule III, are quite different. F and G are preferred to B, and all three rank above A, which gives the same expected return with certainty. For the risk lover, the greater unpredictability associated with E reinforces its superiority in expected return; as under risk-neutral schedule I, E ranks first. The investor whose subjective valuations are described by schedule IV behaves like the risk averter of schedule II with respect to all portfolios except those involving possible returns of .30 or more. The high valuation he attaches to large gains leads him to place G ahead of the other three portfolios with expectations of return of .05, and to place D ahead of C, and E ahead of D. The preference of A over F indicates a customer for insurance; to avoid the 1 percent chance of total loss, this investor would accept an assured return somewhat smaller than .05. At the same time, the preference for G indicates a customer for a lottery ticket; even if the expectation of return were somewhat less than .05, he would prefer the gamble to the certainty of .05.

4.1.3 Characterizing Risk Aversion

The examples in the previous section suggested that risk aversion is related to the concavity of the utility function. In this section, this idea is made more precise with the concepts of risk aversion developed by Arrow (1965) and Pratt (1964). The role of initial wealth will also be examined.

An investor has initial wealth W_0, which he can invest in a portfolio divided between a safe (perfectly predictable) asset and a risky (imperfectly predictable) asset. The safe asset has a fixed gross rate of return of s, and the risky asset has a stochastic gross rate of return of γ ($\gamma = 1+r$), with its distribution function denoted by prob($\gamma \le g$) $= F(g)$. Letting x be the share of wealth invested in the risky asset, final wealth W is given for $\gamma = g$ by

$$W = W_0[(1 - x)s + xg] = W_0[s + x(g - s)]. \tag{4.1}$$

The utility of wealth is such that $U(0) = 0$, $U'(W) > 0$ for all W. The sign of $U''(W)$ captures the investor's attitude toward risk: $U'' > 0$ for a risk lover and $U'' < 0$ for a risk averter. In the intermediate case $U'' = 0$, the investor is risk neutral. Strictly speaking, this is a local characteristic. The same investor may switch from one category to another at different values of W. Expected utility of wealth is

$$EU(W) = \int_0^\infty U(W)\, dF(g) = \int_0^\infty U\{W_0[(1 - x)s + xg]\}\, dF(g), \tag{4.2}$$

which is a function of x and W_0, given the probability distribution of g.

Risk neutrality. Risk neutrality holds for a linear utility function, as in schedule I of Fig. 4.1. Algebraically, $U(W) = cW$ and expected utility is

$$EU(W) = cW_0 \int_0^\infty [s + x(g - s)]\, dF(g) = cW_0\{s + x[E(g) - s]\}, \tag{4.3}$$

where $E(g)$ is the expected value of g. $U' = c$ and $U'' = 0$. In this instance, to maximize expected utility, the investor chooses x as large as possible if $E(g) > s$, and x as small as possible if $E(g) < s$. If short sales and borrowing are ruled out, this means that either $x = 1$ or $x = 0$ unless the two assets happen to have the same expected return, in which case x is indeterminate.

Risk-loving behavior. If marginal utility is increasing, the utility function is convex, as in the example of schedule III where $U(W) = cW + bW^2$ and $U'' = 2b > 0$. With convex utility, the investor will always set $x = 1$ (or higher if borrowing is possible) as long as $E(g) \ge s$, as in the risk-neutral case. Intuitively, this is because the investor's increasing marginal utility of wealth implies that the gain in utility from favorable outcomes more than outweighs the loss from unfavorable outcomes, compared to a safe investment with the same expected value. Unlike the risk-neutral case, a risk lover may invest entirely in the risky asset even if $E(g) < s$. That is, the safe asset would only be held if its return is considerably in excess of $E(g)$. The main point is that with risk-seeking behavior, as with risk neutrality, the investor will nearly always be at a corner solution, holding at least 100 percent of his wealth in one of the two assets. Only with risk aversion is there a possible motive for diversification.

Risk-averse behavior. (For technical details and proofs of the material of this section, see Appendix 4A.) With risk-averse behavior the marginal utility of terminal wealth is decreasing. The investor's problem, to choose x so as to maximize expected utility (4.1), may have an interior solution, found by setting marginal expected utility equal to zero. Marginal expected utility is the expected value of marginal utility; like expected utility itself, it is an integral over all possible values of g weighted by their probabilities. The first-order condition is a maximum, at least a local maximum, at a value of x where that integral is zero, provided the second derivative of $EU(W)$ is negative. This too is a probability-weighted integral, this time of the second derivatives at every value of g.

$EU(W)$ is a function not only of the decision variable x but also of initial wealth W_0. A question of interest is how the choice of x is related to the investor's initial wealth. The answer, it is intuitively clear, depends on the shape of his utility-of-wealth function. If, for example, marginal utility is quite insensitive to wealth, x will be quite unresponsive to W_0.

In this the Arrow-Pratt concepts of *relative* and *absolute* risk aversion are informative. *Relative risk aversion* is the negative of the elasticity with respect to wealth of the marginal utility of wealth. Suppose it is a positive constant c. Then a 1 percent increase in initial wealth will, if x remains the same, mean a 1 percent increase in W and a c percent increase in the absolute value of marginal utility at every possible realization of g. If that x made the probability-weighted average of marginal utilities zero at the original W_0, it will still do so with W_0 1 percent bigger. Constant relative risk aversion implies constant x: Whatever initial wealth, it will be split in the same proportions between the risk asset and the safe asset. Relative risk aversion increasing with wealth implies x declining as initial wealth increases. Becoming more risk averse as his wealth increases, the investor shifts asset proportions in favor of the safe asset. The reverse is true if relative risk aversion declines with wealth.

The utility function that has the property of constant relative risk aversion everywhere equates the log of utility of wealth to a linear function of the log of wealth. (See Appendix 4A.)

Absolute risk aversion is simply the change in marginal utility per unit of marginal utility. If this is a constant, the investor will place all of any increment of initial wealth in the safe asset. This will change marginal utility, up or down, by the same percentage at every possible g, so that the average of all the marginal utilities will remain zero. This is clearly a more conservative policy than the one associated with constant relative risk aversion. Constant absolute risk aversion everywhere implies and is implied by a negative exponential utility function.

In this book constant relative risk aversion with respect to wealth is generally assumed. That is, choices of percentage asset shares in portfolios are taken to be independent of absolute wealth. Utility is taken instead to depend on the proportionate change in wealth, namely $(W - W_0)/W_0$. The Arrow-Pratt risk-aversion concepts are then relevant to the utility function thus redefined.

4.2
MEAN-VARIANCE ANALYSIS

4.2.1 The Measurement of Risk as Standard Deviation of Return[4]

The previous sections show that, except in the case of the risk-neutral investor, described by a linear utility schedule, preferences among portfolios are determined not simply by the expectation of return but by other properties of the probability distribution of returns on the available portfolios. It would be very convenient to be able to summarize these other properties in a single number, a simple measure of unpredictability of outcome, risk. Such a simplification can be made only at the expense of generality, but it may be well worth the cost. A number of measures of unpredictability or risk might be used, all in some way capturing the spread or dispersion of the probability distribution. The measure adopted here is the standard deviation. Its principal advantages are technical: (a) if the central tendency of the probability distribution is described by the mathematical expectation, the standard deviation is for reasons of probability theory the natural measure of dispersion; (b) the standard deviation of return of a compound portfolio can be easily derived from the standard deviations, and correlations, of the returns on the constituent portfolios; and (c) it is the natural parameter in the case of the normal distribution.

The standard deviation of a distribution is the square root of the variance, which is computed as follows: For each possible outcome, calculate the deviation of the return from expectation. Find the weighted average of the squares of these deviations, using as weights the outcome probabilities. In the final column of Table 4.1 are listed the standard deviations of the seven portfolios of Section 4.1.1. Portfolios C and D have equal standard deviations. So do F and G. Although D has a wider range of possible outcomes than C, the extreme values have lower probabilities. In the case of F and G, one is the mirror image of the other; the standard deviation takes no account of the direction of deviations from expectation but attributes the same risk to both.

The desired simplification is to make the investor's ranking of a portfolio depend only on the two numbers, expectation and standard deviation, rather than on the entire probability distribution of returns. If two portfolios have the same expectation and standard deviation (like C and D or like F and G), the simplifying assumption is that the investor is indifferent between them, regardless of how their probability distributions of return may otherwise differ. A theory of portfolio choices based on this assumption is only one parameter more complex than the classical theory founded on the still simpler premise that if two portfolios are alike in the one parameter expectation of return, the investor is indifferent between them. But this one step makes it possible to acknowledge that not only risk-neutral investors but also risk averters and risk lovers inhabit the world.

Mean-variance analysis is identical with expected utility maximization in two important special cases: quadratic utility functions and normally distributed returns.

---

[4]This reduction to a two-parameter problem, known as mean-variance analysis, was pioneered by Markowitz (1952a). Tobin (1958) introduced a safe asset. See Markowitz (1959) for a comprehensive exposition and Markowitz (1989) for a recent survey.

Quadratic utility. Table 4.2 shows two cases, schedules II and III (in addition to the trivial case of schedule I), in which simplification of choice to a comparison of the two parameters expectation and standard deviation does no violence to the rankings resulting from the more general approach. On each schedule, portfolios C and D, which have the same expectation and "risk," have the same expected utility, and likewise for F and G. This happens to be true because each schedule is simply a parabola. If the parabola is $U(r) = cr + br^2$, then the expected value of utility is simply $c\mu + b\mu^2 + b\sigma^2$, where μ is the expectation of return and σ is the standard deviation. Thus for schedule II ($c = .8, b = -.2$) and schedule III ($c = 2, b = 1$) of Table 4.2, expectation of utility can be computed from the last two columns of Table 4.1 without any reference to the first two. Table 4.2 also shows one case, schedule IV, where the simplification to two parameters goes wrong, judging from the rankings of expectations of utility. Although C and D are the same with respect to expectation and risk as measured by standard deviation, the investor of schedule IV prefers D. He prefers a distribution with more extreme values, and with more probability of the central value. Similarly he chooses G over F, valuing highly a small chance of a large gain. Inability to take account of choices of this kind, of which schedule IV is only one example, is the price paid for the analytic and expository convenience of reducing portfolio choice to a two-parameter problem.[5]

Normality of asset returns. Quadratic utility suffices to legitimate analysis of portfolio choice in terms of the two parameters mean and standard deviation, whatever the nature of the probability distribution of portfolio returns. Conversely, a normal distribution of returns suffices to legitimate the same analysis, whatever the nature of the utility function. The reason is that the normal distribution is a two-parameter family and the two parameters are precisely the mean and standard deviation, μ and σ. Like quadratic utility, normality is a sufficient but not necessary condition for writing expected utility as a function of the two parameters mean and standard deviation.[6]

---

[5]One problem with assuming quadratic utility is that some values of wealth must be ruled out to avoid the implication that marginal utility of wealth is negative. Another is that quadratic utility implies increasing absolute risk aversion. However, Markowitz (1989, p. 195) notes that a number of studies have found "mean-variance approximations to be quite accurate for a variety of utility functions and historical distributions of portfolio returns." Moreover, the problem of increasing absolute risk aversion can be mitigated by allowing the quadratic approximation of expected utility to vary over time. Put differently, one can consider the expected utility of return at a given level of initial wealth to be approximated by a quadratic function.

[6]Tobin (1958, p. 252) suggested that any two-parameter distributions could be characterized by mean and standard deviation. "For example, the investor might think in terms of equally likely gains or losses, centered on zero. Or he might think in terms that can be approximated by a normal distribution. Whatever two-parameter family is assumed—uniform, normal, or some other—the whole probability distribution is determined as soon as the mean and standard deviation are specified." Subsequent investigation has confirmed this insight, although some further restrictions on the distribution functions are necessary. See Ingersoll (1987, Appendix B to Chapter 4) for a discussion of the general class of distributions for which mean-variance analysis works.

Many asset prices, notably equities, seem to have fatter tails than a normal distribution, but some fat-tailed (leptokurtotic) distributions are consistent with mean-variance analysis. Limited liability implies that returns to corporate equity are not strictly normally distributed, but where the probability of large losses is low this is not a major problem. Another problem is that the normal distribution assigns probabilities to random variables of unbounded values, both positive and negative, which is inconsistent with many economic applications.

For portfolio analysis, a great convenience of the normal distribution is that a linear combination of any two or more normally distributed variables is also normally distributed. Portfolio return is, of course, a linear combination of the returns of the constituent assets.

A less formal but perhaps more convincing justification for mean-variance analysis is that investors use it widely in practice. Given the relative ease of computation and intuitive plausibility, it is not surprising that focusing on mean and standard deviation is more widely practiced than theoretically more sophisticated methods of maximizing expected utility.[7]

4.2.2 Indifference Curves and Budget Constraints

The choice of portfolio is now examined using standard consumer theory. The two "goods" are mean and standard deviation. In Section 4.2.2.1 the shape of the indifference curves is derived before turning to the budget constraint in Section 4.2.2.2. Section 4.2.2.3 brings these elements together to analyze portfolio choice.

4.2.2.1 Risk-expectation indifference curves— loci of constant expected utility

One rigorous basis for the simplification of portfolio choice to a two-parameter problem, as discussed above, is the assumption that the utility schedule is quadratic throughout the range of possible returns. Given the coefficients of the parabola, it is possible to compute all the different combinations of expectation and risk of return that lead to a given expectation of utility. The combinations can be plotted in a diagram like Fig. 4.2a, where the axes represent expectation of return and risk. They form loci like II' of combinations of equal expected utility—all equivalent to a certain return of OI; between portfolios on this locus the investor would be indifferent. Locus II' is upward sloping for a risk-averting investor as depicted in Fig. 4.2a: more risk must be compensated by higher expectation of return. Points above II' are preferred to those on II'; for example, JJ' is the indifference curve for a higher level of expected utility, the locus of combinations equivalent to a certain return of

---

[7]Also, as noted earlier in this chapter, an increasing body of evidence, surveyed in Machina (1987), is inconsistent with expected utility maximization. Given the unsettled nature of the debate about the nature of preferences regarding uncertain outcomes, it can be argued that plausible approaches such as mean-variance analysis are not necessarily inferior to rigorously deriving asset demands from expected utility maximization.

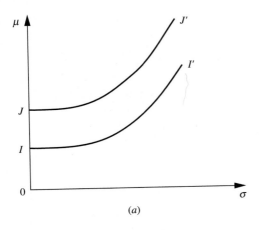

(a)

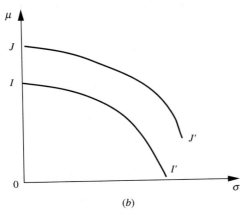

(b)

FIGURE 4.2
Indifference curves in expected return
(μ) and standard deviation (σ). (a) Risk
averter; (b) Risk seeker.

OJ. Similarly points below and to the right of II' represent inferior combinations.
The increasing slopes of II' and JJ' are not accidental. They are implications of
the derivation of the indifference curves from a quadratic utility function. Another
implication is that all indifference curves leave the axis with zero slope. For risk
lovers, the indifference curves are downward sloping as shown in Fig. 4.2b, since
both risk and return are desired.

These properties can be demonstrated as follows. Consider the quadratic utility
function

$$U(r) = cr + br^2. \tag{4.4}$$

This implies

$$E(U) = c\mu + b(\mu^2 + \sigma^2). \tag{4.5}$$

The assumption of positive marginal utility from expected return ($EU'(\mu) > 0$) requires the restriction that $c + 2b\mu > 0$ or $\mu < -c/2b$. Along an indifference curve,

$E(U)$ is constant, that is, $E(U) = k$. This implies that its slope is

$$\frac{d\mu}{d\sigma} = \frac{-2\sigma b}{c + 2b\mu}. \tag{4.6}$$

The denominator $c + 2b\mu$ is the marginal utility of return at μ, which is assumed to be positive as noted above. The numerator is nonnegative for b negative—declining marginal utility of return—and zero for $\sigma = 0$. The convexity of the indifference curve is demonstrated by the second derivative

$$\frac{d^2\mu}{d\sigma^2} = \frac{-2b[(d\mu/d\sigma)^2 + 1]}{c + 2b\mu}, \tag{4.7}$$

positive for b negative.

For a risk lover, like the investor of schedule III in Fig. 4.1, b is positive. Equations 4.6 and 4.7 imply that the indifference curves begin with a zero slope at zero risk and become negative in slope, increasingly so for higher levels of risk, as in Fig. 4.2b. Indeed, the indifference curves are northeast quadrants of circles.

As noted previously, there is a second route by which indifference curves of the same general properties can be derived from the expected utility hypothesis. Instead of restricting utility schedules to a particular two-parameter family of curves—quadratic—one may restrict the probability distributions of outcomes to a particular two-parameter family. In the case of normally distributed returns it can readily be shown that the indifference curves have the same general shape as those in Fig. 4.2: upward sloping for a risk averter, downward sloping for a risk lover, and horizontal at zero σ.

4.2.2.2 Opportunities for expectation and risk

Economy of risk from diversification. As everyone intuitively appreciates, diversification of investments rests on the principle summarized in the adage "Don't put all your eggs in one basket." Risk can be lowered by spreading over a number of independent ventures—independent in the sense that if one fails the others do not necessarily fail too. If the chance of overturning a basket of eggs and losing the whole of its contents is $\frac{1}{5}$, spreading the eggs among two baskets reduces the probability of total loss to $\frac{1}{5} \times \frac{1}{5} = \frac{1}{25}$. But it does so only on the assumption that the fates of the two baskets are independent. If the catastrophe envisaged is that a small boy carrying the eggs may fall down, it will avail little to spread the eggs between two baskets, one in his right hand and the other in his left. Better to entrust one basket to each of two small boys. Even then, if they walk together or even follow the same route, the same circumstances that might make one fall down will make more likely the fall of the other.

Less familiar perhaps is the fact that risk can be reduced by diversification to include independent ventures of greater individual risk. Suppose that one egg messenger has a probability of $\frac{1}{5}$ of falling, while the other one, a less reliable type, has a probability of $\frac{1}{2}$. The course of prudence is not to entrust all the eggs to the more reliable messenger but to divide them, not necessarily equally, into two baskets, and directing the boys to follow separate paths. Thus the risk of total loss will be reduced from $\frac{1}{5}$, if all the eggs were put in the more secure basket, to $\frac{1}{5} \times \frac{1}{2} = \frac{1}{10}$.

But there are two sides to risk, gain and loss. If diversification minimizes the chances of total loss, the price is a considerable sacrifice of chance for gain. In the example, the two-basket policy makes the probability that all the eggs will be safely delivered only $\frac{4}{5} \times \frac{1}{2} = \frac{2}{5}$, whereas under the policy of concentrating on the better messenger, this probability would be $\frac{4}{5}$.

In Table 4.1, the investor was confronted with seven portfolios and asked to choose one among them as the vehicle for his entire investment balance. The implicit assumption was that each portfolio was an indivisible unit. It was not open to the investor to choose to put half his balance, say, in C and half in D, or in any other way to divide his wealth among two or more of the seven portfolios. In fact, of course, mixtures or compound portfolios of this nature are possible. The investor would have to choose not only among the seven basic portfolios but among all possible blends of the seven. These basic portfolios may indeed be identified as the individual assets available to the investor—securities, bank deposits, and so forth. Every portfolio then consists of an assignment of a proportion of wealth to each asset, such that the proportions are nonnegative and add up to one. (The meaning of negative proportions, and their implications, will be reserved for later discussion.) Among the portfolios that can be constructed from the seven assets of Table 4.1 are the following:

	Share of wealth in asset						
	A	B	C	D	E	F	G
Portfolio I	1.0	0.0	0.0	0.0	0.0	0.0	0.0
Portfolio II	0.0	0.5	0.0	0.5	0.0	0.0	0.0
Portfolio III	0.1	0.15	0.0	0.0	0.3	0.25	0.2
Portfolio IV	0.0	0.03	0.7	0.27	0.0	0.0	0.0

Obviously the possibilities are innumerable. The direct technique of Table 4.1—listing all the available choices and looking for the best one—will have to be superseded by a more economical way of summarizing the opportunities available to the investor.

First it is necessary to see how the expectation of return and the risk on a compound portfolio are related to the expectations of return and the risks of constituent assets. The expectation of return on a portfolio is simply an average of averages, a weighted average of the expectations of return of the constituent assets, each weighted by its share in the portfolio. For example, a portfolio composed half of B and half of D has an expectation of .075.

The risk on a compound portfolio is a more complicated function of the constituent risks. As the story of the eggs suggests, the relation depends on the degree of independence of the outcomes for the individual assets. The eggs story also suggests that, to the extent that there is independence among the separate risks, diversification

TABLE 4.3

Outcomes of mixed portfolio assuming independence

Outcome			Return on $\frac{1}{2}$B, $\frac{1}{2}$D	Portfolio $\frac{1}{2}$B, $\frac{1}{2}$D	
B	D	Probability		Expectation	Risk
.10	.30	.028	.20		
.05	.30	.028	.175		
.00	.30	.028	.15		
.10	.10	.276	.10		
.05	.10	.276	.075	.075	.046
.00	.10	.276	.05		
.10	−.10	.028	.00		
.05	−.10	.028	−.025		
.00	−.10	.028	−.05		

leads to a risk *smaller* than the weighted average of the separate risks. As an example, consider the possible outcomes of the portfolio (0.5B, 0.5D) on the assumption that the risks on B and D are independent. These are given in Table 4.3.

Comparing the mixed portfolio with D shows how the dispersion of possible outcomes has been compressed, from a range of (−.10, .30) to (−.05, .20). The risk on the mixed portfolio is .046, very little more than the risk on B and much less than a simple average of the risks of B and D. By increasing the proportion of B in the mixture, it is possible to make the risk smaller than the risk on B, while the expectation of return remains higher than that of B. Consider the portfolio (.8B, .2D). Its expectation of return is .06. Its risk as measured by the standard deviation is only .037. In these circumstances, B would be for a risk averter an *inefficient* portfolio.

Positive correlation between the returns on two assets would reduce and, in the extreme, eliminate the possibilities of reducing risk by mixing them. The extreme case will make the point. Suppose that a .10 return on B is invariably accompanied by a .20 return on C, a .05 return on B by a .10 return on C, and a .00 return on B by a .00 return on C. The possible outcomes of the portfolio (0.5B, 0.5D) are then simply .15, .075, and .00, each with probability $\frac{1}{3}$. The risk, as well as the expected return, is simply an average of the two constituents. The risk is .061, and the expected return is .075. If instead the returns on these two securities were independent, the risk would be only .046.

At the other extreme, perfect negative correlation between the returns of two assets would make possible complete avoidance of risk, perfect hedging. Suppose that a .10 return on B is invariably accompanied by a .00 return on C, a .05 return on B by a .10 return on C, and a .00 return on B by a .20 return on C. Consider the portfolio ($\frac{2}{3}$B, $\frac{1}{3}$C). No matter what the outcome, the return on the portfolio will be .067.

From a given basic set of assets an infinite variety of mixed portfolios can be constructed, and the expectation and risk of every portfolio can be derived. Each portfolio can then be represented by a point in a diagram with coordinates expectation and risk, like those of Fig. 4.2. These combinations of expectation and

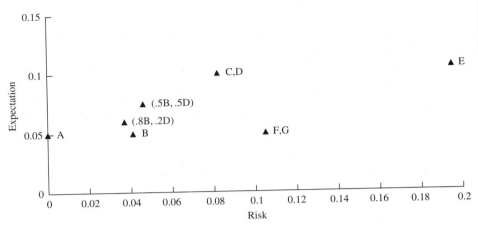

FIGURE 4.3
Return and risk for various assets and portfolios.

risk constitute the opportunities available to the investor. For example, Fig. 4.3 gives the combinations for certain of the portfolios based on Table 4.1, but by no means all of them, on the assumption of independence of risks. Filling in the entire set of opportunities is not a simple task, even when there are only seven assets to be combined.

Two-asset portfolios. It is instructive to approach this task by trying to build the complete set of opportunities, in terms of expectation and risk, made available to an investor by two assets. To give some anticipatory aid to the argument of Chapter 5, let the two assets be currency and capital. Let x_1 be the share of the portfolio in currency and $x_2 = 1 - x_1$ the share in capital; neither share can be negative. Expectation and risk of return on currency reflect possible changes in the price level of consumer goods. Both the yield on capital and the value of capital relative to consumer goods are also matters of uncertainty.

To begin with the simplest case, suppose that the investor regards the consumer goods price level as certain to remain constant. Thus he estimates both the expectation μ_1 and the risk σ_1 on currency to be zero but assesses both the expectation μ_2 and risk σ_2 of return on capital as positive. The opportunities available to him are shown in Fig. 4.4a; they lie along the line from the origin to the point labeled (0, 1). Both expectation and risk are proportional to x_2, the share of capital in the portfolio. The combinations available to the investor extend from zero expectation and risk for a 100 percent currency portfolio (1, 0) to expectation μ_2 and risk σ_2 for a 100 percent capital portfolio (0, 1). Nothing significant is altered if a nonzero return on currency is introduced.

The opportunities available to the investor are somewhat more complicated if he does not regard the real value of currency as perfectly predictable. Suppose that his expectation of real capital gain or loss on currency is zero but that he is not certain of this prospect. Suppose, further, that he regards the risks on capital and

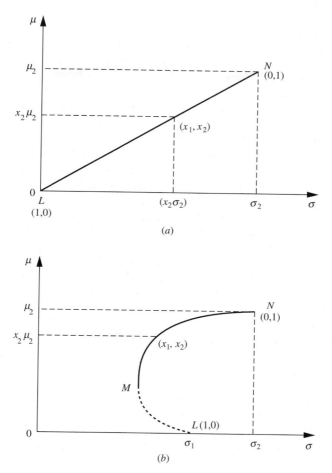

FIGURE 4.4

Efficiency locus in a currency-capital economy. (*a*) Perfectly
predictable currency; (*b*) Risky currency.

currency as independent. That is, whatever happens to the price of consumer goods,
the chances of rises and falls in the real value of capital remain the same. They have
the same likelihood when consumer goods prices rise as when they fall. Suppose, finally, that capital is higher both in risk and in expectation of return. In this situation,
unlike the previous one, all available portfolios entail some risk. The minimum-risk
portfolio is not 100 percent currency. As noted above, it includes each asset in inverse
proportion to its variance. Since the expectation of return is proportional to x_2, the
share of capital in the blend, portfolios with less capital and more currency than the
minimum-risk portfolio are, for a risk averter, inefficient. That is, for no greater risk
it is possible to obtain a higher expectation of return. The available portfolio choices
are shown in Fig. 4.4*b*. The hyperbola *LMN* represents the combinations of risk and

expectations available, going from 100 percent currency at L to 100 percent capital at N. The shares of capital and currency in the portfolio corresponding to any point on the locus are indicated by the proportions in which that point divides the vertical distance from L to N. The minimum-risk portfolio, which involves some capital, gives the combination M of risk and expectation of return. Only the solid part of the hyperbola, MN, represents efficient portfolios for a risk averter.[8]

Currency and capital may not be regarded as independent risks. The investor may feel, for example, that if the price level of consumer goods rises, the chances are that the price of capital goods will rise even more. Or he may believe that if there are capital losses on currency, the chances are that there will also be exceptionally low gains or perhaps losses from holding capital. What are the consequences of beliefs of this nature for an investor's estimate of the opportunities available to him?

To take first one of the extremes, suppose the investor believes in a perfect negative correlation between the return on currency and the return on capital. As will be shown, he can then, if he chooses, avoid all risk by complete hedging, making the share of each asset in the portfolio inversely proportional to its risk. Departures from the no-risk portfolio in the direction of greater concentration in either asset will add to risk. But clearly only one direction leads to greater expectation. The situation may be graphed as in Fig. 4.4b above, except that point M lies on the vertical axis.

If, at the opposite pole, returns on currency and capital are regarded as having a perfect positive correlation, there is no opportunity for reducing risk by hedging or by diversification among independent risks. The minimum-risk portfolio is 100 percent in the lower-risk asset; the maximum-risk portfolio is of course 100 percent in the other asset. The risk of any other portfolio is simply a weighted average of the risks of these two extremes, with weights equal to the portfolio shares of the two assets. Since the expectation of return on a portfolio is a similarly weighted average of the expectations of the two assets, the opportunity locus is, as shown in Fig. 4.5, the straight line LN. If currency had the higher risk as well as the lower return, this line would be negatively sloped, and only its highest point, corresponding to 100 percent capital, would be efficient for investors other than pronounced risk lovers.

The cases discussed, with variation in assumptions about correlation, are summarized in Fig. 4.5. Imperfect correlations, positive and negative, give rise to opportunity loci between the pure cases pictured. The opportunity loci for two-asset portfolios are hyperbolas, except in the special cases in which they degenerate to straight lines.

In the general case the algebra is as follows. Let ρ_{12} be the coefficient of correlation of r_1, the return on asset 1, and r_2, the return on asset 2. Then

$$\mu = x_1\mu_1 + x_2\mu_2, \qquad \text{and} \qquad (4.8)$$

$$\sigma^2 = x_1^2\sigma_1^2 + x_2^2\sigma_2^2 + 2\rho_{12}x_1\sigma_1x_2\sigma_2. \qquad (4.9)$$

---

[8]If short selling of currency (borrowing) is permitted, the efficiency locus will extend beyond N. For further discussion of borrowing see Section 4.3.

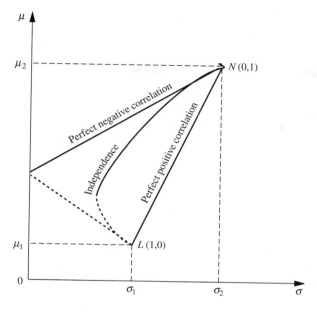

FIGURE 4.5
Opportunity loci for
alternative assumptions
about correlation.

The portfolio that minimizes risk is

$$\{x_1, x_2\} = \left\{ \frac{\sigma_2^2 - \rho_{12}\sigma_1\sigma_2}{\sigma_1^2 + \sigma_2^2 - 2\rho_{12}\sigma_1\sigma_2}, \frac{\sigma_1^2 - \rho_{12}\sigma_1\sigma_2}{\sigma_1^2 + \sigma_2^2 - 2\rho_{12}\sigma_1\sigma_2} \right\} \tag{4.10}$$

provided that both these values are nonnegative.

In case of independence $\rho_{12} = 0$, the minimum-risk portfolio includes the two assets in inverse proportion to their variances and has a risk of

$$\left[2\frac{\sigma_1^2\sigma_2^2}{\sigma_1^2 + \sigma_2^2} \right]^{1/2}. \tag{4.11}$$

In case of perfect negative correlation, $\rho_{12} = -1$, the risk of a portfolio is $|x_1\sigma_1 - x_2\sigma_2|$. The minimum-risk portfolio includes the two assets in inverse proportion to their standard deviations and has a risk of zero. In case of perfect positive correlation, the risk of a portfolio is simply $x_1\sigma_1 + x_2\sigma_2$, and the minimum-risk portfolio is $(0, 1)$ if $\sigma_1 > \sigma_2$ or $(1, 0)$ if $\sigma_1 < \sigma_2$.

Portfolios of more than two assets. When there are only two basic assets, the available portfolios all lie along a single curve—a line or a hyperbola—in the risk-return space. But for three or more basic assets the available opportunities cover an area. The delineation of the attainable set of mean-standard-deviation combinations and of its efficient frontier is a complicated computational task. Procedures are described in detail in Markowitz (1959), to which the interested reader is referred. Some insight into the nature of the problem can be obtained by considering the possibilities added by the availability of a third asset. Suppose that assets 1 and 2 are initially available, and a third one, 3, can then be introduced into the portfolio.

The correlation of the return on the third asset with the return on a blend of assets 1 and 2 will be different for different blends. The degree of economy of risk achievable by mixing asset 3 with a blend of assets 1 and 2 will depend on this correlation. In Fig. 4.6, assets 1, 2, and 3 are represented by points A_1, A_2, and A_3, respectively. The efficiency locus can be found by combining all possible blends of assets 1 and 2 with asset 3 and finding the upward-sloping part of the envelope. Two examples of such asset mixes are shown as the broken lines XMA_3 and YNA_3. If for some blend X of assets A_1 and A_2 the correlation of X and asset 3 is nearly -1, the hyperbola from joining the third asset to X will be strongly bowed, having a minimum-risk point near zero. But if the correlation is nearly $+1$, the hyperbola will degenerate into a virtually straight line.

The efficient frontier will have the general shape MNA_2 illustrated in Fig. 4.6 and will usually include holdings of all three assets. By adding a fourth asset, then a fifth asset, and so on, it is clear that the set of expectation-risk opportunities can be constructed for any number of assets. Certain general conclusions about this set and its efficient (from the standpoint of a risk averter) frontier are important. First, the efficient frontier is concave—it is either a line or a curve convex from above, or in special cases a single point. Second, the minimum-risk portfolio is generally a diversified portfolio; the exceptions occur when there are high positive correlations among asset returns or when there is a riskless asset. Third, the maximum-risk portfolio is, of course, an undiversified portfolio, concentrated on the asset of highest risk.

The efficient frontier is a hyperbola if short positions in each asset are allowed, that is, if asset shares are not constrained to be between 0 and 1. The frontier is not a hyperbola but is straightforward to compute if short positions are not allowed or are limited. Markowitz showed how to do the calculations when constraints on asset shares are introduced.

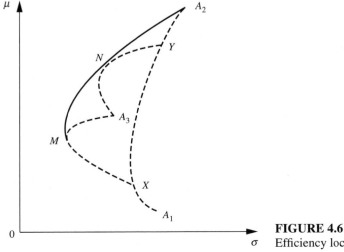

FIGURE 4.6
Efficiency locus with three assets.

EXAMPLE 1: CURRENCY, BONDS, AND CAPITAL. A three-asset example has been constructed both to illustrate the derivation of the opportunity locus and to simulate certain broad characteristics of actual money and capital markets. Three assets are available to wealth owners: cash, bonds, and equities. Cash bears no interest but changes in purchasing power. The investor is assumed to expect on balance no change in the price level, but he grants some probability both to a rise and to a fall. Bonds bear interest; they can, like cash, change in purchasing power. In addition, they are subject to money capital gains or losses because of changes in the interest rate. These capital gains and losses are assumed to have zero expected value. Equities in goods or physical capital have a higher expected rate of return than bonds. But the return is not guaranteed and is subject to the considerable risks of changes in the value of capital relative to consumer goods. This example illustrates the way risks on assets can be derived from the variation of the fundamental factors driving the economy and therefore asset returns, an old idea associated with what has come to be known as the arbitrage pricing theory, which is discussed further in Chapter 6.

Consider two states of the world, a and b, with different expected returns:

	Expected return per year	
	a	b
Cash	.00	.00
Bonds	.03	.06
Equities	.10	.10

Risks are assumed to be the same in both states of the world.

	Standard deviation	Kind of risk
Cash + bonds	.03	Purchasing power change
Bonds	.02	Interest rate change
Equities	.12	Relative price changes

A rough measure of the magnitude of the risks may be obtained by recalling that, if the probability distribution is normal, the probability of a deviation in each direction greater than two standard deviations is 2.3 percent. Thus, the investor thinks the probability is only 2.3 percent that the dollar will lose 6 percent or more of its purchasing power during the year and similarly that there is only 2.3 percent probability that it will gain more than 6 percent in purchasing power during the year. The investor believes the probability is more than 95 percent that the money price of bonds a year hence will be between 96 percent and 104 percent of the current price. The three risks are assumed to be uncorrelated in the investor's view: That is, interest rates and prices, both absolute levels and relative prices, move independently. This does not mean that the three assets have independent risks. Both cash and bonds have purchasing-power risk.

Figure 4.7 shows the efficient portfolios available to a risk-averting investor. On the left panel of Fig. 4.7 are shown the proportions of each of the three assets in efficient

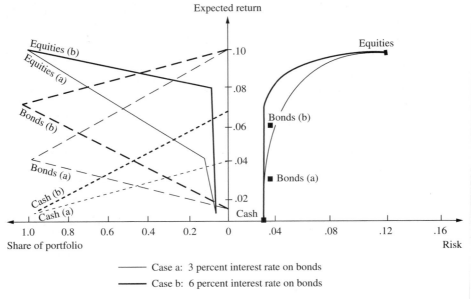

FIGURE 4.7
Portfolio shares and efficiency locus for a three-asset economy.

portfolios of various levels of expected return. The curves (expectation-risk loci) in the right panel tell the corresponding levels of risk. In case a, for example, at an expected portfolio return of .0059, the efficient portfolio is .941 cash, .059 equities, and no bonds. It is not possible to find a portfolio that promises a yield of .0059 or more and has a risk less than .029. (It is in fact not possible to find any portfolio, no matter how low its yield, with a risk less than .029. Note that the all-cash portfolio would yield zero expected return, with a risk of .03.) The least risky way to obtain an expected portfolio return of .03 is .28 cash, .62 bonds, and .10 equities. At an expected return of .039, the cash component of the portfolio becomes zero. Up to this rate additional yield could be obtained substituting bonds, mainly, and equities, partly, for cash. Consequently, below .039 additional yield costs very little in increments to risk, as the steep slope of the risk-return opportunity locus in the right panel of Fig. 4.7 indicates. Since negative holdings of cash are impossible (one cannot borrow at zero interest), the only way to increase expected yield above .039 is to substitute equities for bonds. As the risk-return locus shows, this entails a greater addition to risk for every unit increase in expected return. Given that negative holdings of bonds are likewise impossible, the highest return (.10) and riskiest (.12) available portfolio is 100 percent equities.

Case b is shown to indicate the difference made by a change in the bond rate from .03 to .06. This is one of the principal weapons available to the monetary authority. The nominal return on cash (aside from biased expectations of changes in purchasing power) is assumed to be fixed at zero; for institutional reasons, currency and demand deposits do not bear interest. By open-market operations, the monetary authority varies the supply of the middle asset, bonds, relative to the supply of cash, and thus affects the bond rate and indirectly the willingness of wealth owners to hold equities. The power of open-market operations depends on the strength of this indirect effect.

An increase in the bond rate changes the risk-return opportunity locus, making it possible generally to have less risk and/or more return. The share of equities in the portfolio decreases for one or both of the following reasons: (a) the investor chooses a less risky portfolio, that is, moves to the left, as well as up, on the expectation-risk diagram; or (b) the efficient portfolio, even for a given degree of risk, may contain less equities and more bonds or cash.

EXAMPLE 2: INTERNATIONAL PORTFOLIO DIVERSIFICATION. Movements of capital across regional and national boundaries, and across currencies, have exploded in volume, thanks to the dismantling of currency and exchange controls and other financial regulations, and to revolutionary economies afforded by new technologies of communication and transactions. Figures 4.8 and 4.9 show the trends of American-owned wealth abroad and foreign ownership of American wealth. The latter has been growing especially rapidly since around 1980, a period when the U.S. net wealth position vis-à-vis the rest of the world deteriorated sharply and turned negative. While internationalization has grown over time, these figures show that it remains quite modest in both directions. As of 1992, both U.S. foreign assets and foreign liabilities represented less than 10 percent of U.S. domestic asset supplies, by any of the measures in Figs. 4.8 and 4.9. For most other countries, international portfolio diversification also remains quite limited.[9]

The strong home asset preference exhibited by investors in most countries is by no means an implication of portfolio theory. Returns on foreign and domestic assets are likely to have probability distributions that are weakly correlated because these returns are subject to different economic shocks. If so, risk-averse investors can reduce risk and/or increase return by holding part of their marketable wealth in foreign assets.

The advantages of international diversification depend on whether the assets in question are nominal or real. The risks of nominal assets are those of commodity-price fluctuation, interest-rate variation, and default. Economies with different currencies, geographies, and central governments will be more independent of each other in these dimensions than, for example, the states of a federal union. Exchange risk may work either way. Here it is necessary to consider the correlations of deviations of exchange rates from expected trends with the other risks of nominal assets. If a foreign currency appreciates when home inflation increases and depreciates when foreign inflation is relatively high, foreign currency assets are a hedge against purchasing-power risk. If the foreign currency depreciates when home interest rates move up, foreign securities are not a good hedge against capital losses on home bonds.

Equities and direct investments in real properties in foreign countries present opportunities and risks quite different from those of currency-denominated assets. In particular, the avoidance of exchange risk applies with considerably less force. Equities, and the real capital assets to which they are claims, are not entitlements to specified amounts of any currencies. An extreme view is that goods are goods, capital goods are capital goods, factories are factories, wherever they are located. Earnings of multinational companies come from worldwide sales in numerous currencies. Neither the earnings nor the value of the shares in any currency need be particularly correlated with the price of the currency of the country where the company is domiciled. Indeed if a company is leveraged by debt in its home currency, owners of its equity are going short in that currency.

Consider Japanese direct investments in the United States, say in particular the acquisition of facilities for producing internationally traded goods like automobiles.

---

[9]Adler and Dumas (1983) provide a survey of the theory and evidence on international portfolio diversification. Golub (1990) presents international comparisons of the extent of international portfolio diversification.

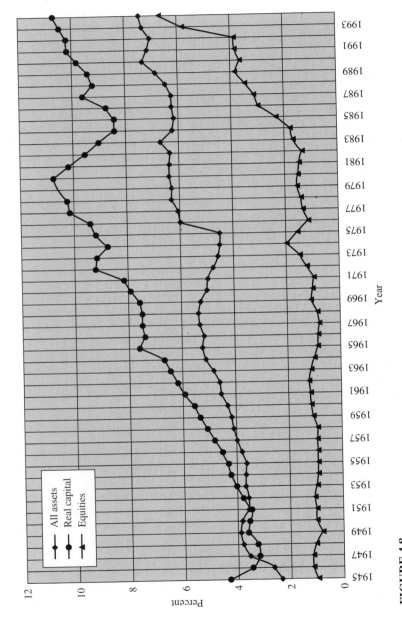

FIGURE 4.8
U.S. private holdings of foreign assets, in percent of U.S. domestic asset supplies.

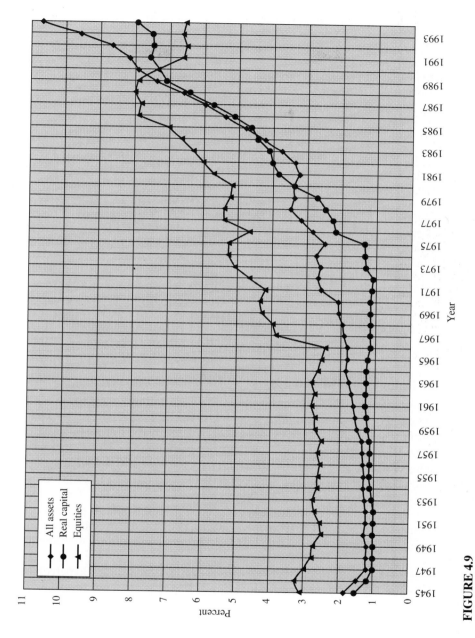

FIGURE 4.9
Foreign private holdings of U.S. assets, in percent of U.S. domestic asset supplies.

85

Japanese investors' demand for nominal dollar-denominated bonds should not decline by the full dollar amount of their direct investments in the United States. The reason is that an automobile factory in Ohio may be a closer substitute for properties and equities in Japan and elsewhere than it is for future dollars qua dollars.

The international car market can be supplied from Tennessee or from Tokyo. The long-run real returns from owning a plant in Tennessee are not very dependent on the dollar/yen exchange rate and not very vulnerable to the factors that might generate losses to Japanese holders of American bonds. U.S. inflation, for example, would raise the dollar earnings from operating the plant at the same time as it depreciated the dollar against the yen. Direct investment of this kind in the United States is a portfolio reallocation vis-à-vis Japanese plants, real properties, and equities more than vis-à-vis dollars per se. Indeed, scattering production for the world market over various locations may diversify risks because of national or regional productivity shocks. The principal location and legal and tax domicile of a business, however, do entangle its earnings with the domestic and exchange value of the currency.

If domestic economic shocks tend to impact capital and labor incomes in the same direction, foreign assets may be a good hedge against the risks associated with domestic labor incomes. This is the same type of consideration that suggests that a risk-averse worker should not invest his retirement savings in the shares of the company that employs him.[10] Nontradeable human labor is the bulk of most people's wealth. If foreign assets are indeed useful hedges against major shocks to domestic wage incomes, then the small amount of international diversification depicted in Figs. 4.8 and 4.9 is an even greater puzzle than it appears when only tradeable-asset portfolios are considered.

In the past, home asset preference has been due less to risk-return calculus than to other factors: legal restrictions, transactions costs, and informational gaps. Mean-variance analysis suggests that global diversification will increase over time as these barriers continue to diminish.

4.2.2.3 Optimal portfolio choices

In previous sections, it has been shown how both the preferences of the investor and the opportunities he estimates to be open to him can be expressed in expectation and risk of return. Preferences can be described by a set of indifference curves, or loci of constant expected utility. Opportunities can be delimited as a set of attainable combinations of risk and expectation, of which only a subset will be efficient. The investor will choose the attainable combination that lies on the highest indifference curve, that is, the one that promises the highest expectation of utility. This choice may be one of the extreme points of the set of attainable combinations or it may be an intermediate point. Figures 4.10 and 4.11 depict choices of extreme points and intermediate points, respectively. Dotted lines represent the investor's indifference curves.

Extreme points correspond to undiversified portfolios—investing 100 percent in one asset—or, in the case of multiperiod investment strategies, to sequences of undiversified portfolios. As the figures show, risk lovers always choose extreme points; diversification can never add to the chances of the exceptional returns that they seek.

---

[10]See Brainard and Tobin (1992) and Golub (1994) for further discussion of this point and empirical evidence.

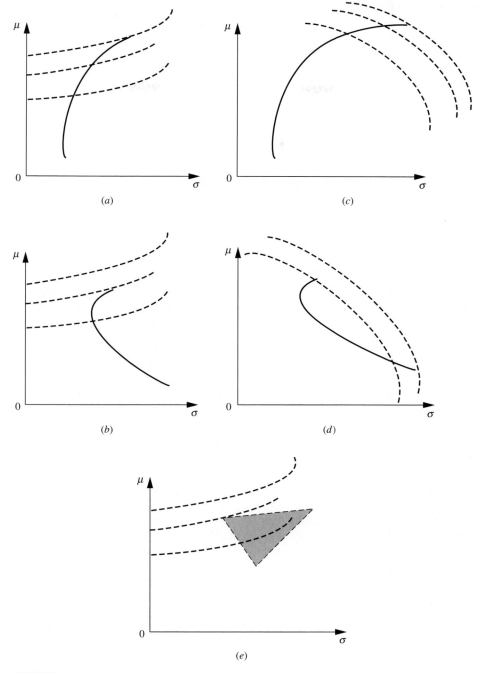

FIGURE 4.10
Choices of extreme points. (*a*) Maximum risk and return, chosen by a risk averter;
(*b*) Maximum return (and maximum risk, on an efficient locus) chosen by a risk averter;
(*c*) Maximum risk and return, chosen by a risk lover; (*d*) Maximum risk, chosen by a risk
lover; (*e*) Minimum risk, chosen by a risk averter.

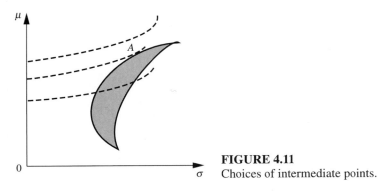

FIGURE 4.11
Choices of intermediate points.

Risk averters sometimes choose extreme points, finding the cost of greater safety, in sacrifice of expectation of return, too high to justify diversification.

Usually risk averters will choose intermediate points, diversified portfolios. Geometrically a chosen intermediate point is a tangency between an indifference curve and the efficient opportunity locus, as in Fig. 4.11 at point A. (If a tangency happens to occur at an extreme, this can be treated as an intermediate point.) At a chosen intermediate point, the terms on which the market is to offer additional expectation in return for the bearing of additional risk are just the terms required to induce the investor to assume added risk without loss or gain of utility.

What will happen to the investor's choice if the opportunities confronting him change as a result of new estimates of expectations and risks of one or more assets? As the diagrams make clear, the same extreme point will remain the choice of a risk lover in the face of considerable shifts of the opportunity locus. A major shift might send him from one extreme point, corresponding to one undiversified portfolio, to another. For a risk averter, the change in the nature of the investor's choice depends on the slopes of successive indifference curves. Suppose there is an improvement in the terms on which the investor can "purchase" additional expectation of return at the expense of assuming additional risk. Diagrammatically, there is a counterclockwise rotation in the efficient opportunity locus, as from MN to $M'N'$ in Fig. 4.12. As all students of the theory of consumer choice know (see also Section 3.1.2.3 of Chapter 3), the reaction to such a rotation can be decomposed into a substitution effect and an income effect. Suppose that the investor was initially at point A, the tangency of MN with an indifference curve I. The substitution effect can be discerned by accompanying the rotation of the locus with an imaginary parallel shift downwards, from $M'N'$ to $M''N''$. At every risk level, $M''N''$ has the same slope as $M'N'$, but $M''N''$ goes through the point A. Thus the shift from MN to $M''N''$ does not permit the investor to enjoy any higher expectation than before unless he also takes more risk. This he would do, thanks to the better terms—steeper slope—of $M''N''$, finding at A'' a new tangency, with an indifference curve I''. The movement from A to A'' is the substitution effect, or incentive effect. The income effect is then the change from A'' to a new position A' because of the parallel upwards shift from $M''N''$ to $M'N'$, a shift that permits the investor to enjoy a greater expectation at the same level of risk—as if the returns on all assets increased in the same proportion while their risks

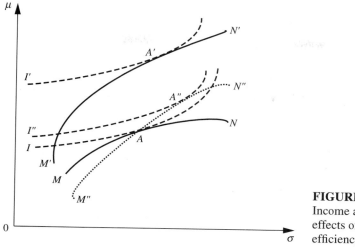

FIGURE 4.12
Income and substitution effects of a shift in the efficiency locus.

remained unchanged. Here the income effect is not literally a question of income but rather the opportunity to enjoy both more expectation and more security (less risk) at the same time. If both expectation and security are, in the parlance of demand theory, normal goods, the investor will divide the expansion of opportunity between them. This is the kind of reaction depicted in Fig. 4.12, where the movement from A'' to A' is a reduction of risk as well as an increase in expectation. As shown, A' is still a position of greater risk than the initial position A; the substitution effect is stronger than the income effect. But it is not excluded that the income effect may be the stronger, that the position of I' relative to I and I'' leads to an adjustment at smaller risk than A. Strong income effects have been detected by market observers who refer to some portfolio managers as "reaching for income" at times of generally reduced yields, that is, increasing equity investments at the expense of bonds to maintain the average portfolio return. At the opposite pole, it is also possible that A' will be to the right of A'', a fortiori of A. The income effect then reinforces the substitution effect. Security from risk is—again using the parlance of demand theory—an inferior good.

4.3
THE SEPARATION THEOREM

Suppose now that there is one riskless asset in addition to a number of risky assets. The riskless asset has a rate of return of s. As Tobin (1958) first showed in an application to the demand for money, the investor's portfolio choice can be separated into two steps. First, the optimal mix of risky assets is determined as in Section 4.2.2.3. This yields an efficiency locus like KK' in Fig. 4.13. The riskless asset is then combined with the risky assets, which yields the efficiency locus NMN', tangent to KK'.

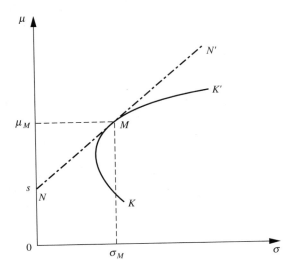

FIGURE 4.13
Efficiency locus with a riskless asset.

The investor's portfolio decision is reduced to selecting the share of wealth invested in the riskless asset and an invariant mix of the risky assets M, with mean return μ_M and standard deviation σ_M. Now, if all investors are also assumed to face the same probability distribution of asset returns and the same safe rate of return, they all have the same efficiency locus NMN'. In that case, all these investors hold the same mix of risky assets regardless of their risk preferences, with relatively risk-averse investors holding a higher proportion of the riskless asset.

All efficient portfolios are on the line NMN', which implies a linear relationship between portfolio expected return μ_p and risk σ_p.

$$\mu_p = s + \frac{\mu_M - s}{\sigma_M}\sigma_p. \tag{4.12}$$

For an algebraic derivation of the separation theorem and an exposition of its relation to the capital asset pricing model, see the following chapter.

If borrowing is precluded, the efficiency locus is confined to NMK' in Fig. 4.13. If borrowing is possible at the same rate s the efficiency locus becomes NMN'. Points on the MN' part of the locus represent negative holdings of the safe asset, that is, borrowing the safe asset so that more than 100 percent of wealth is invested in the bundle of risky assets. In general, however, borrowing rates exceed lending rates. Let s_L be the lending rate and s_B be the borrowing rate. The resulting efficiency locus $NMM'N'$ depicted in Fig. 4.14 consists of three segments. Points on NM represent blends of positive holdings of the safe asset (lending) at a return of s_L and a mix of risky assets M. Points on $M'N'$ represent borrowing at a rate s_B to hold levered positions in the mix of risky assets M'. The intermediate range MM' consists of holdings of risky assets only. The risky-asset portfolio at M is not the same as the one at M', and those between M and M' differ from both.

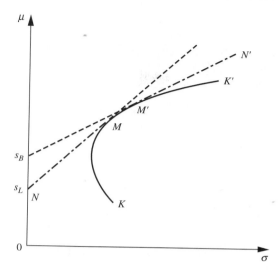

FIGURE 4.14
Efficiency locus when borrowing and lending rates are different.

4.4
MULTIPERIOD INVESTMENT

The description of investment opportunities among assets of uncertain prospects presented above has been cast in terms of immediate returns, expectations, and risks. It has obvious application, therefore, to an investor who plans an early consumption of his wealth, who plans to make no portfolio changes between now and the date of consumption because the time is too short to make it worthwhile to undergo the costs of intermediate changes in holdings. As noted in Chapter 3, the length of time within which portfolio shifts are not economical is different for different investors. For wealthy, knowledgeable, and decisive investors with experience and easy access to asset markets, able to exploit the economies of scale in financial transactions, it may be measured in days or hours. Individuals of modest means and limited knowledge and experience, for whom financial transactions and decisions are difficult, uncongenial, and time consuming, may regard portfolio choices as irrevocable for several years. The utility schedule underlying the preferences of the short-horizon investor regarding current expectation and risk reflects simply his valuations of smaller and larger amounts of consumption at the planned date of liquidation. In particular, the meaning of risk is that consumption may be smaller or larger than expectation.

For an investor with more distant objectives of wealth accumulation, the relevant choices are among portfolio sequences rather than among simple portfolios. If the planned date of consumption is not immediate but, for example, ten years ahead, the utility basic to investment preferences reflects valuations of larger or smaller prospects of consumption ten years from now. Returns, expectations, and risks can all be reckoned over ten years; indifference curves—loci of constant expected utility—can be interpreted accordingly. But the investor need not hold the same portfolio for the entire decade. He can plan to shift his holdings from time to time, guiding himself by expected changes in the prospects of different assets and taking into account the costs of the shifts themselves. Each possible portfolio sequence will have a probability distribution of ten-year return, from which can be derived its expectation and risk. The investor chooses the sequence with the highest expectation of utility. His immediate portfolio choice is simply the first step in the optimal sequence.

Some of the relevant sequences may be contingent sequences, or strategies. A contingent sequence is one that includes a planned move that is, like a chess player's third move, conditional on the situation at the time: For example, hold portfolio A for a year, then shift to portfolio B if B has returned more than 10 percent during that year, otherwise continue to hold A. There are two basic reasons why investors may choose contingent sequences. First, if future events will add to the investor's information about the further future, it may be wise to follow a strategy that exploits this gain in information. If the probabilities governing returns on various assets in year 2 are affected by the returns actually realized in year 1, then the investor will know better what to expect in year 2 after year 1 is over. His portfolio choice at the beginning of year 2 may need to depend on what has happened in year 1, not only to the assets he has held but to others available to him. Similarly, he may learn more about the distribution of his income and consumption requirements as time unfolds. The second reason that an investor may choose a contingent sequence is that the fortunes, good or bad, of his initial investments may change his position in relation to his ultimate consumption target. This may affect the mixture of expectation and risk he wants to have in subsequent portfolios in a way that depends on his risk aversion. For example, extremely good luck the first year will lead the investor to hold a higher proportion of the safe asset to safeguard a consumption level virtually attained if the investor has increasing relative risk aversion, as discussed in Section 4.1.3. This reason for contingent strategy may apply even if the first one does not, that is, even if asset returns in different time periods are statistically independent. This section begins with the case of an investor with a single planned date of consumption in the future and analyzes his portfolio problem in isolation from his saving-consumption decision. The more general problem is briefly discussed subsequently.

4.4.1 Portfolio Choice with a Single Future Consumption Date

For illustration of the nature of choice among portfolio sequences, consider an investor who knows that he will need wealth ten years from the date of portfolio decision, no sooner or later, for example, to pay for his daughter's college education. Suppose that he is certain of the stability of the prices of the goods he wishes to purchase on that future date. Thus his choice is not complicated by risks of changes in the purchasing power of currency. Some of the alternative sequences available to him are the following:

1. Hold currency or demand deposits for ten years. This eliminates all risk but also all return.
2. Hold a discount bond, for example, a government savings bond redeemable at a specified value at the end of ten years. (Whether it is redeemable at earlier dates is immaterial in the present instance.) This avoids all risk, bears some return, and therefore is clearly better than strategy 1.

3. Hold savings accounts, in which periodic interest earnings are accumulated. Or, what amounts to much the same thing, hold a succession of three-month Treasury bills, buying new ones with the maturity proceeds of each issue. It is certain that the value of such a portfolio at the end of ten years will be no smaller than that of strategy 1. How much larger it will be depends on the rates of interest on these assets over the decade. The fluctuations of these rates cannot be perfectly predicted; hence this strategy is riskier than strategy 2.

4. Hold coupon bonds of no default risk, matured at the end of ten years. Again it is certain that the value of the portfolio will be no smaller than that of strategy 1. How much greater it will be, and at how much risk, depends on the disposition of the interest coupons. As they come due, they could be invested without danger of loss in any of these same four alternatives—cash, discount bonds redeemable at the target date, savings accounts or bills, or coupon bonds maturing at the target date. How much interest could be compounded from investment of the coupons is not entirely predictable, as it depends on interest rates prevailing as the coupons become due. Although this strategy does not provide the degree of certainty of strategy 1 and strategy 2, it is less risky than strategy 3.

5. Hold a marketable coupon bond with maturity later than ten years. The value of the bond at ten years is not wholly predictable, and there is not even a guaranteed minimum. This sequence is riskier than any of the preceding ones; the degree of risk depends on the manner of investing the coupons.

6. Follow strategy 3, successive short-term investments, unless and until the rate of return on bonds maturing by the target date exceeds, say, 6 percent. In that event, shift to policy 4.

7. Hold equities, unpredictable both in value and in yield, and reinvest the yields in equities. This is riskier than the other strategies but quite likely to have a higher expectation of return.[11]

The ranking of assets, portfolios, sequences, and strategies in riskiness is often not an absolute property of the assets themselves but is relative to the timing of the accumulation objectives of the investor. A three-month Treasury bill is generally regarded as less risky than a ten-year marketable bond. In terms of three-month return, this is true; an investor with short-term objectives would take less risk in bills than in bonds. But in terms of ten-year return, the reverse is true, as comparison of strategy 3 with 2 or 4 in the discussion above indicates.

For any future date there will be one or more portfolio sequences of least risk. Indeed if risks of changes in the purchasing power of money are ignored, there will be at least one zero-risk sequence for every date. Cash, as in strategy 1 of the illustration above, is always available. But an all-cash sequence is generally inefficient. It is dominated, for any given date, by assets of equal predictability and higher return. The initial portfolio in an efficient least-risk sequence will be different for different

---

[11]MaCurdy and Shoven (1992) found that equities always outperformed bonds for any 40-year period ending between 1916 and 1990, except for the 40-year period ending in 1942 when it was a virtual tie. Stocks also outperformed bonds for all but five of the 25-year investment horizons ending between 1901 and 1990.

target dates. To gain higher expectation of return by his target date, the investor can choose a sequence of higher risk. In the illustration, he can seek higher return in sequences involving short-term securities whose yields are imperfectly predictable, or he can choose sequences involving longer-term bonds or equities, whose values at the target date are also uncertain. How far he will depart from the efficient least-risk portfolio depends on his basic utility schedule.

Once allowance is made for unpredictability of the real value of currency, ranking portfolio sequences in terms of risk is not so easy. Within the category of obligations expressed in terms of currency, the ranking remains the same as if the price level were predictable. But none of these alternatives is free from risk; they are all equally subject to changes in real value from inflation or deflation. As remarked in Chapter 2, neither the market nor the government offers assets perfectly predictable in real value, even for a single future date.[12] But in view of the long-run correlation of capital-goods values and consumer goods prices, the minimum-risk portfolio sequences, at least for more distant target dates, very likely involve diversified holdings of equities.

4.4.2 Modeling Multiperiod Portfolio Choice

Consider an investor with target date T who must make T period-by-period portfolio choices. The principles of portfolio selection developed in the previous sections apply, but calculation of T–period expectations and risks is much more complex than in the single-period case. In particular, the simple manner in which the expectation and risk of a compound portfolio can be derived from the expectations and risks of its constituent assets has no analogue for portfolio sequences.

Two kinds of portfolio sequences can be imagined. A stationary sequence is one in which the same portfolio is maintained throughout; if the proportions of different assets tend to change because of different rates of appreciation, the investor restores the desired proportions periodically. The frequency of bringing the portfolio back into line will depend on the costs of asset exchanges to the investor. A variable sequence is one in which the portfolio is changed, either as deliberate policy or as its assets appreciate at different rates.

Assume that asset returns are independently distributed over time and that portfolio rebalancing is costless. Let g_t, μ_t, and σ_t be the gross portfolio return, expected gross return, and standard deviation in period t, and g, μ, and σ be the terminal T–period return, expected return, and standard deviation, respectively. Tobin (1965) set forth the following relationships.

$$g = \prod_{t=1}^{T} g_t, \tag{4.13}$$

---

[12] As noted above, the U.S. Treasury proposes to issue inflation-indexed securities, as the United Kingdom and other countries already do.

$$\mu = E\left[\prod_{t=1}^{T} g_t\right] = \prod_{t=1}^{T} \mu_t \qquad \text{where } \mu_t = E(g_t). \qquad (4.14)$$

Plugging in the relationship $\sigma_t^2 = E(g_t)^2 - \mu_t^2$ into (4.14) gives

$$\sigma^2 = E(g)^2 - (E(g))^2 = E\left[\prod_{t=1}^{T} g_t^2\right] - \mu^2. \qquad (4.15)$$

$$\sigma^2 = \prod_{t=1}^{T}(\sigma_t^2 + \mu_t^2) - \mu^2. \qquad (4.16)$$

If portfolio choices are stationary at $\sigma_t = \sigma_1$ and $\mu_t = \mu_1$ for all t, (4.14) and (4.16) become, respectively,

$$\mu = \mu_1^T, \qquad (4.17)$$

$$\sigma^2 = (\sigma_1^2 + \mu_1^2)^T - \mu_1^{2T}. \qquad (4.18)$$

Tobin (1965, p. 43) argued that, if probability distributions of single-period asset returns are independent over time and stationary, then the sequence of portfolio choices will be stationary. Under the stationarity and independence assumptions, "It is never an optimal plan to seek the advantages of diversification purely in time, holding different assets in succession. Better to keep a diversified portfolio at all times." He asserted that the minimum multiperiod risk for any given target return was to maintain the same portfolio the whole time.

This proposition is valid in many cases, as simple two-period examples showed. However, Stevens (1972) showed that the Tobin proposition was not always true and exhibited a counterexample. In his setup, there are two periods and the asset menu in each period is familiar: two assets, one safe and one risky. The one risky asset can be, in accordance with the separation theorem, the efficient portfolio of many risk assets. In each period the portfolio decision is what fraction to put in the risky asset. In this problem, there are two decision variables. They can be taken to be the expected gross returns in the two periods. The risk-asset fraction and the portfolio risk in the period depend linearly on the expected gross return. The constraint is that the product of the two gross rates of return must equal the target two-period gross rate of return. Which of the portfolio pairs that meet the constraint has the least two-period standard deviation of return?

Stevens shows that the first-order condition sets equal to zero a fourth-degree polynomial in one of the returns. Of the four solutions, one is meaningless, a negative number. One is the Tobin stationary solution. Two are the conjugate roots of a quadratic equation. When these roots are real, their product is the constraint, and the corresponding two different portfolios minimize the two-period risk. When the quadratic's roots are imaginary, the stationary Tobin solution is the optimum.

Unfortunately, this optimization problem, simple as it seems and confined to two periods, has still other possible solutions. There seems to be no valid generalization to replace the stationary-portfolio strategy.

4.4.3 Sequential Portfolio Decisions

In the previous section the investor had to choose the T-period sequence of portfolios irrevocably at the beginning. What if he can make his portfolio decisions period by period, knowing the outcomes of prior decisions before he chooses his next portfolio? As before, he is aiming at a particular T-period return, seeking to hit that target with minimum variance. At the beginning of the final period—the second period in the simplest case—he can make a choice such that the only source of deviation from the target will be that arising from the random element in that last period's return. How risky a final portfolio it takes to obtain the target expected value of T-period return will depend on the luck of the previous draws, but these portfolios will have been chosen with knowledge that subsequent plans can be contingent on their outcomes. As a result, any feasible expectation of T-period return can be achieved with smaller variance than with once-for-all choices. The expected portfolio sequences will, of course, be different in the two cases.

Levy and Samuelson (1991) pose the problem of optimal portfolio choice for a single future composition date T, in which the investor can make a new decision each period. There is a riskless asset in each period, so that the separation theorem equation (4.12) holds for each period considered in isolation, as in the previous section. Levy and Samuelson demonstrate that the sequence of efficient portfolio choices will satisfy (4.12) for each period whenever single-period mean-variance analysis is justified. The proof is as follows for the quadratic utility case. Suppose that the investor has made decisions for all periods except a single period i. Now let Fig. 4.13 represent the situation in period i. For any feasible portfolio off NMN' there is another portfolio on NMN' that has the same mean but lower standard deviation. The T-period variance (Eq. 4.16) will be reduced while the T-period mean will be unchanged, by selecting a portfolio on NMN' in period i that has the same mean but lower variance than a portfolio to the right of NMN'. A similar argument can be made for any other period j. Therefore, all single-period portfolios that constitute part of a T-period optimal sequence will lie on lines such as NMN', so that the separation theorem holds for each period. A similar but more elaborate proof is made for the case of normally distributed single-period returns.[13]

Now suppose that the distribution of asset returns is stationary. This implies that each period's efficiency locus is identical and each period's optimal portfolio will mix a time-invariant bundle of risky assets like point M in Fig. 4.13 with the safe asset. The proportions of the mix are not time-invariant. Essentially for the reason given above, they depend on the actual sequence of random draws.

Mossin (1968) gives another reason why the actual history during the T periods matters, namely that each period's initial wealth depends on that history. That criticism does not apply to the model of this book, which assumes constant relative risk aversion with respect to absolute wealth, though not with respect to change in wealth.

---

[13]The proof for the case of quadratic utility cannot be used directly, since T-period returns are not normally distributed, so T-period portfolio choice cannot be reduced to mean-variance analysis.

If there is no safe asset or if the efficient portfolio of risk assets is not invariant, then all that can be said is that multiperiod risk can always be reduced by moving on to the single-period frontier. The sequence of efficient points, however, may not be stationary over the investment horizon.

4.4.4 Multiperiod Consumption and Portfolio Choice

Investors are not, of course, generally characterized by single target dates for wealth accumulation, nor do they know how their income and consumption requirements will evolve over time. It is a convenient fiction to imagine the investor to divide his total wealth into as many portfolios as he has target dates, their relative sizes depending upon expected consumption requirements in relation to other income at the various dates. Some assets are designed to minimize risk not for single target dates but for certain patterns of accumulation objectives. Thus investment in consols provides without risk a constant perpetual income for an investor who weights equally consumption, whether by himself or his remote heirs, at all future dates. A life annuity accomplishes the same objective for an individual whose horizon is limited to his own lifetime.[14]

The general features of the problem can be modeled using a dynamic programming approach, as follows.[15] Suppose there is one safe and one risky asset. As in Section 4.1.3, W is wealth, g and s are gross rates of return on the safe and risky assets, respectively, and x is the share of wealth held in the risky asset. A subscript t indexes time. Let income other than that from asset returns be Y_t and consumption be C_t.

The investor seeks to maximize expected utility over time between $t = 0$ and $t = T$:

$$\max E\left(\sum_{t=0}^{T} U(C_t, t)\right),$$ (4.19)

subject to the requirement that consumption is given by income less saving:

$$C_t = Y_t + W_{t-1}[s + x(g - s)] - W_t.$$ (4.20)

The dynamic programming approach separates the objective function into two components—the utility from current consumption and the expected utility J of future consumption, which depends on wealth, recognizing the tradeoff between current consumption and wealth accumulation embodied in Eq. 4.20:

$$\max\{U(C_t, t) + E_t[J(W_t, t)]\}.$$ (4.21)

---

[14]Joan Robinson (1964) has characterized individuals who seek a minimum-risk constant stream as desiring "income certainty," in contrast to investors who, seeking assets of predictable value at all future dates, desire "capital certainty."

[15]The dynamic programming approach was pioneered by Mossin (1968), Samuelson (1969), and Merton (1969). See Breeden (1989) and Ingersoll (1987, Chapter 11) for surveys.

The first-order condition for maximizing consumption is to set the marginal utility of wealth equal to the marginal utility of consumption:

$$\frac{\partial U}{\partial C} = \frac{\partial J}{\partial W}. \tag{4.22}$$

Equation 4.22 can be regarded as determining the saving-consumption decision, which determines investible wealth. If so, the portfolio decision can then be solved in the same way as in the previous section.

In general, however, as noted earlier, the two decisions are interrelated. The marginal utility of wealth may depend on the size of wealth, which in turn depends on the portfolio decisions. Dynamic programming solves for the investor's consumption and portfolio choice in the terminal period T and then works backward in time. This book is focused primarily on portfolio choice. As explained in Chapter 10, Section 10.2, separation of overall wealth accumulation from the allocation of wealth among assets, though somewhat unrealistic, is a convenient simplification. It permits a deeper and broader treatment of portfolios and balance sheets, with attention to their institutional settings.

APPENDIX 4A: MEASURES OF RISK AVERSION

Risk-averse behavior. With risk-averse behavior ($U'' < 0$ as in schedule II of Fig. 4.1) there may be an interior solution for x at $0 \le x \le 1$, although this is not guaranteed—short sales of an asset may be optimal even for a risk-averse investor.

The first-order condition for an interior solution is found by differentiating Eq. 4.2 with respect to x and setting to zero:

$$\frac{\partial^2 EU(W)}{\partial x^2} = \int_0^\infty U'(W)(g - s)W_0 \, dF(g) = 0. \tag{4A.1}$$

This is a maximum if the second order condition $\partial^2 EU/\partial x^2 < 0$ is met:

$$\frac{\partial^2 EU(W)}{\partial x^2} = \int_0^\infty U''(W)(g - s)^2 W_0^2 \, dF(g) < 0. \tag{4A.2}$$

A sufficient condition for (4A.1) to define a maximum is that $U''(W) < 0$ for all W, that is, risk aversion. A necessary condition is that $U''(W) < 0$ for some W.

Consider now how the share of the portfolio held in the risky asset varies with initial wealth. The question is the sign and size of the derivative $\partial x/\partial W_0$. Equation 4A.1 can be interpreted as making x implicitly a function of W_0, given s. Let this implicit function be $H(W_0, x; s) = 0$, where H is $\partial EU(W)/\partial x$ as evaluated in Eq. 4A.1. Differentiating $H = 0$ with respect to W_0 gives:

$$\frac{dH}{dW_0} = \frac{\partial H}{\partial W_0} + \frac{\partial H}{\partial x}\left(\frac{\partial x}{\partial W_0}\right) = 0. \tag{4A.3}$$

$\partial H/\partial x$ has already been found in Eq. 4A.2. It is $\partial^2 EU(W)/dx^2$.

$$\frac{\partial H}{\partial W_0} = \frac{H}{W_0} + \int_0^\infty U''\{W_0[s + x(g - s)]\}[s + x(g - s)](g - s)W_0 \, dF(g), \quad (4A.4)$$

of which the first term is zero.

Consequently,

$$-\frac{\partial x}{\partial W_0}\left[\frac{\partial^2 EU(W)}{\partial x^2}\right] = \frac{\partial H}{\partial W_0} = \int_0^\infty U''(W)W(g - s) \, dF(g), \quad (4A.5)$$

which may be positive or negative or zero.

Relative risk aversion is defined as $\psi(W) = -[U''(W)W]/[U'(W)] > 0$. Thus Eq. 4A.5 can be written as

$$-\frac{\partial x}{\partial W_0}\left[\frac{\partial^2 EU(W)}{\partial x^2}\right] = -\int_0^\infty \psi(W)U'(W)(g - s) \, dF(g). \quad (4A.6)$$

Now if $\psi(W)$ is constant at ψ, the right-hand side of Eq. 4A.6 is $\psi H = 0$, by the first-order condition Eq. 4A.1. Thus constant relative risk aversion implies that $\partial x/\partial W_0 = 0$, that is, the share of risky assets in the portfolio is independent of the level of initial wealth.

If $\psi(W)$ is monotonically declining in W, the right-hand side of Eq. 4A.6 is positive because the integral is negative and because low values of g, hence negative values of $g - s$, are associated with low wealth and thus high $\psi(W)$. That is, the negative values for $g - s$ are more heavily weighted in the integral than the positive outcomes. Similarly, if $\psi'(W) > 0$, the right-hand side is negative.

Summarizing,

$$\psi'(W) \text{ negative implies } \partial x/\partial W_0 > 0,$$

$$\psi'(W) \text{ positive implies } \partial x/\partial W_0 < 0, \quad (4A.7)$$

$$\psi'(W) \text{ zero implies } \partial x/\partial W_0 = 0.$$

It can also be observed that constant relative risk aversion restricts the form of the utility function: $U''(W)/U'(W) = -(\psi/W)$, which implies the following:

$$d \log U'(W) = -\psi d \log W$$

or $\log U'(W) = -\psi \log W + \log C$, where C is an arbitrary constant

$$U'(W) = CW^{-\psi}$$

$$U(W) = \frac{C}{1 - \psi} W^{1-\psi} + B.$$

If $U(0) = 0$ then $B = 0$.

Absolute risk aversion is defined as $\phi(W) = -[U''(W)]/[U'(W)] > 0$. This is not a pure number like relative risk aversion. Its dimension is (change in marginal utility) per (unit of marginal utility). Using the definition of $\phi(W)$, Eq. 4A.5 can be rewritten as

$$-\frac{\partial x}{\partial W_0}\left[\frac{\partial^2 EU(W)}{\partial x^2}\right] = -\int_0^\infty \phi(W)U'(W)W(g-s)\,dF(g)$$

$$= -\int_0^\infty \phi(W)U'(W)W_0[s + x(g-s)](g-s)\,dF(g) \qquad (4A.8)$$

$$= -sW_0\int_0^\infty \phi(W)U'(W)(g-s)\,dF(g)$$

$$- \frac{x}{W_0}\int_0^\infty \phi(W)U'(W)(g-s)^2 W_0^2\,dF(g).$$

Since $\phi(W)U'(W) = -U''(W)$, the last integral in the expression is simply $-[\partial^2 EU(W)/\partial x^2]$. As a result,

$$-\left[\frac{\partial^2 EU(W)}{\partial x^2}\right]\cdot\left[\frac{\partial x}{\partial W_0} + \frac{x}{W_0}\right] = \left[\frac{\partial^2 EU(W)}{\partial x^2}\right]\left(\frac{\partial(xW_0)}{\partial W_0}\right) \qquad (4A.9)$$

$$= -sW_0\int_0^\infty \phi(W)U'(W)(g-s)\,dF(g).$$

If $\phi(W)$ is constant at ϕ, then Eq. 4A.9 is zero by Eq. 4A.4 again, and $\partial(xW_0)/\partial W_0$ is zero. That is, the absolute size of the holding of the risky asset is constant, and all incremental initial wealth is invested in the safe asset. Similarly, diminishing absolute risk aversion implies that some fraction of marginal wealth is invested in the risky asset, whereas increasing absolute risk aversion implies that the amount invested in the risky asset actually decreases as wealth increases.

Constant absolute risk aversion restricts utility to a negative exponential function, as follows. $U'' = -\phi U'$ implies $U' = Be^{\phi W}$, which implies $U = C - (B/\phi)e^{-\phi W}$.

CHAPTER 5

Portfolio Balance: Currency, Capital, and Loans

The aggregate net private wealth of a closed national economy can be divided, according to the analysis of Chapter 1, into two basic components: privately owned real capital and net indebtedness of government. At any moment, the supplies of these two kinds of assets are given by the past. Certain stocks of capital goods are in existence, and along with them, certain forms and amounts of government debt. These supplies must find welcome homes in the portfolios of the ultimate private owners of wealth, either directly or through the intermediation of financial markets and institutions. For if wealth owners are not content with the existing mixtures of assets in their portfolios, they are free to sell some and to buy others. They may wish to sell real capital and in exchange acquire more government debt, or they may wish to do the reverse. A situation of equilibrium or *portfolio balance* obtains when, at the prevailing prices of assets, owners of wealth are content to hold the existing supplies. In particular, equilibrium means that the terms on which real-capital assets can be exchanged for government-debt assets are such that owners of wealth are content with their relative holdings of capital and government debt. Any portfolio balance is necessarily a temporary equilibrium in a dynamic economy, in which saving is continuously adding to the wealth that must be allocated among various assets.

In this chapter the nature and consequences of portfolio balance will be given precision first in a simple and imaginary situation, a two-asset economy. Real capital will be assumed to be homogeneous; likewise, all government debt will be supposed to take a single form, that of currency. Moreover, it will be assumed that there are no intermediate financial institutions or markets. These simplifying assumptions will be gradually removed in this and subsequent chapters by the introduction of a market for private loans, of banks and other financial intermediaries, and of various forms of public and private debt.

5.1
PORTFOLIO BALANCE IN A TWO-ASSET ECONOMY

In the most primitive situation, the entire government debt is in the form of currency, bearing no interest. Currency is the sole means of payment of the community. One source of demand for currency is the holding of transactions balances; as shown in Chapter 3, the demand for balances of means of payment depends directly on the volume of transactions and inversely on the sacrifice of return involved in holding cash. In addition, there will be an investment or portfolio demand for currency holdings. In the two-asset world, there are no near moneys to dominate cash as a portfolio asset. The rate of return on currency is the change in its purchasing power over consumer goods. The investor's estimates of the expectation and risk of the asset depend on his view of the probabilities of rises and falls of various amounts in consumer-goods prices.

The total supply of currency to the economy is equal to the government debt, and the supply changes only as the debt increases or decreases with government deficits or surpluses. The reckoning of government debt and of government expenditures and receipts must follow the accounting principles of Chapter 1 rather than those of conventional government budgeting. Thus purchases of commodities like gold and silver for direct or indirect coinage count as expenditures that increase the national debt, just like any other government purchases of goods and services in excess of tax receipts. In the two-asset economy, all deficits, not just those incurred to purchase precious metals, are financed simply by issuing currency.

The second asset is a homogeneous capital good. The assumption of homogeneity means that all capital goods are the same wherever and whenever produced and used. They depreciate continuously at the same percentage rate no matter how old they are. Aging destroys the effective productive capacity of all capital goods in existence at the beginning of the year at a (continuously compounded) rate of 100δ percent per year. This assumption implies that capital goods never wear out completely. After t years from its origin a unit of capital has physically declined to an amount $e^{-\delta t}$ of capital. This remaining amount has the same usefulness in production as an equivalent amount of new capital, or of capital produced at any other time. The rate of depreciation depends only on time; it is independent of intensity of use. This exponential evaporation assumption makes it possible to regard capital as a durable asset suitable as a store of value for savers, without entering at this stage into the complexities involved in recognizing that there are as many varieties even of a single durable good as there are vintages.

The rent of capital for a period of time is the price that must be paid for the use of a physical unit of capital during the period. In a well-developed rental market, contracts would be available in any desired length; at any moment one would be able to rent capital for twenty years ahead or merely for the next day. Here, in order not to complicate the simple institutions of the two-asset world by speculation and arbitrage in rental contracts, it is assumed that the market deals only in short-term and nonnegotiable rentals. Short-term in this context means short relative to the investment period of wealth owners, the length of time during which asset exchange costs make it unprofitable to shift portfolios. In effect, the user of capital cannot for any significant time enjoy its use at a rent lower than the market rate for new short-term rentals. Nor can the owner for any significant period profit from a contractual rent higher than the current market rent. Indeed many or most owners "rent" their capital to themselves.

Capital is used, with labor, in the production of both consumer goods and capital goods. The marginal physical product of capital in the making of capital goods is the amount by which the output of capital goods, per unit of time, could be increased by the use of an additional unit of capital, holding constant the input of labor. In the consumer-goods industry, the corresponding marginal physical product is the addition to the rate of output due to the use of an additional unit of capital. Assuming that capital is costlessly mobile between these two uses, the value of its marginal product will be the same in both uses.

In a competitive economy the rent on capital per year will be equal to the value of the annual marginal product of a dollar's worth of capital. Rent, in this usage, is a proportion, a pure number, like an interest rate. It is equally the money return per dollar investment in capital, the quantity of additional capital goods yielded by ownership of a unit of capital goods, and the quantity of additional consumer goods yielded from investment in capital of an amount equivalent to one unit of consumer goods. Thus the rent of capital is equal to the marginal product of capital in making capital goods and to the marginal product in making consumer goods times the ratio of the price of consumer goods to the price of capital goods. To the owner of capital, the net rate of return is the rent he earns less the real rate of depreciation δ per year, plus the expected rate of increase per year in the value of capital goods relative to consumer goods. For after receiving this return, which may be either positive or negative, he still owns capital of the same value in terms of consumer goods.

Besides the rental market, which prices flows of goods and services, there is a financial market, which prices stocks of assets, where the exchange of currency against capital permits wealth owners to adjust their portfolios at will and establishes continuously the money value of capital. When wealth owners have relatively too much currency and are trying to exchange it for capital, the value of capital will tend to rise; when they are relatively oversaturated with capital, its value will tend to fall. So long as new capital goods are being produced, the value of capital as determined in the market for capital goods must in equilibrium be the same as the supply price of capital goods producers. Old and new capital goods are interchangeable in use. If old capital goods are valued more than the marginal cost of producing new capital goods, new production will be stimulated by the profit opportunity. When new capital goods are not being produced, the commodity-market value of capital goods can, indeed must, be below the supply price of capital goods producers. Financial markets value titles to capital goods and to their yields. In principle those valuations in equilibrium should correspond to commodity-market prices, but this arbitrage works slowly and imperfectly.

The ownership of capital in this simplified economy entails two risks. First, the rent of capital is uncertain, because it is not a contractual obligation but is determined and renegotiated almost continuously in the market. Within a period when an investor is effectively committed to a certain amount of capital equity because of the difficulty or cost of portfolio shifts, the rent on capital can change. Second, the real value of capital—the quantity of consumer goods equivalent in value to a unit of capital—is subject to the uncertainties of the asset markets. As the volume of production of capital goods varies in relation to the output of consumer goods, the relative prices of the two kinds of output will change. Should capital become so plentiful that its current production ceases altogether, its real value will fall drastically.

The "normal" investors of this chapter estimate the expectation of return on capital to be larger than on currency, the returns on the two assets to have some degree of statistical independence, and the risk of the return on capital to be greater than on currency. An investor who thinks that on balance absolute prices, relative prices, and capital rents will remain unchanged will estimate the expectation of return on capital to be its current rent less depreciation, and the expectation of return on currency to be zero. But it is quite conceivable that some investors, or in some circumstances all investors, have price and rent forecasts that imply a greater expectation of return on currency than on capital. Similarly it is entirely possible that investors may regard the absolute price level of consumer goods as more chancy than the relative price of capital goods. Chapter 4 describes the capital-currency portfolio adjustments of investors, both risk averters and risk lovers, with a variety of attitudes about the future prospects of the two assets.

How do the relative supplies of the two assets required for portfolio balance depend on the rent of capital? How does a change in the rent on capital, other things held equal, affect the proportions in which investors desire to split their wealth between capital and currency? The other things held equal include investors' beliefs about the future of prices and the variability of rents, and the volume and costs of transactions as well as the institutional arrangements for handling them. The imagined change in the rent on capital is a change in its expectation of return, relative to the risks on both assets and to the expectation of return on currency. The aggregate reaction to, say, an increase in the return on capital is a compound of several responses. First, there is reduction in the transactions demand for currency; the higher the return on capital, the more worthwhile it is to assume the trouble and cost of asset exchanges designed to keep more of the average transactions balance in the higher-yielding asset (Chapter 3). Second, risk averters at intermediate points (Chapter 4, Section 4.2.2.3) will increase the share of capital in their portfolios if the substitution effect dominates but diminish it if the income effect prevails. The general assumption here is that the substitution effect is the stronger. Third, the portfolios of investors already 100 percent in capital will not be changed. A risk seeker who is holding 100 percent currency either because he estimates currency to have the higher expectation but lower risk or because he regards it as having the lower expectation but greater risk might be shifted to a 100 percent capital portfolio by an increase in the return on capital. (See Figs. 4.10a–e in Section 4.2.2.3, Chapter 4.) A risk averter holding 100 percent currency, regarding currency as the asset of higher expectation, might shift partly into capital as a result of an increase in its return (Figs. 4.10 and 4.11).

Figure 5.1 shows the relative demands for currency and capital as a function of the return on capital. On the horizontal axis the proportion of aggregate private wealth in currency is measured from left to right, and the proportion in capital from right to left. The vertical axis is the return on capital. The curve then shows, for any level of the return on capital, how owners of wealth desire to apportion their holdings.

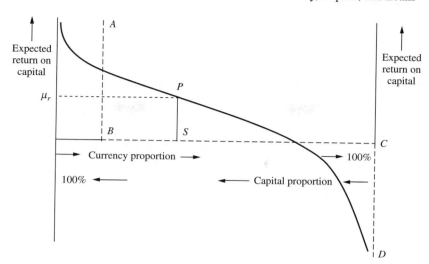

FIGURE 5.1
Portfolio balance with two assets.

The position of the curve, of course, depends on the other things held equal in the preceding paragraph; as those things or other data change, the curve will shift. For example, an increase in the level of money income (wealth held constant), bringing with it greater need for transactions balances, would shift the curve to the right.

The curve of Fig. 5.1 stands in contrast to the broken line *ABCD,* the picture of the relative demands for money and capital implicit or explicit in the traditional quantity theory of money and frequently in its modern incarnation, monetarism. According to that picture, the transactions demand for currency depends only on the volume of transactions and not at all on the earnings lost by holding currency rather than an alternative asset. Supposing that the expectation of real capital gain is zero on both assets, the traditional theory would allow no room for currency in investment portfolios as long as the return on capital exceeds zero and no room for capital if its return is negative. At zero returns the composition of the portfolio would be indeterminate.

5.2
CAPITAL MARKET EQUILIBRIUM WITH TWO ASSETS

The relationship illustrated in Fig. 5.1 is a demand curve; it describes the quantities of currency and capital that wealth owners would demand, given their wealth, the expected return on capital, and other relevant data. In market equilibrium the stocks demanded must be equal to the supply of currency and the money value of the supply of capital, respectively. Thus a point on the curve, such as P, is in equilibrium only if the relative supplies of currency and capital are those indicated by S and the real return on capital is μ_r.

The supply of currency at any time is inherited from the past. It is simply the cumulative net total of government deficits less surpluses—outlays financed by printing money instead of by taxes. The real value of this inherited supply, however, depends on the current level of consumer-goods prices, and its anticipated real return depends on the expected change in the price level. The supply of capital, in physical terms, is also inherited from the past, reflecting the history of real investment, depreciation, and obsolescence. Given the price of capital goods relative to consumer goods, the supply of capital is, as noted earlier, also determined in real value. The current return on capital is its marginal productivity net of depreciation plus expected increase in the relative price of capital goods. There is no guarantee that these supplies, prices, and rates of return will always add up to a situation of portfolio balance like point P in Fig. 5.1. What if they do not? What can adjust to restore equilibrium?

There are several possibilities. First, the price level can adjust the relative supplies of currency and capital. Suppose that at the prevailing real rates of return on the two assets, the supply of currency is too large relative to that of capital. People want to hold the assets in the proportions indicated by S, but the actual proportion of currency is larger. A general rise in commodity prices will diminish the real quantity of currency while leaving the stock of capital unchanged in real amount. Total private wealth in real terms will be diminished, and, what is significant for the present purpose, the share of currency will be diminished too. Similarly, if the currency proportion is smaller than demanded, a fall in the price level can bring it into line. Since numerous events might upset portfolio balance, the price fluctuations necessary to maintain equilibrium might be considerable. These fluctuations would be passed on to the markets for new production and for employment, and if they were capable of absorbing them there would be no problem. But given the inevitable stickiness of prices and money wages, the general price level may not be flexible enough fast enough to maintain portfolio balance without causing severe fluctuations in output and employment (Tobin, 1955).

The second possible equilibrator, at least in the short run, is the ratio between the market valuation of the capital stock and the reproduction cost of the same stock. This ratio is commonly known as q following Brainard and Tobin (1968). See Chapter 6, Section 6.1.3 for detailed discussion. Conceptually the normal value of q is 1, but it is quite volatile and can deviate from 1 in either direction for extended periods.

Here old capital, adjusted for depreciation, and new are perfect substitutes in production. Therefore they should, as argued above, generally command the same price, at least in equilibrium. However, the arbitrage necessary to maintain this parity does not operate instantaneously. A boom in the stock market increases the valuation of the plants and machines to which the owners of common shares hold title. The prices of new plants and machines do not rise as fast or as much. They will rise only as new orders are placed, production is raised, and marginal costs are increased. Meanwhile the discrepancy of market value from reproduction cost, of q from 1, of the valuation of existing capital from the price of new capital goods, works in two ways to restore portfolio balance equilibrium temporarily.

First, if the supply of currency is too large and that of capital too small, increasing the market valuation of capital tends to correct the proportion by raising the share of capital in private wealth. Second, an increase in the market valuation of existing capital means a reduction in its market return. Wealth owners will therefore be satisfied to hold a smaller share of their wealth as capital. The marginal productivity of capital is a technological fact and is not altered by events in the stock market or other markets for used capital. It is the value of the yield of a unit of capital. But if the market price that must be paid to obtain the yield of a unit of capital exceeds its replacement cost, the return on the market price is smaller than the marginal productivity. Suppose that 100 units of capital, valued at reproduction cost, yield in productive use a return of 10 per year. If the corresponding shares command 200 in the stock market, their market return is 5 percent instead of 10 percent. All this can occur within the financial and capital markets themselves, without any repercussions on commodity prices, production, and employment.

A third way that equilibrium can be restored is that arbitrage opportunities stimulate—or in the opposite case deter—the production of new capital goods. Discrepancy of market valuation from reproduction cost, with the corresponding discrepancy in the opposite direction of market return from marginal productivity, cannot be a permanent equilibrator of asset demands and supplies. The arbitrage opportunity—for example, buy a machine for 100 and collect 200 by selling shares in it—will presumably induce actions that tend somehow to eliminate the discrepancy.

This third equilibrator mechanism is slower and more fundamental. Any sustained and abnormal excess of the market value of capital goods over their costs of reproduction is an incentive to production of new capital goods. Or, to put the same point another way, capital formation is stimulated when the market return from owning capital goods is smaller than their marginal productivity. An increase in the physical stock of capital may gradually take the place of the previous inflated valuation of the smaller existing stock. Moreover, relative abundance of capital will drive its actual marginal productivity down toward its market return. In this way a portfolio balance that initially required a large discrepancy of market value over reproduction cost can be maintained while the discrepancy is being eliminated. In a sense the stock market acts out in advance and in purely financial terms the subsequent and much slower adjustment of the physical stock of capital and its basic return.

A fourth possibility of adjustment is change in the expected real return on currency. If the supply of currency is excessive, one way to make wealth owners content is to increase the expected return on currency, to make them expect price deflation or slower inflation. Note, however, that the natural reaction to an excess supply of currency is to *raise* prices, as people try to buy capital. As already observed, the higher level of prices works in an equilibrating direction. But the rising prices themselves, and expectations of future price inflation, work the other way, damping the demand for currency and increasing demand for capital.

Thus the interaction of asset demands and asset supplies can be an important determinant of the course of prices and economic activity, as will be further discussed in subsequent chapters. The purpose of the remainder of this chapter is to add a third asset, private loans, to the primitive financial system so far considered.

5.3
THE LOAN MARKET

Suppose that private borrowing and lending are possible. What are the consequences for portfolio balance? The aggregate net worth of private individuals will still be the sum of net government debt and private capital. In the absence of borrowing and lending, the proportions of these two components required for portfolio balance at each expected yield on capital were depicted in Fig 5.1. The introduction of borrowing and lending shifts the curve to the left. That is, at a given expected rate of return on capital, portfolio balance requires a smaller proportion of aggregate net worth to be in government debt and a larger proportion to be represented by equity in physical capital. To put the same conclusion in a different way, a given combination of net government debt and physical capital will, once private borrowing and lending are introduced, be a portfolio balance combination at a lower expected capital return than before.

Private obligations to pay money are often called inside assets and debts, in contrast to the outside debts of government to private creditors. The analysis considers first situations in which outside and inside assets and debts coexist in private wealth owners' portfolios. A pure inside-money regime will follow—one in which private interest-bearing debts entirely supplant currency and take over its functions. Inside-money economies function quite differently from outside-money regimes.

It takes two kinds of people, at least, to make a market. In the two-asset regime of Chapter 4, there were two possible kinds of individual adjustments: intermediate points and extreme points (see Chapter 4, Section 4.2.2.3). It is the investors at extreme points, those who hold 100 percent capital, who are potential borrowers in a loan market. Consider, for example, the investors pictured in Figs. 4.10a and 4.10b, assuming that capital is both the riskier and the more remunerative of the two assets. In both cases the investor would seek more risk and return if it were possible for him to do so, that is, if the opportunity locus were extended to the right. In both cases, the individual was frustrated from holding more capital by the constraint that his capital holding could not exceed his net worth. The opportunity to borrow relaxes that constraint. It now becomes possible to hold more than one's net worth in physical goods. Naturally these potential borrowers will pay something for the opportunity to add to their expected return and risk. Indeed, the risk seekers among them will pay for the privilege of taking more risk even at a borrowing cost that reduces their expected return.

The other side of the market, the potential lenders, are investors who in a two-asset regime would choose to hold both currency and capital. They are exemplified by Fig. 4.11. These diversifiers can be induced to put a third asset, loans, into their portfolio if the terms are attractive. They will be willing to substitute loans for part of their currency holdings, even though they are somewhat riskier, because loans have a higher yield. They will substitute loans for part of their capital holdings, even though loans may bear a lower expected return, because loans are less risky.

With given aggregate stocks of currency and capital, the broad results of the introduction of a loan market will be as follows: Borrowers will, with the help of loans, hold more of the capital stock. Diversifiers will hold less, substituting loans for the capital they transfer to borrowers. They will still hold the stock of currency. The loan market will establish an interest rate and other terms on loans that induce these portfolio shifts. But these terms and the new rate of return on capital cannot in combination be so attractive as to make the diversifier-lenders unwilling to continue to hold the stock of currency. The rate of return necessary to lodge the capital stock will be lower because the loan market shifts the capital to more eager holders.

5.4
ANALYSIS OF THE LOAN MARKET: FIRST APPROXIMATION

To analyze these effects of a loan market with more precision, it is necessary to make some simplifying assumptions. In actual fact loans differ widely in many respects—maturity, interest rate, collateral, denomination, credit rating of borrower, and so on. For present purposes most of these differences are not essential. The loans contracted in the market can be imagined to be bills denominated in currency, with both principal and interest payable in currency at the end of one period—the common period of portfolio planning and decision. They can be assumed to be divisible, that is, available in any denomination.

Two essential features of a loan are determined in the market. One, of course, is the interest rate. The other is the collateral or margin requirement. The risk of partial or complete default by a borrower depends on the amount of his debt relative to his net worth. Consequently, the attractiveness of a loan, both to lender and to borrower, depends on this ratio. Let γ be the amount that can be borrowed on the basis of a dollar of net worth. Then for every dollar of capital a borrower holds, he is allowed to borrow $\gamma/(1 + \gamma)$. His margin requirement is $1/(1 + \gamma)$. For example, if γ is 2, a borrower can hold physical capital in value up to three times his net worth. His equity, or the margin in his holdings, is one-third.

Two analyses of the behavior of borrowers and lenders in the loan market will be presented. The first approximation is a simple extension of the model of portfolio choice previously set forth. This tells much of the story, but it does not take proper account of default risk and therefore does not explain how margin requirements are determined in the market. The second analysis will try to repair these defects.

5.4.1 Borrowers

Consider a potential borrower whom the loan market enables to go into debt at a given interest rate r_L up to a proportion γ of his net worth. In Fig. 5.2 the risk-return opportunity locus available to him in the original two-asset world is shown as OK. Here currency is assumed to be riskless and to bear zero yield. Point K represents the 100 percent-capital, no-currency portfolio, whose expected return and risk are simply the expected return μ_r and risk σ_r on capital itself.

The opportunity to borrow extends the opportunity locus beyond K. Here the debt is regarded as having the same risk as the currency in which it is denominated. Where, as in Fig. 5.2, the borrower sees no possibility that currency will change in real value, he likewise sees no possibility that the real burden of debt will become lighter or heavier through a change in prices. Moreover, he views the debt, including interest, as an inescapable obligation. As a result, the opportunity to borrow γ per dollar of net worth simply increases the maximum available risk from σ_r to $(1+\gamma)\sigma_r$. In Fig. 5.2, γ is taken to be 1, that is, the margin requirement is one-half; hence the opportunity to borrow doubles the maximum risk available. The maximum risk portfolio consists of no currency, 200 percent of net worth in capital, 100 percent of net worth in debt.

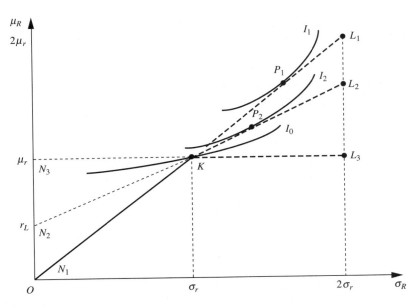

FIGURE 5.2
Equilibrium for a risk-averse borrower.

The slope of the extension of the opportunity locus depends on the net interest rate on loans r_L. If this rate were zero, debt would simply be negative currency, and the opportunity locus would be extended with the same slope, to point L_1. By borrowing an amount equal to his net worth, an individual can expect to earn on his net worth twice the return he could expect when constrained to point K in the two-asset world. If, for example, capital investments are expected to yield on the average 8 percent, the investor can earn 8 percent on his own equity and another 8 percent by the investment of borrowed funds, so that the expected return on his net worth is 16 percent. But if the loan rate were the r_L indicated on the vertical axis, greater than zero but less than the expected return on capital μ_r, the extension would be a line from K to L_2. To continue the previous numerical example, if r_L were 5 percent, the maximum portfolio return would be 11 percent. An intermediate point on this locus can be illustrated by imagining that the borrower's debt is only half of what is permitted. Then his expected earnings on capital are 12 percent of his net worth ($1\frac{1}{2}$ times 8 percent), and his interest charges are $2\frac{1}{2}$ percent of his net worth ($\frac{1}{2}$ times 5 percent), so that his expected portfolio return is $9\frac{1}{2}$ percent. The slope of this extension is the same as the slope of the line N_2K, which would describe opportunities to mix lending, rather than borrowing, with the holding of capital. If the loan interest rate were equal to μ_r, then this line would be horizontal and the new opportunity locus would be OKL_3. If the loan rate exceeded μ_r, then the extension would be downward sloping.

As previously noted, potential borrowers may be risk averse, risk neutral, or risk seeking. Figure 5.2 pictures the change in adjustment of a risk averter. In the two-asset world with no borrowing opportunity, I_0 was the highest attainable indifference curve, and it was reached at point K. If interest-free borrowing were possible, the investor would move along OKL_1 to point P_1 on his indifference curve I_1. An interest charge such that the opportunity locus became OKL_2 would induce him to borrow enough to reach P_2 on indifference curve I_2. (P_2 is to the right of K because K was a corner solution. P_1 is to the right of P_2 as a consequence of the assumption that substitution effects of changes in expected yield are more important than income effects.) Were the interest rate on loans to equal or exceed the expected return on capital μ_r, the risk averter would see no advantage in borrowing and would stay at point K.

A risk-neutral or risk-seeking investor, however—with horizontal or downward-sloping indifference curves—would move to maximum risk points, like L_1 and L_2, whenever the interest charged on loans was smaller than the expected return on capital μ_r. Indeed, a risk seeker may well do so even at higher interest rates on loans, paying in certain interest charges for additional chances to get higher than average returns on capital. He likes a high debt-equity ratio, high leverage in the suggestive jargon of the financial markets.

Interest charges are an effective device for limiting the borrowing of risk averters but not for restricting the borrowing of risk-neutral and especially risk-seeking investors. Risk seekers' borrowing is normally limited only by the limit on their lines of credit, the margin requirement. The possibility of default may be of little concern to the potential defaulter, but it is of course of considerable moment to the conservative, risk-averse types who constitute the lending side of the market. That is why a more satisfactory theory must consider risks of default explicitly and relate them to the margin requirement.

In Fig. 5.2 the yield on currency is taken as certain and zero, and loans are also taken to be riskless. Figure 5.3 concerns a situation in which the future purchasing power of currency, and therefore of loans denominated in currency, is uncertain. For illustration, moreover, currency is assigned a positive expected real yield. The government might somehow pay nominal interest—exchange your dollar bills in January and get a free postage stamp? More likely, people expect on balance a decline in prices; expectations of change in the purchasing power of a dollar are positive. Let the expected real return on currency be r_c and its risk be σ_c. The yield of loans, or their cost to a borrower, is in purchasing-power terms the sum of the nominal interest rate on loans r_L and the change in the purchasing power of currency r_c (an approximation ignoring the second-order term $r_L r_c$). Therefore, the expected return on loans is $r_c + r_L$, and its risk is σ_c, the same as the risk on currency. For example, in the diagram point N_2 represents loans, just as M corresponds to currency and K to capital. Here, as throughout this first approximation, the additional risk due to default is ignored. Figure 5.3, like the preceding diagram, is based on a credit line $\gamma = 1$.

As before, the maximum-risk portfolio is one with 200 percent of net worth in capital, 100 percent in debt. But now the risk associated with such a portfolio is not 200 percent of σ_r, the risk of a no-debt 100 percent capital portfolio. The new extreme portfolio involves not only additional risk due to the holding of additional capital but also additional risk due to the possibility of change in the purchasing power of a loan. If the price level falls, the debtor will lose; he will have to repay the loan in more valuable dollars than those he borrowed. If the price level rises, he will gain by being able to repay the loan in cheaper dollars. Assuming that the risks of

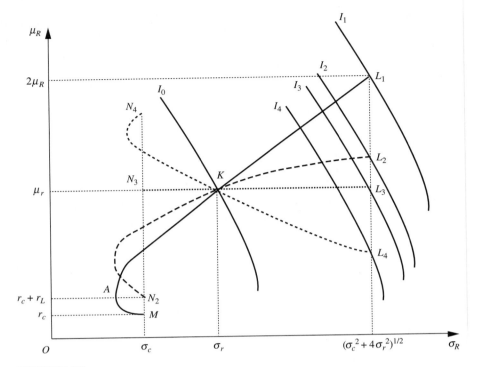

FIGURE 5.3
Risk-seeking borrower; Nonzero risk on currency.

capital investment and of fluctuation in the price level are independent of each other, the variance of return for the new maximum risk portfolio is $4\sigma_r^2 + \sigma_c^2$. Its standard deviation, the measure of risk, is $\sqrt{(4\sigma_r^2 + \sigma_c^2)}$, which is more than twice as big as σ_r, the risk of the 100 percent capital portfolio.

The three alternative extensions, to L_1, L_2, and L_3, correspond as in Fig. 5.2 to expected real returns on loans equal respectively to the expected return on currency, to a return between that expected for currency and capital, or to the expected return on capital. That is, they correspond to loan interest rates, in terms of currency, of respectively $0, 0 < r_L < \mu_r$, and μ_r. In the first case—zero interest on loans—the extension is simply a continuation of the hyperbola MK to the point L_1. In the other two cases there are kinks at point K. The extension to L_2 is part of a hyperbola from N_2 through K to L_2 where, as in Fig. 5.2, the segment to the left of K, N_2K, displays opportunities from combining capital and positive lending. The extension to L_3 is a horizontal line. Figure 5.3 also displays a situation, the locus ending at L_4, in which the real expected cost of borrowing exceeds the expected return on capital. In this case the real rate of return and risk of a portfolio devoted wholly to positive lending is indicated by N_4. The indifference curves pictured in Fig. 5.3 are those of a risk seeker. As mentioned in the discussion of Fig. 5.2 but not illustrated there, a risk seeker may borrow to the limit in all the cases. An investor with the preferences drawn in Fig. 5.3 would do so unless the cost of borrowing were so high that the extension of the locus falls to the left and below indifference curve I_0. Indifference curves with negative slopes but becoming flatter as risk increases could lead to only partial use of credit lines.

5.4.2 Lenders

So far the discussion has concerned the borrowers' side of the market, the demand for loans. On the other side of the market are the potential lenders, owners of wealth who in a two-asset world would hold both currency and capital. Now they also have the opportunity to hold loans. The model has been rigged, however, so that they have no reason to hold both currency and loans. So far as risk of purchasing-power variation is concerned the two are perfect substitutes, and this is the only risk on loans yet considered. Default risk has not yet been analyzed, and the assumptions that loans are one-period bills rather than multiperiod debts relieves them of the risks of capital gains or losses from interest-rate variation. Furthermore, transactions costs, which would give currency the advantages explained in Chapter 3, Section 3.2, are absent from consideration here. In these circumstances one of the two assets, currency or loans, will completely dominate the other, or else investors will be indifferent between them. If their expected returns are the same, if the money rate of interest to lenders is the same as on currency, then investors will be indifferent between them; the allocation of the noncapital portion of their portfolios between currency and loans will be indeterminate. If loans bear a higher yield than currency then there will be no demand to hold currency at all. Even though both these cases are unrealistic, it will be illuminating to consider the marketwide implications of both of them.

Their realism—especially the plausibility of the first case, in which lenders are indifferent between currency and loans—can be somewhat retrieved by one simple amendment. As drawn, Figs. 5.2 and 5.3 assume that the effective interest rate for borrowers is the same as for lenders. The opportunities for lenders to mix loans and capital (to the left of point K) fall along the same line or curve as the opportunities for debtors to extend their holdings of capital by incurring debt (to the right of point K). See, for example, curves N_2KL_2 in both diagrams.

However, it is easy to imagine costs of lending and borrowing that have the effect of making the lender's return lower than the borrower's cost. Such costs are one of the reasons for the existence of financial middlemen or intermediaries. They provide economies of specialization and scale. In the process they also frequently differentiate the form of the ultimate borrower's debt from that of the ultimate lender's asset. Through the intermediations of commercial banks, for example, the lender's asset becomes a deposit, which is much more the equivalent of currency than are the promissory notes of the bank's loan customers. The fact that the depositor receives less interest than the borrower pays reflects in part the service and risk taking the bank provides in effecting this transformation of the nature of the asset.

A difference in borrowing and lending interest rates will give a line or curve like N_2KL_2 a kink at point K, so that its slope at K is greater going to the left than to the right. Thus, if the lender's rate is zero, so that loans have no advantage over currency, the borrower's rate is positive by an amount that covers the costs of bringing borrower and lender together. This situation is depicted in Fig. 5.4 (which like

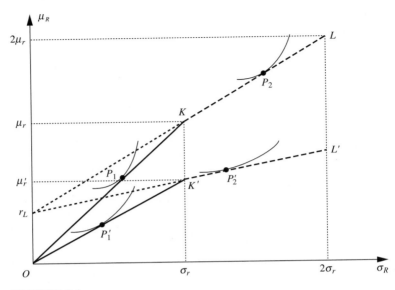

FIGURE 5.4
Different borrowing and lending rates.

Fig. 5.2 assumes for simplicity that currency and loans have neither return nor risk).
Once again the credit line parameter γ is for the time being taken, unsatisfactorily, as
an arbitrary constant, perhaps legally or institutionally fixed. The opportunity locus
for both borrowers and lenders is OKL, assuming that both have the same estimates
of the expected return and risk of holding capital. A typical diversifying risk averter
will arrive at a point like P_1, in the stretch of the locus OK. A typical risk-averse
borrower will arrive at a point like P_2, in the stretch of the locus KL. And a typical
risk-seeking borrower will arrive at L. Curve $OK'L'$, and points P_1', P_2', and L', represent the same situation except that the expected return on capital has been reduced
to μ_r'. The typical diversifier shifts partially from capital to currency-cum-loans (P_1'
is to the left of P_1). The typical risk-averse borrower does likewise; that is, he borrows less and holds less capital (P_2' is to the left of P_2). The typical risk seeker still
holds as much capital as his net worth and credit line allow.

5.4.3 Market Equilibrium: Return on Capital as Equilibrator

In market equilibrium the sum of demands for capital by all types of investors must
equal the capital stock; the sum of demands for currency, all due to diversifiers,
must equal the stock of currency; and of course the demand for loans by borrowers
must equal their supply by lenders. One of these conditions necessarily is implied by
the other two—"Walras's law." This follows from the fact that the algebraic sum of
asset holdings by each investor equals his net worth. For each individual, currency
holdings + capital holdings + loans = net worth. Loans are positive for lenders,
negative for borrowers. Summing over all individuals gives currency stock + capital
stock = aggregate net worth.

These are identities. They must be met, but they are not automatically met for every set of expected returns on the various assets. In that sense they are equilibrium conditions that determine those variables. In the present instance, the only rate that can vary is the expected return on capital. The expected real return on currency is assumed constant at zero, and the lenders' return on loans is stuck at zero by the condition that loans cannot dominate currency; otherwise the currency stock will find no homes in lenders' portfolios. The borrowers' interest rate is then determined by the cost of loan transactions or intermediation. But if the demand for capital exceeds the available stock when its expected return is high, demand may be brought into equilibrium with supply at a lower expected return.

In Fig. 5.4 for example, suppose that the demand for capital was excessive at expected return μ_r. Borrowers of the two types want to borrow more than lenders want to lend. A lower expected return like μ_r' could produce an equilibrium. Lenders are induced to lend more, and risk averse borrowers to borrow less, or even to become lenders. Their demands for capital are correspondingly reduced. In these ways excess demands for loans and for capital are eliminated.

Thus the introduction of a loan market where there was none before shifts the aggregate capital-currency portfolio balance curve in the manner described at the beginning of this chapter. The same relative holdings of currency and capital will be in portfolio balance at a lower expected rate of return on capital. At any given expected return, wealth owners will want more capital and less currency. Similar consequences would follow from improvement of an existing loan market—reducing borrowing costs or liberalizing credit lines.

These effects of the introduction or improvement of a loan market are shown diagrammatically in Fig. 5.5, similar to Fig. 5.1. The proportion of aggregate private wealth in currency is measured from left (0) to right (1) on the horizontal axis, and the proportion of aggregate private wealth in physical capital is measured from right (0) to left (1) on the same axis. Curve ABC applies to the two-asset regime and shows, for any expected rate of return on capital, wealth owners' desired division

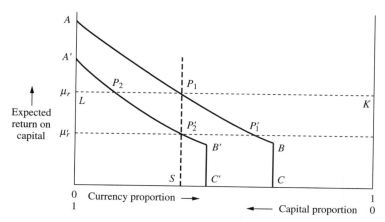

FIGURE 5.5
Portfolio balance with currency, capital, and loans.

of total private wealth between currency and capital. The distance to the right of C represents mainly the demand for capital by risk seekers. It also includes the amounts of capital that risk averters will hold to minimize risks; these amounts will be positive so long as currency is considered to involve some risk of change in purchasing power. Both these demands are insensitive to the rate of return on capital. At any rate of return below B, risk averters, actual or potential diversifiers, will hold no capital at all beyond these minimal amounts. But higher rates will induce at least some of them to hold additional capital.

The introduction (or improvement) of a loan market shifts the curve to $A'B'C'$. At the same expected return on capital μ_r, the demands for capital and currency are now indicated by P_2 instead of P_1. The distance between P_2 and P_1 does double duty. The demand for capital is now KP_2. Diversifiers' demand for currency, or for loans that serve the same function, is still LP_1. But it now takes only LP_2 of currency proper to satisfy this demand, since the remainder P_2P_1 is satisfied by loans. It now takes a lower rate of return on capital, μ'_r, to contain the demand for capital to KP_1 and to allow sufficient room in diversifiers' portfolios for the initial amount of currency LP_1. In addition, diversifiers would at μ'_r hold $P'_2P'_1$ in loans, having transferred to borrowers the title to an equivalent amount of capital.

Exogenous changes in the expected real returns on currency proper and on loans, so far assumed to be equivalent to currency in lenders' views, could be considered. In this model, they would reduce the demand for capital and bring about an increase in its equilibrium rate of return.

5.4.4 Market Equilibrium: Financial Market Value of Capital as Equilibrator

In the preceding discussion only the *demands* for capital and currency have been discussed. The object has been not to describe all the consequences of introducing or improving loan markets or financial intermediation but to trace the consequences only for the demand side of the asset markets. The complete story cannot be told without considering also the relative supplies of the two assets.

If in the short run, introduction or improvement of the loan market throws asset markets out of equilibrium, and neither the stock of capital nor its marginal productivity can immediately adjust to restore equilibrium, for example, at P_2 or P'_2 in Fig. 5.5 or anywhere else on the new portfolio balance curve. Neither can the supply of currency in money units suddenly contract to accommodate the reduced demand for currency relative to capital due to the substitution of loans.

However, as pointed out earlier in Section 5.2, increases in the q ratio raise the money value of a given physical stock of capital relative to the given quantity of currency. In the short run changes in asset demands can be reconciled to unchanged asset supplies by changes in q.

In Fig. 5.5 equilibrium can be preserved by a sufficient increase in q to alter the proportions of capital and currency in total wealth from those indicated by point P_1 to those indicated by point P_2. This is not the whole story, because the q increase has the side effect of altering the distribution of wealth in favor of borrowers, who are

100 percent or more in capital, relative to lenders, who hold some assets that do not rise in money value. The redistribution further raises the demand for capital. This process is further described in Chapter 6.

5.5
THE LOAN MARKET: SECOND APPROXIMATION, A MODEL WITH NO CURRENCY

The preceding sections have examined a model in which loans supplement but do not supplant currency. Consequently the interest rate on loans is essentially determined by the established rate on currency, and it is the return on capital or the market price of capital that must adjust to preserve equilibrium. As suggested earlier, an alternative possibility is that loans take the place of currency altogether. A unit of currency could still be the unit of account, in which loan contracts among other things are written. But currency itself would disappear from public circulation, dominated by private promises to pay currency.

In this regime, the left-hand parts of the loans-capital opportunity loci of Figs. 5.2 and 5.3 apply to lenders, just as the parts to the right of K apply to borrowers, and the currency-capital locus is superseded. (There would be a kink in the loans-capital opportunity locus at K if the borrowers' rate exceeded the lenders' rate.) Now, however, the loan rate can adjust to preserve equilibrium of the demand and supply of capital, at whatever expected rate of return on capital economic and technological conditions have produced.

This mechanism is illustrated in Fig. 5.6. The expected return on capital is given at μ_r, and as before point K represents the 100 percent capital portfolio. The locus NKL represents the opportunities for combining loans and capital—lending to the

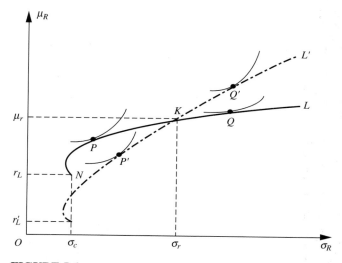

FIGURE 5.6
Effects of an endogenous loan interest rate.

left of K, borrowing to the right—with a loan rate of r_L for lenders (and possibly somewhat higher for borrowers). A typical lender will choose a point like P, a risk-averse borrower Q, and a risk-seeking borrower the maximum risk point L. As above, the credit line parameter γ is arbitrarily fixed. Suppose, however, that given the distribution of wealth among the three types, these portfolio choices add up to an excess supply of loans and an excess supply of capital. A lower loan rate—for example, r_L' for lenders (and its counterpart for borrowers)—will lead toward equilibrium. Diversifiers at point P' will wish to lend less and to hold more capital; risk-averse borrowers will want to borrow more and hold more capital; risk-seeking borrowers will still borrow as much, and hold as much capital, as their credit lines permit.

In this regime the improvement of the loan market—reduction of the costs of intermediation or increase in credit lines—does not necessitate either reduction in the expected return on capital or rise in the money valuation of capital. The loan rate itself does the adjusting. Likewise the loan market will adjust to exogenous shifts in portfolio preferences or in the expected profitability of capital.

Regimes involving government-issued currency are outside-money models—at least one asset that is a constituent of private wealth is supplied to the private economy from the outside. Regimes like the two-asset loans-capital model just discussed are inside-money models—all the assets are generated by market processes within the private economy. In the outside-money model, market interest rates are controlled by the necessity for outside assets to be competitive with inside assets. The fixed nominal rate of zero on government-issued currency acts as an anchor for other money interest rates. Therefore disturbances to equilibrium cannot be absorbed in private loan markets and loan rates but have important consequences outside financial markets—in the demand for capital relative to its supply, in prices of capital and other goods, and very possibly in production and employment. By the same token, government policy—for example, changing the supply of currency or allowing more or less financial intermediation—can have important real consequences. In a pure unregulated inside-money model, on the other hand, interest rates are not anchored. Consequently disturbances can be absorbed in private loan markets without consequences for the markets for capital, other goods, and labor. Likewise there is no room for government monetary or financial policy.

5.5.1 Default Risk and Credit Limits

As pointed out above, the first approximation does not do full justice to private loans, because it does not take account of default risk. One consequence of this is that a credit limit or margin requirement, although it is necessary to bound the borrowing of risk seekers, appears as an unexplained deus ex machina. Nevertheless, the first approximation does delineate many of the essential features and consequences of the loan market. Now it is time to backtrack and to analyze the portfolio choices of lenders and borrowers, with explicit attention to default risk and credit lines. This will be done first on the assumption that loans and capital are the only two assets. This analysis will pave the way to bring currency back into the picture.

Three types of investors are assumed: risk-averse diversifiers (the lending side of the market), risk-averse borrowers, and risk-seeking borrowers. Each group is considered to be internally homogeneous in preferences, and all share the same estimates of risk and return. Lenders are more risk averse than either type of borrowers. The initial distribution of wealth among the three groups is given. λ_1 will represent the ratio to lenders' net worth of the net worth of risk-averse borrowers, and λ_2 the corresponding ratio for risk seekers. Lenders offer two types of loans, each with its own pair of terms, interest rate, and credit line, (r_{L1}, γ_1) and (r_{L2}, γ_2). The second type has a higher loan rate, and a higher credit line as well; these are the loans for the risk-loving borrowers. Loans as shares of lenders' net worth amount to l_1 and l_2. Both the terms and the loan volumes are determined in the loan markets.

Note that in this model, although there are two kinds of loans, there is only one kind of capital, an asset held by all three classes of players. The expected yields and risks on capital are the same for all the holders. They are taken to be given for the purposes of this model of the loan market. So is the aggregate physical capital stock K, whose aggregate asset value qK is the total net worth of the lenders and borrowers. The loan market allocates the capital stock among them.

As above, r represents the realized return per dollar of capital. Its probability density function $\phi(r)$ is taken to be objectively given, or at least agreed upon by all participants in the market. In this respect, the model here differs from recent models of risky loans, in which borrowers and their projects differ in degrees of credit risk, often in ways better known to borrowers than to lenders. See for example Stiglitz and Weiss (1981).

5.5.2 Lenders

For convenience in exposition, consider first lenders' behavior in offering a single type of loan.

The realized return on a loan is, of course, not always the same as r_L, the contracted interest rate. It may be less but not more. Borrowers may not be able to meet their obligations in full. In this case, they go bankrupt and pay their creditors all they have, on a pro rata basis. It is assumed that borrowers have no labor income to draw upon to meet their obligations or are not compelled to draw on resources other than the collateral of the loan. The debt of a borrower, relative to his initial net worth, is at the end of the period $\gamma(1 + r_L)$. The value of his capital at that time is $(1 + \gamma)(1 + r)$. If the value of capital permits, the lender is repaid in full, $\gamma(1 + r_L)$. Otherwise the borrower must default and the lender receives $(1 + \gamma)(1 + r)$.

Formally, let x_L be the return actually realized per dollar of lending. This is a random variable, correlated with r as follows:

I: $$x_L = r_L \qquad \text{if } (1 + \gamma)(1 + r) \geq \gamma(1 + r_L) \tag{5.1}$$

that is, if borrowers end up with enough capital to pay their debt.

II: $$\gamma(1 + x_L) = (1 + \gamma)(1 + r); \qquad \text{thus } x_L = r + (1 + r)/\gamma$$
$$\text{if } (1 + \gamma)(1 + r) < \gamma(1 + r_L)$$

that is, if borrowers cannot repay in full but must transfer their capital to their creditors.

The dividing line between situations I and II occurs when $r = T = (\gamma r_L - 1) \div (1 + \gamma)$. If r exceeds T, situation I occurs. If r is less than T, situation II applies.

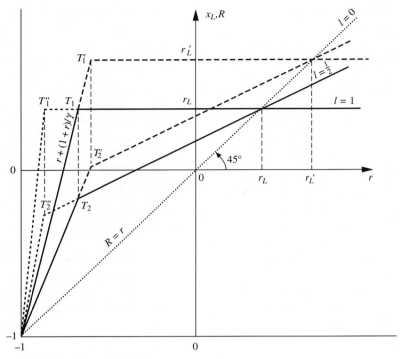

T_1, T_1', T_1'' correspond to $l = 1$
T_2, T_2', T_2'' correspond to $l = \frac{1}{2}$
$'$ corresponds to a rise in r_L
$''$ corresponds to a fall in γ

FIGURE 5.7
Portfolio return with endogenous loan default risk.

The relation of x_L to r and r_L is pictured in Fig. 5.7. Here the return on capital r is measured horizontally and the lender's return to loans x_L vertically. The portfolio return R is also measured vertically. Both x_L and r have a floor at -1; in either asset an investor cannot lose more than he puts in. The relation of x_L to r is the solid line marked $l = 1$. The return on capital at which debtors barely remain solvent is T_1. For $r \geq T_1$, this relation is horizontal, at the level of the loan rate r_L. For $r < T_1$, it is a line connecting the points $(-1, -1)$ and (T_1, r_L).

Let l be the proportion of a typical risk averter's wealth placed in loans; the remainder $1 - l$ is held in capital. Let R be the portfolio rate of return. Then

$$R = lx_L + (1 - l)r = r - l(r - x_L) \tag{5.2}$$

or

I: $$R = lr_L + (1 - l)r = r - l(r - r_L) \qquad \text{for } r \geq T$$

II: $$R = l\left(r + \frac{1 + r}{\gamma}\right) + (1 - l)r = r + l\frac{1 + r}{\gamma} \qquad \text{for } r \leq T$$

In Fig. 5.7 the path designated $l = 1$ represents the return on a portfolio invested 100 percent in loans. The 45-degree line, of course, represents the return on capital itself; it would be the portfolio return for l set equal to zero. By mixing loans and capital, the investor can obtain portfolio outcomes in between these two extremes, for example, the dashed line $l = \frac{1}{2}$. Loans give the investor the opportunity to avoid possible heavy losses on capital, in return for forgoing possible large gains.

The expectation of return on loans $E(x_L)$ is, of course, smaller than r_L, but may be, depending on r_L and γ, either smaller or larger than μ_r, the expected return on capital. A risk-neutral investor will choose $l = 1$ when the expectation of returns on loans $E(x_L)$ exceeds the expected value of the return on capital μ_r. But a risk-averse investor will not necessarily do so. This may seem paradoxical. The reason is that the losses or gains because of diversification—due to including capital as well as loans in the portfolio—must be translated into losses or gains of utility. Marginal utility is low where departures from $l = 1$ produce gains and high where it produces losses. This, of course, works in favor of the $l = 1$ policy. But in the loss range, marginal utility is especially high in the left-hand extremes where the advantage of loans over capital is small. Where loans give substantial protection, in the middle range, the marginal utility of a dollar of protection is lower. Taking all probabilities into account, therefore, a risk averter may not find the full protection of loans worth the complete surrender of choices for higher profits, because the protection is poorest when it is most needed.

A higher interest rate on loans, given the credit line parameter γ, improves the performance of loans in all contingencies. See the dotted line through T_1' and r_L' in Fig. 5.7. The same portfolio choice l still provides the same protection at the low end of the r scale (up to T_1) but provides greater returns at the high end (above T_1). So the balance is tipped in favor of an increase in l. The loss of possible income for high r is diminished in utility terms, while the utility value of the added protection for low r is still the same. This is why an increase in r_L leads unequivocally to an increase in l. See Appendix 5A for proof.

Given the loan interest rate, a decline in γ swings the line $r + (1 + r)/\gamma$ to the left, as illustrated by the steep dotted line to T_1'' in Fig. 5.7. Now if l remains unchanged, for example, at $\frac{1}{2}$, default protection has been improved, but outcomes above T remain as before. As to the advantages of an increase in l, there are two conflicting considerations. In favor of such an increase is the fact that a given change in l now buys a larger dollar improvement in outcome in all cases of default. The difference between $r + (1 + r)/\gamma$ and r is larger, and a given change in l buys a fraction of this difference. On the other hand, the range over which this improvement occurs is reduced, as compared with the range above T and T'', where higher l means symmetrically lower losses and lower gains. The upshot is that a reduction in γ may change l in either direction. However, if l were initially zero, with the investor just on the margin of making some loans, a reduction in risk will tilt the balance in favor of some lending, a positive l.

One limiting case is $\gamma \to 0$, $T \to -1$—loans are, in the limit, sure things. If the interest rate r_L exceeds μ_r, risk-averse investors will put all their wealth into loans. For interest rates below μ_r, they may choose mixed portfolios. Here the standard analysis of Chapter 4, concerning portfolio choices with one risky asset and one safe asset, applies.

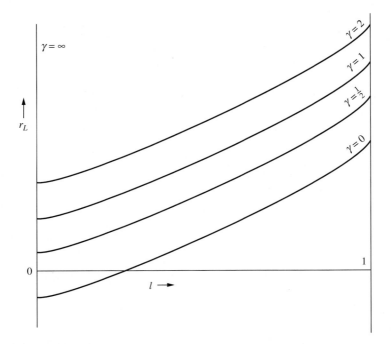

FIGURE 5.8
Lenders' portfolio choice as function of credit limit and interest rate.

At the other extreme, $\gamma \to \infty$, $T \to r_L$. Loans are no different from capital for $r < T$, and not as good as capital for $r > T$. Obviously loans are dominated by capital and no loans will be made.

In summary, l depends jointly on γ and r_L, in a manner illustrated in Fig. 5.8. In the diagrams, l is taken throughout as an increasing function of r_L and a decreasing function of γ; the possibility that in some range l may rise with γ for given r_L is not pictured.

5.5.3 Borrowers

Now consider the other side of the market, risk-averse and risk-seeking borrowers. Borrowing γ for every dollar of their net worth, they hold $1 + \gamma$ dollars of capital. Their return per dollar of net worth is

I: $R = r + \gamma(r - r_L)$ for $r \geq T = (\gamma r_L - 1)/(1 + \gamma)$, and

II: $R = -1$ for $r < T$,   (5.3)

for in this case they must surrender all their capital, whether held on borrowed funds or on their own funds, to their creditors.

This relation of R to r and r_L is shown in Fig. 5.9. Portfolio return R is equal to -1 so long as r falls short of T. For r above T, R increases by $1 + \gamma$ for every unit increase in r. For r below r_L, the return is smaller than the return on an unlevered portfolio, that is, one with no debt and all net worth invested in capital. For r above

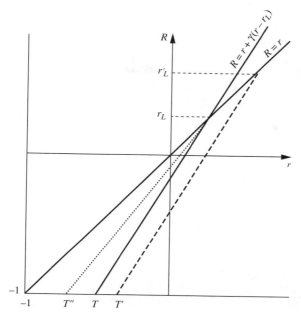

FIGURE 5.9
Returns to borrowers.

r_L, the outcomes are more favorable than those on an unlevered portfolio. When the expected value of R exceeds or equals that of r, a risk seeker will prefer R, and indeed he will usually do so even when the expected value of R is less than that of r. The effect on R of a rise in the loan interest rate to r'_L is to extend the default range ($R = -1$) to T', from which a line, dashed in Fig. 5.9, of the same slope $1 + \gamma$ as before, represents the relation of R to r. The effect on R of a reduction of the credit line to γ'', holding r_L unchanged, is to limit the default range to T'' and to lower the slope of the continuing line.

A risk-seeking (or risk-neutral) borrower will borrow either the permitted maximum γ, at a given interest rate r_L, or nothing. He can be imagined to calculate whether, starting with the 45-degree line, he would like to rotate the outcome line counterclockwise about the point (r_L, r_L). The advantage of this rotation is to give the investor higher return when $r > r_L$; the disadvantage is to give him lower returns when $r < r_L$. The advantages and disadvantages, however, are not symmetrical; he cannot do worse than $R = -1$, and the rotation increases the range to which this limit applies. Consequently, if a small rotation is good, a large rotation is better. A larger rotation increases the high gains to which high marginal utility is attached and increases further some possible losses and/or the probabilities of their occurrence. But small marginal utility is attached to diminishing these losses anyway. Thus competition among risk seekers will put r_L, for any given value of γ, at the maximum value that makes borrowing to the limit as desirable as zero borrowing. (See Eq. 5.A5 in Appendix 5A.)

A risk-averse borrower will prefer loans with smaller credit lines and lower interest rates. As shown in Appendix 5A, these borrowers will normally incur less debt, and require lower credit lines, the higher the loan rate. Actually they behave like lenders choosing to lend negative amounts.

5.5.4 Market Equilibrium with No Currency

How are the values of the two r_L and the two γ determined in a competitive market? On one side of the market are many lenders, here assumed to have identical utility functions. On the other side are the two sets of borrowers.

The equilibrium credit lines and loan rates must be such that lenders' supplies of each kind of loans equal borrowers' demands. Credit lines are set so that they are fully used at the market interest rates. Consequently, the following relationships must hold when the loan markets are cleared:

$$l_1 = \gamma_1\lambda_1, \qquad l_2 = \gamma_2\lambda_2, \tag{5.4}$$

where the λ are the two ratios of borrowers' to lenders' wealth. Thus if a γ is $\frac{1}{2}$, the corresponding l must be $\lambda/2$; if γ is 1, l must be equal to λ, and so on. Since $l_1 + l_2$ cannot exceed 1, the maximum possible $\gamma_1\lambda_1 + \gamma_2\lambda_2$ is 1. The various curves of Fig. 5.8 display the relation of an l to its r_L for alternative values of γ. But if account is taken of the marketwide links imposed by the distribution of wealth between borrowers and lenders, then only one point on each curve is feasible, the point at which $l = \gamma\lambda$.

For example, in Fig. 5.10 λ is taken to be $\frac{1}{2}$. The dashed locus of Fig. 5.10 represents the effective supply of loans by lenders in relation to the loan interest rate r_L and the credit line γ. Normally this will have a positive slope. A higher interest rate will be needed to induce more lending, especially since more lending is inevitably

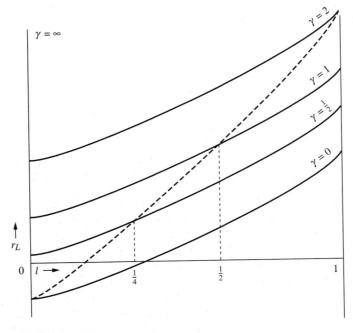

FIGURE 5.10
Derivation of the loan supply curve.

riskier lending. But as observed above, there may be a range for which an increase in risk, as measured by γ, would actually induce an increase in lending at a given interest rate. An increase $\Delta\gamma$ might conceivably induce more than $\lambda\Delta\gamma$ increase in the desired loan fraction l. If so, then a decline in the interest rate would have to occur to keep lending within bounds. The dashed curve of Fig. 5.10 would have a declining slope in such a range. See Appendix 5B.

The result is that there are for each loan type two relations between γ (and l) and r_L—one for lenders (taking into account the identity $l = \gamma\lambda$) and one for borrowers. Normally, as Figs. 5.11a and 5.11b illustrate, the one for borrowers is negatively sloped, and the one for lenders positively sloped. The market equilibrium values of γ and r_L must satisfy both these relations.

As for borrowers, the interest rate at which risk averters will exhaust entire credit lines is lower the more generous the credit line. Risk seekers, of course, always

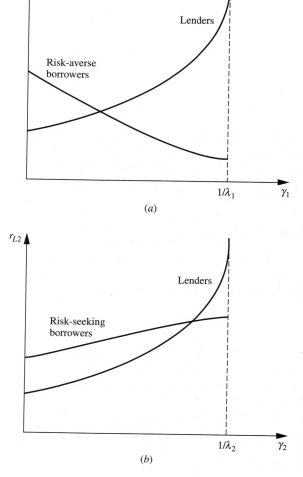

(a)

(b)

FIGURE 5.11
Equilibrium loan rates and credit lines.

borrow as much as they are allowed—provided only that the loan rate is not so far above the expected return from capital that they choose not to borrow at all.

A redistribution of wealth in favor of borrowers—an increase in one λ—would shift the lenders' curves in Fig. 5.11 upward and to the left. The loan rate will be higher and the credit line smaller. But the fraction of lenders' wealth devoted to those loans ($l = \gamma\lambda$) will be greater. A rise in the expected return on capital will, of course, raise the equilibrium loan rates, making both lenders and risk-averse borrowers more anxious to hold capital. In Fig. 5.11a both curves shift upward. Equilibrium γ may either rise or fall.

5.6
MARKET EQUILIBRIUM WITH CURRENCY, LOANS, AND CAPITAL: SECOND APPROXIMATION

To return to an outside-money model, now suppose that lenders have the opportunity to hold currency in addition to loans and capital. (Borrowers have the opportunity also, but are not interested in it as a portfolio investment.) Suppose that currency is a perfectly safe asset with zero return. Loans and capital share a common risk, exhibiting it in the different manners already outlined. Let m be the fraction of their wealth that lenders put into currency, l_1 and l_2 the fractions in loans of the two kinds, and $1 - l_1 - l_2 - m$ the proportion in capital.

Suppose that the relative amounts of total loans l and capital k are decided. The question then is how much of the portfolio should be in currency and how much in loans-cum-capital. The considerations in this decision are illustrated in Fig. 5.12, which, for simplicity, assumes there is only one kind of loan.

Like previous diagrams, Fig. 5.12 shows the outcomes R of various lenders' portfolios for all possible outcomes r of capital investment. The returns on a 100 percent capital portfolio are shown, as before, by the 45-degree line; the returns on a 100 percent loan portfolio by the broken line; and the returns on a 50 percent capital, 50 percent loans portfolio by the dashed line halfway between these two lines. A 100 percent currency portfolio corresponds to the horizontal axis, and this of course can be averaged with any of the mixtures of loans and capital exhibited in the diagram or with any other mixture. The dotted broken line represents a 50 percent currency, 25 percent loans, 25 percent capital portfolio. It falls halfway, vertically, between the horizontal axis and the dashed line. Mixing in currency reduces proportionately both losses and gains. A risk-averse investor may choose m greater than zero because he finds the reduction in risk worth the loss of expected return.

In general, the relative proportions of loans and capital, l and k, chosen when three assets including currency are available, will not be the same as the proportions chosen when no currency is available. Currency makes it possible to avoid risk more fully than loans. If currency becomes available, a risk-averse investor will substitute it more for loans than for capital, reducing l.

However, the separation theorem of Chapter 4 tells us that under certain conditions the loans-capital mixture in the three-asset regime, although not the same as in the two-asset regime, might be independent of the degree of risk aversion of the investor. That is, an investor who became more risk averse would not alter the

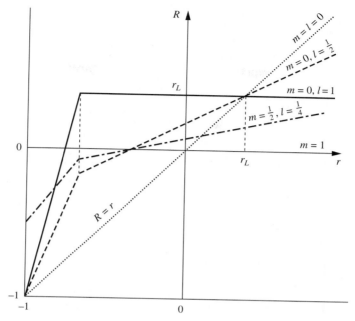

FIGURE 5.12
Portfolio return with three assets and endogenous default risk.

relative proportion of loans and capital but would substitute currency for both of them pro rata. To put the point another way, two investors with differing degrees of risk aversion would hold differing proportions of currency. But their loans-capital ratios would be the same.

A sufficient condition for this uniformity is that utility functions are quadratic. In that case, the situation may be pictured in Fig. 5.13. Here the locus LK represents the combinations of risk and expected return available by mixing loans and capital. Yields of the two assets are positively and imperfectly correlated, though their relationship is nonlinear. The availability of a riskless asset, currency, brings about a new opportunity locus OMK. A risk-averse investor who was at point Y in a two-asset regime will shift to point X. At point X he will hold capital and loans in the proportions indicated by M; that is, l will be the vertical distance from K to M as a proportion of the vertical distance from K to L. Any other risk-averse investor who takes advantage of the opportunity to reduce risk by holding currency will also mix loans and capital in the proportions indicated by M. He may, however, choose a different point on the line OM. The currency fraction m is the distance XM as proportion of OM.

If currency is not riskless the separation theorem does not apply, even if utility functions are quadratic.

In general, the familiar war of income and substitution effects leaves ambiguity about the responses of portfolio shares to expected rates of return and risk. Normally lenders will increase their loans, at the expense of both capital and money, when the

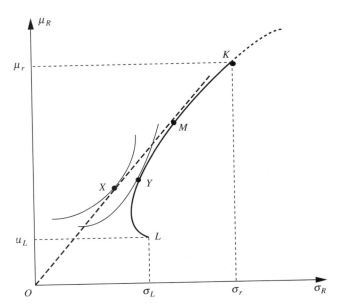

FIGURE 5.13
Separating equilibrium with three assets.

loan rate rises or the credit line extended to borrowers is reduced. They will increase their capital holdings, at the expense of both money and loans, when the expected return on capital rises.

How is market equilibrium determined? The supply of currency and the physical stock of capital, the constituents of private wealth, are given. With two types of loans, there are four assets for which demand and supply must be equated. Market-clearing equations for any three of the assets will suffice, since the fourth equality of demand and supply will simply show the residual disposition of wealth. Two more equilibrium conditions are that both classes of borrowers fully use their credit lines. These five equations determine not only the two dimensions of the two types of loans, r_{Li} and γ_i, but also an expected return on capital μ_r. In this system, unlike the moneyless model of the previous section, the return on capital is an endogenous variable. The return on currency is exogenous.

Let the yield of a physical unit of capital, in terms of its own replacement cost, be MPK, a stochastic variable with expected value $E(\text{MPK})$ and standard deviation σ_{MPK}. The equity market value of a unit of capital is q. Consider the return on market value MPK/q. Its expected value μ_r is $E(\text{MPK})/q$ and its standard deviation σ_r is σ_{MPK}/q. In the short run, when the stock of capital K at replacement cost and the distribution of its marginal productivity are both given, variation in q changes inversely its market return μ_r. Of course, the total return to a stockholder includes changes in q.

According to Appendix 5C, exogenous increases in currency supply raise q, lower μ_r, and also lower loan rates. Effects on credit lines are ambiguous. There is only one value of m^* that is consistent with $q = 1$.

In the long run, as mentioned above, net investment responds positively to positive deviations of q from 1, raises the size of the capital stock, and lowers its expected return on replacement cost $E(\text{MPK})$. This process is described in detail in Chapter 6, Section 6.1.3.

5.7
THE MONETIZATION OF CAPITAL

The principal message of this chapter is that financial markets and the intermediary institutions that play important roles in those markets in effect monetize capital. Loans permit the more adventurous members of society, those who are willing to assume risks, to invest in enterprise capital in excess of their net worth. The lenders, in return, acquire assets tailored to their more conservative tastes—less risky, more liquid, more reversible, more predictable.

Many of these assets are, for them, close if not perfect substitutes for government-issued currency. These inside loans, debts of some private agents to other private agents, do double duty. They finance borrowers' holdings of capital, and they substitute, albeit imperfectly, for lenders' holding of currency. The greater the extent of this "monetization" of capital, the greater is the aggregate demand for capital and the smaller the net aggregate demand for currency proper. In Chapters 7–10 this process is examined in greater detail, in particular the essential roles of commercial banks and other financial intermediaries.

Inside assets and liabilities, including inside money, are central features of capitalism. Clearly they cannot be understood without recognizing the differences of tastes and circumstances between lenders and borrowers, or between savers and investors. In this chapter risk seekers were distinguished from risk-averse diversifiers, and diversifiers were in turn divided between those with short and long positions in means of payment and near moneys. Models of "representative agents" miss the phenomena modeled in this chapter.

Another implication of the approach here is that both sides of private asset transactions are important in understanding their consequences. This would seem obvious were it not for the one-sided fixation of monetarists on the monetary aggregates, M_1, M_2, M_3, etc. Such concentration on the liabilities of financial intermediaries to lenders neglects the asset side of the institutions' balance sheets. But the credit side is bound to affect substantially the macroeconomic consequences of their transactions. Suppose, for example, that banks simply hold short-term government debt. Their depositors are spared some inconvenience by such intermediation, but the economy would not look much different if those same lenders held Treasury bills directly instead of indirectly. Those bills and bank deposits, especially certificates of deposit, are close to being perfect substitutes. This is what banks were doing for the most part during the Great Depression and World War II, until well into the 1950s. When they shifted from government securities to commercial loans and mortgages, banks contributed to a boom in investment and economic activity even though monetary aggregates were held in check.

The extent of monetization of capital in the United States is described in detail in Appendix 5D.

APPENDIX 5A: ALGEBRA OF LENDERS' AND BORROWERS' PORTFOLIOS

The algebraic basis of the results in Section 5.5.4 is as follows: Consider $U(R)$, the investor's utility-of-return function, with $U(-1) = 0$ and marginal utility $U'(R)$ positive but declining with R. Expected utility is, after substituting in equation (5.2),

$$E(U(R)) = \int_{-1}^{T} U[r + (l/\gamma)(1 + r)]\phi(r)\,dr$$

$$+ \int_{-1}^{\infty} U[r - l(r - r_L)]\phi(r)\,dr. \tag{5A.1}$$

$$\partial E(U(R))/\partial l = \int_{-1}^{T} U'[r + (l/\gamma)(1 + r)][(1 + r)/\gamma]\phi(r)\,dr$$

$$- \int_{T}^{\infty} U'[r - l(r - r_L)](r - r_L)\phi(r)\,dr.$$

Setting this derivative equal to zero determines l, unless the maximum of $E(U(R))$ occurs at $l = 0$ or $l = 1$. To determine how l responds to variations in r_L and in γ, the condition for the maximum must be differentiated with respect to those two variables. Recalling that $T = (\gamma r_L - 1)/(1 + \gamma)$, note that the integrands in the two integrals in the expression are identical at $r = T$. This means that derivatives with respect to the limits of integration T (a function of r_L and γ) will cancel out.

Differentiating with respect to r_L thus gives

$$\partial l/\partial r_L = \text{NUM/DENOM},$$

where

$$\text{DENOM} = \int_{-1}^{T} U''[r + (l/\gamma)(1 + r)][(1 + r)/\gamma]^2\phi(r)\,dr$$

(5A.2)

$$+ \int_{T}^{\infty} U''[r - l(r - r_L)](r - r_L)^2\phi(r)\,dr,$$

and

$$\text{NUM} = \int_{T}^{\infty} U''[r - l(r - r_L)]l(r - r_L)\phi(r)\,dr$$

$$- \int_{T}^{\infty} U'[r - l(r - r_L)]\phi(r)\,dr.$$

Both terms in DENOM are negative, and NUM is unambiguously negative. Consequently $\partial l/\partial r_L$ is positive; not surprisingly, more loans are supplied when the loan rate is higher.

Similarly

$$\partial l / \partial \gamma = \text{NUM}'/\text{DENOM}', \qquad (5A.3)$$

where $\text{DENOM}' = \text{DENOM}$, and

$$\text{NUM}' = \int_{-1}^{T} U''[r + (l/\gamma)(1 + r)][l(1 + r)^2/\gamma^3]\phi(r)\, dr$$

$$+ \int_{-1}^{T} U'[r + (l/\gamma)(1 + r)][(1 + r)/\gamma^2]\phi(r)\, dr.$$

DENOM' is negative, as before. But NUM' contains a negative term followed by a positive term. The importance of the negative term depends on l. As stated above, $\partial l / \partial \gamma$ is negative for $l = 0$ but may become positive for high l.

As mentioned above, there will generally be more than one type of loan, two in the particular model at hand. Each type will have its own r_{Li}, γ_i, x_{Li}, and T_i. Let l_1 and l_2 be the proportions of a typical risk-averse lender's wealth placed in loans of the two types; the remainder is held in capital. Let R be the portfolio rate of return. Then

$$R = l_1 x_{L1} + l_2 x_{L2} + (1 - l_1 - l_2)r. \qquad (5A.4)$$

There are four regimes for (x_{L1}, x_{L2}). The algebra becomes tedious, but qualitatively the portfolio strategy of the lenders is the same as in the simpler case with one type of loan and two regimes.

Risk-seeking borrowers. Let $V(R)$ be the utility of return for a typical risk-seeker, where $V'(R)$ is a positive increasing function of R, and $V(-1) = 0$. Expected utility is

$$E(V(R)) = \int_{T}^{\infty} V[r + \gamma_2(r - r_{L2})]\phi(r)\, dr. \qquad (5A.5)$$

Compare the expected utility of an unlevered portfolio:

$$E(V(r)) = \int_{-1}^{\infty} V(r)\phi(r)\, dr. \qquad (5A.6)$$

$$\partial E(V(R))/\partial \gamma_2 = \int_{T}^{\infty} V'[r + \gamma_2(r - r_{L2})](r - r_{L2})\phi(r)\, dr. \qquad (5A.7)$$

$$\partial^2 E(V(R))/\partial \gamma_2^2 = \int_{T}^{\infty} V''[r + \gamma_2(r - r_{L2})](r - r_{L2})^2 \phi(r)\, dr \qquad (5A.8)$$

$$+ V'(-1)\phi(T)(1 + r_{L2})/(1 + \gamma_2)^3.$$

Given that $V''(R) \geq 0$, $\partial^2 E(V(R))/\partial \gamma_2^2$ is positive. Consequently if $\partial E(V(R))/\partial \gamma_2$ is positive at $\gamma_2 = 0$, it is always positive.

Therefore, a borrower who chooses to borrow at all will use his entire credit line. Consider, therefore, what is the maximum interest rate r_{L2} a borrower will pay when his credit line is γ_2. This is the rate at which $E(V(R)) = E(V(r))$, that is, the rate which leaves him indifferent between borrowing nothing and borrowing γ_2. This is given implicitly by

$$\int_T^\infty V[r + \gamma_2(r - r_{L2})]\phi(r)\,dr = \int_{-1}^\infty V(r)\phi(r)\,dr. \qquad (5A.9)$$

Differentiating this with respect to γ_2 gives

$$\int_T^\infty V'[r + \gamma_2(r - r_{L2})][(r - r_{L2}) - \gamma_2(\partial r_{L2}/\partial\gamma_2)]\phi(r)\,dr = 0, \qquad (5A.10)$$

and $\qquad \partial r_{L2}/\partial\gamma_2 = \dfrac{\int_T^\infty V'[r + \gamma_2(r - r_{L2})](r - r_{L2})\phi(r)\,dr}{\gamma_2\int_T^\infty V'[r + \gamma_2(r - r_{L2})]\phi(r)\,dr}.$

The numerator is positive if borrowing is at all worthwhile. The denominator is positive. Therefore $\partial r_{L2}/\partial\gamma_2$ is positive. That is, risk-seeking borrowers will pay more for high credit lines than for low ones.

Risk-averse borrowers. While a risk-averse borrower will not necessarily use the entire amount of any arbitrary credit line, the market will set γ_1 so that he chooses to use it fully. Since there is no advantage in borrowing to hold money, his capital holding will be $1 + \gamma_1$ times his net worth. Let $Z(R)$ be the utility of return for a typical risk-averse borrower, where $Z(-1) = 0$, and marginal utility $Z'(R)$ is a declining function of R, that is, $Z''(R) < 0$. Choosing γ_1 so as to maximize expected utility

$$E(Z(R)) = \int_T^\infty Z[r + \gamma_1(r - r_{L1})]\phi(r)\,dr$$

gives

$$\int_T^\infty Z'[r + \gamma_1(r - r_{L1})](r - r_{L1})\phi(r)\,dr = 0. \qquad (5A.11)$$

This relates γ_1 implicitly to r_{L1}, and

$$\partial\gamma_1/\partial r_{L1} =$$

$$\dfrac{\int_T^\infty Z'[r + \gamma_1(r - r_{L1})]\phi(r)\,dr + \gamma_1\int_T^\infty Z''[r + \gamma_1(r - r_{L1})](r - r_{L1})\phi(r)\,dr}{\int_T^\infty Z''[r + \gamma_1(r - r_{L1})](r - r_{L1})^2\phi(r)\,dr}.$$

At $\gamma_1 = 0$, this derivative is necessarily negative—less borrowing the higher the cost—but at higher values of γ_1 it may have either sign. The substitution effect of an increase in the loan rate r_{L1} always works in favor of a reduction in γ_1. But a borrower who is already in debt is made worse off by an increase in r_{L1}, and the income effect normally works in favor of taking more risk. As throughout the book, it is assumed that the substitution effect predominates.

APPENDIX 5B: MARKETWIDE CONSTRAINTS

Algebraically, each condition $l_i = \gamma_i \lambda_i$ can be substituted in Eq. 5A.1, giving for loan market

$$0 = \int_{-1}^{T} U'[r + \lambda_i(1 + r)][(1 + r)/\gamma_i]\phi(r)\,dr$$

$$- \int_{T}^{\infty} U'[r - \gamma_i \lambda_i(r - r_{Li})](r - r_{Li})\phi(r)\,dr. \qquad (5B.1)$$

Differentiating this with respect to γ_i,

$$\partial r_{Li}/\partial \gamma_i = \qquad\qquad\qquad\qquad\qquad\qquad\qquad\qquad (5B.2)$$

$$\frac{\int_{-1}^{T} U'[r + \lambda_i(1 + r)][(1 + r)/\gamma_i^2]\phi(r)\,dr - \lambda_i \int_{T}^{\infty} U''[r - \gamma_i \lambda_i(r - r_{Li})](r - r_{Li})^2\phi(r)\,dr}{\int_{T}^{\infty} U'[r - \gamma_i \lambda_i(r - r_{Li})]\phi(r)\,dr - \lambda_i \int_{T}^{\infty} U''[r - \gamma_i \lambda_i(r - r_{Li})](r - r_{Li})\gamma_i\phi(r)\,dr}.$$

The numerator of this expression is unequivocally positive. But the denominator can be negative for large values of $\gamma_i \lambda_i$.

APPENDIX 5C: ASSET MARKET EQUATIONS

The model of the market in Section 5.6 is as follows. Let $l_i(r_{L1}, r_{L2}, \gamma_1, \gamma_2, \mu_r)$ be the fraction of their wealth that lenders wish to hold as loans of type i ($i = 1, 2$). Recall that μ_r is the expected rate of return on capital. Let $\gamma_1 = f_1(r_{L1}, \gamma_1, \mu_r)$ represent the fraction of their wealth that risk-averse borrowers wish to borrow. Let $\gamma_2 = f_2(r_{L2}, \gamma_2, \mu_r)$ represent the fraction of their wealth that risk-seeking borrowers wish to borrow. As before, λ_1 and λ_2 are the ratios of the wealth of each class of borrowers to that of lenders. In market equilibrium four equations determine the two loan rates and credit lines.

$$l_i(r_{L1}, r_{L2}, \gamma_1, \gamma_2, \mu_r) - \gamma_i \lambda_i = 0 \qquad (i = 1, 2)$$
$$\gamma_i = f_i(r_{Li}, \gamma_i, \mu_r) \qquad (i = 1, 2). \qquad (5C.1)$$

Assuming the partial derivatives of the l_i and f_i have the normal signs shown above, the results of the text can be derived.

The equations are the same as Eq. 5C.1 augmented by one for currency:

$$m(r_{L1}, r_{L2}, \gamma_1, \gamma_2, \mu_r) = m^* \qquad \text{currency (lenders' demand = exogenous supply)}$$
$$l_1(r_{L1}, r_{L2}, \gamma_1, \gamma_2, \mu_r) - \gamma_1 \lambda_1 = 0 \qquad \text{\#1 loans (lenders' supply = borrowers' demand)}$$
$$l_2(r_{L1}, r_{L2}, \gamma_1, \gamma_2, \mu_r) - \gamma_2 \lambda_2 = 0 \qquad \text{\#2 loans (lenders' supply = borrowers' demand)}$$
$$f_1(r_{L1}, \gamma_1, \mu_r) - \gamma_1 \lambda_1 = 0 \qquad \text{(risk-averse borrowers borrow up to limit)}$$
$$f_2(r_{L2}, \gamma_2, \mu_r) - \gamma_2 \lambda_2 = 0 \qquad \text{(risk-loving borrowers borrow up to limit)}$$

$$(5C.2)$$

Here m is the fraction of lenders' wealth that they hold in currency, and m^* is the supply of currency expressed as a fraction of lenders' wealth. On the normal assumptions about the partial derivatives of m, l_1, l_2, f_1 and f_2, it can be shown that the equilibrium yield of capital goes down when the currency supply is increased relative to lenders' wealth, that $\partial r_K/\partial m^*$ is negative, that the two $\partial r_L/\partial m^*$ are negative, while the two $\partial \gamma/\partial m^*$ may be of either sign.

APPENDIX 5D:[1] ASSET STATISTICS

Tables 5.1 and 5.2 present a historical breakdown of American private wealth into capital, money, and loans. Column one is the capital column. *Private capital* (PC) is the dollar value of the domestic private capital stock (business equipment and structures, inventories, residential structures, consumer durables, privately owned land) plus net foreign assets.

Net monetary assets (NMA) is the sum of currency outside the Treasury and the Federal Reserve System, bank reserves in Federal Reserve Banks, and U.S. government interest-bearing debt held outside Federal Reserve Banks and outside federal trust funds and agencies, minus deposits of the Treasury in private banks. NMA can be thought of as the assets in the private sector balance sheet that are canceled in the national balance sheet by government liabilities. Together NMA and PC represent net *Private Wealth* (PW).

TABLE 5.1
Assets in U.S. economy (in units of $ billion)

	Private capital, PC	Monetized capital, MC	Net monetary assets, NMA	Gross monetary assets, GMA
1920	342.0	30.3	30.5	60.8
1929	390.5	52.7	22.6	75.3
1941	365.6	36.4	83.9	120.3
1945	500.4	32.3	274.2	306.5
1950	940.3	71.9	277.0	348.9
1955	1277.2	130.1	300.4	430.5
1960	1633.7	204.9	304.3	509.2
1965	2075.6	364.9	331.1	696.0
1969	2897.9	491.2	381.0	872.2
1973	4340.7	836.2	479.9	1316.1
1979	9420.9	1485.2	867.5	2352.7
1983	12,827.9	2049.4	1430.8	3480.2
1989	17,540.6	3215.8	2993.8	6209.6
1992	17,545.5	3042.6	4209.9	7252.5

[1]Prepared by Joseph Boyer.

TABLE 5.2
**Shares of monetized capital (MC) in private
capital (PC) and in private wealth (PC + NMA)**

	MC/PC	MC/(PC + NMA)
1920	8.9	8.1
1929	13.5	12.8
1941	10.0	8.1
1945	6.5	4.2
1950	7.6	5.9
1955	10.2	8.2
1960	12.5	10.6
1965	17.6	15.2
1969	17.0	15.0
1973	19.3	17.3
1979	15.8	14.4
1983	16.0	14.4
1989	18.3	15.7
1992	17.3	14.0

   Gross monetary assets (GMA) is the sum of NMA and the net creation of money by the financial system, the monetary assets that have corresponding liabilities in the private balance sheet. It is calculated as the sum of NMA and deposits in commercial and mutual savings banks, savings and loan associations, credit unions, and the postal savings system, minus the deposits and currency held by these institutions, their reserves at the Fed, and their holdings of interest-bearing U.S. government debt. GMA is the holdings of monetary assets by the nonbank private sector.
   The monetization of capital by the banking system, then, can be calculated by subtracting NMA from GMA. This is column two, *Monetized capital* (MC). It can be thought of as both the net creation of money by the banking system (the creation of deposits minus bank holdings of monetary assets) and the loans made by banks to finance holding of capital.
   The sources of data for Table 5.1 and the accompanying figures are given in detail at the end of this appendix.
   Figure 5.14 breaks down GMA into NMA and MC by year. The height of the bar is NMA/GMA. MC/GMA is $1 - $ NMA/GMA and can be read as the distance between the top of the bar and the top of the graph.
   The ratio NMA/GMA depends on three factors: the money multiplier (m),[2] the ratio of privately held U.S. government interest-bearing debt (PHGD) to the monetary base H (PHGD/H), and the propensity of banks to hold government debt rather than to make private loans. The first and third factors determine how efficiently the banking system uses a given monetary base to monetize capital; a higher money multiplier means that more deposits are created from a given monetary base, and a lower propensity of banks to buy government debt means that a larger share of deposits finances private loans. The second factor determines what portion of NMA

---

[2]Here, what is meant by the money multiplier is the ratio of the nonbank public's currency and bank deposits of all kinds to the monetary base. See Chapter 9 for further discussion.

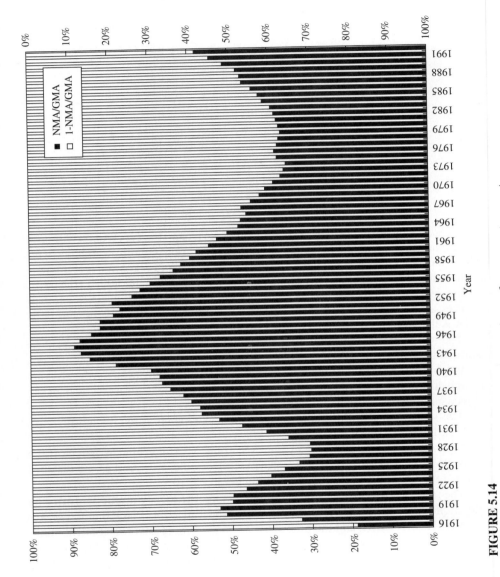

FIGURE 5.14
Net monetary assets and monetized capital as shares of gross monetary assets.

136

is available for the banking system to use for deposit expansion. If PHGD/H were to rise while NMA remains the same, private holdings of bank deposits would be smaller, and NMA/GMA would rise because more of the monetary base H would take the form of currency instead of bank reserves.

The NMA/GMA ratio rose during World Wars I and II chiefly because of an increase in government interest-bearing debt (and thus in PHGD/H). This has also accompanied the upward drift in the ratio since 1974 (Fig. 5.14). Movements in the money multiplier were the main force behind changes in NMA/GMA in the 1920s and 1930s. An increase of 250 percent in the money multiplier helped during the postwar decades, along with a 33 percent drop in PHGD/H, to bring the ratio down to 36 percent by 1974.

Changes in banks' holdings of government debt have also contributed to the movements in Fig. 5.14, especially during the Great Depression and World War II. At year-end 1945, banks held 47 percent of all interest-bearing U.S. government debt.

Figures 5.15 and 5.16, which graph those ratios in which the denominator is private wealth (PW, the sum of NMA and PC), show the importance of NMA, GMA, and MC in the private portfolio from 1916 to 1992. The black bar in Fig. 5.15 marks off the ratio NMA to PW. Large deficits to finance World Wars I and II greatly expanded the importance of government debt in the private portfolio—in World War II, NMA accounted for as much as a third of private wealth. After World War II, government debt declined in importance for four and a half decades, but today NMA/PW is back to the level of the mid 1950s. The insignificance of NMA in the private portfolio in 1916 serves to highlight the fact that the average NMA/PW ratio has been quite high in this period by historical standards.

The white bar in Fig. 5.15 denotes the ratio of GMA/PW, which need not follow NMA/PW for reasons explained above. Recently monetary assets have been as important in the national portfolio as in any other peacetime period.

Monetized capital has grown in importance over time, but irregularly. The difference between the two bars in Fig. 5.15, the difference between GMA/PW and NMA/PW, is MC/PW. This can be interpreted as an indicator of the contribution of the banking sector to the financing of capital accumulation. We can see from Fig. 5.16 that the relative importance of the monetization of capital in the national portfolio has varied substantially. In 1945 MC amounted to only about 4 percent of PW (6.5 percent of PC), whereas in the early 1970s MC was over 17 percent of PW and nearly 20 percent of PC.

Variations in MC/PW and MC/PC (Fig. 5.16) can occur for several reasons. They depend on the monetary base that banks have to work with and on how effectively that base is levered into bank loans. Another important factor has been increase in federal borrowing, which, by raising NMA and lowering MC (if banks buy part of the new debt), has tended to lower MC/PW.

Figure 5.17 compares GMA with a popular monetary aggregate, M2. The differences between the two are that GMA includes so-called large time deposits and interest-bearing government debt held by the nonbank public.[3] The figure shows

---

[3]Large time deposits comprise only a small part of the difference. Through most of the period, they amount to less than 5 percent of M2.

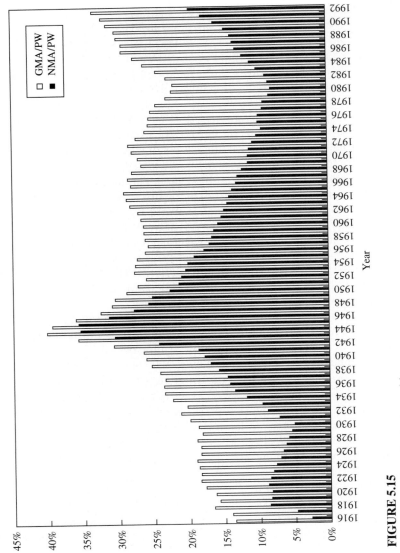

FIGURE 5.15
Monetary assets and private wealth.

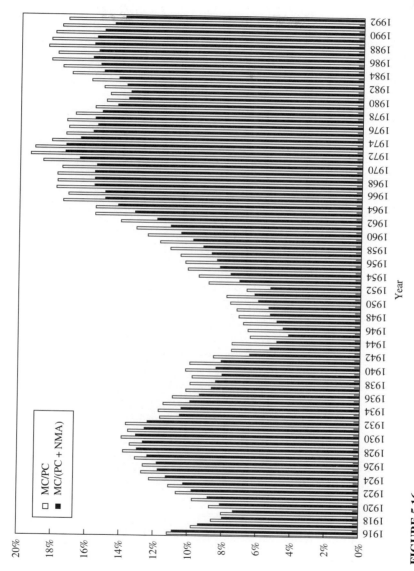

FIGURE 5.16
Monetized capital relative to private wealth.

139

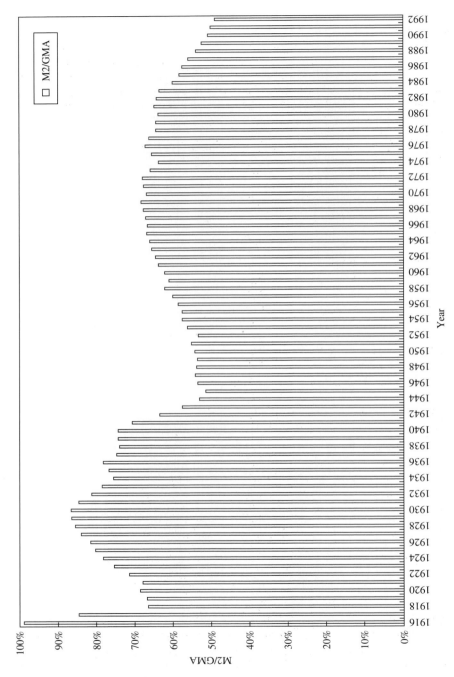

FIGURE 5.17
M2/GMA.

140

considerable variations in M2/GMA over long time periods, demonstrating that the two aggregates do not move in step. When government borrowing increases, GMA will tend to increase relative to M2. An increased propensity by banks to hold government bonds rather than private sector loans will decrease GMA relative to M2; in such an event, GMA may be a more successful indicator of how expansionary a particular monetary stance is, as discussed above. Increases in the monetary base or the money multiplier, ceteris paribus, will increase M2/GMA. The reasons for the movements in Fig. 5.17 are very similar to those for Fig. 5.14.

Sources of Data for Tables 5.1 and 5.2 and Figures 5.14, 5.15, 5.16, and 5.17

The following time series are non-seasonally-adjusted, end-of-year levels unless otherwise noted. Sources (in parentheses) are identified below.

Private capital

+Business inventories

1916–1944: (1) Column 13 minus column 17
1945–1992: (2) Included in "Reproducible Tangible Assets"

+Business plant and equipment, and residential structures

1916–1924: (1)
1925–1944: (12) Table A13, column 12
1945–1992: (2) Included in "Reproducible Tangible Assets"

+Consumer durables

1916–1924: (1)
1925–1944: (12) Table A18, column 2
1945–1992: (2) Included in "Reproducible Tangible Assets"

+Land

1916–1944: (1) Column 9 minus column 24
1945–1992: (2)

+Net foreign assets

1916–1948: (1) Column 25
1949–1970: (3) Series U26 minus series U33 minus series X417
1971–1992: (4) Various issues

Note: Net foreign assets here is the value of U.S. holdings of foreign assets, not counting the value of the U.S. monetary gold stock, minus the value of foreign holdings of U.S. assets. Between 1971 and 1989, the "net international investment position" series that values direct investments at book value was chosen. Between 1990 and 1992, the series that values direct investments at market value was used, for lack of an alternative. The value of the gold stock is subtracted from these series to obtain the one used here.

Net monetary assets

+ Currency in circulation

1916–1940: (7)
1941–1970: (6)
1971–1992: (5) "Monetary Authority" table, "vault cash of commercial banks" plus "currency outside banks"

+ Depository institution reserves in Federal Reserve Banks

1916–1937: (7) Table 85
1938–1944: (10) Table 29
1945–1992: (5) "Depository institution reserves" under "total liabilities" in "Monetary Authorities" table.

+ U.S. government debt

1916–1939: (7) Table 146
1940–1950: (6) Table 13.4
1951–1960: (9) Various issues
1961–1969: (6) Table 13.4
1970–1992: (9) Various issues

Notes: Includes debt of U.S. government agencies guaranteed by the Treasury between 1916 and 1960. Thereafter, includes only the debt of the U.S. Treasury. However, after 1960 there was very little guaranteed debt—less than $1.7 billion in 1978, less than $1.3 billion in 1988, none in 1992. Debt is valued at par.

− U.S. government deposits in banks

1916–1944: (8)
1945–1992: (5) "Checkable Deposits and Currency" table, "U.S. government deposits in commercial banks" plus "U.S. Government" table, "time deposits" under "assets"

− Trust fund and U.S. government agency holdings of U.S. government debt

1916–1941: (7)
1942–1950: (6)
1951–1960: (9) Various issues
1961–1970: (6)
1971–1992: (9) Various issues

Notes: Debt is valued at par. From 1916 to 1960, includes holdings of U.S. government agency debt guaranteed by the Treasury. After that, includes only the debt of the U.S. Treasury. Before 1935, year-end data are not available, so the June 30 holdings are used.

− Federal Reserve Bank holdings of U.S. government debt

1916–1939: (7)
1940–1970: (6) Table 13.4
1971–1992: (9) Various issues

Notes: Debt is valued at par. Includes Treasury and guaranteed debt until 1950; thereafter, excludes guaranteed debt.

Gross monetary assets: NMA +

+ Checking and other deposits

1916–1922: (8) Table 1.

Note: This data excludes U.S. government deposits. This was taken account of in constructing GMA.

1923–1937: Deposits in banks, (7) page 17 column 1, plus postal savings, (7) Table 154 column 1, plus savings and loan shares, (8) Table 1

1938–1944: Deposits in banks and the postal savings system, (10) Tables 27 and 28, plus savings and loan shares, (8) Table 1

1945–1964: Postal savings, (9), plus time deposits and savings accounts, (5), plus checkable deposits, (5)

1965–1992: Same as 1945–1964 less postal savings.

Note: After 1964 these postal savings were insignificant—$0.05 billion in 1967, 0 thereafter.

− Currency and deposits held by depository institutions

1916–1922: Vault cash of commercial banks, below, plus postal savings system holdings of currency and deposits from (7) Table 154

1923–1937: Vault cash of commercial banks, below, plus postal savings system holdings of currency and deposits from (7) Table 154 plus interbank deposits from (7) Table 2 column 8

1938–1944: (10) Table 27 line a3 plus line a20 plus Table 28 line b1

1945–1992: (5) "Commercial Banking" table, "vault cash of commercial banks" plus "currency and deposits" under "assets" plus currency and deposits held by thrifts, obtained from various tables

Notes: The deposits data for 1916–1922 are net of interbank deposits, so there was no need to obtain a separate series. Likewise, the Flow of Funds data used for commercial bank deposits in 1945–1992 net out most holdings of deposits by commercial banks.

− Depository institution holdings of U.S. government debt

Postal savings system

1916–1937: (7) Table 154

1938–1953: (10) Table 28

1954–1963: (9) Various issues

Notes: After 1963, PSS holdings are not included in depository institution holdings of U.S. government securities, but they were insignificant—$0 after 1968. These data do not include PSS holdings of guaranteed agency debt, except for the period 1938–1953.

Credit unions

1964–1992: (5) "U.S. Government Securities" table

Notes: Before 1964, credit union holdings are not included in depository institution holdings of U.S. government securities, but they were insignificant before that. (They were $0.3 billion in 1964.) These data do not include holdings of guaranteed agency debt.

Banks

1916–1939: (7) Table 2 column 5 and Table 7 column 5
1940–1963: (6) Table 13.4
1964–1992: (5) "U.S. Government Securities" table

Note: These data exclude guaranteed agency debt after 1950.

Savings and loans

1916–1963: (3) Series x840
1964–1992: (5) "U.S. Government Securities" table

Note: These data exclude holdings of guaranteed agency debt.
Note: All securities are valued at par.

   −**Depository institution reserves in Federal Reserve Banks (defined above).**

M2

M2

1916–1944: GMA minus U.S. government debt plus trust fund and U.S. government
   agency holdings of U.S. government debt and depository institution holdings of U.S.
   government debt.
1945–1958: calculated same way as 1916–1944, but large time deposits are also
   subtracted.
1959–1992: (11)

Large time deposits

1945–1958: (2)

Note: These are large time and savings deposit holdings of households and nonfinancial private business, plus $\frac{1}{2}$ of foreign holdings of U.S. time deposits.

Sources of error

The time series detailed above deviate from year-end, non-seasonally-adjusted levels of the time series they are intended to measure in the following minor ways:

Some of the observations from (1) may not be year-end.
The figures for the monetary gold stock of the United States, used to calculate net
   foreign assets, are annual averages rather than year-end.
All data from (8) are seasonally-adjusted.
The data on holdings of U.S. government debt by banks, savings and loans, federal
   trust funds, and U.S. government agencies are June 30 figures until 1935.
Between 1916–1944, savings and loan holdings of cash are included in GMA.
Between 1938 and 1944, the measure for holdings of cash by banks may include slight
   double-counting of holdings by mutual savings banks and the postal savings system.
Deposits in credit unions are not included in GMA in the prewar period.
Guaranteed agency debt, which perhaps should be created no differently than Treasury
   debt, is not included in NMA after 1960. See above concerning the subtraction of
   holdings of guaranteed agency debt by depository institutions from GMA.
The textbook definition of M2 is currency plus "small' time deposits minus the
   holdings thereof by the U.S. government and depository institutions. Here the
   measure of M2 includes all time deposits before 1945, and between 1945 and 1958
   subtracts a constructed measure of large time deposits.

These sources of error are relatively minor, probably amounting to less than 1 percent of the value of year-end GMA in all years except 1917–1918 and 1932–1935. In those years, depository institutions' holdings of U.S. government debt were growing, and the data used to subtract them from year-end GMA are June 30 figures. This may cause year-end GMA to be understated in those years by a few percentage points.

Sources

(1) Goldsmith, Raymond, *A Study of Saving in the United States*, Vol. 3, Table W-1.
(2) Board of Governors of the Federal Reserve System, *Balance Sheets for the United States Economy*, 1945–1993.
(3) *Historical Statistics of the United States.*
(4) Bureau of Economic Analysis, *Survey of Current Business.*
(5) Board of Governors of the Federal Reserve System, *Flow of Funds Accounts.*
(6) Board of Governors of the Federal Reserve System, *Banking and Monetary Statistics of the United States, 1941–1970.*
(7) Board of Governors of the Federal Reserve System, *Banking and Monetary Statistics of the United States, 1943.*
(8) Friedman, Milton, and Anna Schwartz, *Monetary Statistics of the United States.*
(9) Board of Governors of the Federal Reserve System, *Federal Reserve Bulletin.*
(10) Board of Governors of the Federal Reserve System, *Flow of Funds in the United States, 1939–1953.*
(11) Citibase.
(12) Bureau of Economic Analysis, *Fixed Reproducible Tangible Wealth in the United States, 1925–1989.*

CHAPTER 6

Financial Markets and Asset Prices

Chapters 3 and 4 examined portfolio choices of individuals facing asset prices given by the market and calculating their expectations of returns and their risks. This chapter turns to the dual problem of how asset prices are determined given their economy-wide supplies and the portfolio preferences of agents. It considers also the role of asset prices in stimulating new capital investment. A two-way relationship exists between the supplies of reproducible assets and their prices. The existing stocks, along with the market demands for them, determine asset prices. These prices in turn influence flows of new capital assets, altering the outstanding supplies.

The previous chapter introduced the concept of asset-market equilibrium in the context of a currency-capital economy, with and without a loan market. Consider again the currency-capital model without loans. In market equilibrium the stocks demanded must equal in money values the supplies of currency and capital. What if actual supplies and demands are not equal at existing prices and rates of return? Chapter 5, Section 5.2 discussed various adjustment processes.

Section 6.1 focuses on the way prices of existing capital assets relate to their replacement costs and influence the quantity of new investment. The role of the ratio of market value to replacement cost, q, is explained. Section 6.2 discusses standard models of asset prices—the capital asset pricing model (CAPM) and the so-called arbitrage pricing theory. Section 6.3 modifies CAPM to show how "fundamental" valuations of assets can be derived from expectations and risks of earnings, abstracting from other sources of variability in returns on assets.

6.1
VALUATIONS OF CAPITAL ASSETS AND THE q RATIO[1]

6.1.1 New and Used Goods

Markets for used durable producer and consumer goods are a central feature of capitalist economies. These may be markets for the goods themselves or for claims to them and their fruits. Direct used-goods markets provide ever changing market valuations of both nonreproducible real assets, like land and mineral deposits, and reproducible assets, like buildings and equipment. In the case of reproducible assets, the current cost of producing identical or competitive goods is obviously an important factor in the valuation of an existing good. Thus a rise in residential construction costs can be expected to raise the value of existing homes, and a rise in the price of new cars is good for the prices of previous years' models. The reverse is also true. High valuations of existing stocks will lead both to increased production and to higher prices of newly produced substitutes.

New and used prices can diverge significantly for extended periods of time, and the valuations of existing assets are more volatile than the costs or prices of their newly produced counterparts. An increase in the market valuation of houses relative to current cost of building will encourage residential construction. The incentive is the gain to be made by the excess of market price over replacement cost.

This profit is not wiped out immediately because construction takes time, and rapid construction is especially expensive, both for the individual builder and for the economy as a whole. In the longer run, however, the increase in the stock brings market value in line with replacement cost, lowering the former and possibly raising the latter. In equilibrium the volume of construction will meet demands for replacement and normal growth, and the size of the stock will be such that its market value is the same as its marginal production cost for the equilibrium volume of construction.

6.1.2 Business and Corporate Capital

The same mechanism applies to nonresidential structures and producers' equipment. But there is an important difference. The various physical assets of a business enterprise are often designed, installed, and used in complex combinations specific to the technology. It is costly or impossible to detach and move individual assets or to apply them to alternative purposes. The valuation of the business as a whole as a going concern is generally much more relevant than the separate valuations of the assets on used-goods markets.

Markets for businesses take several forms. Small unincorporated businesses are bought and sold directly or through brokers; see, for example, the advertisements in any Sunday *New York Times* or in trade journals. Corporations acquire other companies by buying their assets or their stock. Mergers and leveraged buyouts are heavily influenced by the market valuation of a company in relation to the expected

---

[1] This section draws on Tobin and Brainard (1977).

profitability of the company's assets as they are and as they would be in the proposed combination.

The most important markets are those for corporate securities. In these markets ownership of corporate businesses, and other claims upon their assets, change hands daily. The securities markets provide a continuing market valuation of each enterprise and thus indirectly of the productive assets of the company. These markets are well organized and technically efficient. Their valuations are sensitive and volatile. Here, even more than in used-goods markets, discrepancies arise and persist between the market valuations and the replacement costs of the assets the market is implicitly valuing. Here too the formation of new businesses and the expansion of existing ones can be expected to respond to those discrepancies.

The point was expressed succinctly by Keynes in *The General Theory* (p. 151):

> The daily revaluations of the Stock Exchange, though they are primarily made to facilitate transfers of old investments between one individual and another, inevitably exert a decisive influence on the rate of current investment. For there is no sense in building up a new enterprise at a cost greater than that at which a similar enterprise can be purchased; whilst there is an inducement to spend on a new project what may seem an extravagant sum, if it can be floated off on the Stock Exchange at an immediate profit.

This is the commonsense justification for paying attention to the ratio q of the market valuation of reproducible real capital assets to the current replacement cost of these assets. In the illustrative case of houses discussed above, q would be the ratio of the market value to the replacement cost, for an individual house or the aggregate stock. The same concept applies to a single business or to corporate business in aggregate, though replacement cost must be interpreted to cover not only physical assets but also other items on the firm's balance sheet. Note that the numerator of the ratio, the securities market value of a firm, includes not only stocks but also debt. The Modigliani-Miller theorem (1958) implies that this aggregate market value is independent of debt-to-equity ratios. This is a good first approximation, because ceteris paribus shareowners have to expect lower returns if a company incurs additional debt. But Section 6.2.3 below gives reasons why in practice market value, and therefore q, may not be independent of financial structure. See Tobin and Brainard (1977) for an empirical estimate of market values for corporations and the economy, in relation to capital structure and other factors.

Economic logic indicates that a normal equilibrium value for q is 1 for any reproducible assets which are in fact being reproduced, and less than 1 for others. Values of q above 1 should stimulate investment, in excess of requirements for replacement and normal growth, and values of q less than 1 should discourage investment.

The simplest model of valuation of an earning asset says that its present value is the sum of its earnings at all future dates, discounted to the present. For a house, the earnings are rents—cash or imputed, net of costs of operation and maintenance, taxes, and so forth. For the durable productive assets of a business, earnings are the gross products of capital earned over their lifetimes, that is, output less payments to other factors of production. For a share of stock, the earnings stream includes future dividends and other disbursements and subtracts allowances for depreciation, depletion, and obsolescence. The securities—debt, preferred stock, common stock—of a corporation are essentially claims to the earnings thrown off by the real productive capital assets of the business. The securities will rise in value when the market revises upward its expectations of future earnings or revises downward its discount rates. The discount rates applied to expected earnings represent, in principle, interest costs: rates of return that the investor must pay to borrow funds to hold the asset or must sacrifice by holding smaller amounts of other assets, adjusted for differences in perceived risk and in other asset properties.

The neoclassical theory of corporate investment is based on the assumption that the management seeks to maximize the present net worth of the company, the market value of the outstanding common shares.[2] An investment project should be undertaken if and only if it increases the value of the existing shares. Ideally, the securities markets appraise the project, its expected contributions to the future earnings of the company, and its risks. If the value of the project as appraised by investors exceeds the cost, then the company's shares will appreciate to the benefit of existing stockholders. That is, the market will value the project more than the cash needed to pay for it, whether the financing is obtained from retained earnings or from external funds. If new debt or equity securities are issued to raise the cash, the successful prospectus leads to an increase of share prices. To state the point another way, suppose the firm announces a project and proposes to finance it by selling additional shares at the going market price. Will the proceeds when invested suffice to purchase the earnings that justify that price? If they do so, with margin to spare, then the joint operation—share issue and investment—benefits the original shareholders.

Clearly it is the q ratio *on the margin* that matters for investment: the ratio of the increment of market valuation to the cost of the associated investment. The crucial value for marginal q is 1, but this is consistent with average q values quite different from 1. A firm with monopoly power, or with other sources of diminishing returns to scale, will have an average q ratio higher than its marginal q. The difference is the market's valuation of its rents or monopoly profits or good will.

A similar but conceptually distinct problem arises from the heterogeneity of capital goods and from technological progress. The average q ratio for existing capital stocks may be a serious understatement of q for new capital goods of a quite different nature. This occurs spectacularly when the new technology renders the old obsolete. This Schumpeterian phenomenon may occur within a single firm, but it is more likely to characterize whole industries or economies during periods of rapid innovation. It is conceivable to observe investment booms during periods when observed average q ratios are low and even declining.

Investment would not be related to q if instantaneous arbitrage could produce such floods of new capital goods as to keep market values and replacement costs continuously in line. Such perfect arbitrage does not occur. Discrepancies between q and its normal value do arise. The speed with which investment eliminates such discrepancies depends on the costs of adjustment and growth for individual enterprises, and for the economy as a whole on the short-run marginal costs of producing investment goods.

---

[2]The use of q does not necessarily imply a thoroughly neoclassical point of view, however, for reasons discussed in this section.

This is a different investment model from what appears to be the investment function of Keynes's *General Theory*. Keynes's condition—that the marginal efficiency of capital equals the rate of interest—determines not the flow of investment but the stock of capital. Specifically, it determines capital/labor and capital/output ratios. In a stationary economy, satisfaction of the condition—at whatever level of the interest rate—means zero net investment. In a growing economy, it means capital accumulation at the natural rate of growth of the economy. (Since the capital stock will be larger the lower the interest rate, gross investment in stationary equilibrium, and both gross and net investment in growth equilibrium, will also be larger the lower the interest rate. But these long-run steady-state relationships are clearly not what Keynes had in mind in postulating an inverse short-term relation between investment and interest rates.)

Since Keynes discusses at length independent variations in the marginal efficiency of capital and the rate of interest, he does not really imagine that investment adjusts the capital stock rapidly enough to keep them continuously equal. Indeed the true message is that investment is related to discrepancies between the marginal efficiency and the interest rate. This is the tradition of Wicksell and of Keynes's earlier work (1930).[3] The q theory of investment is in this tradition. Indeed under special conditions, q could be equivalently defined as the ratio of the marginal efficiency of capital R to the interest rate r_k used to discount future earnings streams.

This can be seen as follows. q is defined as

$$q = \frac{\text{MV}}{\text{RC}}, \tag{6.1}$$

where MV is market value and RC is replacement cost. Denoting the gross marginal product of capital by MPK and the depreciation rate by δ, the return on capital r for the interval is

$$r = \frac{\text{MPK}}{\text{MV}} + \frac{d\text{MV}}{\text{MV}} - \delta. \tag{6.2}$$

Equilibrium in the capital market obtains when the expected return on capital $E(r)$ is equal to the rate of return required by investors r_k. This can be written, from the definition of return in Eq. 6.2,

$$r_k = \frac{E(\text{MPK})}{\text{MV}} + \frac{d\text{MV}}{\text{MV}} - \delta. \tag{6.3}$$

Integrating Eq. 6.3 forward yields the familiar present value relationship, as in Chapter 2, Appendix 2A.

$$\text{MV} = \int_0^\infty E[\text{MPK}(t)]e^{-(r_k+\delta)t}\, dt. \tag{6.4}$$

---

[3]Gunnar Myrdal (1931, 1933) long ago anticipated q, even called it Q! However, his Q was not a ratio but the absolute difference between market value and replacement cost. His articles were in Swedish and German, never English, not known to the authors of q until Klaus Schmidt, a graduate student at Johann Wolfgang Goethe University in Frankfurt called them to the author's attention in 1994. See Schmidt (1995).

Equilibrium in the capital market can be viewed interchangeably as determining r_k or MV, which are inversely related.

The marginal efficiency of capital R is defined implicitly by the net rate of return on replacement cost, that is,

$$RC = \int_0^\infty E[\text{MPK}(t)]e^{-(R+\delta)t} \, dt. \tag{6.5}$$

In the special case where MPK is constant over time $RC = \text{MPK}/(R+\delta)$ and $MV = \text{MPK}/(r_k + \delta)$, so q can be expressed as a function of the marginal efficiency of capital and the discount rate:

$$q = \frac{R + \delta}{r_k + \delta}. \tag{6.6}$$

Several points deserve emphasis. First, the statistic q is observable as a ratio of market valuation to replacement cost, whereas R, r_k, and δ are not easily measured. Second, the discount rate is not any observed interest rate on long-term bonds or other fixed-money value obligations. Those interest rates are the discount factors for streams of payments with the risks and other characteristics of those instruments, while r_k is the discount rate for streams of return with the characteristics of earnings on business capital. The rates are related but not identical. Third, the rates r_k and R are in the same interest-rate *numéraire*. As discount for a stream of dollar earnings, they both would be nominal rates. As discount for a stream of earnings in constant dollars, they would be real rates. The ratio q is the same either way.

"Tobin's q" has been labeled a neoclassical theory of investment[4] and praised or criticized accordingly. There is some truth in the label, but also some misunderstanding. The literature contains q models that are more strongly neoclassical than Tobin's q. As noted above, if stock adjustment is costless, actual and desired stocks will always be equal. Tobin and Brainard (1977) cited the resource costs of adjustment to explain why capital stocks do not jump instantaneously in response to changes in marginal efficiencies and interest rates, but did not introduce such costs into a firm's formal dynamic optimization problem. This has been done by other writers (Hayashi, 1982). The shadow price of investment at any time is a q-like variable, the value to the firm of the future returns to a dollar's purchase of capital goods that makes just worthwhile the current rate of investment. This value will not necessarily be one or any other constant; it will be high when it is optimal for the firm to invest rapidly and incur high adjustment costs, low when it is optimal to invest little and economize on adjustment costs.

The logic here is similar to that of the neoclassical theory of a corporation seeking to maximize shareholder's values. But note that this formal q theory does not require any stock market. This q is not an observed or observable market price but an implicit shadow price. It is not an incentive for investment; rather it is determined jointly along with optimal investment. They are both functions of the data of the optimization problem, including the technologies of production and adjustment, expected prices, interest rates, and taxes.

---

[4]Crotty (1990). See Tobin and Brainard's (1990) reply, from which the next few paragraphs are adapted.

Empirically, it is quite obvious that stock market qs and formal implicit qs are not the same animals. Variations in marginal costs of adjusting capital stocks by investment would have to be implausibly large to be consistent with fluctuations in observed market valuations. Like Keynes's view, the position here is that the stock market does not grind out values by mirroring the rational optimizations of informed managements but generates values of its own. These nevertheless provide incentives or disincentives for investment. Tobin's q is so far from being a thoroughgoing neoclassical theory that it is quite consistent with recognition that corporate managers and other economic agents respond to market noise and are in any case sluggish in responding to the arbitrage opportunities of large deviations of q from par.

Figure 6.1 shows the historical pattern of q for 1900–1995. The effects of Tobin's q on investment have been investigated for many countries and time periods and received mixed empirical support, perhaps because of the practical difficulties of measuring q discussed above as well as the long and variable lags of firms' response to deviation of q from par. For empirical studies on the role of q in determining

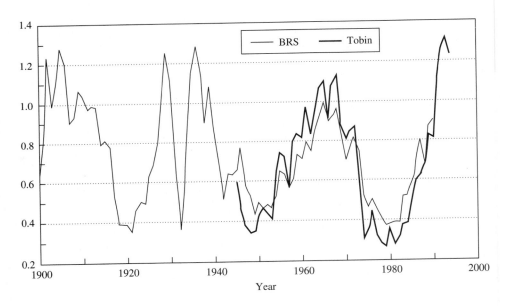

FIGURE 6.1

q ratio, 1900–1995.

Source: BRS estimates come from Blanchard, Rhee, and Summers, "The Stock Market, Profit, and Investment," *Quarterly Journal of Economics* 108 (February 1993), pp. 134–35. Tobin estimates are based on the Board of Governors of the Federal Reserve System's Flow of Funds data, year-end balance sheets for nonfinancial corporations. These reports give estimates of "tangible assets at replacement cost," the denominator of q. For the numerator, these data provide market value of equity but only book value, not market value, of corporate debt. It is necessary to convert book values into market values using series for corporate bond interest rates (Moody's AAA). The numerator of q is the sum of the market values of equity and long-term debt, less the net book values of financial working capital, short-term assets minus short-term liabilities, and land.

investment see, for example, Bischoff (1971), Ciccolo (1975), Von Furstenberg (1977), Summers (1981), Oulton (1981), Gordon and Veitch (1986), Chan-Lee and Torres (1987), Hayashi (1985), and Sensenbrenner (1991). In a recent comprehensive study of six Organization for Economic Cooperation and Development (OECD) countries' investment behavior, Sensenbrenner (1991) concludes that the q model works well when investment inertia is introduced.

6.1.3 A Stock-Flow Model of Investment and q[5]

This section formalizes the interaction of financial markets and the flow of new investment. In Fig. 6.2, the left-hand quadrant represents horizontally stocks at a point in time while the right-hand side depicts flows over a specified time interval. The demand for shares of claims on business—equities—by investors is a stock demand. A share represents one inflation-corrected dollar's worth of capital stock at its replacement cost. The demand for shares varies inversely with the market value of shares q for the two reasons mentioned in the introduction to this chapter. First, since r_k and q are inversely related as explained in the previous section, a rise in q lowers the rate of return on equities and therefore decreases the desired share of wealth in equities. Second, higher q raises the proportion of existing wealth held in equities, so investors need to sell shares just to return the wealth to its original proportion. The relationship between the quantity of capital K demanded at a point in time and q is

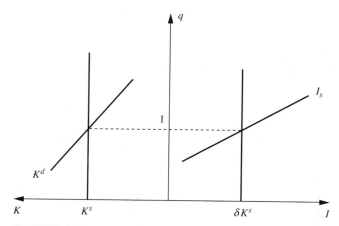

FIGURE 6.2
The stock demand for capital and the flow supply of new capital.

---

[5]Lerner (1940, p. 334) was the first to point out that there was a stock-flow confusion in Keynes's (1936, Ch. 11) investment function. See Clower (1954) and Witte (1963) for early expositions of the role of stock-flow interactions in capital investment. For a rational-expectations version of this model, see Blanchard (1981).

depicted in the left-hand quadrant of Fig. 6.2 as K^d. The stock supply of capital K^s at a point is time is predetermined by the past history of net investment and is therefore a vertical line. Note that net investment adds to the supply of equities outstanding even if financed by retained earnings, using the above definition of shares.

Recalling that δ denotes the rate of depreciation, the dynamic relationship between gross investment I and the capital stock K is

$$K_t = K_{t-1} + I_t - \delta K_{t-1} = (1 - \delta)K_{t-1} + I_t, \tag{6.7}$$

that is, the capital stock increases by the amount of net investment.

The flow supply of new capital goods—gross investment—is an increasing function of q for the reasons given above. Subject to the qualifications regarding marginal and average q, short-run gross investment supply I_s will be positively related to q as depicted in the right-hand quadrant of Fig. 6.2 for any given time period, for example, one year. The slope of I_s depends on the costs of adjustment. If arbitrage between the prices of new and used goods were instantaneous, I_s would be horizontal, that is, an infinite supply of new capital goods would be forthcoming as soon as the market price exceeded production cost. In this case q would always be equal to 1 for reproducible assets. The slower the adjustment process or the shorter the time period, the steeper the I_s curve will be. The long-run investment supply will be horizontal, as arbitrage will eventually eliminate any discrepancies between replacement cost and market value.

Assume for simplicity that the par value of q is 1. A long-run equilibrium for a stationary economy will be where $q = 1$ in the left-hand quadrant and where net investment is zero in the right-hand quadrant, as depicted in Fig. 6.2. In a growing economy, steady-state net investment would be positive to keep the capital/labor ratio constant.

The role of q in dynamic adjustment can be illustrated with an example. Consider a rise in the desired holding of equities by investors, for example, due to a fall in the discount rate r_k. There will be an instantaneous upward shift in K^d to $K^{d'}$ as shown in Fig. 6.3. Since the stock supply of capital is fixed in the short run, equilibrium jumps to point B where $q = q'$. The higher level of q now stimulates an increased flow of new investment I' as shown by point B in the right-hand diagram. Net investment is positive since gross investment now exceeds depreciation ($I' > \delta K^s$). Positive net investment implies a gradual increase in the stock of capital, and the economy converges to a new steady-state equilibrium at point C, where q has returned to 1, the stock of capital has increased to $K^{s'}$, and net investment is again zero. Note that the long-run investment function I_l is assumed to be horizontal as discussed above, and the new short-run investment flow curve passes through C. Also, gross investment is now higher in the new steady state because the capital stock and hence depreciation are higher.

A similar model of stock-flow interaction can be applied to the balance of payments, where the stock variable is the net foreign asset position of a country and the flow is the current account balance (Kouri, 1976). A steady-state equilibrium is where the current account balance is zero. The economy converges to a steady state through current account imbalances which gradually alter the supply of net foreign assets.

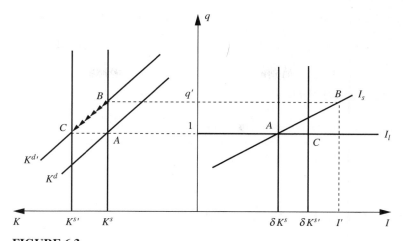

FIGURE 6.3
Adjustment to a rise in the stock demand for capital.

6.1.4 The Saving-Investment Nexus

The q theory concerns the interface between financial markets, including monetary events and policies, and real investments by nonfinancial enterprises and households. In practice, these influences are mostly indirect. Very few securities transactions are sales of new issues, and most new issues are for financial restructuring rather than for new real investments. In 1993, for example, nonfinancial corporations raised about $370 billion gross from security issues but only $75 billion net. Retained earnings of $90 billion, including foreign earnings retained abroad, were more than enough to finance capital expenditures of $85 billion (net of those financed by capital consumption allowances). The federal government, state and local governments, and financial and real estate enterprises all issued more securities than nonfinancial corporations.[6]

Translation of the saving of households into corporate business investment is a process that mainly occurs outside the securities markets, because retention of earnings gradually and irregularly augments equity values. Financial intermediaries facilitate transfers from surplus companies to deficit companies. For example, the traditional role of commercial banks is to facilitate the circulation of funds among businesses, channeling the temporary seasonal and short-run surpluses of some businesses to those businesses with temporary deficits. This circulation is closely connected with the diverse rhythms of accumulation and decumulation of inventories of finished goods, raw materials, and work in process, and of interbusiness accounts receivable and payable.

Although their direct role in financing business investment is limited, financial markets play an important indirect role by establishing asset prices and required rates of return, which influence investment even when financed by retained earnings. Management uses q as a guide whether to plow earnings into new investment or

---

[6]This paragraph is based on data from SEC Monthly Review and Federal Reserve Flow of Funds Accounts.

pay them out to shareowners. And if earnings are retained, large shareholders can nevertheless capture them in cash by selling some shares.

6.2
CAPITAL ASSET PRICING

This section discusses popular theoretical models of asset prices, the capital asset pricing model (CAPM), the consumption capital asset pricing model (CCAPM), and the arbitrage pricing theory (APT). Section 6.3 will then develop an alternative model drawing on the concept of q developed in the previous section.

6.2.1   The Capital Asset Pricing Model

CAPM was developed by Sharpe (1964) and Lintner (1965) by combining the separation theorem with the assumption of market clearing.

Assume that the conditions required for mean-variance analysis hold, that expected utility depends only on the mean μ and variance of return σ^2, and that there is one riskless asset in addition to a number of risky assets. The riskless asset has a rate of return of s. Assume also that all individuals perceive the same distribution of returns on all assets and that they can all borrow as well as lend at the rate s.

Let there be n risky assets, indexed by $j = 1, \ldots, n$, along with the one safe asset indexed by $j = 0$. The market portfolio of risky assets, which contains those assets in the proportions in which they are supplied, w_j, is denoted by m. The risky assets' gross returns have mean μ_j, standard deviation σ_j, and covariance σ_{jk} with other assets k. Individual investors i choose their portfolios; in aggregate, they must hold the market portfolio and the safe asset in the proportions in which they are supplied.

The central proposition of CAPM is

$$\mu_j - s = \beta_j(\mu_m - s), \quad \text{where } \beta_j = \sigma_{jm}/\sigma_m^2. \tag{6.8}$$

This is proved in detail in the appendix to this chapter.

Equation 6.8 can be interpreted to state that the "excess" return, or risk premium s, on any asset j—its expected return minus the returns on the safe asset μ_j—depends on its systematic or undiversifiable risk β_j and not on its own total risk σ_j. This undiversifiable risk β (which may be negative) reflects σ_{jm}, the covariation of the asset's rate of return with an overall market index of rates of return, in which assets are weighted by their relative supplies. If, for example, the asset's returns are independent of those on other assets, its undiversifiable risk reflects only its own weight in the index. An asset 's own risk does matter, but a single firm or particular security issue in a large economy will have a weight close to zero. On average, covariation of returns on business capital tends to be positive. Most equities have some undiversifiable risk. The risk premium of a particular asset depends on the amount of its undiversifiable risk and on a marketwide "price of risk," $\mu_m - s$. This common price of risk, reflecting the aggregate supplies of the riskless and risky assets and the risk preferences of investors, provides all the information required to value the undiversifiable risk associated with any particular asset or portfolio of assets. This simple and plausible interpretation, along with seeming ease of empirical testing, explains the popularity of the CAPM. The CAPM has been widely used in practical applications although empirical tests have yielded mixed results.

6.2.2 Extensions of the CAPM

In the 1970s and 1980s the CAPM was extended in two main directions, the intertemporal capital asset pricing model (ICAPM) and the arbitrage pricing theory (APT).

Merton (1973) generalized the CAPM to an intertemporal framework, using the techniques of stochastic calculus. He showed that a relation similar to Eq. 6.8 holds, but that expected returns on assets are also a function of their correlations with the state variables driving the economic system. That is, systematic risk is no longer characterized by the market portfolio alone but also by a vector of other state variables. Breeden (1979) simplified the Merton model back to a single driving variable, the level of aggregate consumption. In Breeden's model systematic risk is summarized by the behavior of aggregate consumption, so expected returns are determined by the covariance with aggregate consumption instead of the market portfolio as in the CAPM. This version has been labeled the consumption capital asset pricing model (CCAPM). Aggregate consumption, however, is an endogenous variable in macroeconomic and macroeconometric models, more a consequence of the state variables driving the economy than a summary of them.

Ross's (1976) development of the arbitrage pricing theory posited that returns are driven by a set of exogenous factors rather than one factor—the market portfolio or consumption. Undiversifiable risk is then associated with a number of factors, not just the market portfolio or consumption. A similar point was made in Chapter 4, Example 4.1 with a three-asset example—currency, bonds, and capital—and three factors— inflation, interest rates, and the relative price of capital goods. The expected return of a portfolio is governed by the factor loadings of the portfolio (the weights of the various risk factors) and the risk premia associated with each of the three factors. In Tobin and Brainard (1977), the same idea is applied to relate empirically the qs of individual companies to company characteristics as they interact with macroeconomic fluctuations.

6.2.3 Critical Assessment of CAPM and Its Extensions

The simplicity of the CAPM and its extensions reflects the special nature of the underlying assumptions. For example, all these models neglect transactions costs, which will limit the number of assets a typical investor can hold in his portfolio. The undiversifiable risk of a particular asset to him then depends on its covariation not with the entire market but with his own portfolio. Obviously an asset will be a higher proportion of any portfolio in which it is held than of the aggregate market "portfolio." Hence its own variance will be more important. In the extreme case where only one risky asset is held in each portfolio, its own variance is a complete and accurate measure of undiversifiable risk. In principle, it would be possible to relate risk premia to covariations with individualized portfolios, but as a practical matter, these are unobservable. The restrictions or economic limitations on the tradeability of assets make the estimation of undiversifiable risk difficult and increase the importance of assets' own variances.

Relaxing other assumptions—for example, the existence of a riskless asset, the possibility of borrowing and lending at the same rate, the homogeneity of expectations—further complicates matters. These complications not only make it difficult, conceptually and empirically, to measure the relevant risks on particular assets but also make it impossible to speak of, let alone estimate, a single price of risk.

There has been considerable empirical investigation of the effect of risk on the valuation of equities using the CAPM, the CCAPM, and the APT. Serious conceptual problems arise, however, in empirical applications of these models. First, Tobin and Brainard (1977) and Roll (1977) pointed out that even under the restrictive assumptions necessary for the simple CAPM, the list of assets in the market portfolio should not be limited to the stock market. At a minimum, corporate bonds as well as equities should be included. In principle, even the risks on less marketable assets, such as houses, consumer durables, and human capital, are relevant to the valuation of stocks and bonds. The APT and CCAPM were in part developed to deal with this criticism, although the extent to which the usual empirical applications capture the influence of the supplies of all marketable and nonmarketable assets is open to question.

Most people have little or no discretion regarding major components (assets and debts) of wealth in its widest sense. Consider human capital, the present value of future earnings from work, and tax liabilities. Management of the discretionary portfolio has to take into account the covariances of those financial assets with the nondiscretionary components of balance sheets.

Second, the valuation of a firm's productive business assets may depend importantly on the firm's financial structure. It is true that the celebrated Modigliani-Miller theorem says that a firm's valuation should be independent of its financial structure, implying that a firm could theoretically estimate the required rate on a new investment just by looking at the stock market and observing the market's valuation of equities whose distribution of earnings are proportional to those on the contemplated investment. But there are important reasons for believing that the valuation of a firm's physical assets and their returns cannot be divorced from its financial structure. These include corporate income taxation, which is not neutral regarding debt interest and dividends; the implications of leverage for probability of bankruptcy and loss of control; and economies of scale in borrowing, which enable stockholders to borrow more cheaply through the corporation than individually. Looking directly at the market valuation of firms' total earnings, interest as well as common stock earnings, requires less restrictive assumptions than looking separately at the firm's various securities.

Third, and most important, empirical studies of asset pricing rely on ex post data on security prices to estimate the means, variances, and covariances of asset returns.

The distribution of market yields reflects fluctuations of market discount rates as well as fluctuations in the firm's earnings. It is difficult to construct a "bootstrap" model of asset markets in which the risk characteristics of market yields used in the valuation of assets are consistent with the fluctuations in value generated by the market itself. Further, it is difficult to know how firms in making investment and financing decisions should react to changes in the market's valuation of risk that reflect speculative movements, or to changes in capitalization rates in response to investor preferences. The consumption capital asset pricing model is subject to a similar criticism. It makes more sense to relate portfolio (CCAPM) choice to endowment and income risk rather than consumption risk, because the latter is more endogenous to the investor's own behavior. For these reasons, Tobin and Brainard (1977), Tobin (1984a), Brainard et al. (1980), and Brainard et al. (1991) have developed "fundamentals" approaches to asset values, which take the direct and simple expedient of asking how the market values what the firm has to sell, namely the claims on prospective earnings associated with the firm's stocks of physical assets.

6.3
A "FUNDAMENTALS" APPROACH TO ASSET VALUES

The purpose of this section is to provide a reformulation of the capital asset pricing model (CAPM) that, by distinguishing between market valuations and fundamental valuations of equities, avoids the bootstrap circularity just discussed earlier. Here an equity is considered to be a title to the stream of earnings from a unit of physical capital at replacement cost. The fundamental valuation of such an asset is the valuation of those earnings. It excludes speculative capital gains and losses, arising from variations of the market prices of the equities.

The fundamental valuation takes account of earnings whether or not they are distributed as dividends. Reinvestment of retained earnings may be reflected in appreciation of actual equity issues, but such retention is really equivalent to issue of new shares. Thus, a share here is always title to one unit of capital at replacement cost. The purpose is to express the fundamental valuations as functions of the means, variances, and covariances of the joint probability distributions of the earnings per share of the basic risk assets.

The key to the fundamentals approach is a very primitive observation. Expected earnings and risks on equities, as defined above, are given to the economy as a whole independently of asset prices. Yet, the expected returns and risks of any individual investor depend on those asset prices. If MPK_j is the stochastic gross return on an equity at replacement cost and its price is q_j, then the stochastic gross return to the investor at market prices is[7]

$$r_j = MPK_j/q_j. \tag{6.9}$$

The higher q_j is, the lower will be the expected value of r_j, its variance, and the lower will be the absolute value of its covariance with any r_j. The key assumption of

---

[7]Gross return is 1 plus net return.

the fundamentals approach is that q is nonstochastic, that is, asset prices do not vary independently of the fundamentals. In the long run, as discussed at length in Section 6.1, q_j will tend toward 1, so the distinction between r_j and MPK_j holds only in the short run.

Let e_j, v_j^2, and v_{jk} be the expected value, variance, and covariance of MPK_j. As before, μ_j, σ_j^2, and σ_{jk} denote the mean, variance, and covariance of r_j. We can relate these variables using Eq. 6.9:

$$\mu_j = e_j/q_j, \tag{6.10}$$

$$\sigma_j = v_j/q_j, \tag{6.11}$$

$$\sigma_{jk} = v_{jk}/q_j q_k. \tag{6.12}$$

We can now reinterpret the capital asset pricing result, Eq. 6.8, which is restated here for convenience:

$$\mu_j - s = \beta_j(\mu_m - s), \qquad \text{where } \beta_j = \sigma_{jm}/\sigma_m^2.$$

Substituting Eqs. 6.10–6.12 into Eq. 6.8 yields, after some manipulation, the fundamentals version of the CAPM:

$$q_j - e_j/s = b_j(q_m - e_m/s), \tag{6.13}$$

where $b_j = v_{jm}/v_m^2$ is the fundamentals equivalent of CAPM's b. The significance of b is that it is based only on fundamentals: the covariance of an asset's return on replacement cost with the economy-wide return divided by the variance of the aggregate economy's return. Equation 6.13 states that an asset's fundamental value will depend on its fundamental b.

Although the betas here are fundamental, they are not immutable. For example, an increase in the supply of a risky asset relative to the supplies of the other risky assets or an increase in the correlation of its return with the economy-wide return will increase its b.

This fundamentals approach could be extended to a multibeta framework, as in the arbitrage pricing theory (APT). In fact, Tobin and Brainard (1977) in effect used a multiple-factor approach to study the market valuation of firms for 1960–1974. In that study the dependent variable was q for each firm. Cross-section regressions for each year used the following independent variables, meant to capture the characteristics of the firms: (1) the prior growth rate of earnings, (2) the cyclical sensitivity of earnings, (3) the covariance of the firm's earnings with aggregate earnings, (4) the volatility of the firm's earnings around trend, (5) the probability that earnings will fall short of fixed debt service charges, (6) the probability that earnings will fall short of fixed charges plus preferred and common dividends, (7) dividends divided by replacement cost, and (8) earnings divided by replacement cost. Note that (3) corresponds to the fundamental b from Eq. 6.13, while the other variables correspond to other sources of firm-specific or economy-wide risk. This formulation anticipated the APT approach but did not assume that all idiosyncratic risk is arbitraged away. Tobin and Brainard concluded that the theory of fundamental valuations discussed in this chapter was fairly well confirmed, although the weights the market placed on the different characteristics changed from year to year. In the recent parlance of the APT, the risk premia associated with the various factors are time varying.

6.4
FINANCIAL MARKETS IN PRACTICE[8]

6.4.1 Fundamentals and Bubbles

Do financial markets in fact generate fundamental values? There is no doubt that in the United States and other developed capitalist economies these markets are efficient in a technical sense. Stocks and bonds and other assets traded on organized markets are quite liquid—they can be sold at full current value on extremely short notice. And they are quite reversible—bid-asked spreads and other transactions costs are small. Moreover, prices in these markets reflect accurately all the generally available information up to the minute. Only traders with inside information can beat the market. What ordinary people know about a stock issue has already been "discounted," that is, reflected in the market price. While insider trading certainly occurs, the rules of the game in the United States, notably the regulations of the Securities and Exchange Commission, seek to minimize it.

Yet this technical efficiency does not guarantee that the asset prices generated in financial markets are fundamental values, based on rational expectations of the future returns to which ownership of the asset gives title. Efficiency in this sense is by no means implied by the technical efficiency just discussed. There are good reasons to be skeptical.

The fundamentals for a stock are the expected future dividends and other payouts, or what amounts in principle to the same thing, the expected future earnings. The stock's value is the present discounted value of either of these streams. The previous section showed how the discount rate depends on risks and on the rate of return on safe assets. Casual observation suggests that the market moves up and down much more than can be justified by changes in rationally formed expectations or in the rates at which they are discounted. This suspicion has been verified by Shiller and others.[9] Evidently market speculation multiplies several fold the underlying fundamental variability of dividends and earnings.

Shiller (1989, Section III) has also demonstrated the analogous empirical proposition for the bond market. The gross yield of a long-term bond is in principle a geometric average of gross short-term interest rates expected to prevail in sequence from now to the bond's maturity. Bond prices fluctuate much more than the variability of short rates can justify. Likewise, Golub (1983) and others have shown that exchange rates are excessively volatile relative to fundamental determinants such as money supplies and interest-rate differentials.

---

[8]This section draws on Tobin (1984b).
[9]See Shiller (1989, Section II) and Froot and Obstfeld (1991).

The takeover mania of the 1980s, motivated by egregious undervaluations, is testimony to the failure of the market to value corporations correctly. Evidently a takeover mobilizes enough capital to jump the price of the target stock to levels much closer to the fundamental value of the underlying assets. Ordinary investors might have detected the same undervaluations, but could not expect to profit from them unless and until other ordinary investors agreed or a takeover materialized. Takeovers serve a useful function if they bring prices closer to fundamental values. But why did markets not do so on their own?

Stock market crashes, like those of October 1929 and October 1987, during which stocks lost a quarter of their value without any discernible fundamental news, are further evidence of market irrationality. In both cases these losses were mostly reversed within a year. The rises of the Japanese land and stock markets in the mid-1980s and their collapse in the early 1990s seem to be clear-cut cases of bubbles. Similarly, the rise and fall of the dollar in the 1980s is difficult to reconcile with behavior of the fundamentals, and widely accepted exchange-rate models perform badly in tracking the behavior of exchange rates out of sample.

Professional economists generally are disposed to give markets the benefit of doubts, but since 1980 the behavior of securities and foreign exchange markets has spurred a burgeoning literature on bubbles and "noise traders."[10]

Keynes (1936, Chapter 12) likened the stock market—and he referred particularly to the American market—

> to those newspaper competitions in which the competitors have to pick out the six prettiest faces from a hundred photographs, the prize being awarded to the competitor whose choice most nearly corresponds to the average preferences of the competitors as a whole; so that each competitor has to pick, not those faces which he himself finds prettiest, but those which he thinks likeliest to catch the fancy of the other competitors, all of whom are looking at the problem from the same point of view. . . . [W]e have reached the third degree where we devote our intelligences to anticipating what average opinion expects the average opinion to be. And there are some, I believe, who practice the fourth, fifth, and higher degrees.

Speculations on the speculations of other speculators who are doing the same thing—those are bubbles. They dominate the pricing of assets with negligible fundamentals, zero or vague or nontransferable returns, as discussed in Chapter 2, Section 2.1. Gold and collectibles, for example, derive value almost wholly from guesses about the opinions of future speculators. But bubbles are also, as Keynes observed, phenomena for markets in equities, long-term bonds, foreign exchange, commodity futures, and real estate.

Keynes, himself an active and experienced market participant, despaired of "investment based on genuine long-term expectation . . . . There is no clear evidence from experience," he said, "that the investment policy which is socially advantageous coincides with that which is most profitable." He noted that professionals who bet on long-term fundamentals, while everyone else is engaged in short-term

---

[10]See the work by Summers and his coauthors [Cutler et al. (1990), Delong et al. (1990)] on noise traders, and Meese (1990) and Frankel and Froot (1988) for evidence of irrationality in the foreign exchange market.

attempts "to guess better than the crowd how the crowd will behave," run greater risks. Not least of these is the criticism for unconventional and rash investment behavior.

Keynes's views would be confirmed today if he observed how professional portfolio managers seek safety from criticism in short-run performances that match their competitors and market indices. Market participants try to guess how others will react to macroeconomic news items, such as reports of employment and inflation, and bet in the markets that actual news will differ from what others expect. They focus on macroeconomic news that they believe may influence Federal Reserve policy decisions at the coming meetings (eight per year) of the Federal Open Market Committee. Weekly announcements of money supply statistics, M1 and M2 growth rates, were once the obsessive focus of Wall Street. When the Fed was perceived to have abandoned M targets and to gear its policy moves to direct measures of macro performance, unemployment and inflation, those statistical releases replaced the M announcements as the focus of speculative activity. Data thought to worry the Fed about inflation and perhaps to raise short-term interest rates often send bond markets down, and stock markets too—even though the news may be optimistic about business activity and profits. The markets appear to exaggerate the effects of minor blips in monthly time series on Fed policies and of small adjustments in monetary policy on the long-run performance of the economy and corporate business.

Keynes's pessimism on the long-term rationality of securities markets led him to the view that the liquidity these markets provide is a mixed blessing. "The spectacle . . . has sometimes moved me towards the conclusion that to make the purchase of an investment permanent and indissoluble, like marriage [sic!] except by reason of death or other grave cause, might be a useful remedy . . . ." But he concluded that illiquidity would be the worse evil, because it would push savers towards hoarding of money. Today that disadvantage seems less serious than when Keynes was writing, during the Great Depression. Anyway he wrote favorably of a "substantial . . . transfer tax. . . [which] might prove the most serviceable reform available, with a view to mitigating the predominance of speculation over enterprise in the United States." By its very nature a transactions tax discourages short-term in-and-out speculation while leaving long-term investments relatively unscathed.

Similar reasoning may justify an international transfer tax on transactions across currencies (Tobin, 1978). Besides penalizing quick round-trips across currencies, the source of speculative volatility on exchange rates, this tax would give national monetary authorities more independence. The tax would limit the cross-currency arbitrage that tends to equate money market interest rates. The real economies of the world, even the twenty-five major industrialized economies in the Organization for Economic Cooperation and Development (OECD) or the seven big economic powers (G-7), are insufficiently integrated to make a single international currency viable. Consequently national central banks still need autonomy in policy, but ever more massive and mobile private funds leave them with reserves utterly inadequate to protect themselves. The tax would have to be uniformly levied by most or all members of the International Monetary Fund. It would be appropriate to dedicate much of the revenue to international purposes.

As Keynes was pointing out, there is a tradeoff between liquidity (and reversibility) and stability in financial markets. As explained in Chapter 1, the assets traded in those markets are essentially and ultimately claims on quite illiquid and very specific physical capital goods. Individuals can exchange the claims at will, and even consume them, while such transactions in the underlying assets would be difficult, costly, or impossible. What individuals can do one at a time, the society would not be able to do all at once. In that sense the liquidity of financial markets is potentially illusory, like the liquidity of commercial bank deposits. It is a useful property, but some infringement of it may be justified to diminish speculative volatility. As Keynes saw even in his day, the advantages of the liquidity and negotiability of financial instruments come at the cost of facilitating nth-degree speculation which is shortsighted and inefficient.

6.4.2 The Asset Menu

Financial markets perform important functions. They enable individuals and families to adjust the timing of their consumption—month to month, year to year, decade to decade, generation to generation—so that it is not the slave of their cash incomes. Thanks to mortgages and consumer debts, they can enjoy houses, cars, other consumer durables, and vacation trips before they have earned and saved the funds to pay for them. On the other hand, they can save in a variety of forms for annuities in their old age and for support of their dependents and heirs. They can buy insurance against death, disability, ill health, accidents, property losses. As illustrated in previous chapters, they can take more or less risk in their portfolios; markets will allocate the irreducible risks of economic life in accordance with the diverse risk preferences of wealth owners.

Future markets allow businesses and farmers to hedge against events that might alter spot prices of commodities they will be buying or selling. Capital markets enable fundamental risks of business enterprise to be taken by the adventurous, while risk averters content with lower average returns are protected from many possible sources of loss.

But the system could do better. For example, consider the long-term level payment mortgage. It was a great invention. But mortgage instruments with payments that conform closely to typical earnings profiles and are flexible in maturity would be helpful to young families, especially in inflationary times. Likewise, older households whose equity in homes is the major part of net worth do not find it easy to consume such wealth while retaining occupancy and ownership, although home equity loans and reverse mortgages are making this increasingly possible. Consumer credit permits households to advance consumption in time and age, though at what are sometimes exorbitant interest rates. Borrowing against future earnings, against human capital, is much more difficult than against negotiable financial or physical assets. Educational loans would not be generally available without government guarantees and subsidies. They could be longer in term, and lengths and even amounts of repayment could be contingent on the debtors' actual earnings.[11]

---

[11] A number of economists and educators, including Milton Friedman (1962, Ch. 6) have advocated student loans with repayment linked to earnings. Yale University offered such loans for several years but discontinued the plan because these unconventional loans were not eligible for federal subsidies and guarantees.

New financial instruments and markets have proliferated in recent years, and it might be thought that the enlarged menu now spans more contingencies and permits average citizens to insure themselves more fully against risks they confront. But the new options, futures contracts, and elaborate derivatives do not stretch very far into the future. They serve mainly to allow leverage to short-term speculators and arbitragers, and to limit losses in one direction or the other. Collectively, they contain considerable redundancy. Every financial market absorbs private resources to operate and government resources to police. The country cannot afford all the markets and instruments that enthusiasts may dream up.

One obvious contingency that our system left uncovered is inflation, until 1997, when the Treasury began issuing bonds indexed by the Consumer Price Index. Equities should be in principle a good hedge, because they are claims to physical goods whose prices would share any general inflationary trend. But in short runs they are vulnerable to the nexus from inflation to restrictive monetary policy to recession or stagflation, as described above and experienced in the 1970s. Short-term nominal interest rates are better correlated with inflation; consequently variable interest instruments provide some protection to both debtors and creditors. It is not clear why private financial institutions cannot take the next step and develop price-indexed instruments for both savers and borrowers. These institutions are better placed than the general public to assume the risks of deviations of interest rates from inflation rates. Now that the federal government issues indexed bonds, financial intermediaries will be able to offer indexed instruments tailored in maturities and denominations to the needs of savers and borrowers.

What index should be used? The present Consumer Price Index is not wholly appropriate. There is a case for excluding changes in the country's external terms of trade, from shocks to prices of oil or other imports and from swings in the foreign exchange value of the dollar. Likewise there is a case for excluding changes in indirect business taxes. These CPI movements are essentially uninsurable for the nation as a whole. An index purged of them is preferable for wage contracts and social insurance benefits, as well as for new financial instruments. The government would do well to leave betting on these events to the private sector.

CONCLUSION

Like Keynes in the *General Theory,* this chapter has combined skepticism about the efficiency of financial markets with recognition of the important role that financial markets play in a market economy. Keynes's stress on the macroeconomic role of financial markets through their influence on volume of capital investment has been affirmed and extended through the concept of q. But Keynes's characterization of financial markets as a beauty contest also rings as true today as when he wrote it. If financial markets are subject to such fads and bubbles, the implementation of the CAPM and APT with ex post data on security prices or returns is problematic. This is a reason for a fundamentals approach based on the underlying characteristics of the assets rather than the ex post realizations of market returns. The exercise of fundamental valuations focuses on the basic returns that are available to portfolio owners and the basic risks that they must somehow assume, and it asks at what prices these supplies will be equal to the amount demanded. But of course it is not to be expected that these are observed market prices. Deviations from fundamentals are a zero-sum game, in which some investors win and others lose. In this sense the fundamentals approach focuses on social rather than private valuations.

APPENDIX 6A

6A.1
THE SEPARATION THEOREM AGAIN

The individual investor i's optimization problem is to choose the portfolio shares w_{ij} to maximize utility:[12]

$$\max U_i(\mu_i, \sigma_i^2), \quad U_{i1} > 0, \quad U_{i2} < 0. \tag{6A.1}$$

Portfolio expected return μ_i is a weighted average of asset expected returns μ_j, with $\mu_0 = s$, the return on the safe asset.

$$\mu_i = \sum_{j=0}^{j=n} w_{ij}\mu_j = w_{i0}s + \sum_{j=1}^{j=n} w_{ij}\mu_j = s + \sum_{j=1}^{j=n} w_{ij}(\mu_j - s), \tag{6A.2}$$

which makes use of the adding-up constraint $w_{i0} = 1 - \sum_{j=1}^{j=n} w_{ij}$. Portfolio variance is a function of the variances and covariances on all risky assets:

$$\sigma_i^2 = \sum_{j=1}^{j=n}\sum_{k=1}^{k=n} w_{ij}w_{ik}\sigma_{jk}. \tag{6A.3}$$

Using bold characters to denote vectors and matrices, note for use below that Eqs. 6A.2 and 6A.3 can be written respectively as

$$\mu_i = s + \mathbf{w}_i'(\boldsymbol{\mu} - s\mathbf{1}), \tag{6A.2a}$$

$$\sigma_i^2 = \mathbf{w}_i'\boldsymbol{\Omega}\mathbf{w}_i. \tag{6A.3a}$$

$\mathbf{w}_i$ is the vector of portfolio weights, $\boldsymbol{\mu}$ is the vector of expected returns on the risky assets, $\mathbf{1}$ is a vector of ones, and $\boldsymbol{\Omega}$ is the variance-covariance matrix. Substituting Eqs. 6A.2 and 6A.3 into Eq. 6A.1, the first-order condition for a maximum is

$$U_{i1}(\mu_j - s) + 2U_{i2}\sum_{k=1}^{k=n} w_{ik}\sigma_{jk} = 0, \quad j = 1,\ldots,n. \tag{6A.4}$$

---

[12] An alternative way of obtaining the optimal weights, w_{ij}, is to minimize variance σ_n^2 subject to the condition that expected return μ_i is constant.

The second-order condition for a maximum holds under risk aversion; that is, $U_{i2} = \partial U/\partial \sigma_i^2$ is negative.

Equation 6A.4 defines a system of j simultaneous equations. Solving by matrix inversion yields asset demand functions, which can be expressed in matrix form as follows:

$$\mathbf{w}_i = T_i \mathbf{\Omega}^{-1}(\boldsymbol{\mu} - s\mathbf{1}), \tag{6A.5}$$

where $\mathbf{\Omega}^{-1}$ is the inverse of the variance-covariance matrix of returns on the risky assets, and $T_i = -U_{i1}/2U_{i2}$ is a measure of investor i's risk tolerance. Under the assumption that all investors face the same probability distribution of returns, only T_i is specific to investor i.

Equation 6A.5 states the separation theorem (Tobin, 1958). Individual attitudes toward risk are embodied in the parameter T_i. But Eq. 6A.5 implies that the ratio of any two risky asset holdings w_j/w_k is independent of T_i. w_j/w_k is therefore the same for all investors, that is, each investor i will hold risky assets j and k in the same proportions. T_i affects only the proportion of wealth invested in the safe asset relative to the common bundle of risky assets.

The separation theorem has been derived here under the restrictive set of assumptions spelled out above. It fails if, for example, there are different borrowing and lending rates, so that the individual's portfolio choice cannot be reduced to a two-fund problem. See Chapter 4, Fig. 4.14, for a graphical analysis of a simple case where borrowing and lending rates differ. However, a modified separation theorem can be derived when some of the assumptions of the CAPM are dropped.[13] For example, if there is no riskless asset it can be proved that Eq. 6A.5 becomes

$$\mathbf{w}_i = T_i(\mathbf{\Omega}^{-1}\boldsymbol{\mu} - \lambda_i \mathbf{\Omega}^{-1}\mathbf{1}), \tag{6A.5a}$$

where λ_i is a Lagrange multiplier associated with the constraint that $\sum_i w_{ij} = 1$. Equation 6A.5a says that portfolio choice can still be separated into two mutual funds that are independent of preferences, $\mathbf{\Omega}^{-1}\boldsymbol{\mu}$ and $\mathbf{\Omega}^{-1}\mathbf{1}$.

Similarly, when there is a nonmarketable asset H, Eq. 6.13 becomes

$$\mathbf{w}_i = T_i \mathbf{\Omega}^{-1}(\boldsymbol{\mu} - s\mathbf{1}) - \mathbf{\Omega}^{-1}\boldsymbol{\sigma}_{ih}, \tag{6A.5b}$$

where $\boldsymbol{\sigma}_{ih}$ is the vector of covariances of the risky assets with the nonmarketable asset H of individual i. Equation 6A.5b says that holdings of risky assets consist of a mix of a "tangency" portfolio $\mathbf{\Omega}^{-1}(\boldsymbol{\mu} - s\mathbf{1})$, which is the same as the standard CAPM market portfolio, and a "hedging" portfolio $\mathbf{\Omega}^{-1}\boldsymbol{\sigma}_{ih}$. The hedging portfolio derives from the fact that an investor can lower risk by investing in assets that are weakly or negatively correlated with the returns on her nonmarketable asset. That is, holdings of asset k are inversely related to σ_{ikh}, the covariance of asset k with the nonmarketable wealth of individual i. This suggests, for example, that an individual may wish to avoid investing in the stocks of the company she works for, if labor and capital incomes are correlated. See Brainard and Dolbear (1971) for further discussion of the gains from diversifying risks of nonmarketable assets.

---

[13] See Brennan (1989) for more details and references.

6A.2
MARKET CLEARING AND THE CAPM

The capital asset pricing model is derived by combining the separation theorem (Eq. 6A.5) with the assumption that the markets for assets clear. The market-clearing condition is that the outstanding supply Z_k of any asset k, measured in physical units or shares of replacement cost, is equal to the sum of the individual demands for shares, z_{ik},

$$Z_k = \sum_i z_{ik}. \tag{6A.6}$$

To express Eq. 6A.6 in value rather than physical terms, let q_k be the market-clearing price of asset k. Measured at market prices, individual i's wealth W_i, the aggregate market value of all assets MV, and w_{ik}, w_{mk} can then be defined as the shares of asset k in the individual and market portfolios respectively:

$$W_i = \sum_k q_k z_{ik}, \tag{6A.7a}$$

$$MV = \sum_k q_k Z_k, \tag{6A.7b}$$

$$w_{ik} = \frac{q_k \cdot z_{ik}}{W_i}, \tag{6A.7c}$$

$$w_{mk} = \frac{q_k \cdot Z_k}{MV}. \tag{6A.7d}$$

Multiplying both sides of Eq. 6A.7a by q_k and substituting in Eqs. 6A.7c and 6A.7d, we can express the market-clearing condition for asset k,

$$MV w_{mk} = \sum_i w_{ik} W_i, \tag{6A.8a}$$

and in vector format, for all assets

$$MV \mathbf{w}_m = \sum_i W_i \mathbf{w}_i. \tag{6A.8b}$$

Substituting Eq. 6A.5 into Eq. 6A.8b yields, after rearranging,

$$\mathbf{w}_m = T_m \mathbf{\Omega}^{-1}(\mathbf{\mu} - s\mathbf{1}), \tag{6A.9}$$

where $T_m = \sum_i (T_i W_i / MV)$. Equation 6A.9 can be rewritten as

$$\mathbf{\mu} - s\mathbf{1} = T_m^{-1} \mathbf{\Omega} \mathbf{w}_m. \tag{6A.10}$$

Premultiplying by $\mathbf{w}_m$ yields, using the definitions of Eqs. 6A.2a and 6A.3a,

$$\mu_m - s = T_m^{-1} \sigma_m^2. \tag{6A.11}$$

Using Eq. 6A.11 to eliminate T_m in Eq. 6A.10, and premultiplying Eq. 6A.10 by any chosen portfolio p consisting of weights $\mathbf{w}_j$ yields the CAPM relationship:

$$\mu_p - s = \beta_p(\mu_m - s), \qquad \text{where } \beta_p = \sigma_{pm}/\sigma_m^2. \qquad (6A.12a)$$

Alternatively, interpreting the portfolio as a single asset j, the CAPM states

$$\mu_j - s = \beta_j(\mu_m - s), \qquad \text{where } \beta_j = \sigma_{jm}/\sigma_m^2. \qquad (6A.12b)$$

CHAPTER 7

The Banking Firm: A Simple Model[1]

Commercial banks have been historically the most important kind of financial intermediary. In the United States in the 1980s, the distinctions between commercial banks and other banks and certain other institutions were greatly diminished. Savings banks and savings and loan institutions now operate in ways similar to commercial banks, have similar assets and liabilities, compete with each other and with commercial banks for business, and are subject to similar governmental regulations. The official generic term for them is depository institutions, but it is convenient to refer to them just as banks. Banks' liabilities are the closest privately issued substitutes for government currency. Demand deposits serve as means of payment generally acceptable for most transactions. For several reasons, depositors bear very little of the risks of the loans the banks make. There are economies of scale in pooling of default risks specific to borrowers and in specialized administration and appraisal of the loans. The banks' shareholders assume the residual risk; only after their equity is wiped out would depositors' claims be jeopardized. Finally, the government stands behind bank deposit liabilities, both as lender of last resort to tide banks over crises of illiquidity and as insurer of deposits against the contingency of insolvency.

Government monetary and credit policy operates mainly through the banking system, and this is the principal reason today to give special attention to banks. Historically the first reason for government intervention in the banking business was to protect depositors (or in older times bank note holders) against the risks of bank illiquidity and insolvency. But the public regulations and institutions established for this purpose can also be used to regulate credit markets in the interests of economic stabilization, maintenance of the value of the currency, or other government objectives. As the protective purpose of government intervention seemed to have been achieved, these other objectives came to dominate relations of government to the banking system.

This chapter presents a primitive theory of a single banking enterprise. It refers principally to the traditional distinctive function of banks, to buy and hold assets of

---

[1] An earlier version was published as Tobin (1982).

longer maturity and less liquidity than their liabilities. The bank's decision problem is an important example of the *precautionary* motive for holding cash or other safe liquid assets, discussed in Chapter 3, Section 3.2.2.2.

In recent years banks, large banks especially, have increasingly become brokers, buying and selling marketable assets and liabilities more closely matched in maturity and liquidity, and attempting to use their market expertise and access to funds to exploit opportunities for arbitrage and innovation in derivative instruments. The approach of this chapter does not apply to such business.

The models of this chapter, like those throughout the book, refer principally to United States institutions. Because of legal limitations on branch banking, the American system contains many more banking firms and is more decentralized and competitive—monopolistically competitive in Chamberlin's sense—than those of other economies. The legal framework and central banking institutions assumed also conform to American practice. Nevertheless, the basic messages of the model have wide applicability.

7.1
THE PORTFOLIO CHOICES OF A BANK

In a first approximation to understanding the nature of the business decisions confronting a banker, the assets of a bank may be divided into two categories: loans and investments and defensive assets. *Loans and investments* are in the short run either illiquid or unpredictable in value. To be sure of realizing their full value, the bank must hold them to maturity. Consequently, these assets can be available for meeting deposit withdrawals only at some risk of loss. It may indeed be impossible to sell or to borrow against certain loans. *Defensive assets* are, in contrast, assets of very high liquidity. The bank knows that they can be sold, or borrowed against, without loss or delay. Defensive assets include currency, deposits in the central bank, deposits in other banks, overnight loans to other banks (known as federal funds in the United States), well-secured call loans, Treasury bills, and other paper of equivalent quality and eligibility to serve as collateral. In this usage the term covers both *primary reserves* and *secondary reserves,* that is, both those assets that qualify as legal reserves and those that are so readily convertible into legal reserves that the banks can regard them as their virtual equivalent.

Law or convention generally requires the bank to hold a certain quantity of defensive assets, the bank's required reserves. Under the Monetary Control Act of 1980, depository institutions in the United States are required to hold in currency or on deposit in a Federal Reserve Bank 10 percent of demand deposits and other checkable accounts. (For small banks, those with net transactions accounts not exceeding $46.8 million, the requirement is only 3 percent.) Since 1990 no reserves have been required against any other liabilities, even time certificates of deposit. The Board of Governors of the Federal Reserve System has some discretion, within limits set by Congress, to set reserve requirements.

A bank's holdings of defensive assets will almost always exceed its required reserves. But some of these holdings may be offset by short-term or overnight borrowing from other banks or from the central bank. The amount by which the bank's *net* holdings of defensive assets exceed its required reserves will be called its *defensive position.* For it is this margin that measures the bank's ability to meet reserve requirements if it should be confronted with unusual deposit withdrawals or extraordinary demands for loans. In this contingency the bank can draw down its deposits in other banks, or fail to renew overnight loans of federal funds to other banks, or present maturing Treasury bills for cash instead of new bills, or borrow money on the collateral of Treasury bills, or sell bills either outright or with agreement to repurchase them.

The basic accounting identity for the commercial bank (abstracting from its physical assets and other minor accounts) is

Deposits + shareholders' equity = required reserves + defensive position
+ loans and investments.

Figure 7.1 displays this accounting identity graphically, and also sets forth some other definitions and classifications that will be useful.

It is convenient simplification to distinguish three kinds of bank decisions: (1) the sizes of the two broad asset categories, the loan and investment portfolio and the net defensive position; (2) the management of the defensive position: the kinds and amounts of primary or secondary reserve assets held, and the amount of short-term borrowing; and (3) the composition of the loan and investment portfolio. This chapter concerns mainly the first decision, discusses some aspects of the second, and does not treat the third.

7.2
THE BANK'S DEPOSITS

The volume of deposits in a bank is partly within and partly outside its control. The location of a bank, in both a geographic and an economic sense, gives it a natural clientele of depositors. The bank can seek to increase its attractiveness to depositors by the interest rates it offers on deposits, by the quality and costs of its services, and by the usual media of indirect competition—the splendor of the building, the organ music and the lollipops for children, the advertising, the cultivated identification with community service, and so on. However, some of these forms of competition for deposits are at times limited by law or by explicit or tacit convention. In the United States, banks are prohibited from paying interest on demand deposits of businesses. Until the 1980s they could not exceed legal ceilings for interest on other checkable deposits, passbook savings accounts, and certain time deposits.

A bank may be able to influence the level of its own deposits more directly. When a bank makes a loan to one of its customers, it simply credits the amount to the borrower's account. In the first instance, therefore, the bank's deposits are increased dollar for dollar with its loans. As the borrower spends the proceeds by check, some of the recipients will leave the money on deposit with the lending bank, while others will deposit their receipts in other banks or convert them into currency. As these recipients spend their balances and as succeeding generations of transactions occur,

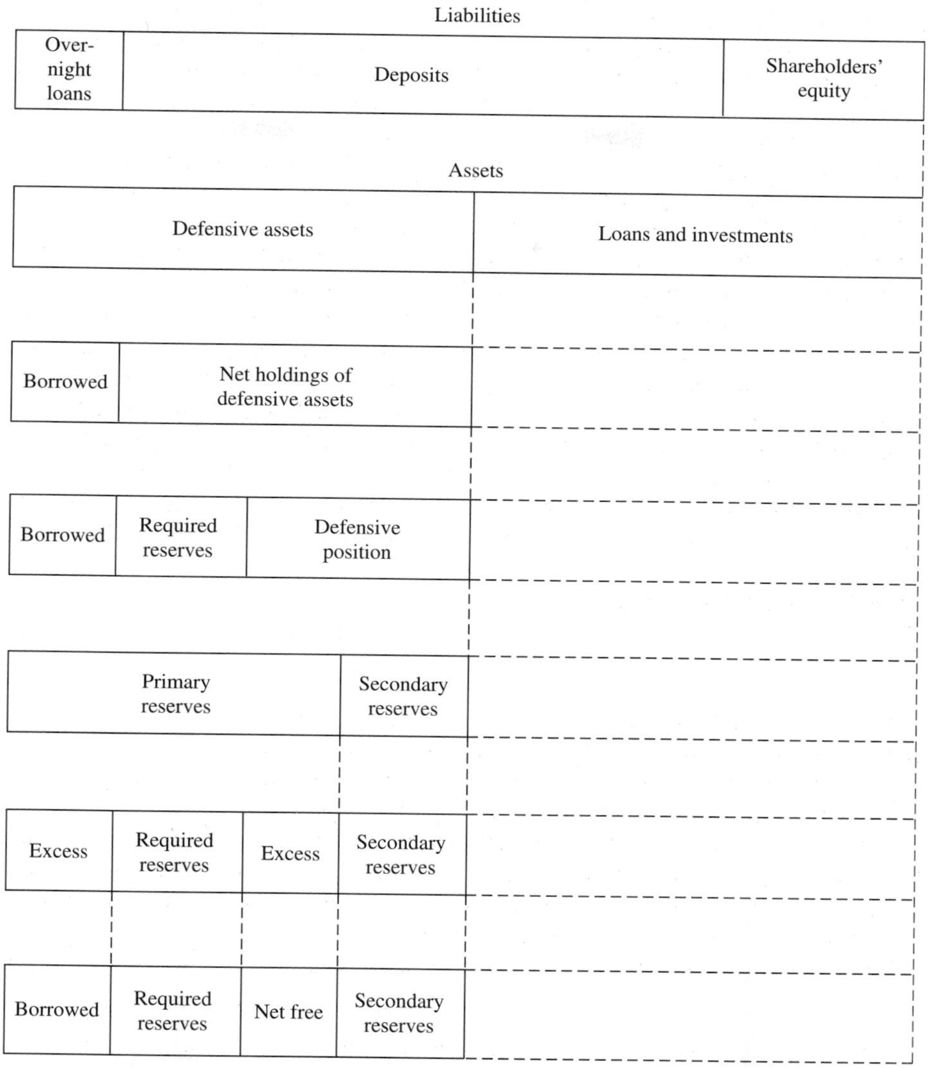

Liabilities

Over-night loans	Deposits	Shareholders' equity

Assets

Defensive assets	Loans and investments

Borrowed	Net holdings of defensive assets	

Borrowed	Required reserves	Defensive position	

	Primary reserves	Secondary reserves	

Excess	Required reserves	Excess	Secondary reserves	

Borrowed	Required reserves	Net free	Secondary reserves	

FIGURE 7.1

Schematic representation of bank balance sheet.

the lending bank will lose more and more of the deposit created by its initial loan. On the other hand, a borrower may build up his deposit in the lending bank toward the end of the term of his loan, in preparation for repaying it.

Sometimes a bank requires the borrower to hold a certain fraction of the loan on deposit during the term of the loan; in effect, the bank has lent less than the nominal amount of the loan. This practice should be distinguished from the "you lend to me now, I'll lend to you later" bargain that often characterizes, with varying degrees of formal and explicit understanding, the relations of a bank and a continuing customer. By the terms of such an understanding, a borrower compensates for his loan with deposits in past or future, not by holding some of the loan itself on deposit. Through these continuing customer relations, a bank's loans affect its deposits, but at some future time. It is equally true that deposits today entail some commitment to provide future loan accommodation. Indeed, one way in which banks compete for deposits with each other, and with other short-term borrowers, is by offering to regular depositors the reciprocal assurance of credit on favorable terms when they want to borrow rather than lend.

The degree to which a bank can expect to retain deposits resulting from its own loans depends on its size relative to other banks. If a bank is the only one in its community, it will retain more than if the local payees of the borrower's checks are scattered among several banks. But even a local monopoly bank will lose deposits as transactions spread to other areas of the economy. And a national monopoly bank, if one existed, would still face leakages to currency holding, foreign balances, and other assets. The restrictions on branch banking in the United States make the leakages from an individual bank typically much larger than in the banking systems of most other countries, where a handful of banks, each with many branches, dominate the scene. Where in England or Canada or Sweden a loan by one branch increases deposits in another branch of the same bank, in the United States a loan by one bank increases deposits in another bank.

The leakage is naturally greater and quicker for bank investments in nationally marketable securities than for loans to local businesses. An individual bank, even a large one, can be assumed to retain virtually nothing at all of amounts placed in defensive assets. A bank's decision to hold currency, or deposits in the central bank, or the debts of other banks, or Treasury securities does not lead to any significant increase in the amounts that others choose to leave on deposit with the bank.

7.3
BANK PORTFOLIOS AND PROFITS

In considering the bank's broad portfolio choice, between loans and investments and defensive position, it will be simplest to begin with a bank whose deposits are costless and independent of the bank's own portfolio decisions. Moreover, the bank is assumed to know with certainty what its deposits will be over the period of time that its funds are committed. This assumption abstracts, of course, from the essential problem of banking, the unpredictability of deposits and withdrawals, and it will be removed shortly. Beginning with the unrealistic case of certainty is an analytic and expository convenience.

In Fig. 7.2, assets are measured horizontally and deposits vertically. The basic accounting identity behind the diagram is the same one given above, translated into symbols as follows:

$$D + E = kD + R + L.$$

Thus the horizontal distance to the dashed line $D + E$ represents total assets, and the horizontal distance to the solid line kD represents required reserves. The horizontal

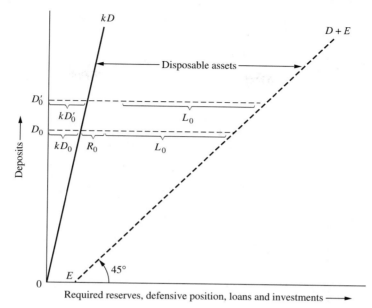

FIGURE 7.2
Loans, required reserves, and disposable assets in relation to deposits.

distance between these lines represents disposable assets, the amount that can be divided between defensive position R and loans and investments L. If loans and investments exceeded disposable assets, the defensive position would be negative.

Now suppose that the bank earns a rate of interest r on its defensive position R (or pays interest at this rate on a negative position) and earns on a loan and investment portfolio of size L a total revenue $P(L)$ (net of administrative costs and actuarial allowance for default). Its deposits are a given amount beyond its control, D_0, and its equity is fixed at E. The bank will seek to maximize the total net revenue on its portfolio, $P(L) + Rr$, subject to the balance sheet constraint $L + R = E + (1 - k)D_0$. If the marginal revenue from loans $P'(L)$ is constant and greater than r, this maximization puts no limit on the loan and investment portfolio other than the bank's ability to borrow to finance a negative defensive position. If the marginal revenue from loans $P'(L)$ is always smaller than r, the bank will simply hold all its deposits and equity in defensive assets.

A situation in which declining marginal revenue sets a positive limit on the loan and investment portfolio is shown in Fig. 7.3. Here loans and investments L are measured horizontally. L_c is the point at which loans and investment exhaust disposable assets, that is, $L_c = E + (1 - k)D_0$. To the left of L_c, defensive position R is positive; to the right, negative. Total net revenue from loans and investments is measured vertically upward from the origin, and total revenue from defensive position is measured in the opposite direction, downward from the origin. A negative defensive position means, of course, negative revenue from this source; in Fig. 7.3 this is shown when the lower revenue curve rises above the horizontal axis. Thus total revenue from the two sources combined appears in Fig. 7.3 as the difference between the two curves. Indeed the lower line—revenue from defensive position—may be regarded

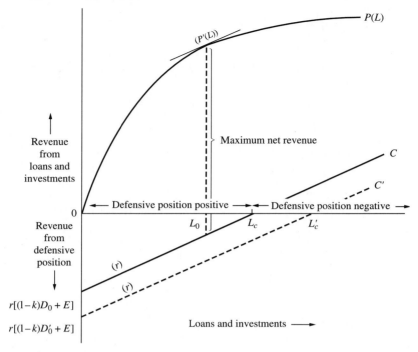

FIGURE 7.3
Maximizing net revenue from loans and defensive position.

as the cost curve, albeit opportunity cost, to the loans and investments revenue curve. In Fig. 7.3 a revenue maximum occurs at L_0, where marginal revenue is the same from the two sources. The slope of a line or curve is indicated in the diagram in parentheses; for example, the slope of line C is r.

A higher level of deposits will enable the bank to enjoy a stronger defensive position at any given volume of loans and investments. Suppose, for example, that deposits rise from D_0 in Fig. 7.2 to D_0', so that the bank now has, after meeting reserve requirements of kD_0', disposable deposits of $D_0'(1 - k)$. Then the point of zero defensive position L_c in Fig. 7.3 will shift to the right, for example, to L_c', by the amount $(1 - k)(D_0' - D_0)$. There will be a parallel shift to the right, from C to C' in the line representing the revenue from the defensive position in Fig. 7.3. The bank will have no reason to change its volume of loans and investments. The volume that equated the marginal revenue and marginal opportunity cost of lending still does so. Given the required reserve ratio k, a dollar increase in deposits means an increase of required reserves of k and an increase in defensive position of $1 - k$.

7.3.1 Penalties for Negative Defensive Position

So far it has been assumed that the bank can always borrow short term at the same rate r that positive holdings of defensive assets yield. If so, the marginal opportunity cost of lending is the same for negative defensive positions as for positive. But more likely the bank must pay a higher rate to borrow, or—what amounts to the same thing—must liquidate assets that would have yielded a higher rate than r. Let the effective rate for negative positions be $r + b$. In addition, there may be a fixed cost of net borrowing, independent of the amount borrowed, attributable to the costs and inconveniences of arranging a loan or to the loss of prestige involved in displaying a shortage of owned reserves. In Figs. 7.4a, 7.4b, and 7.4c, the curve C representing revenue from defensive position increases in slope at L_c from r to $r + b$. In Fig. 7.4a, no fixed cost is involved in having a negative defensive position. But in Figs. 7.4b and 7.4c, the existence and amount of a fixed cost a are shown by the upward jump in the curve C.

These changes in the opportunity cost curve at L_c have no effect on the bank's decision if the decision is in any case to lend an amount less than or equal to L_c, that is, to hold a positive or zero defensive position. This will be true whenever $P'(L_c)$, marginal revenue from loans at the point L_c, is smaller than or equal to r. But the extra costs of a negative position are relevant if $P'(L_c)$ exceeds r. Here there are several possibilities:

1. $r < P'(L_c) \leq r + b$ (not diagrammed). The best portfolio for the bank is the one corresponding to L_c, a zero defensive position.
2. $r + b < P'(L_c)$, no fixed cost (Fig. 7.4a). Here the bank will choose a volume of loans and investments higher than L_c and a negative defensive position.
3. $r + b < P'(L_c)$, positive fixed cost (Figs. 7.4b and 7.4c). Here the bank may, as in case 2, proceed to a point beyond L_c where $P'(L) = r + b$. This is illustrated in Fig. 7.4b. It is also possible, however, that the revenue at such a point is smaller than the revenue at L_c because of the fixed cost of borrowing. This outcome is illustrated in Fig. 7.4c.

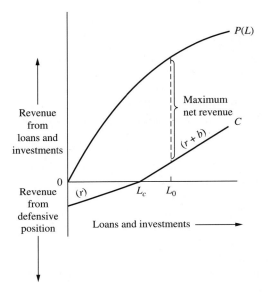

FIGURE 7.4
(a) Maximizing net revenue, given penalty interest for borrowing;

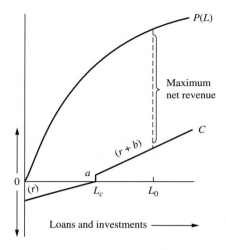

FIGURE 7.4 (continued)
(*b*) Maximizing net revenue, given penalty interest and fixed cost;

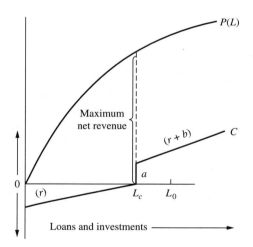

FIGURE 7.4 (continued)
(*c*) Maximizing net revenue, corner solution.

The preceding analysis has assumed that the bank neither earns interest on required reserves nor pays interest on its deposits. These assumptions can be relaxed in some respects without altering the analysis.

Central banking systems differ in respect to the payment of interest to banks on required reserves. In the U.S. Federal Reserve System, member bank reserve balances earn no interest; banks can enjoy the prevailing yield r on defensive assets only to the extent that their defensive positions exceed requirements. Currently, however, there is considerable agitation for payment of interest on reserves, because banks are increasingly competing for deposits with money market funds and other institutions not required to hold reserves.

In other banking systems, for example, the United Kingdom and Canada, two reserve requirements or conventions have sometimes been in effect simultaneously—a liquid-assets convention and within that a cash requirement. In the United

Kingdom, for example, there were both primary and secondary reserve requirements before 1971. Banks could earn the prevailing rate r on all their defensive assets including those qualified for the 30 percent liquid-assets convention, except for the 8 percent of deposits required to be held in cash or with the Bank of England.

If interest, at a legally or administratively set rate, is earned on required reserves, these earnings add a constant amount to the bank's revenue from its given volume of deposits. This addition does not affect the calculations that determine the optimal allocation of those deposits between loans and investments and defense assets.

Likewise, the analysis applies when the bank must pay interest to its depositors so long as the deposit interest rate is regulated, and fixed below what the bank can earn on a dollar of deposits. It is still in the bank's interest to accept as many deposits as are available to it. The interest outlay is then a fixed cost, the same whatever is the bank's portfolio.

Although these interest receipts and outlays do not affect the maximum-profit portfolio, they do affect the bank's profits. They may be relevant, therefore, to the shareholders' decision whether to stay in the business or not.

7.3.2 The Value and Cost of Equity

How much is a dollar of new equity worth to the bank? More precisely, how much additional profit will the bank earn if an additional dollar of capital is subscribed? With the exception of the case illustrated in Fig. 7.4c, additional capital will simply be invested in an increased defensive position and will thus yield either r or $r + b$. Since r or $r + b$ is also the marginal revenue from lending, it is equally true to say that the value of new capital is $P'(L)$. In the exceptional case, the new equity will go into loans and investments; it will yield the marginal revenue $P'(L)$, which exceeds $r + b$. If the existing shareholders of the bank can attract a new stock subscription of a dollar by the prospect of a dividend yield no larger than these marginal contributions to profit, it will be worth their while to do so. In the long-run equilibrium of the banking firm, the marginal cost of equity capital will just equal the marginal profit. The bank may nonetheless be making monopoly profits that would attract new firms, assuming entry into the industry is not legally restricted.

7.3.3 The Value and Cost of Deposits

How much is a dollar increase in deposits worth to the bank? As noted above, an increase in deposits of $1 will normally mean an increase of $1 − k$ in the defensive position and an increase of k in required reserves. Therefore, assuming no interest is paid on required reserves, a dollar more in deposits will permit the bank to add $(1 − k)r$ to its earnings if its defensive position is positive, or $(1 − k)(r + b)$ if its defensive position is negative. Since in these situations $P'(L)$ is equal to r or $r + b$, the value of deposits can also be expressed as $(1 − k)P'(L)$.

The situation pictured in Fig. 7.4c is again something of an exception. There an influx of deposits will push the jump in the opportunity cost curve to the right. It will still be profitable for the bank to lend up to the jump, the point of zero defensive position. Hence an increase in deposits will increase loans and investments rather than defensive position. It will, as in the other cases, add $(1 - k)$ times the marginal revenue of lending, $(1 - k)P'(L_c)$, to the bank's revenue. But this is greater than $(1 - k)(r + b)$.

The marginal value of deposits to the bank is smaller than the marginal value of equity in the proportion $(1 - k)$, because of the reserve requirement against deposits. But of course it is generally easier to attract deposits than to attract capital.

If interest is paid at rate r' on required reserves, then the marginal cost of deposits will be equated to a weighted average of r' and the marginal return on disposable assets, with weights k and $1 - k$ respectively. So long as r' is the smaller, one effect of an increase in the required reserve ratio k is to lower the value of deposits to the bank.

Banks generally accept more than one kind of deposit. Suppose l is the reserve requirement on a particular category of time deposits T. Then if r' is zero, the additional earnings made possible by \$1 additional time deposits is $(1 - l)P'(L)$. Assuming l is smaller than the reserve ratio k required for demand deposits—as noted above, l is currently zero in the United States—the gross marginal value of time deposits lies between the corresponding values of equity and demand deposits. But of course the net value of time deposits depends also on the interest that must be paid to attract them.

7.3.4 Unrestricted Competition for Deposits

So long as competition for deposits is effectively limited by laws or gentlemen's agreements prohibiting or limiting interest payments to depositors, the firm and the industry are in disequilibrium. These devices permit the banking industry as a whole to receive rents that under effective competition would be paid to depositors. In the long run the competition of new banking firms could reduce the marginal revenue from lending until the value of deposits is brought down to their cost. But in practice entry is not free. In the United States entry is regulated by federal and state chartering authorities.

For many years the legal ceilings on interest rates payable on demand, time, and savings accounts in the United States were so low that they prevented effective rate competition for them. Raising or lifting of ceilings, beginning in 1962 and culminating in their virtual elimination in the 1980s, led to vigorous and open rate competition. As would be expected, the rates banks offer for time deposits, which have small or zero reserve requirements, are close to the yields they can earn on defensive assets. Rates available on transactions deposits are smaller, because of the reserve requirement and other costs these accounts impose on the bank.

In a full equilibrium, without deposit rate ceilings, the banking firm will equate the marginal cost of each class of deposits to its marginal value, that is, to the addition to earnings on assets that an additional dollar of deposits will permit. Moreover, the optimal portfolio will generally be such that this addition to earnings will be the same no matter in which asset the new deposit is invested. If the value of an additional deposit exceeds its cost, the bank will seek to attract deposits by raising the rate of interest paid depositors or by other competitive devices.

The marginal cost of attracting deposits may exceed the average interest rate on deposits and may rise with the bank's volume of deposits. For one thing, some of the costs of attracting deposits are not payments to depositors at all but diffuse costs of administration, promotion, advertising, and atmosphere. In paying depositors, moreover, the bank may be a monopsonist, just as it has some monopoly power in selling loans to borrowers. No doubt the bank can to some extent discriminate among depositors, as it can among borrowers. Thus if it takes 12 percent to attract a new depositor, the bank is not necessarily forced to pay 12 percent to all its depositors. As noted above there are indirect ways of giving a depositor special remuneration, for example, in ancillary services or in promises of preferred treatment when the depositor wishes to borrow.

7.4
UNCERTAINTY ABOUT DEPOSITS

7.4.1 The Function of Reserves and Defensive Assets

So far it has been assumed that the bank knows for sure what its deposits will be. The bank holds defensive assets beyond its reserve requirements only to the extent that their yield is competitive with the marginal revenue from lending. In this analysis the properties of defensive assets—highly liquid and predictable in value—were quite inessential. Any other assets with comparable yields might find their way into bank portfolios with loans and investments.

The principal reason that banks hold defensive assets—generally at lower yields than the marginal returns from lending—is to defend themselves against deposit withdrawals that they cannot perfectly foresee. Many factors outside the bank's power either to control or to predict can change the bank's deposits from week to week, from day to day, even from hour to hour. For example, expansion or contraction of the lending of other banks will spill deposits and reserves into the bank or suck them from it. The bank must commit itself to illiquid assets *before* it knows what its deposits will be. Therefore, in deciding the volume of its loans and investments, the bank must consider the consequences of large if improbable withdrawals.

At one time the consequence might have been literal inability to honor demand obligations. The bank would "fail" not because its loans and investments were bad but simply because they were illiquid. The original and historic purpose of reserves was to protect the bank and its depositors from this kind of failure.

Modern financial institutions have virtually eliminated this danger. As a lender of last resort the central bank can prevent banks from failing simply from lack of liquid funds to meet deposit withdrawals. The possibility of a contagious loss of confidence in a particular bank or in banks in general is greatly reduced both by the availability of a lender of last resort and by government guarantees of deposits. A bank may fail because of poor management or extraordinarily bad luck in making loans and investments, not because these assets are illiquid but because they are of insufficient value even if held to maturity and beyond. The stockholders' capital in the enterprise is the depositors', or the deposit insurers', cushion against this kind of misfortune. Failures of savings and loan associations in the 1980s demonstrated that the capital cushions were inadequate to cover losses when regulations and conventional fiduciary scruples were drastically weakened. This experience cost taxpayers $200 billion to fulfill insurance guarantees to depositors. In response to this and similiar incidents, internationally agreed-upon regulations of banks now insist on higher ratios of capital to risky assets.

In any case, the historic function of reserves as a cushion against failure due simply to illiquidity has been rendered obsolete. The modern function of reserves is to provide a mechanism of monetary control over the economy by the central bank. Why do banks hold reserves? They hold reserves because they are required to do so by law or by convention with the virtual force of law. These required reserves are—paradoxically in view of the original function of reserves and indeed of reserve requirements—unavailable to meet deposit withdrawals. Why do banks maintain a net defensive position in excess of reserve requirements? They hold secondary reserves for fear that they might not pass the required reserve test without incurring the special costs of borrowing or of liquidating high-yielding investments. The consequence of deposit withdrawals is not the disaster of insolvency but the additional cost, including perhaps inconvenience and damage to prestige, involved in meeting the reserve test. Given these costs, uncertainty about the future level of deposits may lead to a lower volume of lending and to a higher defensive position than in the profit maximization discussed earlier.

The analysis will assume that only demand deposits are subject to uncertainty. If the bank also has time deposits, these are assumed to be no less illiquid than loans. Thus the making of loans need not be deterred by fear of losing time deposits, for the loans will be repaid soon enough to meet such withdrawals. This means that time deposits play much the same role as equity, with the exception that they entail interest payments and possibly reserve requirements. This assumption is unrealistically extreme, but it is qualitatively in the right direction. Time deposits are less volatile and unpredictable than demand deposits, and a bank with a high proportion of time deposits has less to fear from unanticipated withdrawals.

7.4.2 The Portfolio that Maximizes Expected Profit

Once the bank has chosen a volume of loans and investments, a dollar change in deposits will mean a $(1 - k)$ change in defensive position. An influx of deposits will increase the defensive position at least temporarily; if the bank becomes convinced it is a permanent gain, presumably it will choose a new and higher volume of loans and investments. A loss of deposits will lower and perhaps wipe out the defensive position. Again, this outcome may be only temporary. If the loss of deposits proves to be permanent, the bank will in time lower its volume of loans and investments and reconstitute its defensive position.

In Fig. 7.5 let L_0 represent, as in Fig. 7.2, the volume of loans and investments chosen by the bank. Let D_0 be the expected volume of deposits, in the probabil-

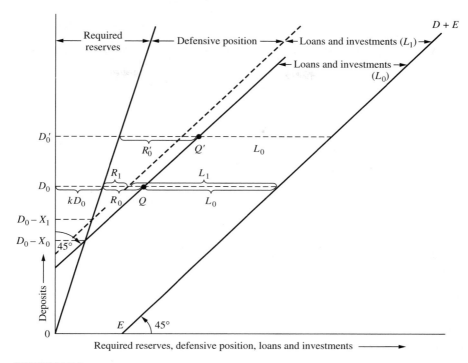

FIGURE 7.5
Balance sheet outcomes depending on deposits realized after loans decided.

ity sense, the next week. In Fig. 7.2 the bank was sure of D_0; now various deposit levels both higher and lower are possible, and D_0 is just the mean of a probability distribution. Correspondingly, R_0 in Fig. 7.5 is the expected defensive position. Through point Q in Fig. 7.5, a 45-degree line has been drawn, parallel to the line $D + E$. Given the volume of loans and investments L_0, the actual outcome for deposits and defensive position will be somewhere on this line. If more deposits come to the bank, the outcome will be on this line above and to the right of Q. If there are deposit withdrawals beyond expectation, the outcome will be to the left of and below Q. A reduction of deposits by X_0, from D_0 to $D_0 - X_0$, would wipe out the defensive position.

The relevant probabilities of future deposits are not objective ones, if indeed these exist, but probabilities estimated by the bank in the light of its past experience. In Fig. 7.6, curve $\rho(D)$ represents the cumulative probability distribution of deposits. Any point on the curve is to be read as follows: The ordinate gives the probability that the future deposits will not exceed the abscissa; for example, the probability is $\rho(D_0 - X_0)$ that deposits will not be greater than $D_0 - X_0$. As in Fig. 7.5, $D_0 - X_0$ represents the deposit level at which the defensive position is zero; therefore $\rho(D_0 - X_0)$ is the probability that the bank will have to borrow or liquidate investments. Suppose there is an increase in expected deposits, say from D_0 to D_0' in Figs. 7.5 and 7.6, because the bank has become through external circumstances or

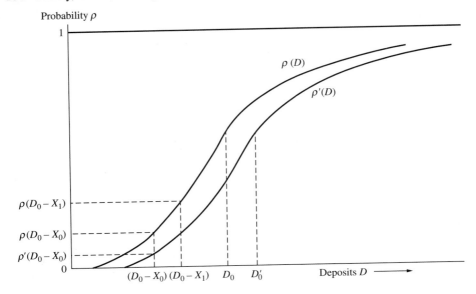

FIGURE 7.6
Cumulative probability distribution of deposits.

through its own competitive measures a more attractive depository. This is assumed to shift the entire cumulative distribution to the right, from $\rho(D)$ to $\rho'(D)$ in Fig. 7.6. The expected defensive position is increased from R_0 to R'_0 in Fig. 7.5. The deposit level at which the defensive position is zero remains the same, $D_0 - X_0$, but the probability of encountering a negative defensive position is reduced to $\rho'(D_0 - X_0)$.

It is assumed that the probability distribution shifts in a special way when expected deposits change, namely that the probability that actual deposits will not exceed any given fraction or multiple of expected deposits remains unchanged. Thus, in the example above, $\rho(xD_0) = \rho'(xD'_0)$ whether x is $\frac{1}{10}$ or $\frac{1}{2}$ or 1 or 3 or any other positive number.

Given the original probability distribution of deposits, $\rho(D)$, an increase in loans and investments will lower the expected defensive position, reduce the safety margin it provides against losses of deposits, and increase the probability of a negative defensive position. Consider, for example, an increase in loans and investments from L_0 to L_1 in Fig. 7.5. This lowers the expected defensive position from R_0 to R_1, reduces the safety margin from X_0 to X_1, and increases the probability of a negative defensive position to $\rho(D_0 - X_1)$.

Every increase in loans thus increases the probability that the bank will be subject to the special costs of meeting a negative defensive position. The opportunity costs of making loans and investments must be reckoned as the *expected* costs of providing the funds, taking into account the reduction in expected defensive position and safety margin. Therefore the expected special costs must be included. They contribute to marginal as well as to total expected costs.

7.4.3 Effects of Uncertainty

The nature of the change in opportunity costs introduced by uncertainty about deposits is indicated in Fig. 7.7, which should be compared to Fig. 7.4. In Fig. 7.4a, L_c (equal to $D_0(1-k)+E$) is shown as the volume of loans and investments corresponding to a zero defensive position. At this critical volume, the opportunity cost curve increases in slope from r to $r+b$. And in Figs. 7.4b and 7.4c, the cost curve

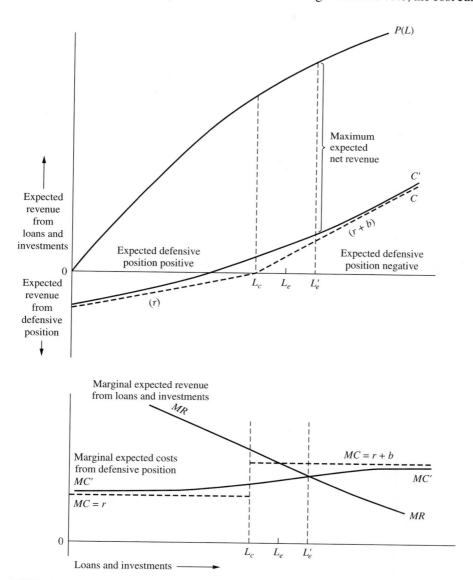

FIGURE 7.7
Maximizing expected net revenue with deposits uncertain: (a) Penalty rate and no fixed cost;

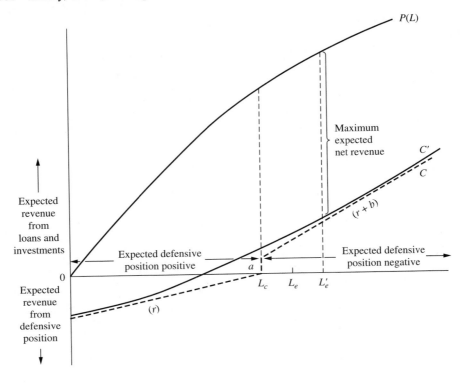

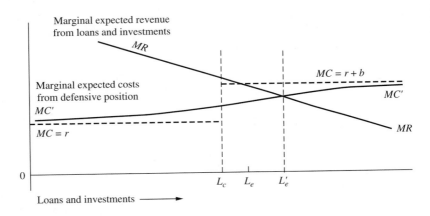

FIGURE 7.7 (continued)
Maximizing expected net revenue with deposits uncertain: (*b*) Penalty rate and small fixed cost;

also jumps at this point, reflecting a once-for-all cost of borrowing *a*. In Fig. 7.6, the same volume of loans and investments L_c now corresponds to an *expected* defensive position of zero. But the probability of a negative defensive position is no longer zero to the left of this point and one to its right. Rather this probability grows con-

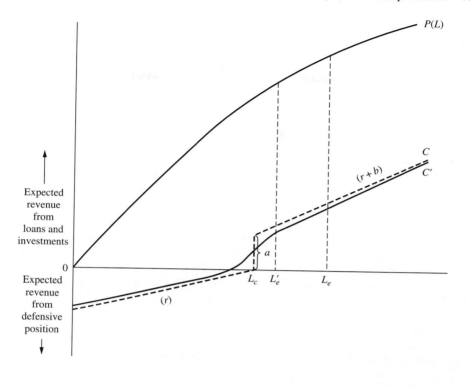

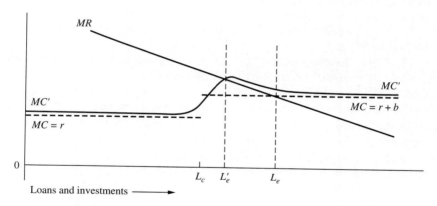

FIGURE 7.7 (continued)
(c) Penalty rate and large fixed cost.

tinuously as L increases. Consequently, the expected opportunity cost for every level of L must include an allowance for the probability that the defensive position will turn negative and impose special costs on the bank—an allowance that is greater the higher the chosen volume of loans and investments. This allowance has the effect of smoothing the cost curve C', as illustrated in Fig. 7.7.

Formally, as shown in the appendix, marginal expected cost is

$$r + bF(X) + \frac{a}{(1-k)D_0} f(X).$$

Here X is a function of L such that $D_0(1+X)$ is the level of deposits $(L-E)/(1-k)$ at which the defensive position would be zero, $F(X)$ is the probability that deposits will not exceed this crucial level, and $f(X) = dF(X)/dX$ is the corresponding probability density. The bank equates this marginal cost to the marginal revenue of lending $P'(L)$.

How does uncertainty affect the volume of loans and investments?

In Fig. 7.7a, there is no fixed cost of borrowing, no jump in the cost curve under certainty (curve C in Fig. 7.7a). Uncertainty results in an expected total cost curve like C' in Fig. 7.7a, above C everywhere and asymptotic to C at both ends. The corresponding change in marginal cost is shown in the lower panel. The jump in marginal cost MC, at L_c, is now distributed throughout the new marginal cost curve MC'. With uncertainty about deposits, marginal cost rises continuously, and always lies between r and $r + b$. Therefore, if the maximum-profit volume of loans and investments were previously below L_c, implying a positive defensive position, deposit uncertainty leads to a *lower* volume of lending and a *larger* expected defensive position. But if the maximum-profit volume of loans and investments under certainty were greater than L_c, implying a zero or negative defensive position, uncertainty leads to a *higher* volume of lending and a *smaller* defensive position, that is, more expected borrowing. This second result is the one illustrated in Fig. 7.7a by the shift in equilibrium lending from L_e to L'_e. The third possibility is that the equilibrium under certainty is exactly at L_c—the marginal revenue curve goes through the jump in MC at that point. In this event uncertainty may either increase or decrease lending, depending on whether marginal revenue is greater or less than the new marginal cost MC' at that point.

In Fig. 7.7b there is a jump in total cost C at L_c, a once-for-all cost of borrowing. But this cost is small relative to the additional interest b incurred on a negative defensive position. The results are qualitatively the same as in the previous case. If the equilibrium under certainty were at L_c but marginal revenue $P'(L)$ exceeded $r + b$, as illustrated in Fig. 7.4c, then of course the introduction of uncertainty will lead to increased lending and to a negative defensive position.

In Fig. 7.7c, however, the fixed cost of borrowing, a, is large relative to the extra interest charge b. As a result, the total cost curve under uncertainty, C', lies below the corresponding curve under certainty, C, for values of L above L_c, that is, for negative expected defensive positions. Also, the marginal cost curve MC' eventually rises above $(r + b)$, and then approaches $r + b$, the marginal cost under conditions of certainty. The new marginal cost MC' is smooth, but it is not continuously rising. If the defensive position would be positive under certainty, then it will be increased—and lending curtailed—under uncertainty. This is the same conclusion as in the two previous cases. For negative defensive positions, the situation is more complicated than in the previous two cases. Even there the introduction of uncertainty *may* so increase marginal cost as to reduce lending and increase (algebraically) the defensive position. This is the possibility illustrated in Fig. 7.7c. These results may be summarized in Table 7.1.

TABLE 7.1

Effect of uncertainty about deposits on volume of loans and investments and expected defensive position

		Equilibrium under certainty	
		Positive defensive position	**Negative defensive position**
(i)	Fixed cost of borrowing zero or small (Figs. 7.7a and 7.7b)	Lending diminished; defensive position increased	Lending increased; defensive position reduced
(ii)	Fixed cost of borrowing large (Fig. 7.7c)	Lending diminished; defensive position increased	Result uncertain

The possibility that uncertainty increases the bank's loans and investments seems surprising, and the cases in which this result occurs are probably not of great empirical importance. These are cases where the defensive position is negative or zero. Ordinarily, banks in the United States are not in this situation. These analytical possibilities may have greater relevance in certain foreign banking systems, where banks customarily lend and invest funds borrowed from the central bank.

7.4.4 Value and Cost of Deposits

What are the disposition and the value of an increase in expected deposits, as from D_0 to D_0' in Figs. 7.5 and 7.6? A shift of this kind moves L_c to the right in Fig. 7.7. At any given volume of loans and investments, say L_e' in the diagrams, the penalties of a negative defensive position are less probable and have less weight in the calculation of marginal cost. Therefore the marginal cost curve is moved to the right and generally down. The result is an increase in the equilibrium volume of loans and investments. It is not true, as it was with certainty about deposits, that an influx of deposits goes entirely into defensive assets.

Correspondingly, the value in added expected earnings of an addition to expected deposits is $(1 - k)$ times the marginal revenue of lending, or, what is in equilibrium the same thing, $(1 - k)$ times the marginal expected revenue from defensive position. Even when the expected defensive position is positive, deposits are worth more than $r(1 - k)$. An increment in expected deposits acquires additional value by lowering the probability that random deposit loss will inflict on the bank the penalty costs of a negative defensive position.

An exception may occur when the marginal cost curve has the hump shape of Fig. 7.7c. Sliding this curve to the right will raise it at certain points. If the previous equilibrium had occurred on a declining stretch of the curve (not as depicted in Fig. 7.7c), then the new equilibrium will involve a lower volume of loans and investments. The increase in expected deposits derives considerable value from lowering the probability of incurring the fixed penalty cost, but to exploit this improvement the bank must plan a much higher defensive position than before.

As in the case of certainty, two situations may be distinguished with respect to the supply of deposits to the individual bank:

1. The expected volume of deposits is externally determined, beyond the bank's control. A market interest rate may have to be paid on deposits, but given the limited supply of deposits available to the bank, their value exceeds this interest rate. In these circumstances the cost of deposits affects the expected profits of the bank but not its optimal portfolio.
2. The bank can influence its expected volume of deposits by its interest payments and other outlays. Total costs of deposits are uncertain because deposits themselves are uncertain. A simple and natural assumption is that the average cost of deposits is a function of expected deposits, generally an increasing function. Given this average cost, actually realized total costs depend on the random element in deposits. For example, the bank sets an interest rate but is uncertain what volume of deposits it will attract. In these circumstances, the bank will equate the marginal cost of expected deposits to their value. Decisions about deposit levels and about portfolio composition are intertwined. For example, if the marginal costs of attracting a given volume of expected deposits decline, the bank will accept more deposits and make more loans. But as the marginal revenue of loans declines, the bank will shift relatively more of any new funds into defensive assets.

In Fig. 7.8 this complete equilibrium is illustrated. The horizontal axis measures either the bank's expected disposable funds, $E + (1 - k)D_0$, or their balance

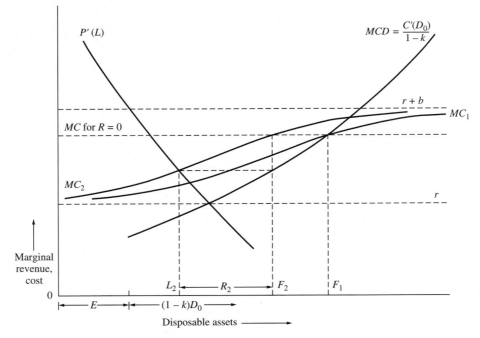

FIGURE 7.8
Full equilibrium of a bank.

sheet equivalent, $L + R$. Curve MCD represents the marginal cost of the disposable funds; if $C'(D_0)$ is the marginal cost of \$1 of expected deposits, then $C'(D_0) \div (1 - k)$ is the marginal cost of \$1 available for lending or placing in defensive assets. MC represents, as in previous diagrams, the marginal opportunity cost of lending, measured by the expected return from defensive position. But in this diagram the level of expected deposits is not fixed. Instead the MC curve slides laterally, with the point of zero defensive position L_c always corresponding to the abscissa $E + D_0(1 - k)$. Thus if disposable funds are F_1, the proper MC curve is MC_1, whereas if disposable funds are F_2, the applicable curve is MC_2. Now F_1, with zero defensive position, is clearly not an equilibrium. Suppose lending is set equal to F_1 so that defensive position is zero. Although the value of defensive assets equals the cost of deposits, the marginal revenue of lending falls short of both of them. There is too much lending; and to cut it back deposits should be lowered and defensive position increased. This process leads to F_2, which is an equilibrium, with loans of L_2 and defensive position of R_2.

7.5
THE BANK'S RESPONSE TO EXTERNAL CHANGES

7.5.1 Exogenous Changes in Expected Deposits

What is the bank's response to an exogenous decrease in expected deposits D_0? For a reference point, consider the following first approximation: The bank places all of its capital funds in loans and investments, meets its expected reserve requirements, and divides the remainder of its expected deposits in constant proportions between loans and expected defensive position. A bank following this policy would respond to a 10 percent cut in expected deposits by a 10 percent cut in $L - E$, the amount of deposits placed in loans. The logic of the policy is that the bank is still protected against the same percentage downward deviation of deposits from expectation; the probability of a negative defensive position remains the same. This may be illustrated by a numerical example, showing expected and contingent balance sheets before and after the change in expected deposits, as in Table 7.2A. Here the required reserve ratio is assumed to be 10 percent.

TABLE 7.2A

Assets		Liabilities	
Expected required reserves	10	Expected deposits	100
Loans, etc.	64	Equity	10
Expected defensive position	36		

Committed to loans of 64, the bank could lose 40 percent of its expected deposits before running out of defensive position (see Table 7.2B).

TABLE 7.2B

Assets		Liabilities	
Required reserves	6	Deposits	60
Loans, etc.	64	Equity	10
Defensive position	0		

Now the bank's expected deposits are cut by 10 percent, and the first approximation policy indicates a proportionate cut in $L-E$, originally 54, and in expected defensive position, originally 36 (see Table 7.3A).

TABLE 7.3A

Assets		Liabilities	
Expected required reserves	9.0	Expected deposits	90
Loans, etc.	58.6	Equity	10
Expected defensive position	32.4		

The bank is still protected against a 40 percent "loss" of deposits, that is, its defensive position will be positive unless deposits fall as low as 54 (see Table 7.3B).

TABLE 7.3B

Assets		Liabilities	
Expected required reserves	5.4	Expected deposits	54
Loans, etc.	58.6	Equity	10
Expected defensive position	0		

What might cause the bank to deviate from this policy? For one thing, the marginal revenue of lending $P'(L)$ might rise as L is reduced. By itself, this would lead the bank to a smaller curtailment of lending than the first approximation strategy suggests.

On the other hand, the marginal value of defensive assets may also rise. This marginal value depends on r, b, and a, all of which are constant. It depends also on X, the crucial percentage downward deviation of deposits at which the defensive position would be negative. This is also constant under the assumed policy. But it depends further on the level of expected deposits D_0 itself, provided the penalty a is positive and constant. The reason is that each dollar increase in expected defensive position lowers the crucial deposit level by the same dollar amount whether expected deposits are high or low. (In the tabular example above, reducing loans by 9 and correspondingly increasing the expected defensive position lowers the critical deposit level by 10, to 50 and 44 respectively, whether expected deposits are 100 or 90.) But the same dollar amount is a larger percentage when deposits are low, and therefore a greater reduction in the probability of trouble. (In the example, it was equally likely that with expected deposits of 100, actual deposits would be as low as 60, and that with expected deposits of 90, actual deposits would be as low as 54. But it is less likely that 90 will turn out to be 44 or lower than that 100 will turn out to be 50 or lower.) The presence of a fixed penalty leads to a kind of economy of scale of deposits: The marginal opportunity cost of lending is higher when expected deposits are lower.

The first approximation policy would be optimal if the marginal revenue of lending $P'(L)$ were constant and if there were no fixed penalty ($a = 0$). Otherwise, following this policy in the face of a decline in expected deposits will raise both the marginal revenue and the marginal cost of lending. The optimal cut in lending may be either smaller or greater than indicated by the pro rata reduction in $L - E$.

When deposits are endogenously responsive to the bank's own payments to attract them, any rise in the marginal value of assets will lead the bank to "buy" more deposits. The bank will not fully acquiesce in an unfavorable shift in expected deposits but will partially offset it by incurring greater average and marginal costs to attract deposits.

7.5.2 Other Changes in Available Funds

If additional funds become available as equity or time deposits, they can be placed in loans and investments without altering the bank's margin of safety. The first approximation, therefore, is that all of $1 additional equity, and $(1 - l)$ of an additional $1 of time deposits, will go into loans.

This leaves the size and marginal value of defensive position unchanged. But unless the bank is operating in a purely competitive loan market, the marginal revenue of lending will decline. Thus the first approximation overstates the loan response. To keep its alternative investments equally valuable on the margin, the bank will have to use some of its additional funds to improve its expected defensive position.

7.5.3 The Yield of Defensive Assets

With given expected deposits (Fig. 7.7), an increase in r will raise the marginal opportunity cost of lending. The bank will substitute defensive assets for loans and investments. When expected deposits and the costs of attracting them are endogenous (Fig. 7.8) along a given supply curve of deposits to the bank, an increase in r will also induce the bank to seek and accept more deposits, at higher marginal cost. Defensive position gains from new deposits as well as from curtailment of loans. Reductions in r have the opposite effects.

One source of variation in r is monetary policy, and indeed it is largely through changes in interest rates on defensive assets in the money market that the individual bank feels the impact of monetary policy.

7.5.4 Penalties for Negative Defensive Position

An increase in the variability penalty b will raise both the level and the slope of the marginal cost curve, with consequences similar to those of an increase in r just discussed. The same is true of an increase in the fixed penalty a—except that for high values of L relative to D_0, this lowers the slope of the MC curve.

For the individual bank an increase in penalties may arise from a number of sources: greater expectation or risk of a future rise in interest rates, meaning greater losses if investments must be liquidated to cover a negative defensive position; greater interest charges and transactions costs in arranging loans from other banks or the central bank; greater estimates of damage to future credit-worthiness involved in near-term borrowing.

7.5.5 Required Reserve Ratio

One very direct way in which the monetary authorities affect the bank is by setting the legal reserve ratio, k. With given expected deposits, a rise in k means that the bank must provide for higher expected required reserves, by curtailing either loans or expected defensive position or, most likely, both. How much will loans be curtailed?

Consider, to begin with, the same first approximation used in Section 7.5.1 in connection with deposit inflows. This suggests the following reaction to a change in reserve requirement: The bank adjusts its loans so as to maintain unchanged the probability of a negative defensive position. This means that $(L-E)/(1-k)$ remains constant; the elasticity of $L-E$ with respect to $1-k$ is one. For example, suppose that the bank had chosen the balance sheet shown in Table 7.2A when the required reserve ratio was 10 percent. The bank is protected for deposits as low as 60, as shown in Table 7.2B. Now let the required reserve ratio be raised to 20 percent. The following plan in Table 7.4A will maintain the same protection as before.

TABLE 7.4A

Assets		Liabilities	
Expected required reserves	20	Expected deposits	100
Loans, etc.	58	Equity	10
Expected defensive position	32		

Once again the bank is protected for deposits as low as 60 (see Table 7.4B).

TABLE 7.4B

Assets		Liabilities	
Required reserves	12	Deposits	60
Loans, etc.	58	Equity	10
Defensive position	0		

The bank lends out its capital (10) and beyond that maintains the same relative dispositions of its disposable deposits. In Table 7.2A the expected disposable deposits of 90 are divided between three-fifths loans (54) and two-fifths defensive position (36). In Table 7.4A the expected disposable deposits, now 80, are divided in the same proportions: three-fifths loans (48), and two-fifths defensive position (32).

This approximation would be exact if it maintained equality of marginal revenue from lending and expected marginal revenue from defensive position. But both of the elements of this equality will, in general, be changed. Reduction in the volume of loans L will raise their marginal revenue $P'(L)$ unless the bank is operating in a purely competitive loan market. Recall that the second element, the marginal revenue from defensive position, is equal to

$$r + bF(X) + \frac{a}{(1 - k)D_0} f(X), \qquad \text{where } X = \frac{L - E}{(1 - k)D_0} - 1$$

is the percentage deviation from expected deposits at which defensive position would be zero (-40 in the tabular illustration above), $F(X)$ is the probability of deviations as bad as that or worse, and $f(X)$ is $dF(x)/dx$ evaluated for $x = X$, the corresponding probability density function at X.

The approximation keeps X constant, and r, b, a, and D_0 are all constant. But unless a is zero, the rise in k increases the third term of this marginal opportunity cost of lending. When jumping over the line to a negative defensive position entails a fixed cost, the fact that a \$1 increase in loans and investments increases the probability of crossing the line must be charged against it. Furthermore, the amount by which an additional \$1 of lending raises this probability is greater when the reserve requirement is higher. A \$1 increase in L raises the critical level of deposits by $1/(1 - k)$, for example by 10/8 when the required reserve ratio is 20 percent, compared to 10/9 when it is 10 percent. With both the marginal revenue and marginal cost of lending higher, it is not possible to say in general in which direction the first approximation errs. The first approximation—the unitary elasticity of $L - E$ with respect to $1 - k$— is exact if marginal revenue from lending $P'(L)$ is constant and if the fixed penalty a is zero.

The foregoing analysis of changes in reserve requirement refers to the case of exogenous deposits. What of the other case, where the bank can determine its own volume of expected deposits? Clearly an increase in k raises the cost of obtaining, via additional deposits, funds to place in loans or in defensive assets. The bank will seek a smaller volume of expected deposits, and therefore curtail its loans even more than in the first case.

7.6
RETENTION OF DEPOSITS

The preceding analysis has assumed that the bank's volume of deposits is independent of the size of its loans and investments. Deposits may depend on the interest rates and services the bank offers depositors and on its advertising and public relations expenditures. But so far they do not depend on the bank's portfolio choice. For reasons outlined earlier in Section 7.2, this is an extreme assumption, and it is time to examine the implications of its removal.

Suppose instead that, given the attractions the bank offers potential depositors, the volume of its deposits is the sum of an autonomous element D_0 and an induced element $\phi(L)$ that depends on its loans and investments. With zero loans and investments, deposits are just D_0, that is, $\phi(0) = 0$. The function $\phi(L)$ may be called the bank's deposit retention function, and its slope $\phi'(L)$, which lies between zero and one, its marginal retention ratio.

Note that the bank is assumed to be unable to affect its deposits by acquiring defensive assets; its marginal retention ratio from this part of its portfolio is zero. Indeed, it is only because its deposits depend on how the bank divides its portfolio among alternative assets that deposit retention may become a relevant factor in its portfolio choices. The fact that loans are more likely to be redeposited than other bank asset purchases may dispose the bank to favor loans.

The advantage that deposit retention gives to loans may be illustrated most clearly in the first deterministic model, in which deposits are exogenous, costless, and foreseen with certainty. An expansion of $1 of loans and investments now increases deposits by $\$\phi'(L)$ and lowers the defensive position not by $1 but only by $\$(1 - \phi')$. Required reserves increase by $\$k\phi'$. Defensive position is reduced by $\$(1 - \phi' + k\phi')$. Thus the marginal opportunity cost of lending $1 is $r[1 - \phi'(L)(1 - k)]$ instead of r for defensive position positive, or $(r + b)[1 - \phi'(L)(1 - k)]$ instead of $r + b$ for defensive positive negative. This marginal cost is lower, and the marginal retention ratio is higher. The higher the retention ratio, the greater the volume of loans and deposits and the lower the defensive position.

The previous diagrammatic analysis can be easily reinterpreted. Take D_0—the wholly autonomous volume of deposits assumed in Figs. 7.2, 7.3, and 7.4—to be the volume of deposits the bank can have without making loans at all. Then the effect of deposit retention is to rotate downward the cost curve of Figs. 7.3 and 7.4, pivoted on its intersection with the vertical axis, and to give it a lower slope, still positive but not necessarily constant. With this amendment, the previous analysis and conclusions still hold. Note, however, that the size of the required reserve ratio k now affects the marginal opportunity cost of lending, which is higher the larger the fraction of induced deposits that must be placed in interest-barren required reserves.

The advantages of deposit retention, however, are partially or even wholly lost if the retained deposits impose interest or other costs on the bank. For example, if an interest rate $C'(D)$ is paid to depositors, the marginal cost of lending is raised by $\phi'(L)C'(D)$. If the bank is in complete equilibrium, and if retained deposits cost as much as any other deposits, their marginal cost is equal to their value in any investment use. Hence $C'(D)$ is equal to $r(1 - k)$—or $(r + b)(1 - k)$—and the retained deposit has no net value. The marginal cost of lending reduces once more to r, or $r + b$, and portfolio choice is independent of deposit retention.

Deposit retention entails similar modification and reinterpretation of the analysis of the effects of uncertainty about future deposits. But the conclusions, including the variety of possible cases, remain qualitatively the same.

7.7
RISK NEUTRALITY OR RISK AVERSION?

The preceding analysis assumes that the bank is risk neutral. The firm maximizes expected profits, and this also maximizes its expected utility of profits. Of course the hazards of deposit fluctuation affect the bank's decision. But they do so through their calculable effect on expected costs rather than through any assumed disutility of variance of profits. To some degree the two approaches are interchangeable. The fixed cost *a* of a negative defensive position has been treated above as a definite pecuniary cost. It might alternatively be regarded as a psychological cost, that is, an approximate pecuniary equivalent of the disutility of adverse fluctuations of deposits. In any case, superimposing risk aversion on the model as presented would tilt the bank's decision further toward a conservative portfolio policy, reducing illiquid loans and investments relative to defensive assets.

Risk neutrality seems the appropriate assumption for the firm. A bank is managed by specialists engaged in taking a long sequence of risks of deposit fluctuation and can expect bad luck and good luck to average out. That is, the long-run variance of the profits associated with any given policy is much smaller than the short-run variance. It is true that the firm might not survive a sequence of heavy losses. In the preceding model, this danger enters the model through the size of the parameters *a* and *b*; if they are large enough relative to loan and deposit opportunities, the firm will follow a cautious policy, perhaps accepting no illiquidity risks at all.

The variance of profits of a risk-neutral bank will be taken into account by the shareowners, who may be risk-averse individuals. In a system without deposit insurance, the risks of illiquidity taken by a bank would also be considered by depositors gauging the chances that the bank will be unable to meet its liabilities. The portfolio choices of the bank would then affect its supply of deposits in a manner that works in a direction opposite to the loan retention mechanism discussed above: A more conservative balance sheet would attract more deposits. Deposit insurance has largely eliminated this consideration. It has not done so entirely, because legally it covers only the first $100,000 of a deposit and because there may be delays in receiving payment. Moreover, the surveillance formerly exercised by depositors is in some degree replaced by the surveillance of the insurer.

7.8
CONCLUDING REMARKS

The simple model of a commercial banking firm presented in this chapter examines the choice between reserves and other defensive assets, on the one hand, and less liquid loans and investments, on the other. The bank must make this choice before it knows what its volume of deposits will be. A drain of deposits to other banks, for example, an adverse balance in interbank check clearing, has to be met by disposal of assets of one kind or the other or by borrowing. The same problem arises for banks in the aggregate if the public withdraws deposits in order to hold currency.

Meeting a drain by selling loans and investments or by borrowing is typically more expensive than drawing on reserves or selling liquid defensive assets. The additional expense of a negative defensive position is modeled to consist of a fixed cost plus a penalty proportional to the size of the shortfall. The bank weighs the probability of incurring such expense against the probability of forgoing profit by holding less remunerative defensive assets in redundant amounts if deposit experience turns out to be favorable.

The behavior of the bank in this model is a prime example of what Keynes called the *precautionary motive* for holding money and other liquid assets. This was discussed in general terms in Chapter 3. Other economic agents face problems similar to those of banks and exhibit similar behavior. Thus the model, in spirit though not in institutional detail, applies generally to households, businesses, financial institutions, and other agents who make illiquid commitments in the face of uncertainties about their future streams of receipts.

In its simplicity the model ignores several important aspects of the decision problems of real-world banks: First, it is a static model and does not deal with the intertemporal structure of bank liabilities and assets. Their maturities, for example, will affect the bank's defensive positions for many—in principle for all—future dates. Second, assets, liabilities, and borrowing capabilities are not so neatly divisible into two categories but constitute a spectral menu of liquidity and other characteristics. Consequently the model's separation of the bank's decision on defensive position versus loans and investments from portfolio choices within those categories is somewhat artificial. Third, the model does not explicitly handle uncertainties other than those connected with deposits. These include calls on lines of credit committed to long-term customers who use the bank both as a depository and as a contingent source of credit, fluctuations in interest rates and prices of marketable securities, and possible defaults on commercial loans.

Nevertheless the model captures in essence the distinctive features of bank portfolio choice most relevant to banks' crucial role in the monetary system. It provides therefore a *micro*economic foundation for analysis of the *macro*economic effects of monetary policy instruments under various institutional and regulatory regimes. Among the policy instruments and structural variations of interest are the procedures and targets of central bank open-market operations, the nature and level of reserve requirements, the payment or nonpayment of interest on reserve assets, the costs and terms of central bank lending to banks, the existence and level of legal ceilings on deposit interest rates, and the number and competitive structure of firms in the banking industry. A tractable model of the banking firm is a prerequisite to economy-wide analysis of financial and monetary systems that rely heavily on intermediation and inside money.

APPENDIX 7A: CERTAINTY ABOUT DEPOSITS

7A.1
DEPOSITS EXOGENOUS AND COSTLESS

In the first model deposits are assumed to be known with certainty, but possibly to depend on the loans and investments of the bank. They are assumed exogenous in the sense that the bank cannot influence the quantity of deposits by varying its outlays for deposit interest, depositor services, or advertising.

The balance sheet identity for the bank is

$$[D_0 + \phi(L)](1 - k) + E - R - L = 0, \tag{7A.1}$$

where $D_0 + \phi(L) =$ deposits
$k =$ the required reserve ratio
$E =$ shareholders' equity
$R =$ defensive position
$L =$ loans and investments
$\phi(L) =$ the deposit retention function: $\phi(0) = 0, 0 \le \phi'(L) < 1$.

The profits per year of the bank are

$$\Pi = P(L) + Y(R) \tag{7A.2}$$

where $P(L)$ is the net revenue from loans and investments and $Y(R)$ the net revenue from the defensive position. Marginal revenue from lending $P'(L)$ is assumed positive but declining with L:

$$Y(R) = \begin{cases} rR & R \ge 0 \\ (r + b)R - a & R < 0. \end{cases} \tag{7A.3}$$

Here r is the interest rate earned on a positive defensive position; $r + b$, with $b \ge 0$, the interest rate paid on a negative defensive position; and $a \ge 0$ the fixed penalty cost per annum of a negative defensive position.

It is assumed, in conformity with U.S. institutions, that no interest is earned on required reserves.

Using Eqs. 7A.1 and 7A.3, Eq. 7A.2 can be rewritten:

$$\Pi_1(L) = P(L) + r\{[D_0 + \phi(L)](1 - k) + E - L\} \quad (R \ge 0)$$
$$\Pi_2(L) = P(L) + (r + b)\{[D_0 + \phi(L)](1 - k) + E - L\} \quad (R < 0). \tag{7A.4}$$

The problem is to maximize Eq. 7A.4 with respect to L. Let L_c be the value of L such that $R = [D_0 + \phi(L)](1 - k) + E - L = 0$. Let L^* be the value of L, if one exists, such that

$$P'(L^*) = -Y'(R)\frac{\partial R}{\partial L} = Y'(R)[1 - \phi'(L^*)(1 - k)]$$

$$= \begin{cases} r[1 - \phi'(L^*)(1 - k)] & (L^* \le L_c) \\ (r + b)[1 - \phi'(L^*)(1 - k)] & (L^* > L_c). \end{cases} \tag{7A.5}$$

There are several cases:

(a) $L^* \le L_c$; L^* is the solution.
(b) $L^* > L_c$ and $\Pi_2(L^*) > \Pi_1(L_c)$; L^* is the solution.
(c) $L^* > L_c$ but $\Pi_2(L^*) < \Pi_1(L_c)$; L_c is the solution.
(bc) $L^* > L_c$ but $\Pi_2(L^*) = \Pi_1(L_c)$; both L_c and L^* are solutions.
(d) $r[1 - \phi'(L_c)(1 - k)] < P'(L_c) \le (r + b)[1 - \phi'(L_c)(1 - k)]$; L_c is the solution and profits are $\Pi_1(L_c)$.

When the maximizing value of L is L^*, it is not altered by exogenous changes in E or D_0. The marginal values of such changes reflect simply their investment in defensive assets. $\partial\Pi/\partial D_0 = (1-k)(\partial\Pi/\partial E)$ because k of every incremental deposit must be placed in interest-barren reserves.

$$\frac{\partial\Pi}{\partial E} = \begin{cases} r & (L^* \leq L_c) \\ r+b & (L^* > L_c). \end{cases} \tag{7A.6}$$

When the maximizing value of L is L_c, then

$$\frac{\partial\Pi}{\partial E} = \frac{\partial\Pi_1}{\partial L_c} \cdot \frac{\partial L_c}{\partial E} = \frac{P'(L_c)}{1 - \phi'(L_c)(1-k)}. \tag{7A.7}$$

Again, $\partial\Pi/\partial D_0$ is $(1-k)$ times this quantity.

7A.2
DEPOSITS EXOGENOUS AT A GIVEN COST

A variant on this model would require the bank to pay a fixed interest rate on deposits, though at this rate it could not obtain more deposits than $D_0 + \phi(L)$. Assume this rate d to be smaller than $r(1-k)$. Then Eq. 7A.5 must be revised to reflect the smaller value of retained deposits:

$$P'(L^*) = Y'(R) - \phi'(L^*)[Y'(R)(1-k) - d]. \tag{7A.5$'$}$$

If d exceeds $r(1-k)$ but does not exceed $(r+b)(1-k)$, it is clearly not to the bank's interest to accept deposits and invest them in defensive assets. Instead the bank will be fully loaned up, with $R = 0$, and with $D \leq D_0 + \phi(L)$. The volume of loans and investments will be such that

$$P'(L^*)(1-k) = d, \qquad \left[D = \frac{L^* - E}{1-k} \leq D_0 + \phi(L^*) \right]. \tag{7A.5$''$}$$

If $P'(L_c)(1-k) > d$, the bank may find it profitable to accept all the deposits available at d and obtain additional lendable funds by borrowing at rate $(r+b)$. Then Eq. 7A.5$'$ applies once more.

If d exceeds $(r+b)(1-k)$, the bank will accept no deposits and simply borrow at rate $(r+b)$ to finance any lending beyond its capital:

$$P'(L^*) = r+b, \qquad (R = L^* - E). \tag{7A.5$'''$}$$

A model in which the several margins are met simultaneously is given in the next section.

7A.3
DEPOSITS ENDOGENOUS

The second model assumes that the bank can choose its volume of deposits by incurring a cost $C(D)$ of a total volume of deposits $D = D_0 + \phi(L)$. The bank may now be regarded as having two decision variables, D_0 and L. Then Eq. 7A.4 becomes

$$\Pi_1(L, D_0) = P(L) + rR - C(D) \qquad\qquad (R \geq 0)$$
$$\Pi_2(L, D_0) = P(L) + (r + b)R - C(D) - a \qquad (R < 0). \tag{7A.8}$$

At $R = 0$, Π_1 can be written solely as a function of L, namely:

$$\Pi_1 = P(L) - C\left(\frac{L - E}{1 - k}\right) \qquad (R = 0). \tag{7A.9}$$

Given $R = 0$, the maximizing L, call it L_c, is such that

$$(1 - k)P'(L_c) = C'\left(\frac{L_c - E}{1 - k}\right). \tag{7A.10}$$

As before, L^*, if it exists, will be a solution to one of the following two pairs of equations:

$$\left.\begin{array}{l} \dfrac{\partial\Pi_1}{\partial L} = P'(L) + [r(1 - k) - C'(D)]\phi'(L) - r = 0 \\[2em] \dfrac{\partial\Pi_1}{\partial D_0} = r(1 - k) - C'[D_0 + \phi(L)] = 0 \end{array}\right\} (L \leq L_C). \tag{7A.11}$$

$$\left.\begin{array}{l} \dfrac{\partial\Pi_2}{\partial L} = P'(L) + [(r + b)(1 - k) - C'(D)]\phi'(L) - (r + b) = 0 \\[2em] \dfrac{\partial\Pi_2}{\partial D_0} = (r + b)(1 - k) - C'[D_0 + \phi(L)] = 0 \end{array}\right\} (L > L_C). \tag{7A.12}$$

These may be rewritten as follows:

$$\left.\begin{array}{l} P'(L^*) = r \\[1em] r(1 - k) = C'[D_0^* + \phi(L^*)] \end{array}\right\} (L^* \leq L_c), \tag{7A.11'}$$

$$\left.\begin{array}{l} P'(L^*) = r + b \\[1em] (r + b)(1 - k) = C'[D_0^* + \phi(L^*)] \end{array}\right\} (L^* > L_c). \tag{7A.12'}$$

There are several cases, as above:

(a) $L^* \leq L_c$; (L^*, D_0^*) is the solution.
(b) $L^* > L_c$ and $\Pi_2(L^*, D_0^*) > \Pi_1(L_c)$; (L^*, D_0^*) is the solution.
(c) $L^* > L_c$ but $\Pi_2(L^*, D_0^*) < \Pi_1(L_c)$; L_c is the solution.
(bc) $L^* > L_c$ but $\Pi_2(L^*, D_0^*) = \Pi_1(L_c)$; both L_c and (L^*, D_0^*) are solutions.
(d) $r < P'(L_c) < r + b$; L_c is the solution and profits are $\Pi_1(L_c)$.

Note that when deposits are endogenous the degree of loan retention is irrelevant. On the margin, a deposit costs as much as it earns. Hence the bank does not gain by having part of a loan end up as a deposit for which it must pay. (This would not be true if the marginal cost of a deposit obtained from loan retention were lower than the marginal cost of other deposits.)

In general,

$$P'(L^*) = Y'(R)[1 - \phi'(L^*)(\partial\Pi/\partial D_0)]. \tag{7A.13}$$

In the first model (Section 7A.2), $\partial\Pi/\partial D_0$ is $Y'(R)(1 - k)$ or $Y'(R)(1 - k) - d$, and this leads to 7A.5 or 7A.5'. In the second model (Section 7A.3), $\partial\Pi/\partial D_0$ is zero, and this leads to 7.11' or 7.12'.

APPENDIX B: UNCERTAINTY ABOUT DEPOSITS

7B.1
DEPOSITS EXOGENOUS BUT RANDOM

Now assume that deposits are $D_0(1 + x) + \phi(L)$ where $x \geq -1$ is a random variable with mean zero. Let $F(X)$ be the probability that $x \leq X$, and let $f(x)$ be the corresponding probability density function. The value of L is set prior to the deposit outcome. Therefore, defensive position R is also a random variable, equal to $[D_0(1 + x) + \phi(L)](1 - k) + E - L$. For given L, the critical value X at which R is zero is given by

$$XD_0 = \frac{L - E}{(1 - k)} - E(D) = -\frac{E(R)}{(1 - k)} \tag{7B.1}$$

where $E(R)$ is expected defensive position and $E(D) = D_0 + \phi(L)$ is expected deposits. Every dollar increase in lending raises XD_0 by $1/(1 - k) - \phi'(L)$.

Profits are $\Pi(L, x) = P(L) + Y(R)$:

$$\Pi_1(L, x) = P(L) + rR \qquad\qquad (x \geq X)$$
$$\Pi_2(L, x) = P(L) + (r + b)R - a \qquad (x < X). \tag{7B.2}$$

Therefore,

$$E(\Pi) = P(L) - r(1 - k)XD_0 - b(1 - k)XD_0F(X)$$
$$+ (1 - k)bD_0\int_{-1}^{X} xf(x)\,dx - af(X). \tag{7B.3}$$

$$\frac{\partial E(\Pi)}{\partial L} = P'(L) - r[1 - (1 - k)\phi'(L)] - b[1 - (1 - k)\phi'(L)]F(X)$$
$$+ \frac{\partial X}{\partial L}[-b(1 - k)XD_0f(X) + b(1 - k)XD_0f(X) - af(X)]. \tag{7B.4}$$

Maximum expected profits are obtained when

$$P'(L) = [1 - (1 - k)\phi'(L)][r + bF(X) + af(X)/D_0(1 - k)]. \tag{7B.5}$$

The term on the right is the marginal expected revenue from defensive position, the marginal opportunity cost of making loans. Since both $F(X)$ and $f(X)$ will generally be rising in the relevant range, marginal cost is increasing. But for high L and X, $f(X)$ declines with X, and from this arises the possibility that marginal cost declines in some range. Assuming that $f(X)$ goes to zero at both extremes of X, marginal cost approaches r as L goes to zero, and approaches $r + b$, from either above or below, as L and X become indefinitely large.

The value of additional equity E is

$$\frac{\partial \mathbf{E}(\Pi)}{\partial E} = P'(L)\frac{\partial L}{\partial E} + \frac{\partial \mathbf{E}[Y(R)]}{\partial L}\frac{\partial L}{\partial E} + \frac{\partial \mathbf{E}[Y(R)]}{\partial E}. \tag{7B.6}$$

From Eq. 7B.5 we know that the first two terms add to zero. To evaluate the third term, differentiate $\mathbf{E}(\Pi) - P(L)$ in Eq. 7B.3 with respect to E, noting that $\partial X/\partial E = -[1/(1-k)D_0]$.

$$\frac{\partial \mathbf{E}(\Pi)}{\partial E} = r + bF(X) + \frac{a}{(1-k)D_0}f(X). \tag{7B.7}$$

Similarly,

$$\frac{\partial \mathbf{E}(\Pi)}{\partial D_0} = r(1-k) + b(1-k)F(X) + \frac{a}{D_0}f(X)(1+X). \tag{7B.8}$$

7B.2
DEPOSITS ENDOGENOUS AND STOCHASTIC

As in the case of deposit certainty, an alternative model would permit the bank to influence its own deposits by means other than making loans. In this case interest payments or other outlays by the bank shift the parametric value D_0 around which the probability distribution $F(x)$ pivots. Indeed D_0 may be regarded as a decision variable for the bank, along with the volume of loans L. The total cost of deposits is, like the volume of deposits itself, a random variable. The bank, by setting L and D_0, also establishes an average cost of deposits, for example, an interest rate. The total volume of deposits bearing this established rate then depends on the random element x. The cost of deposits satisfies

$$C = C[D_0 + \phi(L)](1+x) \tag{7B.9}$$

Expected deposits $\mathbf{E}(D)$ are determined ex ante by the bank's choices (D_0, L) and are equal to $D_0 + \phi(L)$. Actual deposits realized are $D = \mathbf{E}(D)(1+x)$. Realized defensive position will be stochastic:

$$R = \mathbf{E}(D)(1+x)(1-k) + E - L. \tag{7B.10}$$

The critical value of x at which defensive position is zero is X, given by

$$(1-k)X\mathbf{E}(D) = L - E - (1-k)\mathbf{E}(D). \tag{7B.11}$$

Actual defensive position realized can be rewritten:

$$R = (1-k)(x-X)\mathbf{E}(D). \tag{7B.12}$$

Similarly, the cost of deposits, and its partial derivatives with respect to the two decision variables can be expressed in terms of $\mathbf{E}(D)$:

$$C(D) = C\left(\mathbf{E}(D)\right)(1 + x), \tag{7B.13}$$

$$\frac{\partial \mathbf{E}(C)}{\partial D_0} = C'\left(\mathbf{E}(D)\right) \quad \text{and} \quad \frac{\partial \mathbf{E}(C)}{\partial L} = C'\left(\mathbf{E}(D)\right)\phi'(L). \tag{7B.14}$$

Profits are as follows:

$$\begin{aligned} \Pi_1(L, D_0, x) &= P(L) + rR - C\left(\mathbf{E}(D)\right)(1 + x) &\quad (x \geq X) \\ \Pi_2(L, D_0, x) &= P(L) + (r + b)R - C\left(\mathbf{E}(D)\right)(1 + x) - a. &\quad (x < X) \end{aligned} \tag{7B.15}$$

Note the following partial derivatives:

$$\begin{aligned} \partial\left(X\mathbf{E}(D)\right)/\partial L &= 1/(1 - k) - \phi'(L); \\ \partial\left(X\mathbf{E}(D)\right)/\partial D_0 &= -1; \\ \partial X/\partial L &= 1/\left[\mathbf{E}(D)(1 - k)\right] - [\phi'(L)(1 + X)]/\mathbf{E}(D); \\ \partial X/\partial D_0 &= -(1 + X)/\mathbf{E}(D). \end{aligned} \tag{7B.16}$$

The expected value of profits can be written in terms of $\mathbf{E}(D)$:

$$\mathbf{E}(\Pi) = P(L) - r(1 - k)X\mathbf{E}(D) - C\left(\mathbf{E}(D)\right) - b(1 - k)X\mathbf{E}(D)F(X)$$

$$+ b(1 - k)\mathbf{E}(D)\int_{-1}^{X} x f(x)\, dx - aF(X). \tag{7B.17}$$

The first-order conditions are

$$\frac{\partial \mathbf{E}(\Pi)}{\partial D_0} = r(1 - k) + b(1 - k)F(X) - C'\left(\mathbf{E}(D)\right)$$

$$+ b(1 - k)\int_{-1}^{X} x f(x)\, dx + af(X)(1 + X)/\mathbf{E}(D) = 0 \tag{7B.18}$$

$$\frac{\partial \mathbf{E}(\Pi)}{\partial L} = \phi'(L)\left(\frac{\partial \mathbf{E}(\Pi)}{\partial D_0}\right) + P'(L)$$

$$- \left[r + bF(X) + af(X)/\left(\mathbf{E}(D)(1 - k)\right)\right] = 0.$$

Therefore:

$$P'(L) = r + bF(X) + af(X)/\mathbf{E}(D)(1 - k)$$

$$\frac{C'(\mathbf{E}(D))}{(1 - k)} = P'(L) + b\int_{-1}^{X} x f(x)\, dx + af(X)X/\mathbf{E}(D)(1 - k). \tag{7B.19}$$

In words, marginal loan revenue exceeds the marginal cost of deposits not only because of the reserve requirement k but also because additional expected deposits enlarge the shortfalls on which penalty interest is charged. (The second term in the last equation is likely to be negative and the third term close to zero.)

CHAPTER 8

The Monetary and Banking System of the United States: History and Institutions

The purpose of this chapter is to set the stage for the analysis of the monetary and banking system of the United States that will follow in Chapters 9 and 10. A peculiarly American institutional framework has evolved over two centuries; the first eight sections of this chapter review the history. The remaining five sections describe the accounting and the mechanics of the relations among federal debt, the Treasury and the Federal Reserve System, and the supplies of currency and bank reserves. Chapter 9 fleshes out this skeleton with economic analysis of the behavior of the banks, the Federal Reserve, and the general public.

In advanced societies over the last two centuries, economic and financial transactions have been largely carried out with media of exchange issued by banks, either notes or deposits. These have been promises to pay the currency of the realm but have supplanted the actual transfer of currency in the majority of transactions, measured in value. Sometimes the currency itself has been a promise to pay gold or silver, and sometimes, as in the last few decades of the twentieth century, the currency has been inconvertible paper, embodying simply a government's fiat.

The association of the supply of transactions money with the business of banking was an unplanned historical development beginning in the fifteenth century in Italy and especially in the seventeenth century in England. Goldsmiths' business was to receive and hold monetary metals for appraisal and safekeeping. Their paper receipts for gold and silver became convenient means of payment, substituting for the coins or metals themselves. Goldsmiths also learned that they could lend some of the deposits entrusted to them at interest, counting on the law of large numbers to protect them from many depositors' requesting redemptions all at once. Goldsmiths became bankers.

8.1
BANKING IN THE UNITED STATES TODAY

The U.S. banking system included in 1992 some 13,500 depository institutions, private enterprises which incur liabilities to pay dollar currency on demand to depositors or on their order. Including their branches, there were 65,000 banking offices. Of the 13,500 depository institutions—"banks" for short in this book—11,000 were commercial banks, traditionally oriented to lending to businesses. The rest were thrift institutions—savings banks and savings and loan associations (S&Ls). Commercial bank assets totalled $3.5 trillion, and those of the thrifts $1 trillion. In addition there were 12,500 credit unions, small mutual cooperatives with aggregate assets of only $250 million. They too do a banking business, offering their members checking accounts, consumer credit, and mortgage finance.

Deregulation in the 1970s and 1980s has blurred the institutional difference among savings institutions and between them and commercial banks. Commercial banks are no longer the only depositories allowed to offer the public deposit accounts payable and checkable on demand. On the asset side, too, the depositories have been converging in the classes of borrowers they serve and the types of loans and securities they acquire. S&Ls have now become savings banks, and account for a majority of all savings institutions. S&Ls were originally chartered to specialize in residential mortgage finance. Most of them were initially mutual institutions, theoretically owned by their depositors, who were called shareowners. Over the last forty years they gradually evolved into stock companies; in other respects too, they have become more and more like commercial banks. Traditional savings banks are still nonprofit or mutual institutions. While participating actively in residential mortgage markets, they generally had more diversified asset portfolios than S&Ls.

The U.S. system is unique in its large number of banks. However, $3.25 of the $4.75 trillion assets are concentrated in the 475 institutions, almost all commercial banks, with over a billion dollars of assets each, and $2.5 trillion in the 238 institutions with $3 billion or more of assets (U.S. Department of Commerce, Statistical Abstract of the United States 1994, Table #776). About 9000 banks, accounting for 95 percent of deposits, are wholly owned subsidiaries of bank holding companies. All but 1000 of the 6000 holding companies own just one bank. The holding company device was designed to escape regulations that restricted the activities and locations of banks proper and to raise in the open market funds that the holding company could invest as capital in its bank or banks. In response, legislators and bank regulators have sought tighter control of bank holding companies.

8.2
A QUICK HISTORY OF U.S. BANKING

So decentralized a banking system was not what Alexander Hamilton, George Washington's Treasury Secretary, had in mind. He established the First Bank of the United States on the model of the Bank of England. The First Bank was owned 80 percent by private shareholders and 20 percent by the federal government. The First Bank was the Treasury's depository and financier. It also engaged in ordinary commercial banking; its notes, convertible on demand into gold or silver dollars, circulated as currency. Its central office was in Philadelphia, and it had branches in commercial centers throughout the young nation. Hamilton chartered few competitors and kept the states out of the banking business too.

Populist and anti-federalist resentment prevented the First Bank from being rechartered by Congress in 1811. It was missed during the War of 1812. The Second Bank of the United States, similar and larger, was chartered in 1816. Rechartering became the major political issue in the 1830s: agrarian populism versus Hamiltonian concentration of financial power. Andrew Jackson succeeded in killing the Second Bank and any possibility of another such bank.

With Jackson's encouragement, state-chartered banks rushed in to fill the vacuum. Free banking replaced Hamilton's federally centralized banking. The state banks issued notes that circulated as currency. They were supposedly secured by state government securities. They were theoretically convertible into U.S. dollars, that is, into gold or silver, on demand. Sometimes people could not find the "wildcat banks" whose notes they sought to redeem. Bank notes were discounted as they changed hands in circulation, to reflect the inconveniences and risks of redeeming them and the credibilities of the issuers. Despite the wildcat epithet, however, recent revisionist studies of the era of free state banking grade it higher than its legendary reputation (Schuler and White, 1992).

The pendulum swung back from states to nation in 1864. The National Banking Act inaugurated free chartering by the comptroller of the currency in the U.S. Treasury. National banks were empowered to issue notes backed by U.S. government bonds; as a further safeguard, note issue could not exceed the paid-in capital of the bank. These notes were official U.S. currency; the Treasury would assume the liability if the bank failed. Thus national bank notes were guaranteed to exchange at par, no matter what bank issued them. In effect, the Treasury was paying these banks the interest on the bonds that stood behind the notes, letting the banks pocket the seignorage on the currency.

In 1866 Congress taxed state bank notes out of existence; the incident gave rise to the famous adage "The power to tax is the power to destroy." But state banks were not destroyed, because they could accept deposits, which grew rapidly as a medium of exchange alternative to paper currency. Deposits became the main liabilities of national banks too. By substituting doubly guaranteed national bank notes for state bank notes, Congress made sure that banking panics could not occur by the public's losing confidence in bank notes. But Congress did nothing to guard against public runs to convert deposits into currency and gold, the source of future banking crises.

The national banks had the advantage of issuing both media, but they were subject to stricter regulatory surveillance than banks with state charters. National banks lost their right to issue bank notes in 1935; currency became a monopoly of the Treasury and the Federal Reserve.

The dual system of chartering and regulating survives to this day. One of its consequences was that no banks, state or national, could expand into another state without that state's permission. This is one reason there are so many banking companies in the United States. However, the rules against interstate banking are now rapidly eroding.

In 1997 it appears that the country may be returning to free banking and decentralized issues of currency, this time electronic currency embodied in any desired amount in *smart cards* sold by private financial companies, not even necessarily banks (Gleick, 1996). These cards obviously have great advantages in convenience over ordinary currency—divisible, anonymous, compact—and also over checks in many uses. Like credit cards, an electronic currency card of a particular brand will be usable to make payments until it is exhausted, to anyone who has agreed to honor it. The payee's bank account will automatically be credited, and the original issuer's account correspondingly debited. Presumably any such card could itself be passed from hand to hand, like old-fashioned currency, so long as it has a positive balance.

To potential issuers, the attraction is the fee charged the buyer of the card and, more important, the interest earned on the float during the time it takes for the card to be used up. The danger is, as in the era of free banking, that issuers may be unable or unwilling to redeem their cards. If laissez faire prevails, they will not be chartered and regulated, and their liabilities will not be federally insured. The issuers look to be new species of banks, free of the disciplines to which old species are subject. Yet so far, federal officials have not viewed private electronic currency with any concern or considered the issue of federal electronic currency. The government should not give up its constitutional monopoly so thoughtlessly.

8.3
BANKING PANICS

Banking is an inherently risky business, as explained in previous chapters, especially Chapter 7. Banks borrow short. Their principal liabilities are deposits payable on demand or on short notice or on definite dates only weeks or months away. They lend long. Their assets are commercial loans maturing in six months or a year or several years, mortgages payable over many years, and long-term bonds. Their liabilities are fixed in dollars and are extremely liquid. Their assets may not be salable at all before their maturity or may be liquidatable only at prices below their maturity values. Loans made to a bank's commercial customers are often completely illiquid. Longer-term interest-bearing assets, bonds and mortgages, are usually marketable, but at prices that vary unpredictably with interest-rate fluctuations and with changes in the credit standings of the debtors. A fraction of assets are cash reserves, but these are mostly tied up by reserve requirements, thus not available to meet deposit withdrawals.

The capital of the bank is the difference between the value of the assets and the deposit liabilities. This is the buffer, the safety margin—the amount by which the aggregate value of the assets can fall without impairing the ability of the bank to meet withdrawals. (See Chapter 7.) Typically this is a single-digit percentage of assets. To level the playing field of global banking competition, major governments have agreed to common capital ratio requirements. These differ with the riskiness of asset categories. The highest ratio applies to commercial loans and to private bonds and mortgages. It is only 8 percent, but many U.S. institutions still fall short of these internationally agreed-upon requirements.

In short, banking is a highly levered business. When the bank makes a loan of $100, the owners are lending less than $10 of their own money and more than $90 of other people's money. It is not surprising that banks sometimes fail, inflicting heavy losses on their depositors and other creditors. Nor is it surprising that depositors' and note holders' withdrawals, triggered by nervousness about the possibilities of failure, sometimes bring on failures, not just of individual banks but by contagion of many banks. Prominent in the history of banking are endless efforts by governments to prevent failures and especially epidemic failures. Governments charter banks and regulate their activities. Public or quasi-public central banks lend to troubled banks. Governments guarantee to the public that bank liabilities will be paid.

After the demise of the Second Bank of the United States, the nation had nothing that resembled a central bank. No institution assumed responsibilities, like those of the Bank of England, for the system as a whole until Congress established the Federal Reserve System in 1913. Meanwhile, the U.S. Treasury, lacking any official banker, learned to carry out some central banking functions on its own. Its Independent Treasury System involved a chain of regional offices to collect and disburse government funds. By accumulating balances and managing the timing and geography of their disbursement, the Treasury could respond to seasonal and regional variations in needs for currency. Nevertheless, there were periodic panics. Six occurred before the Civil War and six more before World War I.

A panic is a sudden rush to convert bank notes or bank deposits into government currency. Until 1933—with the exception of 1863–1879, the period of inconvertible government "greenbacks," originally issued to finance the Civil War—this meant turning bank promises to pay into gold or silver or their dollar equivalent. Of course, an individual bank might at any time suffer a run because its note holders, depositors, and other creditors lost faith in its ability to meet its liabilities. It could be thought to be insolvent because of bad loans or illiquid because its loans would become good too late. A panic is an undiscriminating loss of faith in banks in general. The distrust is a self-fulfilling prophecy because the run itself renders the banks illiquid and incapable of filling the demands upon them. Moreover, even note holders and depositors who had trusted their banks will join a run if they fear that other creditors will force their banks to fail.

Under the pre-1914 gold standard a run to gold also had international dimensions. Gold and British pounds sterling were essentially equivalent. Americans and foreigners could be running from dollar paper and dollar deposits to sterling.

The usual therapies for bank panics were concerted efforts by local clearinghouse associations of banks to pool their reserves and borrowing resources to stand behind all members. These appear to have been fairly successful (Gorton, 1992). With respect to panics, the national banking system was a mixed blessing. National bank notes were required to be maintained and exchanged at par, in contrast to the former state bank notes, which could be discounted. The discounts were a safety valve, a sort of automatic partial bankruptcy. When national banks, on the other hand, couldn't redeem their notes and deposits, they had to close.

Between financial panics and economic recessions there are two-way cause-and-effect connections. Panics contribute to economic downturns because credit becomes scarce, interest rates rise, depositors lose their savings, debtors are wiped out.

Recessions can turn into depressions, and both can breed panics. In the other direction, recessions and depressions can cause panics. Bad times result in loan defaults, endangering the solvency of many banks, breeding distrust of all banks, triggering epidemic runs.

Effects in both directions were operative in the decade of the Great Depression, 1890–1896. The decade was a critical period in the monetary economics and politics of the nation. Gold was leaving the country, contributing to the price deflation and credit stringency afflicting the nation's many farmers. Bank failures and panics (in 1890 and 1893) resulted and in turn exacerbated the depression. This story, which involves the politics and economics of gold and silver, is continued later in Section 8.7.

Prosperity returned as the century ended and continued in the new century. Yet another serious panic occurred in 1907, crystallizing the belief in financial and political circles that a new central banking institution must at long last be established.

8.4
THE FEDERAL RESERVE ACT OF 1913

The act set up twelve district Federal Reserve Banks, hybrid public-private institutions, each "owned" by member banks in its district and governed by a board of directors composed of bankers, business managers, and public members, administered by a governor (now president) appointed by the district Bank board, subject to approval of the Federal Reserve Board in Washington (now the Board of Governors of the Federal Reserve System.) That Board is governmental, its members either ex officio (before 1935 the Treasury Secretary and the Comptroller of the Currency) or appointed by the President of the United States and confirmed by the Senate. All national banks were required to be Federal Reserve members, and state banks too could choose to be members. In practice, big metropolitan state banks joined, but most state banks did not. A member bank was allowed to borrow from its Federal Reserve Bank, by rediscounting its commercial loans, that is, pledging them as collateral and receiving somewhat less than the face value of the loan. That discount rate is legally set by the district Federal Reserve Bank, with the approval of the Board. Originally it was thought that discount rates could vary among districts, responding to their particular economic and financial conditions. Even in 1914, however, the country was too financially integrated to make such differences in money market rates viable. Now the common discount rate for the twelve Federal Reserve Banks is de facto a systemwide decision.

The privilege of borrowing at the "discount window" was an advantage of membership. Disadvantageous were the reserve requirement and reserve discipline enforced by the Board, which were much tougher than those generally imposed by state banking authorities. Moreover, membership made a state-chartered bank subject to Federal Reserve surveillance on top of regulation by its state. In 1980 all commercial banks, national or state, and indeed all other depository institutions, were made subject to members' reserve requirements and in return were given access to the discount window. Membership was no longer an issue of importance.

The Federal Reserve Act authorized the Federal Reserve Banks to issue U.S. currency, Federal Reserve notes, which became the major currency in circulation and nowadays the only type issued. The Federal Reserve Banks also take deposits from banks, the Treasury, foreign governments, and international institutions. Unlike the Bank of England and other foreign central banks, Federal Reserve Banks have never been retail banks dealing directly with the general public. They are bankers' banks.

In the first twenty years of the system, it was not clear where would be the center of power, New York or Washington. The New York Bank was and is in the financial center, where the financial transactions of the system and the Treasury are executed, where the governor (later president) was in regular contact with the financial leaders of the nation and the world. In the 1920s the agenda of the system emphasized stabilization of financial markets, domestic and international. It was natural for the New York Bank to take leadership, and Benjamin Strong, its governor from 1914 until his untimely death in 1928, outclassed the Board in Washington. He was the dominant figure in the conferences and committees the governors organized on their own, independent of the Board, including one that coordinated their operations in money and securities markets.

With the inauguration of President Franklin D. Roosevelt in 1933, however, the health of the domestic economy became first priority for the federal government, the Federal Reserve System included. With a strong Board chairman close to the president, Marriner Eccles, and in the absence of anyone of Strong's stature among the banks, the Board in Washington took charge. A Federal Open Market Committee (FOMC) led by the Board chairman became the monetary policy-making authority. On the FOMC all seven Washington governors had votes, but only five of the twelve Bank presidents did. Domestic goals took precedence over foreign exchange, and the economy took priority over financial markets.

8.5
THE GREAT DEPRESSION AND THE BANKING CRISIS OF 1932–1933

Established to prevent recurrence of panics, the Federal Reserve System failed its first big test. In several ways, the episode was a replay of the 1890s. Bank insolvencies became increasingly frequent during the agricultural recessions of the 1920s, followed by the severe nationwide and worldwide collapse of economic activity in 1930–1932. Bank failures were not the cause of the depression, but they reinforced and aggravated the decline of business activity. In several bouts of nonconfidence, the public drained currency from the banking system and precipitated scrambles for reserves among banks. As in the 1890s, there was also an external drain of gold, triggered by Britain's forced departure from the gold standard and devaluation of the pound in September 1931. Finally, in the winter 1932–1933 between the November presidential election and the March inauguration, an acute panic, a run from bank deposits to currency and gold, brought epidemic bank failures. President Roosevelt's first acts were to close all banks—those that had not already failed and closed—and suspend the convertibility of dollars into gold.

In theory the Federal Reserve should have been able to prevent the contraction of bank reserves and bank credit that resulted from the public's massive shift from deposits to currency. If the public wanted more currency, the Federal Reserve could in effect just print it and supply it. Open-market purchases of government securities, or of private paper, would have replenished the banks' reserves. Why this was not done in the degree needed has been debated ever since. There were some technical problems, relating to the adequacy of the system's holdings of assets legally required as backing for Federal Reserve notes, 40 percent gold and 60 percent either gold or private paper eligible for rediscount. Friedman and Schwartz (1963, pp. 399–419) convincingly refute this excuse. The problem was remedied by legislation in February 1932, allowing government securities to back the notes, and this could have been requested earlier. Mainly, the officials of the system just did not think big enough; they were timid, scared of upsetting financial markets, and petrified by the possibility of losing gold if they acted too strongly. Friedman and Schwartz, and several other historians of the period, suspect that Benjamin Strong's death in 1928 deprived the system of leadership that might have been equal to the challenge.

8.6
THE BANKING AND FINANCIAL REFORMS OF THE 1930s

After the bank holiday at the outset of the new administration, the federal government nursed the banking system to life. Commercial banks were fewer, stronger, and wiser. The obvious urgent problem of the day was to forestall recurrent banking crises and panics. The solution adopted by Congress was federal insurance of deposits. National banks and other Federal Reserve members were required to join the Federal Deposit Insurance Corporation (FDIC); nonmember state banks had discretion, but most eventually joined too. The deposit insurance system worked well for a half century and still functions. A parallel system of insurance was established for federal savings and loan associations. It ran into trouble in the 1980s, not because of depositor panics but because many associations took advantage of deregulation of their balance sheets in the 1980s to make excessively risky loans and investments, with both managers and depositors secure in the knowledge that the insurance funds, and ultimately federal taxpayers, would pay off the depositors if their adventures did not pan out.

Other banking reforms in the 1930s included the following: (a) National bank notes were taken over by the Treasury as its direct obligations, and eventually disappeared from circulation. (b) Interest on demand deposits was prohibited, and ceilings on interest on time deposits were imposed. The motivation was the belief that banks endangered their solvency by raising deposit interest rates to compete with each other for deposits. These rate regulations were phased out in the 1980s (see Chapter 3, Section 3.2.4). (c) Banks were forbidden to underwrite securities issues or sell them to the public. Commercial banking and investment banking were forcibly divorced. The separation is generally referred to as Glass-Steagall, after the authors of the Banking Act of 1933, which includes this provision. The theory was that securities abuses by banks had contributed both to securities market crashes and to insolvencies of banks. Neither this theory nor the hypothesis that deposit interest-rate competition made banks unsound has withstood recent research.

A New Deal priority was to expand the nation's housing stock and in particular to promote home ownership. Building and loan associations had been around a long time. Now the federal government would charter them, and the number grew rapidly. At the same time, the federal government was insuring and subsidizing home mortgages.

The Banking Act of 1935 augmented the power of the Federal Reserve vis-à-vis the executive branch, the President, and the treasury secretary. Within the system, the act elevated the Board, which became the Board of Governors, composed of seven members appointed by the President, each for a term of fourteen years. Ex officio members of the Board were dropped. The secretary of the treasury had been the Board chairman. Now the chairman is one of the governors designated by the President for a four-year term. In practice, when the chairmanship is vacant, the President always has the governor slot of the outgoing chairman to fill by whomever the President wants to appoint as chairman.

Management of the balance sheet of the system, formerly dominated by the district Banks, was entrusted to the Federal Open Market Committee (FOMC), the Board plus five of the twelve presidents of Federal Reserve Banks. The nonvoting Bank presidents attend FOMC meetings. The New York Bank always has a vote; Cleveland and Chicago take annual turns; the other three votes rotate among the remaining nine districts. These allocations are economically outdated, as indeed is the geography of the districts—only one bank, San Francisco, is west of Dallas, Kansas City, and Minneapolis, but there are four along the Atlantic seaboard and two in Missouri.

8.7
GOLD AND SILVER IN THE U.S. MONETARY SYSTEM

Gold and silver have histories going back many centuries as the moneys of choice of many societies and as international media of exchange. Copper coinage antedated them, but copper became too abundant and was relegated to subsidiary coins—worth less in metallic content than as coins, called token coins in contrast to full-bodied coins. Gold and silver, one or the other or both, were the basic moneys of Europe and of European dominions and settlements throughout the world from the seventeenth century or before until the latter decades of the twentieth century.

Sovereigns minted these precious metals on demand into coins of their realms, embossed with their own names and heads. Many of these full-bodied coins circulated across national boundaries, with values equivalent to their weights. The original monetary unit of the United States was the silver dollar of Spanish America. Until the late nineteenth century, silver was more prevalent than gold as a monetary commodity. England's pound sterling was initially a weight of silver.

Many countries, including both England and the United States, coined both silver and gold. But there were frequent periods when bimetallism degenerated into one standard or the other. This happened when their prices at the mint diverged enough from their relative values in other countries or in commerce to offset the costs of arbitrage. Then Gresham's law would take over: The metal undervalued at the mint, the "good money," would disappear from monetary circulation, "driven out" by the "bad money" overvalued at the mint. Note that, contrary to popular metaphorical usage, Gresham's law works only when somebody, here the mint, buys and sells two commodities at prices relative to each other different from the terms on which one can be converted into the other elsewhere, for example in the mines. "Good" and "bad" do not refer to intrinsic worth. The mint could contrive to make gold bad and silver good, so that gold gets coined while silver is used in industry and the arts.

Indeed Isaac Newton, master of the Royal Mint, did just that in 1717. He inadvertently overvalued gold, pushing silver out of circulation and putting England de facto on the gold standard, a switch formalized in 1816. Alexander Hamilton supplemented the new American republic's silver dollar with gold coins. Only in the late nineteenth century did gold displace silver as the basic money of the United States. The gold values of sterling and dollar set by Newton and Hamilton, implying an exchange rate of $4.86 per pound, lasted until 1931, except for several wartime interruptions. The heyday of the international gold standard was 1880–1914, when all major national currencies were convertible into gold at fixed prices per ounce and therefore into each other at fixed rates.

In the United States the last two decades of the nineteenth century were characterized by financial panics, deflation, and depression, especially in agriculture. Silver became undervalued relative to gold at the mint, and tended to drop out of monetary circulation. At the same time, gold was scarce, credit was tight, and interest rates were high. Thanks to internal bank panics, people were moving from dollars to foreign currencies and gold was leaving the United States. The administration of Grover Cleveland, a conservative Democrat, and the New York financial establishment made defense of the gold value of the dollar their highest priority. Populists agitated for free coinage of silver, at a higher mint price per ounce, sixteen times that of gold, as a means of liberating the economy from the effects of the gold shortage. They succeeded in capturing the 1896 presidential nomination of the Democratic party for William Jennings Bryan who, with some justification, chided the establishment, "You shall not crucify mankind upon a cross of gold." Bryan's defeat gave political sanction to the gold standard. Gold flowed back in. At the same time, by lucky coincidence, discoveries of new gold deposits in South Africa and technical economies in the mining and refining of gold remedied its scarcity and set the monetary foundation for prosperous growth until World War I.

Silver was demoted to token-coin status like copper and nickel. The populists and the silver miners prevailed upon Congress from time to time to purchase silver for coins and for backing of new issues of silver certificates. But silver never regained the status of gold. The Treasury's commitment to buy silver was always limited in amount and flexible as to price. The silver in a silver dollar or "behind" a paper-dollar silver certificate was worth less than a dollar, either at the market price or at the price paid by the Treasury. The difference was the government's profit, its seignorage; the money coined or printed paid not only for the metal and paper involved but for other government expenditures as well.

In the 1960s, with the price of silver rising, the Treasury stopped issuing silver certificates, redeeming outstanding certificates in silver, and coining silver dollars. The mint cut the silver content of half-dollars and eliminated silver from other token coins. In the 1980s, the market price of silver rose nearly to its monetary value. The notorious Texas Hunt brothers tried to corner the market. The Treasury actually sold silver from its stockpile to industrial users to keep the price from rising to the point where melting down of outstanding silver coins would be profitable. That was the occasion for retiring silver certificates as they gravitated to the Federal Reserve Banks and the Treasury, replacing them with Federal Reserve notes. Although the silver bubble burst, issues of silver dollars and certificates have not been revived.

After its victory at the turn of the century, gold was unchallenged as the basic official money of the United States. Until 1971, except for the greenbacks issued to finance the Civil War, which remained inconvertible into gold (or silver) until 1879, the U.S. dollar was defined in ounces of gold or reciprocally by the dollar price of an ounce of gold. The Treasury was committed to buy gold and sell gold at a fixed price, which remained $20.67 as Hamilton had set it, until 1933.

To cope with the monetary and banking crisis he confronted on taking office in March 1933, President Roosevelt suspended convertibility; then he gradually raised the price at which the Treasury would at its discretion buy gold. At the end of the year the price was fixed at $35. Gold coins and gold certificates were permanently withdrawn from circulation, and private holding of gold within the United States, except the modest amounts used in art or industry, was prohibited. Some outstanding Treasury bonds had promised payment in dollars of the original gold content, but the administration argued that payment in dollars would suffice and prevailed at the Supreme Court. However, the Treasury resumed its commitment to buy and sell gold at the new price on demand of foreign governments and central banks, and likewise to buy newly mined gold.

After the crisis of 1932–1933, the Treasury and the Federal Reserve confronted a very different gold problem. They were not losing the stuff anymore; they were being overwhelmed by it. The Treasury was offering a price nearly 75 percent higher than before. American citizens were required to exchange their gold coins and hoards of gold for paper dollars. Gold newly mined throughout the world returned underground at Fort Knox, Kentucky, the Treasury's safe deposit vault. At the same time, the growing political perils of Europe made the United States the attractive safe haven for wealth. As foreigners bought American assets with European currencies, their banks and central banks had to buy the necessary dollars with gold. A popular book in undergraduate money and banking courses in the mid-1930s was *The Golden Avalanche* (Graham and Whittlesey, Princeton University Press, 1939). By the monetary mechanics explained in Section 8.12, Treasury gold purchases translate into banks' reserve balances in Federal Reserve Banks. Saturated with zero-interest reserves far in excess of requirements, banks sought interest-bearing loans and securities in which to invest them and brought market interest rates down close to zero. The glut of gold continued through World War II, and America entered the postwar world with 60 percent of the world's monetary gold stock.

8.8
THE BRETTON WOODS SYSTEM, 1945–1971

At Bretton Woods, New Hampshire, in 1945, forty-four nations agreed to the American design of a new world monetary system. Other countries pegged their currencies to the dollar, and the United States affirmed the dollar–gold linkage established in 1934. Beginning in 1959, however, as U.S. official gold reserves, once embarrassingly large, dwindled, the ability of the Treasury to honor the commitment to pay out gold for dollars on demand from foreign governments came into question. Speculation threatened to raise gold prices in private markets overseas above the official $35 price. Feeding those markets to hold the price down was draining U.S. official gold reserves. In 1968 the Treasury ceased intervening, and the free price rose tenfold.

Finally, in 1971–1973, the United States abandoned its Bretton Woods commitment. The dollar and other currencies were cut loose from gold. As a result, gold is no longer a commodity of monetary significance. Once the dollar was no longer convertible into gold, other countries had no further obligation to peg their currencies to the dollar. The world entered a new monetary regime. Many exchange rates, including those between major currencies, float continuously in free markets. Some governments choose to peg their currencies to others, subject to discretionary changes. The nations of western Europe have established a regional monetary system along the lines of Bretton Woods, with deutsche marks playing the Bretton Woods roles of gold and dollars. The European Union is committed by the Treaty of Maastricht to move to a single currency, the euro, in the next few years.

An incidental outcome of the 1971–1973 monetary revolution was that the United States and international official gold price was raised to $42.22. Remaining Treasury gold reserves and U.S. gold deposits in the International Monetary Fund (see item 1 in Table 8.2, Section 8.9) are carried at this value. Obviously no transactions occur at this price, so long as the market price is ten times greater, more or less. It is not clear what keeps the market price of gold so high. It is not commercial and industrial demand. It is not even ornamental and traditional demand among Asians, though this is considerable. It is ultimately a pure speculative bubble, wherein hoarders value gold high today because they think others will value it even higher tomorrow. Some speculators do think that governments will restore gold to its monetary pedestal, but this hope seems irrational, the more so the longer the present world monetary regime continues.

The Federal Reserve Banks used to be subject to reserve requirements imposed by Congress. Formerly they were required to hold reserves in gold certificates both against their currency issues, Federal Reserve notes, and against their deposit liabilities. These requirements were 40 percent and 35 percent, respectively, before World War II. In 1945 they were lowered to 25 percent for both kinds of liabilities.

In 1965 and 1968 Congress dropped these two reserve requirements altogether. When the United States was still on the gold standard but its gold stock was dwindling, there was some fear that these reserve requirements might become embarrassing binding constraints on Federal Reserve policy and also some fear that foreigners' confidence in the dollar might be impaired if they saw gold tied up in these cover requirements. Anyway, the requirement served no useful purpose.

In 1932 the gold cover requirements may have done serious harm. Federal Reserve officials seemed to regard them as constraints on their ability to stem the tide of deflation and bank failure—unnecessarily, according to Friedman and Schwartz (Section 8.5).

The remainder of the chapter describes current American federal financial and monetary institutions, an account that continues analytically in Chapter 9.

8.9
FEDERAL DEBT, BANKS, AND MONEY

The public debt of the federal government plays important roles in the structure and operating mechanism of the U.S. banking and monetary system. Banks, other financial institutions, businesses, and households hold various kinds of federal obligations. Changes in these holdings, often deliberately induced by Federal Reserve policies, are of great monetary and macroeconomic importance. Before World War II the debt was much smaller relative to the size of the economy. Private debt instruments played roles in the monetary and banking system that have since been assumed by federal obligations.

The federal debt consists of financial claims against the federal government, inclusive of the Federal Reserve System, held by individuals and institutions outside the federal government. These are of several kinds:

Transferable demand obligations. These are perfectly liquid, reversible, and predictable in money value. They include currency issued by the Treasury and Federal Reserve, and deposit obligations of the Federal Reserve.

Marketable securities, short-term and long-term. Securities are promises to pay specified sums of money on specified future dates. Marketable securities can be bought and sold, subject to some exchange costs and to unpredictability of money value because of interest-rate fluctuations. Maturities of Treasury securities outstanding as of 1995 ranged from three months to thirty years from original issue. The U.S. Treasury has in the past issued bonds as long as forty years, and the British government has traditionally offered perpetual bonds (called consols because they were originally put out to consolidate various debts of finite maturities.) There is, of course, no sharp line between short-term and long-term.

Bills are promises to make just one future payment, a specified amount at a specified date. They generally come in short maturities, one year or less. Bills of long maturity are called zero-coupon bonds. Conventional bonds promise a series of periodic payments, coupons, usually every six months, and a final payment of principal, equal to the face value of the bond. Bonds of shorter maturity are often called notes. In Table 8.1, the short-long dividing line is taken to be one year.

Nonmarketable securities. These are not traded. They are obtainable only from the Treasury or its agents and are disposable only by redemption at the Treasury after specified maturities. In terms of the properties of assets of Chapter 2, they are predictable but not liquid or reversible. Savings bonds, designed to accommodate small and unsophisticated savers, are the principal example.

TABLE 8.1

Estimated composition and distribution of federal debt (billions of dollars)

	1962	1972	1982	1992
Total outside Treasury and Federal Reserve				
1. Demand obligations (currency and Federal Reserve deposits)	53.4	97.6	168.3	369.2
2. Short-term marketable debt (maturity < 1 year)	68.0	91.0	293.3	843.4
3. Long-term marketable debt (maturity > 1 year)	94.6	89.2	335.7	1590.9
4. Nonmarketable debt	52.6	80.3	110.7	376.4
Held by depository institutions				
5. Demand obligations	23.3	36.4	39.9	67.7
6. Short-term marketable debt	24.4	25.8	53.9	93.9
7. Long-term marketable debt	54.3	57.2	77.8	256.3
Held by others				
8. Demand obligations	30.1	61.2	128.4	301.5
9. Short-term marketable debt	43.6	65.2	239.4	749.4
10. Long-term marketable debt	40.3	32.0	257.9	1334.6
11. Nonmarketable debt	52.6	80.3	110.7	376.4

Note: Includes only direct debt of the Treasury. Does not include debt of federal agencies and corporations. Figures represent end of December for all years except 1982, which shows figures for June.

Source: Federal Reserve Bulletin, Flow of Funds Accounts; for sources of current holdings by thrifts, see Table 9.2. For 1962–1982, the ratio of short-term debt to total debt held by depository institutions is calculated from data in the *Bulletin* and multiplied by total holdings to obtain estimates above. (Credit unions are omitted for these years.) For 1962 holdings of savings and loans, data are from *Historical Statistics of the United States,* and the maturity distributions are assumed to be the same as for mutual savings banks. For 1992, relative maturity holdings for all types of institutions are assumed to be those calculated for commercial banks for all investment securities from *Assets and Liabilities: Commercial and Mutual Savings Banks,* published by FDIC.

A full balance sheet of the federal government would recognize a vast array of statutory commitments difficult to estimate in amount and timing. They are not unconditional obligations to pay fixed sums of money at specified future dates. Examples are commitments to pay social security benefits, veterans' pensions, other entitlements, and grants-in-aid to state and local governments. Expenditures to meet commitments of this kind amount in the 1990s to a trillion dollars a year. A complete federal balance sheet would also credit the government with assets: loans to the private sector or to foreign governments, public lands, and other real properties. These debts and assets, important as they are in assessing governmental and national wealth (Kotlikoff, 1992) are largely irrelevant to the monetary and financial concerns of this book.

The federal debt for the purposes of this book is the total of the three kinds of financial obligations outstanding at any moment. Its book value is the net accumulation of past federal deficits and surpluses; it grows when federal outlays exceed receipts, and declines when receipts exceed outlays. The course of the total debt over time depends, therefore, on budgetary policies and outcomes year after year. The distribution of the total among the various categories of debt at any moment of time can be altered by the Treasury and Federal Reserve. The size of the debt results from fiscal policies; its composition is the province of debt management and monetary policies. The market value of the debt will vary, and deviate from the book value, as interest rates change and alter the prices of outstanding securities. These are nominal values in dollars. The real values, in purchasing power over goods and services, will depend also on price indexes, whose changes measure inflation and deflation.

The concepts of debt, surplus, deficit, receipts, and outlays must be mutually consistent, and the definitions chosen should be relevant to the choices available to government policy makers. The concepts used in these chapters correspond essentially to those of the National Income and Product Accounts (NIPA). For example, social security and federal retirement trust funds are incorporated within federal government accounts. In this accounting, the federal deficit is the NIPA accrual variant of the commonly used cash unified deficit.

It is worth stressing again that debt here includes non-interest-bearing demand obligations. Accordingly, in reckoning the current deficit, outlays include purchases which, like those of foreign currencies and obligations of the International Monetary Fund, are financed by printing or coining money or creating equivalent Federal Reserve deposit liabilities. These transactions augment public holdings of the government's demand debt.

It is for similar reasons that in reckoning federal debt and its composition the distinction between the Treasury and Federal Reserve is ignored. A debt of the Treasury to the Federal Reserve is a debt of the left hand to the right. It does not enlarge the public's claims. Nor does it enlarge the net interest costs of the Treasury, as the profits of the Federal Reserve Banks, above a fixed payment on the stock member banks are compelled to subscribe, belong to the Treasury. On Federal Reserve Banks' balance sheets, their holdings of Treasury bills and bonds are assets. Corresponding to them are those Federal Reserve Banks' deposit liabilities—to private banks, foreign governments and central banks, and international institutions—and their Federal Reserve note liabilities to holders of U.S. currency throughout the world. Treasury currency is also in circulation, although the Treasury no longer issues new paper notes but confines itself to coins. The user of dollar bills does not care whether it is a Treasury greenback or a Federal Reserve note.

The Treasury's debt issues include long-term bonds bearing high interest rates. But if those bonds are held by the Federal Reserve Banks, which have in turn

TABLE 8.2

Estimated supply and holdings of federal debt demand debt, end of December (billions of dollars)

	1962	1972	1982	1992
Supply of demand debt to the public				
1. Gold and other international reserve assets	16.0	10.8	15.5	21.1
2. Loans to depository institutions	—	1.2	0.7	0.7
3. Treasury currency net of Treasury holdings of currency and Federal Reserve deposits	4.6	6.1	10.5	13.5
4. Float	2.9	4.0	2.7	3.3
5. U.S. government securities (includes repurchase agreements and federal agency securities)	30.8	71.2	148.8	308.5
6. Other assets of the Federal Reserve Banks	0.1	2.1	11.4	30.1
7. Nonmonetary liabilities of the Federal Reserve Banks (including capital accounts)	−1.0	−21	−5.0	−8.0
Holdings of demand debt by the public				
8. By depository institutions:	23.3	36.4	47.0	67.7
a. Deposits at Federal Reserve Banks	17.5	25.6	26.5	32.1
b. Currency	5.8	10.8	20.5	35.6
9. Other deposits with Federal Reserve Banks	0.6	1.2	0.8	0.6
10. Currency held outside depository institutions, Treasury, and Federal Reserve Banks	29.5	60.0	137.0	300.9

Sources: Federal Reserve Bulletin; "Currency held by depository institutions" means vault cash. For 1962 and 1972, currency held by thrifts obtained from FDIC, *Assets and Liabilities: Commercial and Mutual Savings Banks, Flow of Funds Accounts, Federal Reserve Bulletin,* and *Supplement to Banking and Monetary Statistics, Section 12,* Jan. 1966. For these years, currency holdings of thrifts are partly estimated from their cash assets.

incurred demand obligations to banks and public, the debt that matters is a non-interest-bearing demand debt. In Table 8.1 the Treasury and Federal Reserve are consolidated, and the composition of claims against them on two sample dates is shown. In Table 8.2 the details for demand debt are shown.

8.10
MONETARY CONTROL AND DEBT MANAGEMENT

How can the Treasury and Federal Reserve affect the composition of the debt? The Treasury can replace security issues when they come due—at which time they are virtually demand obligations—with new securities. By "advance refunding" offers or conceivably by repurchasing its own debt, the Treasury can convert debt before it matures into new debt, usually lengthening its maturity. The Treasury can increase nonmarketable debt at the expense of other categories by offering more attractive terms on savings bonds. The Treasury can increase the public's holdings of federal demand obligations by drawing down its deposit balance in the Federal Reserve Banks to pay its bills, or by issuing and spending newly minted coins or, as in the past, paper currency.

The Federal Reserve also can change the composition of the debt, principally by its open-market operations. By purchasing short-term securities, for example, the Federal Reserve at the same time increases the quantity of demand obligations outstanding and decreases by an equal amount the quantity of outstanding debt in the short-term marketable category. Federal Reserve sales of long-term securities diminish the outstanding demand debt and increase the outstanding long debt by an equal amount. By purchasing shorts and at the same time selling an equivalent quantity of longs, the Federal Reserve could lengthen the marketable debt, leaving demand debt unchanged. The Federal Reserve does not set the terms of nonmarketable securities kept on tap by the Treasury. But it may influence the demand for such securities indirectly by open-market operations altering yields of marketable debt instruments.

There is no neat way to distinguish monetary policy from debt management, the province of the Federal Reserve from that of the Treasury. Both agencies are engaged in debt management in the broadest sense, and both have powers to influence the whole spectrum, directly or indirectly. But monetary policy refers particularly to determination of the supply of demand debt, and debt management refers to determination of the amounts in the long and nonmarketable categories. In between, the quantity of outstanding short debt is determined as a residuum. Since the early 1950s, this specialization has for the most part been institutionalized. The Federal Reserve controls the size of the demand debt, independently of the Treasury. The Treasury decides the amounts of long-term and nonmarketable debt.

In the 1950s the Federal Reserve announced and followed a bills-only policy, refraining from buying or selling long-term securities. An important motivation was to minimize governmental interventions in the financial markets, leaving long-term markets and rates to private decisions. During the Kennedy administration in the early 1960s, however, the Fed became more pragmatic and on occasion conducted open-market purchases in long bonds. But these interventions are rare, and the vast preponderance of Federal Reserve operations occur at the very shortest end of the maturity spectrum.

8.11
THE SUPPLY OF BANK RESERVES

In Section 8.9, the composition of federal debt was described. Table 8.1 shows the actual composition at ten-year intervals from 1962 to 1992 and also tells how the supplies of four categories of debt were distributed between banks and other holders. Details for demand debt are shown in Table 8.2.

Banks' primary reserves are legally required to be government demand obligations. Likewise, federal short-term debts, generally ninety-day Treasury bills, are banks' principal choices as secondary reserves. Frequently bills are rented by repurchase agreements, called *repos,* rather than bought and sold. That is, the seller agrees to repurchase the bill before it matures, after a specified number of days. Other government securities may also serve as defensive assets.

Banks supplying deposits payable on demand to the owner or by the owner's order to third parties are required to hold certain fractions of their deposits as reserves. These reserve requirements depend on the classification of the bank and the type of deposit, as shown in Tables 8.3A and 8.3B. The tables also show the limits within which Congress gave the Board of Governors discretion to set the required ratios. The tables summarize the rules for 1967 and 1994. At the earlier date and until 1980, only Federal Reserve members were subject to the Fed's requirements. As the table makes clear, both the required ratios and their coverage have become much less severe. Since 1980, these requirements have applied to all depository institutions. (Recall that here the term "banks" refers to that universe which includes both members of the Federal Reserve System and nonmembers; both commercial banks and thrift institutions, that is, savings banks, savings and loan associations, and credit unions; and both state-chartered and federal-chartered institutions. Before 1972 only commercial banks issued demand deposits.)

The assets that count as banks' reserves are deposits in Federal Reserve Banks and currency. The quantity of potential primary reserves, sometimes called

TABLE 8.3A
Reserve requirements, Federal Reserve member banks January 30, 1967 (percent of deposits)

	Net demand deposits		Time deposits	
	In effect	**Permitted range**	**In effect**	**Permitted range**
Central reserve city banks (New York and Chicago)	18.0	10–22	5	3–6
Reserve city banks	16.5	10–22	5	3–6
Country banks	11.0	7–14	5	3–6

TABLE 8.3B

Reserve requirements, all depository institutions June 30, 1994 (percent of deposits)

Type of deposit	In effect	Permitted range
Checkable deposits		
First $4 million	0	0
Next $47.9 million	3	3
Amounts in excess of $51.9 million	10	8–14
Personal time deposits and savings accounts	0	0
Nonpersonal time deposits and savings accounts	0	0–9

high-powered money or the monetary base, M0, supplied by the federal government is divided between the banks and the public at large. Although the nonbank public cannot hold deposits in the Federal Reserve System, it does hold currency. Banks can exchange currency for reserve balances at will. Other things equal, if the public holds more currency, the banks have less reserves in one form or the other.

Banks are subject to periodic reserve tests. For banks that account for the bulk of deposits, the test covers each consecutive two-week period; smaller banks are tested less frequently. From a bank's deposits at the close of each business day can be calculated the average over the test period of those deposits on which reserves are required. Applying the required reserve fractions to the deposit average gives the average required reserves in dollars. Likewise the average end-of-day holdings of reserve assets in dollars is calculated. To pass the test, average reserve holdings must be no less than average required reserves. Excess reserves may be counted against up to 4 percent of the next period's requirement, and deficiencies up to 4 percent may be carried forward. Financial penalties for deficiencies are not severe, interest at the discount rate plus 2 percent per annum and/or additional required reserves in the next test period. The district Federal Reserve Banks have considerable discretion to fit punishments to crimes. The most important sanction is the damage to the bank's reputation at its Federal Reserve Bank and in the financial markets (Board of Governors of the Federal Reserve System, 1994, pp. 53–57).

Consider an individual bank, AnyBank. During the test period, AnyBank keeps track of how it is doing on the reserve test and takes corrective steps if it is running short. What determines AnyBank's holdings of reserves? What actions can AnyBank take to augment its own primary reserves?

1. If AnyBank's customers, old or new, deposit currency in their accounts, AnyBank gains a quantity of reserves equal to its new deposit liabilities. This is true whether AnyBank holds on to the currency or redeposits it in its Federal Reserve Bank account. The reverse occurs if AnyBank's depositors withdraw currency.
2. AnyBank also gains reserves dollar for dollar if its customers deposit checks drawn on other banks and AnyBank deposits these in its Federal Reserve account. As explained in Chapter 7, whether the balance of deposits and withdrawals of

currency, and of interbank check collections, favors AnyBank or not during a particular day or week or month is not wholly controllable or predictable by the bank. This was especially true before the 1980s, when legal ceilings on deposit interest precluded rate competition and limited banks to nonprice attractions. Chapter 7 modeled the difference between regimes with and without deposit rate ceilings.

For the system as a whole, there is a big difference between case 1 and case 2. When currency is deposited, AnyBank gains reserves and no other bank loses. When checks on other banks are deposited, what AnyBank gains in reserves other banks lose.

3. AnyBank can borrow reserve balances, popularly known as *federal funds*, from other banks. Overnight loans of federal funds are arranged in an organized electronic market. The rate of interest set by supply and demand in this market reflects the bite of anticipated requirements for reserves relative to banks' actual reserve holdings. For example, the rate will rise if most banks are approaching the end of the test period with insufficient reserves. The trading of federal funds cannot of course change the total quantity of primary reserves available to the banks collectively.

4. AnyBank can borrow from its Federal Reserve Bank at the posted discount rate. Its Federal Reserve deposit balance will be credited, thereby increasing the reserves AnyBank can count to pass its reserve test. Clearly this borrowing also augments the total reserves of the whole system. AnyBank's borrowing privileges are routinely satisfied so long as AnyBank does not stay in debt to the Fed for more than a few weeks or rely repeatedly on borrowing from the Fed to avoid the consequences of overaggressive risk taking. The Federal Reserve System can, of course, influence banks' demands for loans by varying its discount rate.

Bank reserve accounting may be summarized algebraically. AnyBank's gross holdings of primary reserves, its *total reserves,* tr, are identical to item 8 in Tables 8.1 and 8.2. They include its *unborrowed reserves,* ubr, and its *borrowed reserves,* br, its debt position in federal funds, dff (which could be negative, i.e., a credit position if AnyBank was a net lender of federal funds), and its debt at its Federal Reserve Bank's discount window, dfr (which cannot be less than zero). Its legally *required reserves*, rr, depend on its deposits as described in Tables 8.3A and 8.3B. The reserve requirement may be satisfied by its total reserves, whether borrowed or unborrowed.

TABLE 8.4
Reserve accounting identities for Anybank and for all banks

Anybank		All banks
(9.1A)	tr = ubr + br	TR = UBR + BR
(9.1B)	br = dfr + dff	BR = DFR + 0

(DFF is necessarily zero; if one bank borrows federal funds, another bank must lend them.)

(9.1C)	er = tr − rr	ER = TR − RR
(9.1D)	nfr = er − br = er − dfr − dff	NFR = ER − BR = ER − DFR
(9.1E)	nfr = ubr − rr	NFR = UBR − RR

TABLE 8.5

Aggregate reserve accounts of banks: two hypothetical examples (billions of dollars)

Example A		Example B	
Currency in vault	0.5	Currency in vault	0.5
Reserve balances at F. R. Banks	19.5	Reserve balances at F. R. Banks	19.5
Total reserves	20.0	Total reserves	20.0
−Required reserves (vs. deposits 160)	−16.0	−Required reserves (vs. deposits 190)	−19.0
Excess reserves	4.0	Excess reserves	1.0
−Federal funds borrowed	−2.0	−Federal funds borrowed	−2.0
+Federal funds lent	2.0	+Federal funds lent	2.0
−Borrowed from Federal Reserve	−3.0	−Borrowed from Federal Reserve	−3.0
−Borrowed reserves	−3.0	−Borrowed reserves	−3.0
Net Free Reserves	1.0	Net free reserves	−2.0

The quantity of AnyBank's *excess reserves,* er, is the excess of its total over its required reserves. Its *net free reserves,* nfr, are its excess reserves minus its borrowed reserves, or equivalently, its unborrowed reserves less its required reserves. The unborrowed reserves of the banking system are the sum of the unborrowed reserves positions of all the banks. Table 8.4 shows these identities both for a single bank (lower case) and for the system as a whole (capitals). Table 8.5 illustrates these concepts numerically.

8.12
SOURCES OF CHANGES IN SUPPLIES
OF BANKS' TOTAL RESERVES

The determinants of the supply of primary reserves are listed in Table 8.2. Clearly that quantity, item 8 in the table, will be increased ceteris paribus by an increase in any of the first seven items or by decreases in the ninth and tenth. In normal circumstances, the Federal Reserve can if it wishes control the supply of reserves by open-market purchases or sales of securities (item 5). Nevertheless, it is instructive to review the most important influences that the Federal Reserve must offset:

1. *Gold and other international reserves.* When the United States was on the international gold standard, purchases and sales of gold were important sources of changes in federal demand debt. Transactions changing item 1 of Table 8.2 are rare now, but their domestic monetary mechanics are worth reviewing. Suppose gold was offered to the Treasury by domestic producers or by foreign central banks in need of dollars. In either case the Treasury would pay for the gold by a check on its balance in a Federal Reserve Bank. The check was deposited in the seller's account in an American bank, and in turn deposited in that bank's reserve balance at its Federal Reserve Bank. The bank's reserves were increased, and the Treasury's account was debited. The Treasury replenished its balance by

printing gold certificates and depositing them with the Federal Reserve Bank. Gold certificates were assets on Federal Reserve Bank balance sheets. (Before 1933 but not after, they might circulate as currency. The Treasury might pay for gold directly with gold coins or certificates.)

The same mechanism worked in reverse when the Treasury sold gold. A foreign central bank, for example, might choose to convert its deposit in a New York bank into gold. The Treasury then received a check on that bank, and its Federal Reserve balance rose at the expense of bank reserves. But the Treasury had to use the increase in its balance at the Federal Reserve to withdraw and cancel gold certificates equivalent to the amount of gold it sold. The Treasury's capacity to issue gold certificates to the Federal Reserve depended not only on its gold hoard in ounces but also on the dollar value per ounce set by the Treasury with the permission of Congress. When the official price of gold was raised in 1934 and 1973, the Treasury made paper profits, against which gold certificates could be issued.

The same mechanics apply to increases in special drawing rights at the International Monetary Fund, sometimes called paper gold. They are occasionally created by international agreement to add to the world supply of international reserve assets and assigned pro rata to the member governments. The U.S. Treasury can issue paper-gold certificates analogous to gold certificates, increasing demand debt and bank reserves in the same way.

In fact the Treasury has not issued and deposited to its accounts in Federal Reserve Banks all the certificates that it is entitled to issue as a result of gold revaluations, SDR issues, and foreign exchange transactions. Beginning in 1933 with the $2 billion "profit" from the revaluation of its gold stock, the Treasury has accumulated an Exchange Stabilization Fund now amounting to $36 billion. This is a convenient discretionary slush fund for such transactions as the emergency loan to Mexico in 1994.

2. *Federal Reserve credit to banks.* As explained above, banks may augment their unborrowed reserves by borrowing at the Federal Reserve Banks' discount windows. The Fed can influence the amount of such borrowing both by its discount rate and by the standards and procedures of administering the discount window.

All banks, that is, institutions subject to reserve requirements, are eligible to borrow from Federal Reserve Banks. The borrower's Federal Reserve Bank advances funds against collateral predeposited at the Reserve Bank, by crediting the borrower's reserve account. The usual type of loan, *adjustment credit,* is for overnight or a few days. The purpose is to tide the borrowing bank over an unexpected spell of illiquidity because of deposit withdrawals or natural disasters and other local shocks increasing the credit needs of the bank's customers. Depositories, especially large and well-connected banks, are expected to exhaust other credit sources before applying to the Reserve Bank, and all borrowers are supposed to use the temporary relief of Federal Reserve credit to arrange other solutions. Borrowing at the discount window is always at the Reserve Bank's discretion. It is not an entitlement, and in particular it is not intended to be an auxiliary and inexpensive source of funds for banks to invest at a profit in federal funds or other assets. Banks are reluctant to overborrow both because they may wear out their welcome at the discount window and because bank equity and debt markets may become suspicious. Nevertheless there is a clear positive correlation between adjustment borrowing and the spread of the federal funds rate over the Federal Reserve discount rate, a matter that will be modeled in the next chapter.

There are two other types of borrowing from the Fed—*seasonal credit* and *extended credit*. The former assists mostly small agricultural banks, which borrow in the spring and repay at harvest time. This is probably not an appropriate function for a central bank. *Extended credit* rescues troubled institutions from imminent bankruptcy. On occasion in the 1980s the Fed advanced billions of dollars to banks judged to be too big to be allowed to fail, offsetting the systemwide expansionary monetary effects by open-market sales. While lender of last resort is an essential central bank role, rescue of particular institutions is not. The systemic consequences of their failures was exaggerated in the 1980s, and Congress has strictly limited Federal Reserve participation in the rescue of undercapitalized institutions. (Board of Governors of the Federal Reserve System 1994, pp. 42–53.)

3. *Treasury currency outstanding, net of Treasury holdings of currency and Treasury deposits in Federal Reserve Banks.* If the Treasury makes payments to the public in the form of currency or checks drawn on the Federal Reserve, the supply of reserves is increased. Assuming that the recipients of Treasury payments do not wish to add to their holdings of currency, they will deposit these amounts to their bank accounts. The banks in turn will present them to the Federal Reserve for payment, to be credited to their reserve balances. The process works in reverse when the Treasury uses receipts from the public to withdraw currency from circulation or to increase its balances in Federal Reserve Banks. Under present circumstances Treasury currency outstanding increases only in response to public need for minor coins. The total decreases as old Treasury currency, mostly silver certificates, are withdrawn from circulation and replaced by Federal Reserve notes.

Like any other transactor, the Treasury needs cash balances to bridge gaps between its receipts and its expenditures. These balances may be held in currency, in deposits at Federal Reserve Banks, or in deposits at ordinary banks. The Treasury can increase the supply of primary reserves by shifting deposits from the Federal Reserve to commercial banks, or reduce the supply by shifting deposits in the other direction. These shifts can be used to reduce the impact of seasonal fluctuations in the Treasury's total cash position on bank reserves. In cooperation with the Federal Reserve, the Treasury endeavors to manage the size and location of its cash balance to minimize fluctuations in the total supply of primary reserves.

4. *Float.* In many transactions that involve a transfer of reserve balances from one bank to another, the Federal Reserve Banks credit the receiving bank before they debit the paying bank. The Federal Reserve is thereby lending reserves to the paying bank for a day or two. The paying bank is unaware of its borrowing, because it cannot know what checks its depositors have drawn until they are presented for payment. Thus float borrowing is anonymous and automatic, in contrast

to deliberate and planned borrowing of reserves at the discount window. When float increases because of rising frequency, seasonal or otherwise, of the kind of interbank transfers that give rise to it, then the supply of primary reserves is increased. Speedier clearing, as by the substitution of wire transfers through Federal Reserve banks for checks, diminishes float.

5. *Open-market operations.* The most important determinant of the supply of reserves is the securities holdings of the Federal Reserve Banks. Purchases and sales of securities are the principal instruments of monetary policy. By purchases of securities in the open market the Fed can increase unborrowed reserves, and by sales reduce them. The Federal Reserve pays for securities purchases by checks on itself, and when member banks deposit the checks in their Federal Reserve Banks, the volume of these deposits rises. Similarly, when the Federal Reserve sells a security, it debits the deposit account of the bank on which the purchaser drew the check to pay for it, and the volume of member bank reserve balances falls. As an alternative to open-market purchases the central bank could conceivably buy securities directly from the Treasury; as the Treasury then spent the proceeds, or deposited them in commercial banks rather than leaving them in Federal Reserve Banks, the supply of primary reserves would be increased. Direct Treasury borrowing from the Federal Reserve is severely restricted, evidently on the ground that it would make deficit financing too easy. However, the same effect can be achieved, if both parties are willing, by the Fed's purchasing in the open market the counterpart of what the Treasury is selling there. The important point is that the Federal Reserve can control the supply of unborrowed primary reserves to the banks, offsetting to any desired degree changes in the other sources and uses of high-powered money.

Open-market operations almost always are exchanges of federal demand debt for Treasury securities, in one direction or the other, and the very shortest securities at that. But this need not be so. If the Fed pays out high-powered money, no matter what it buys, the operation has the same effect in increasing the supply of unborrowed bank reserves. Occasionally the Fed buys long-term government bonds and quite frequently buys foreign currencies. Likewise, selling whatever for cash reduces the supply of bank reserves. Conceivably the Fed could buy and sell equities or state and local bonds or home mortgages or corporate debt.

6. *Currency outside banks.* As noted above, if bank depositors wish to increase their holdings of currency, they will withdraw currency from banks. The banks, in turn, unless they happen to have redundant cash in their vaults, will have to withdraw the needed currency from their balances at the Federal Reserve Banks, whose Federal Reserve note liabilities will rise to the extent that their deposit liabilities fall. In the reverse case, the public deposits currency in the banks; the banks deposit it in the Federal Reserve Banks, and reserve balances rise while note liabilities decline.

Individual depositors who withdraw $100 in currency intend to reduce their deposits only by the same amount. But the unintended indirect consequence in the system as a whole could be much larger. The withdrawal, other things equal, deprives banks of $100 in reserves, while their required reserves have fallen only by $10, if the required ratio is 10 percent. As banks scramble to make up the deficiency of reserves, they will be curtailing their loans and deposits. In extreme form, this is the mechanism of panics, as described in Section 8.3. Normally the Federal Reserve offsets shifts in public demands for currency by open-market purchases or sales of securities, to neutralize their consequences on the balance of supply and demand for bank reserves.

Public currency holdings are demand determined. The Fed does not, cannot, determine the quantity of currency in public circulation outside banks. Neither can the banks, either individually or collectively. The members of the nonbank public—individuals, households, businesses, foreigners—hold the amount of currency they want. If they have too much, they deposit it in their bank accounts. If the banks have more than they need, they deposit it in their accounts at the Federal Reserve Banks. If the members of the nonbank public need more currency, they withdraw it from their bank accounts. The banks, in turn, can if they wish, replenish their currency stocks by withdrawing it from their Federal Reserve Banks. Whether they do or not, their reserves have fallen.

The Fed and the banking system may have some indirect influences on public demands for currency, through the interest rates on bank deposits and other substitute assets. But any influences of this kind would normally be small and unintended.

Incidentally, just as the government cannot control the total volume of currency outstanding, neither can the Federal Reserve or the mint determine the quantities in general circulation of the different coins and paper dollars on its menu. For example, people don't like half-dollars. And the attempt to replace the dollar bill with the Susan Anthony coin failed miserably. Canada did succeed with its dollar coin, but only by retiring paper dollars from circulation altogether as they gravitated back to the Bank of Canada, so that the public had no choice.

8.13
MONETARY POLICY OPERATIONS AND TARGETS

Control of unborrowed reserves is the fulcrum of Federal Reserve monetary policy, and correspondingly open-market operations are the Fed's principal instrument. But there are other instruments of policy, which do not work by directly altering quantities of demand debt. The most important of these is the Federal Reserve discount rate, discussed in Sections 8.11 and 8.12. Another is the required reserve-to-deposit ratio for banks, discussed in Section 8.11 and throughout Chapter 7.

Although open-market operations directly affecting unborrowed reserves are the predominant modus operandi of the system, the Federal Reserve need not be aiming at any numerical target for unborrowed reserves. If they were, the target would probably be frequently changed, in response to seasonal and other changes in banking and business situations. The Fed might aim its open-market operations at a numerical target of total reserves or of net free reserves or of required reserves. In any case, the target quantity would be frequently changed or at least reconsidered at the meetings every six weeks of the system's policy-making body, the Federal Open Market Committee (FOMC).

The FOMC need have no particular target for any reserve statistic. Instead, its operations may be aimed at bringing about or maintaining certain conditions in credit markets or in the banking system: certain levels of interest rates, quantities of bank deposits, or of money supplies including both currency and deposits, or of bank lending. Operating in this way, the Fed will let the quantities of reserves adjust as necessary to obtain the results it desires in the credit markets or the banking system or the economy as a whole.

Frequently the Fed's operating targets have been interest rates. An extreme example was the commitment of the Federal Reserve, during World War II and afterwards until 1951, to keep the prices of $2\frac{1}{2}$ percent government bonds from falling below par and correspondingly hold down the interest rates on shorter Treasury securities. When this commitment required the Fed to buy securities in the market, the supply of primary reserves was simply whatever the banks and the economy demanded at those interest rates. This commitment effectively tied the hands of the monetary policy makers. The Fed was liberated from the peg by the Accord of 1951 between the Federal Reserve and the Treasury, engineered by Senator Paul Douglas of Illinois, earlier a distinguished professor of economics.

Since 1951, interest rates have often been used as operating targets but at levels subject to change at any time at the discretion of the FOMC.

In the 1950s and 1960s the Fed appeared to focus on short-term interest rates, represented by the 3-month Treasury bill rate. In what was often described as "leaning against the wind," the Fed raised its bill rate target during cyclical upswings and lowered it in recessions. In the 1970s and since, the overnight federal funds rate took the place of the bill rate as the operating target. It is easy to control, because it is the market interest rate on the reserves the Fed supplies. The supply of reserves will be whatever quantity the banks want at the federal funds rate at which the Fed buys or sells those funds.

In 1979–1982 the FOMC geared its operations to hit quantitative unborrowed reserve targets set and reset at its periodic meetings, rather than federal funds rate targets. The purpose was to implement and demonstrate a resolute anti-inflation policy, which was thought to be impossible if interest rates were pegged even for just a few weeks at a time. Once its anti-inflation objective was substantially achieved in the mid-1980s, the Fed returned to the federal funds rate as its operating instrument.

Operating targets are means to more fundamental and longer-run ends. In the 1970s the FOMC aimed at targets for intermediate monetary aggregates, M1 or M2, announced several quarters ahead; interest-rate or reserve supply targets adopted at FOMC meetings were supposed to achieve those money stock goals. The aggregate M1 is essentially the sum of currency in circulation outside banks and checkable bank deposits; M2 adds time and savings deposits. Since 1975 Congress has required the Fed to report twice a year its targets for growth in these intermediate monetary aggregates. They are, of course, not the ultimate goals of policy, which are measures of macroeconomic performance: real Gross Domestic Product and its growth, unemployment, price inflation, net international claims and terms of trade.

In the 1980s and 1990s the Fed no longer took targets for intermediate monetary aggregates—M1, M2, and others—seriously, although they continued to be announced. They appeared to have lost dependable relationships to the more basic goals. Indeed the Fed formally abandoned M1 altogether. Macroeconomic performance, some pragmatic amalgam of price inflation, unemployment, and real GDP growth, became the Fed's policy goal, and the FOMC fine-tuned its instrument—the federal funds rate—to aim directly at its desired macroeconomic path.

CHAPTER 9

The Monetary and Banking System of the United States: Analytic Description

It is time to put the individual banks analyzed in Chapter 7 together into an economy-wide banking system within the institutional framework described in Chapter 8. This chapter will examine the determinants and properties of equilibrium in the several markets in which the banks operate. In each market, banks' aggregate demand for any asset must equal the total supply less the amount demanded by other economic units: households, business firms, other financial institutions, foreigners. Likewise the banks' aggregate deposit liabilities must be simultaneously an amount that the banks are willing to supply and an amount that the public wants to hold. As in Chapter 5, interest rates and credit lines adjust to bring demands and supplies into line in these interrelated markets. Here, unlike Chapter 5, it is not assumed that government debt is homogeneous, entirely demand debt.

The important markets in which the banks participate are those for (1) federal demand obligations, which serve as primary reserves for banks; (2) government interest-bearing securities, some of which may serve banks as defensive assets or secondary reserves; (3) deposits, both demand and time; and (4) private loans.

9.1
THE MONEY MULTIPLIER

Suppose that the Federal Reserve sets the total volume of unborrowed federal demand debt, that is, demand debt net of bank borrowings from the Federal Reserve. This quantity is often known as the unborrowed monetary base or as high-powered money, M0. What will be the corresponding volume of transactions money, low-powered money, held by the nonbank public, the total of their currency holdings and their checkable bank deposits? At times the Federal Reserve has sought to control this monetary aggregate, M1.

M0 consists of two parts, unborrowed bank reserves and currency held by the nonbank public. Assuming that the bank reserves are 100 percent used as reserves required as a fraction k of deposits, a dollar of unborrowed reserves supports $1/k$ dollars of deposits. Suppose, further, that the public likes to hold a fraction c of M1 as currency and the remaining $(1 - c)$ as deposits. Then the total derived demand for M0 is cM1 + $k(1 - c)$M1. A dollar of public demand for M1 in the form of currency is a dollar demand for base money. A dollar demand for M1 in the form of deposits is a demand for a fraction of a dollar k for base money. The so-called money multiplier, M1/M0 is

$$\frac{1}{c + k(1 - c)}.$$

For example let $k = 0.1$ and $c = 0.4$; then M1/M0 = 2.46.

The formula is an instructive implication of definitional identities. But there is no reason to expect the public to split its holdings of transactions money between currency and deposits in constant proportions c and $1 - c$, and to expect banks to hold net free reserves exactly equal to zero.

9.1.1 Currency versus Deposits

Currency and demand deposits are competing media of exchange. Social and legal conventions designate certain kinds of transactions for currency and others for check. But for many transactions, currency and personal checks are more or less perfect substitutes, as they were treated in Chapter 3. The acceptability of a personal check depends on the assurances the recipient has that the check is good or recourse is available. In some cases these assurances cannot be provided without cost, for example, charges for certification of checks or for telephoning the bank. In other cases currency may be too cumbersome and too vulnerable to loss and theft to use directly to make a payment, for example, to a distant creditor. Holders of currency can nevertheless make such payments, without first acquiring a demand deposit, by going to the trouble and expense of postal money orders, bank drafts, travelers' checks, etc.

There are other quite practical reasons for the continuing strength of the demand for currency in the face of more convenient and remunerative means of payment. Numismatists' holdings cannot account for much. More important, an individual who wishes to conceal his income and wealth from the police or from the tax assessor may prefer the anonymity of large-denomination currency to checks and bank accounts. Evidently a large and recently growing quantity of dollar currency is held abroad, and in many countries dollars are often used in transactions in preference to local currencies.[1]

---

[1] See Sprenkle (1993) for a discussion of the magnitudes.

The factors that influence the proportions in which the public desires to hold currency and deposits are relatively slow to change. Some of them were discussed in Chapter 3, Section 3.2.2.2. The need for currency to anticipate retail purchases and vacation outlays leads to regular weekend and seasonal peaks in public currency holdings. The yearly peak occurs in connection with Christmas shopping, and summer holidays lead to other large drains of currency from the banks. Over the years the dominion of the check has expanded; new credit and identification arrangements have made it increasingly possible to get along without stocks of currency. The weekly pay envelope has gradually been superseded by the paycheck, and wage earners have acquired bank accounts.

Formerly banks could not legally pay interest on checkable deposits. As pointed out in Chapter 3, Section 3.2.4, since 1986 all banks have been free to offer interest at whatever rate they choose on checking accounts (except demand deposits of corporations and federal agencies) as well as on savings and time deposits. This gives deposits an important advantage over currency, one which might be expected to raise the deposits/currency ratio, and then to make the ratio rise when interest rates rise and fall when interest rates fall. But there is little evidence of such effects, even though the ratio has been quite variable since 1970 (Garfinkel and Thornton, 1991).

Competition with banks in transactions management has arisen from other financial institutions. Money market mutual funds offer check privileges. These funds are not banks; they are more risky than bank deposits; they can vary in value; and they are not insured. The checks are written on the fund's deposit in a bank. There is a scale economy here. The fund does not need as large a deposit to handle its customers' check transactions as the customers collectively would need on their own. The same is true of credit cards. The cardholder uses her line of credit, and the credit-card lender pays the merchant. The bank balances the credit-card lender needs to hold against its debtor-customers' purchases, plus those balances the cardholders need for their regular monthly credit-card bills, are much smaller than those cardholders collectively would have needed were they paying for their purchases separately by checks or currency. Efficient innovations like these can be regarded not as new kinds of transactions money but as increases in the velocity of currency and bank deposits. ATM cards; which make it more convenient to withdraw currency from bank deposits, have probably reduced the stocks of currency people need to keep on hand.

9.1.2 Relation of Deposits to the Reserve Base

In this chapter the monetary mechanism is described as if the Federal Reserve fixes the supply of unborrowed reserves. This is a convenient way to describe the mechanics of the system. It is not an assertion that Fed operations normally do in fact fix that supply. Once the mechanics are modeled, alternative operating procedures can be examined.

The money multiplier above assumed that deposits are simply a multiple $1/k$ of unborrowed reserves. Another way to express it is that unborrowed reserves and required reserves are equal. This is a fair first approximation most of the time. It has two important implications, which are also generally closer to being true than false. One is that a change in the net supply of reserves is *sufficient* to cause an equal change in the volume of required reserves. That is, whenever the reserve base is changed, deposits change by the appropriate multiple. The other is that a dollar change in the net supply of reserves is a *necessary* condition of a dollar change in the volume of required reserves. That is, nothing can alter the volume of deposits so long as the reserve base remains unchanged. Deposits will not be reduced even if the public desires and tries to shift from bank deposits to nonmonetary assets, for example, government securities or liabilities of nonbank financial institutions.

These approximations, however, neglect the money markets, in which the Federal Reserve operates to carry out monetary policy. If the simple multiples are good approximations, it is partly because the Fed operates in ways that make them so. What the simple formulas omit are excess reserves and borrowed reserves, or their difference net free reserves, as defined and illustrated in Chapter 8, Section 8.11 and Table 8.4. The formulas assume that the equilibrium demand for net free reserves is a constant, indeed zero. On the contrary, this chapter will argue, the normal or equilibrium level of net free reserves is not constant at zero or any other level. It is the result of economic calculations by the banks, in response to costs and opportunities at the discount window of the central bank, in the money market, and in commercial lending. In particular, it is sensitive to the differential between the Federal Reserve discount rate and money market rates.

The Federal Reserve cannot and surely does not assume that, other things equal, equilibrium net free reserves will remain constant in the face of open-market operations. On the contrary, if the Federal Reserve maintains the discount rate unchanged, there is a systematic tendency for net free reserves to rise by some fraction of a dollar whenever the Federal Reserve augments the supply of primary reserves by one dollar. In the first instance, open-market purchases will raise net free reserves above their equilibrium level. Banks will then try to reduce them to normal. But "normal" will be a higher level than before. Both the open-market purchases of the central bank and the purchases of bills by member banks with surplus net free reserves will lower the bill rate and related money market rates. They will lower, therefore, the incentive of banks to economize cash and to borrow from the Federal Reserve. As a result, banks will be content with a higher quantity of net free reserves. Similarly, the influence of open-market sales will be divided between reduction of net free reserves and reduction of required reserves. In this scenario, although open-market operations affect the supply of bank reserves dollar for dollar, their effect on required reserves is less, because some of the new supply goes into additional net free reserves. This does not mean that required reserves are beyond the control of the monetary authorities. It does mean that to increase required reserves by $1, it may be necessary to augment the supply of unborrowed reserves by more than $1 or to reduce the discount rate.

Likewise, banks may change the normal, equilibrium volume of net free reserves when no open-market operations are occurring, for one of several reasons: (1) The Federal Reserve may change the discount rate, inducing either greater holdings of net free reserves by raising the rate or lower holdings by reducing the rate; (2) Banks' own cash preferences, or expectations of the future of rates and lending opportunities, may change; or (3) the Treasury bill rate and other money market rates may be altered as a result of changes in the asset and debt preferences and demands of the nonbank public. For example, a public shift into bills will lower the bill rate and, other things equal, induce the banks to hold more net free reserves, repaying debt and substituting excess cash for bills. Or a reduction in customer's demands upon the banks for loans will lead to a fall in the bill rate as the banks seek to substitute Treasury securities for loans. The fall in the bill rate, if the discount rate remains unchanged, will induce the banking system to use a given supply of primary reserves less intensively.

As these examples suggest, the volume of bank deposits is not wholly independent of depositors' preferences between bank deposits and nonmonetary assets or of the strength of borrowers' demands for bank loans.

In Fig. 9.1 the constant-multiple story is pictured. Along the vertical axis are measured required reserves, proportional to deposits, and along the horizontal axis, the supply of reserves. Line OR is a 45-degree ray from the origin. A point like B is to be interpreted as follows: The supply of reserves is OA. Required reserves amount to AB. The remainder of the supply BC is net free reserves, positive. In contrast, a point like B' indicates negative net free reserves of $B'C'$. If equilibrium net free reserves are zero, the 45-degree line OR also represents the normal bank demand for reserves. Thus both B' and B are positions of disequilibrium, from which banks will move toward C' and C, respectively.

The mechanics of open-market operations may be described as follows. Suppose the banks are in equilibrium at C', and let the Federal Reserve augment the supply of reserves by the amount $A'A$. Suppose, for simplicity, that the purchases are entirely from banks. In the first instance, therefore, deposits do not change. Required reserves remain at the level $A'C' = AB$. The open-market purchases have created excess

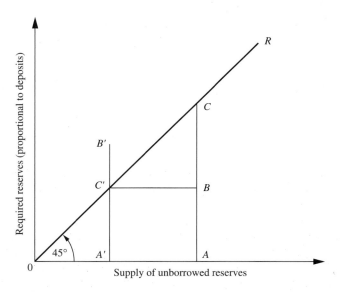

FIGURE 9.1
Reserves supplied and required, the constant-multiple case.

net free reserves of $A'A = BC$. Banks will then acquire earning assets and expand deposits enough to eliminate this excess. The ultimate result, then, is an increase in required reserves of $A'A = BC$, *equal* to the increase in the supply of reserves.

Of course, the Federal Reserve does not necessarily, or even typically, commence open-market operations from a position of equilibrium. If, for example, banks were at point B and the Federal Reserve desired to forestall an increase in deposits and required reserves, the Federal Open Market Committee could wipe out the excess by open-market sales.

The more complete scenario is illustrated by Fig. 9.2*a*. The axes measure the same variables as in Fig. 9.1. But the equilibrium relationship of required to

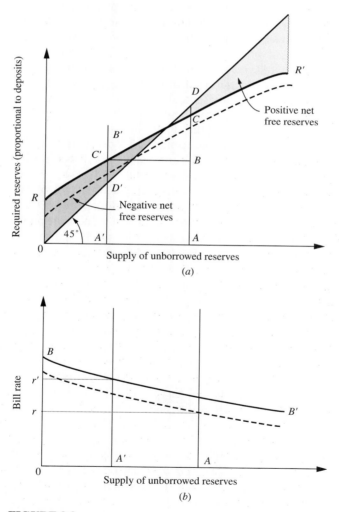

FIGURE 9.2

(*a*) Reserves supplied and required, general case; (*b*) bill rate in relation to reserve supplies.

unborrowed reserves RR' does not coincide with the 45-degree line; it is flatter. This demand curve, it must be emphasized, is drawn on the assumption of a *given* discount rate. As the supply of reserves increases, banks divide the increase between net free reserves and required reserves. Again points B' and B represent positions of disequilibrium, B' with too-small net free reserves, B with too-large net free reserves. C' and C represent positions of equilibrium, to which the banks would move from B' and B respectively. In the illustration, it happens that C' is a position of negative net free reserves ($C'D'$) while C is a position of positive net free reserves (CD). The mechanism of open-market operations is as follows: Suppose the banks are in equilibrium at C'. Suppose the central bank increases the supply of reserves by $A'A$. In the first instance the net free reserve position of the banks is changed from $C'D'$, a negative value, to BD, positive. Banks consider this position excessive, and they expand earning assets and deposits until required reserves are AC, net free reserves CD. The equilibrium volume of required reserves has risen by BC, a fraction of $A'A$, most of $A'A$ but not all.

The reason is pictured in Fig. 9.2b. There the horizontal axis is the same as in the top panel, the supply of reserves. But the vertical axis measures the bill rate, or interchangeably the federal funds rate. Curve BB' shows horizontally the banks' demand for unborrowed reserves at each bill rate r. It is also the equilibrium interest rate corresponding to each level of the supply of reserves, taking the supply to be independent of the bill rate and to be a central bank decision. With a fixed discount rate, the bill rate falls as the supply of reserves increases. This is readily understandable, since the way for the Fed to increase the supply of reserves is to buy bills, or repos. Moving to the right along the horizontal axis, the stock of bills outside the central bank diminishes. Increasing the supply of reserves from OA' to OA reduces the bill rate from r' to r. Indeed it is this reduction that induces the public or the banks themselves to sell bills to the Federal Reserve. As a result banks are willing to hold a larger volume of net free reserves. The lower bill rate gives them less incentive to economize cash or to borrow from the Federal Reserve.

Figure 9.2 also illustrates the manner in which the equilibrium volume of deposits may change *without* any change in the supply of reserves. Suppose that depositors decide to substitute short-term Treasury securities for bank deposits. Or suppose that banks' demand for such securities increases because of a decline in profitable loan opportunities. Then the bill rate corresponding to any given supply of reserves will be lower. Accordingly the demand for net free reserves will be greater; the banks will use as required reserves a smaller proportion of any given supply of reserves. These shifts are shown by the dashed curves in both panels of Fig. 9.2. The same kind of shifts could be engineered by the central bank itself by lowering the discount rate.

Conceivably the supply of reserves could be made so large, and the bill rate driven so close to zero, that further open-market purchases would neither add to the volume of required reserves and deposits nor reduce further the bill rate. The curves on both panels of Figure 9.2 would be horizontal. This state of affairs actually prevailed in the United States in the 1930s, as a result of the depression and the "golden avalanche" described in Chapter 8, Section 8.7. It survives as an exception in expositions of the traditional theory of multiple-deposit expansion. But the exception is just the extreme case of a general qualification to the traditional story.

Variability of the banking system's demand for net free reserves is not just a theoretical possibility, of practical importance only in exceptional times. As Fig. 9.3 shows, the variation of net free reserves relative to required reserves during the period 1959–1992 is far from negligible.[2] As a source of variation in required reserves, changes in net free reserves are sometimes, though not on average, comparable in magnitude to changes in the supply of unborrowed reserves. Figure 9.3a shows monthly the ratios of net free reserves to lagged required reserves; Figure 9.3b shows the month-to-month changes in this ratio. Figure 9.3c pictures the frequency distribution of the ratio, and Fig. 9.3d the frequency distribution of its change. Net free reserves were an important source of variation in required reserves. (Extreme negative net free reserves in 1974 and 1984 arose for Federal Reserve last-resort lending to specific troubled banks.)

Much of the variation in net free reserves undoubtedly reflected temporary disequilibria rather than persisting changes in bank demand for net free reserves. Much of the week-to-week correlation between changes in supply of reserves and changes in net free reserves reflects the same thing. The banks have abnormal net reserve positions as a result of changes in the supply of reserves to which they have not fully adapted. But Fig. 9.3 also makes it apparent that there are swings in the general level of net free reserves around which month-to-month variation occurs. These longer swings cannot usefully be regarded as a series of temporary disequilibria about a constant normal level. Sections 9.3 through 9.5 show how they might be explained as responses to variations in the incentives provided by market interest rates relative to the discount rate.

9.2
SECONDARY RESERVES

A bank needs in addition to its required reserves certain assets of high predictability of money value and nearly perfect liquidity and reversibility. These holdings, as explained in Chapter 7, enable the bank to meet a reserve test in the face of deposit losses or compelling demands for loans from established customers. Excess primary reserves are, of course, one way to meet this need. But since they are barren of interest, banks seek more profitable substitutes. For many small and medium-size banks, deposits in larger banks in financial centers are convenient secondary reserves; these pay interest close to federal funds rates. But of course interbank deposits cannot serve this function for the system as a whole.

Partly in response to the system's need for secondary reserve assets, the money markets relate federal funds to other short-term assets, which those markets themselves help to endow with the requisite liquidity and reversibility. The big financial center banks are the main players in the money markets.

---

[2]The standard deviation of the monthly change in net free reserves (nfr) was $386 million, while the standard deviation of the change in the supply of unborrowed reserves (ubr) was $1083 million. Their correlation was +0.32, indicating that variation in one component of required reserves (rr) tended to offset variation in the other. The variance in the change in the ratio $nfr(t)/rr(t-1)$ was 0.0096, and that of the change in $ubr(t)/rr(t-1)$ was 0.024. Their correlation was 0.39.

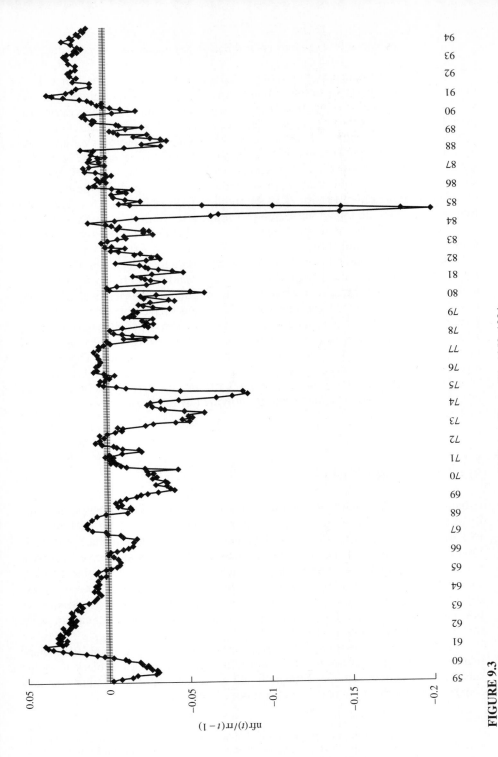

FIGURE 9.3

(a) Net free reserves relative to required reserves, $\text{nfr}(t)/\text{rr}(t-1)$, monthly 1959–1994;

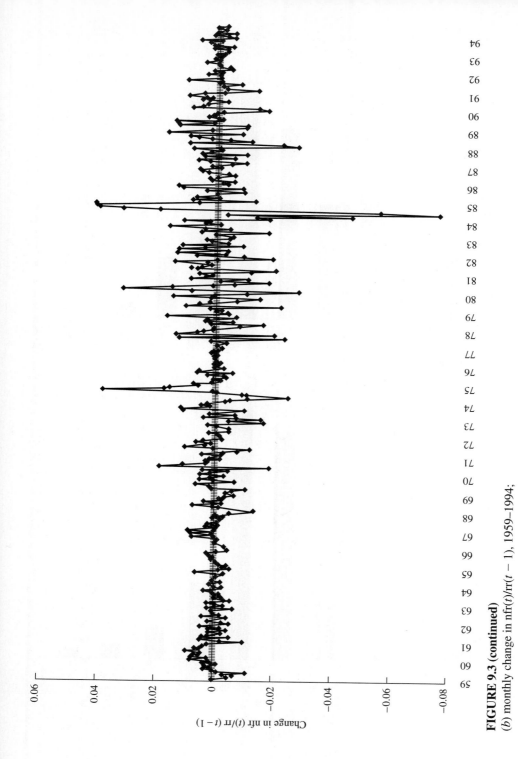

FIGURE 9.3 (continued)

(b) monthly change in $\mathrm{nfr}(t)/\mathrm{rr}(t-1)$, 1959–1994;

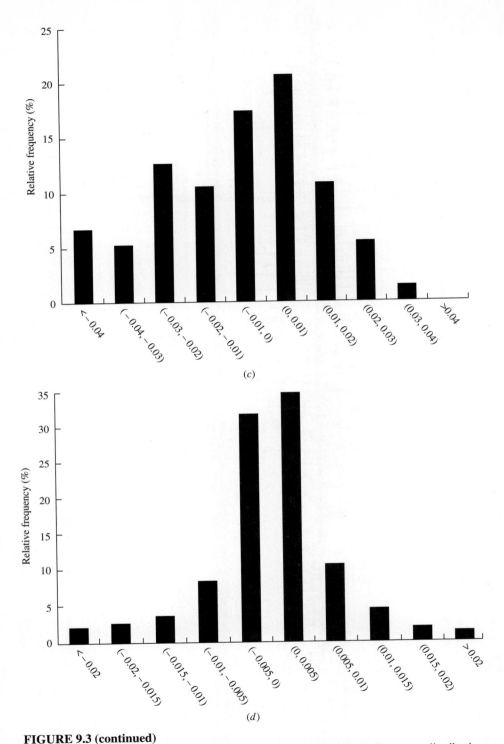

FIGURE 9.3 (continued)
(*c*) frequency distribution of nfr(*t*)/rr(*t* − 1), monthly 1959–1994; (*d*) frequency distribution of change in nfr(*t*)/rr(*t* − 1), monthly 1959–1994.

In the United States, marketable Treasury bills, or agreements to repurchase them, are principal secondary reserve assets. Prime commercial paper, bills issued by impeccable companies, also serve the purpose. Since there are no formal requirements or definitions of secondary reserves, banks use their discretion. Government regulators concern themselves, however, with the soundness of the balance sheets of individual banks and the adequacy of bank capital to prevent losses to depositors or deposit insurance funds. Safe assets are exempt from the required capital/assets ratios.

Treasury bills are obviously suitable secondary reserves. They have a ready market. They are free of risk or default. A large and homogeneous stock is available. They can be used at par to secure advances from the Federal Reserve; borrowing from the Federal Reserve against private paper entails some trouble and delay while the Federal Reserve Bank appraises the eligibility and quality of the note.

There is no definite maturity that sharply divides Treasury securities that are secondary reserves from those that are not. The greater unpredictability of value of longer-term securities makes them less suitable. It is true that any government security, of whatever maturity, can serve as the basis for a Federal Reserve advance at par, even though its market price may be below par. Thus a government bond with twenty years to go will permit a bank to meet a reserve deficiency of a few weeks just as well as a three-month bill. But the central bank will not let the bank meet a persistent reserve deficiency by borrowing. Eventually the bank will have to sell the bond before its maturity and take the loss. It is this risk that makes a bond a less attractive buffer against reserve deficiencies than a bill. The bank with a bill may be able to avoid all loss by borrowing against it until it matures; and even if the bank sooner or later meets its reserve deficiency by selling the bill in an unfavorable market, the loss cannot be large.

There is a certain conventionality and circularity in the process of selection and generation of secondary reserve assets, very much as there is in the social choice of generally acceptable media of exchange. Overnight call loans to brokers against tradable stocks fulfilled this function in New York in the 1920s, and there was a flourishing organized market in them. The secondary reserve function happens to be otherwise handled today. In England and Canada today the principal secondary reserve asset is the day-to-day loan to a dealer in government securities, and to a lesser extent, in other short-term paper. Formerly the London discount house, to which the banks lend their secondary reserves, was a specialist in commercial bills.

Certain intrinsic characteristics, freedom from default risk and high predictability of money value, are essential for secondary reserves. Of assets with the requisite intrinsic properties, only a few acquire the additional essential characteristics of quick and inexpensive marketability; an asset gains these characteristics because and only because the banks and the money market happen to specialize in it. In the United States today, for example, private debtors could generate a much greater volume of short-term obligations with virtually the same attributes as short-term Treasury instruments. If the debtor is a nationally known corporation, or if the IOU has been accepted by a bank, default risk is eliminated. The paper can serve as collateral for Federal Reserve advances to banks. The Federal Reserve used to stand ready to buy acceptances discounted at a rate a bit above its discount rate for advances. Should the supply of short-term Treasury debt by some miracle vanish, there is no doubt that private debt instruments suitable for secondary reserves—commercial paper, sales finance company paper, securities markets call loans, and other instruments—would fill the void. The monetary system would not be quite the same as the one we have now; it makes a difference whether the banks are financing business not only by relatively illiquid commercial loans but also by placing their secondary reserves in commercial paper. The latter practice accomplishes more of the monetization of capital described in Chapter 5.

Under the present system, the supply of secondary reserve assets to the banks is, like the supply of primary reserves, the joint product of decisions by the Treasury and Federal Reserve, on the one hand, and the public outside the banks, on the other. As Table 8.1 showed, in each case the Treasury and Federal Reserve determine the total supply; the nonbank public takes what it wants, and the rest is available to the banks. An important difference between demand debt and short-term debt is that the Treasury and central bank can by varying interest rates have more influence on the public's demand for short-term debt than its demand for currency.

As mentioned in Chapter 8, Section 8.3, in 1988 major central banks and governments agreed on common standards of adequacy of bank capital. As a result U.S. banks are now formally subject to risk-based capital requirements. In determining the requirement each category of assets is weighted by a coefficient scaled to its risk, as estimated by the regulators. Thus the central bank has in effect more power to determine which assets are secondary reserves, and in what degree. Safe assets generally considered secondary reserves are free of capital requirement, while business loans, mortgages, and long-term bonds require equity margins in varying degrees. The buffer of capital assets must equal at least 8 percent of risk-weighted assets.

9.3
COMPOSITION OF BANKS' DEFENSIVE POSITION: NO FEDERAL FUNDS MARKET

The sum of *net free reserves* and *secondary reserves,* for a single bank or for the whole banking system, is its *defensive position.* The strategic questions about the banking system's asset portfolio choices are two. First, what determines the size of the defensive position relative to holdings of less-liquid loans and investments? Second, given the size of the defensive position, what determines its division between its two components? The first was the subject of Chapter 7, so far as an individual bank is concerned, and will be discussed in Section 9.5 for the system as a whole. The second is the subject of this section.

The share of net free reserves in the defensive position can be either negative or positive: correspondingly the share of secondary reserves can range from values above one down to zero. Other things equal, a bank will wish to hold a larger share in secondary reserves the higher the rate of return it can earn on these assets relative to what it can earn on net free reserves. The broad rationale of this relationship is obvious enough; it is simply an application of general principles of portfolio choice

(Chapters 3, 4, and 7). To understand the specifics of this application, it is necessary to extend Chapter 7's theory of the behavior of individual banks.

What is the rate available to a bank on net free reserves? It is the Federal Reserve discount rate if the bank is borrowing from its Federal Reserve Bank or repaying an advance. It is zero on excess reserves. For an individual bank, an overnight debt of federal funds is in effect a negative item in its net free reserves, like a debt to the Federal Reserve. Likewise an overnight loan of federal funds is a positive item equivalent to holding of excess reserves on deposit in its Federal Reserve Bank. One bank's credit position in federal funds is another bank's debtor position; the system as a whole has a zero position. The systemwide role of the federal funds rate will be described in Section 9.4. To prepare for that description, the remainder of this section will describe a system without a federal funds market.

On that assumption, consider a bank's choice between net free reserves and secondary reserves. The important decisions concern expected values of its future holdings of these two kinds of assets. The defensive position serves among other purposes the function of a transactions balance for the bank. Individuals and firms need transactions balances to bridge gaps between imperfectly synchronized receipts and expenditures. Similarly the peaks and troughs of the bank's deposits will generally occur on different days of the week, weeks of the month, and months of the year than those of the loan requirements of its customers. The defensive position will tend to fluctuate correspondingly, rising when deposits are flowing in and loans are being repaid, falling when deposits flow out and loans are being made. But these fluctuations are quite imperfectly predictable. In the face of the uncertainties, the most conservative and inactive policy would be to hold sufficient reserve balances to meet the reserve requirement with high probability in the most stringent circumstances. Net free reserves would fluctuate but unless the very unusual happened they would remain positive at their lowest. Seasonal fluctuations in deposits and loans would not normally give rise to any need to sell secondary reserve assets or to borrow to meet reserve requirements.

In contrast, an active policy of reserve management would entail either frequent purchases and sales of bills or frequent borrowing and repayment at the Federal Reserve or both. Temporarily flush with newly deposited funds, the bank would invest them in the bill market; later when they are needed for reserve requirements, the bank would sell the bills or let them run off as they mature. Or the bank could meet a temporary shortage by an advance from the Federal Reserve, using bills as collateral instead of selling them; correspondingly a surplus could be used to repay debt rather than to expand security holdings. The conservative and inactive policy avoids the bother and expense of frequent money market transactions, as well as the bother and indignity, real or imagined, of relying on Federal Reserve credit. But the bank that follows it earns no income on the defensive part of its portfolio. Active reserve management earns interest, at the cost of numerous money market and discount window transactions, and at the risk of being caught illiquid and short of reserves at high cost in adverse markets. Differences among banks and bankers in circumstance and temperament are to be expected; the costs of active reserve management loom much larger for small country banks than for big New York or Chicago banks. Given the bank, the analogy with the transactions balance of the individual or business firm says that the earning asset will have a greater average share the greater its advantage in interest income.

Figure 9.4 shows how the average cash reserve proportion of a bank varies with the bill rate, at a given Federal Reserve discount rate $0d$. The bill rate is measured on the vertical axis and net free reserves as a proportion of the bank's defensive position on the horizontal axis.

The bank's cash preference behavior has to take account of the basic asymmetry between negative and positive net free reserves: The rate of interest on borrowed reserves is the discount rate; the rate on excess reserves is zero. A bank in debt to the Fed can in effect earn the discount rate on temporary surplus funds by repaying debt. A bank that simply lets such funds pile up as excess reserves earns nothing.

The cash preference function, the solid curve in Fig. 9.4, is a weighted splicing of two relationships, one governed by the discount rate, and the other by the zero rate on excess reserves. The first, which starts in the northwest quadrant of the diagram, shows bill holdings dependent on the differential of the bill rate over the cost of borrowed reserves. This relationship applies when the opportunity cost of bill holdings is unambiguously the bill rate. The second, starting in the southeast corner, shows bill holdings dependent on the absolute level of the bill rate. It applies when the incentive to borrow is absent and the opportunity cost of bill holdings is the zero rate on excess reserves.

Phantom extensions of these relationships, each beyond the range to which it applies, are shown by dotted curves. The extension in the first case can be constructed by imagining that the discount rate is paid on excess reserves, just as it is charged

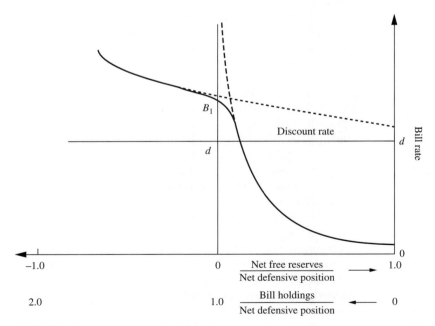

FIGURE 9.4
Bank cash preference curve.

on borrowed reserves. The extension upward of the second relationship, asymptotic to the vertical axis, can be constructed by imagining that borrowing is altogether proscribed.

What accounts for the curvature of the relationships of cash proportions to the two opportunity costs? Both have the shape of Keynesian liquidity preference curves, for essentially the traditional Keynesian reasons. But their application here requires some specific explanation.

Consider first negative net free reserve positions in Fig. 9.4. Such a position does not mean continuous constant indebtedness to the Federal Reserve; it indicates a policy under which expectations of borrowing in some weeks more than offset the excess reserves expected to be held at others. When the bill rate is high relative to the discount rate, the bank has incentive to borrow rather than to sell bills when it is short of reserves and to buy bills rather than repay indebtedness when it has temporary surplus funds.

This incentive, and the behavior to which it leads, is quite consistent with the Federal Reserve's philosophy of the discount window, as described in Chapter 8, Section 8.12, item 2. Under those rubrics there is ample scope both for operation of the incentive given by a favorable differential of the bill rate over the discount rate and for the persistence of such a differential despite the incentive. From a bank's viewpoint the discount window is an imperfect substitute for cash reserves in hand.

High bill rates provide, then, an incentive to maintain large bill holdings, letting seasonal and random fluctuation in deposits and loans be reflected in a fluctuating net free reserve position, sometimes negative and sometimes zero or positive. The limits on frequency and amount of discounting enforced by the Federal Reserve make it more and more difficult as the bill rate rises to increase borrowed reserves in response to the enhanced incentive. As the bill rate falls relative to the discount rate, positive excess reserves at some times will tend to outweigh, on average, borrowings at other times, as shown in the eastern quadrants of the figure.

Consider the second relationship, applicable when the relevant opportunity cost is the zero rate on cash reserves. At a given positive discount rate, a bill rate low enough to discourage all borrowing may yet be high enough to induce considerable active economizing of cash reserves. To keep excess reserves low, the bank will go frequently in and out of the bill market as its defensive position fluctuates from week to week. But at lower bill rates active reserve management becomes less profitable, and the bank will tolerate high cash balances. At some bill rate above zero the costs of transactions in and out of bills and the risks of illiquidity will keep the bank entirely out of bills. The cash preference curve becomes flat, as in Keynes's liquidity trap.

At bill rates in the neighborhood of the discount rate, where the two simple relationships splice, the story is more complicated. There is an incentive to use temporary surplus funds to reduce debt rather than to purchase bills, but at the same time there is an incentive to buy bills rather than to increase idle excess reserves. At these rates the bank will meet shortages of funds sometimes by selling bills and sometimes by borrowing. The lower the bill rate, the less frequent will be the use of the discount window. Below a certain rate, say $0B_1$, there will be no borrowing at any time.

In Fig. 9.4 the critical rate $0B_1$, above which the bank does at least some borrowing from the Federal Reserve, is higher than the discount rate. This need not be the case. Even at a bill rate below the discount rate a bank may on occasion find it cheaper or more convenient to borrow rather than to sell bills, or to buy bills rather than to repay indebtedness. In particular, if a banker expects a fall in the bill rate, he may be willing to borrow at a rate higher than the current bill yield.

A change in the discount rate will shift up or down the first component of the splice, while the second remains in place. For this reason it is not accurate to say that the bank's demands for cash and bills depend just on the differential between the bill rate and the discount rate; they depend also on the absolute level of the two rates. In Fig. 9.5, the cash preference relationship is shown for three levels of the discount rate, including at the bottom a hypothetical discount rate of zero. In general, a rise in both rates, maintaining a constant differential between them, will diminish the demand for net free reserves. For example, if the bill rate and discount rate are equal, there will be more borrowing and less excess reserves with a 5 percent discount rate than a 3 percent rate.

A basic assumption of Fig. 9.5, and of the theory of this chapter in general, is that the administration of the discount window is a constant, that is, that the criteria and standards are applied with the same rigor whether interest rates are high or low, whether money is loose or tight. This assumption corresponds to express statements of the Federal Reserve concerning discount policy (see Chapter 8, Section 8.12).

The curves of Figs. 9.4 and 9.5 have been drawn for a single bank. But qualitatively, at any rate, they can also depict the cash preference relationship for the banking system as a whole.

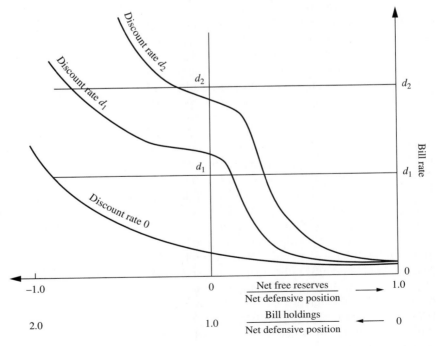

FIGURE 9.5
Bank cash preference at alternative discount rates.

9.4
THE FEDERAL FUNDS MARKET

In the previous section the market in overnight loans of reserve balances between banks was ignored. The basic conclusions stand even when the complication of the federal funds market is introduced. The effect of that market is to shift the banks' aggregative cash preference curve to the left. The federal funds market enables the banking system as a whole to hold at a given bill rate more bills and less net free reserves. The explanation of this shift is quite analogous to the explanation in Chapter 5 of the shift to the left in the public's cash preference curve because of the introduction of the loan market.

In the absence of a federal funds market, banks can be divided into two groups, according to the compositions of their defensive position at a given moment. In one group are banks that would be willing to expand their bill holdings, were credit available or less expensive. In the other group are banks with excess reserves beyond their immediate cash needs; they are holding all the bills they want, even though the opportunity cost of additional bill holding is simply the zero yield on cash. The first group includes banks in debt to the Federal Reserve, and other banks temporarily short of reserves; having exhausted their cash holdings, they must meet any further drains by selling bills or by borrowing. The second group includes firms temporarily flush with reserves, as well as others who do not find the yields of temporary bill holdings worth the transactions costs and risks involved. Obviously banks of the first group are potential borrowers of federal funds, and banks of the second group potential lenders. The lending banks can substitute federal funds sold for excess reserve balances, and the borrowing banks can hold more bills. Thus the banking system as a whole will hold, at a given bill rate, more bills and less excess reserves.

Why are federal funds, from the point of view of the lending banks, a better substitute than bills for reserve balances? They are a much shorter obligation, and unlike bills are free of all risk of capital loss. A bank which has to sell bills to obtain reserves may find that the market has turned against it; indeed if it is a large bank, its very need to sell may cause bill prices to fall. Funds called by the lender are immediately available as reserve balances; transactions are made by wire transfer from one bank to another on the books of the Federal Reserve Banks. The proceeds of a matured or sold bill are not available to meet reserve requirements until the bank receives and deposits the check.

In Fig. 9.6 the cash preference function for the banks in the absence of a federal funds market is shown as curve CC'. With a federal funds market, the cash preference function moves to FF'. The federal funds rate that clears the market is different at different points on FF'.

For example, consider a bill rate of $0R_1$. Without a federal funds market the banking system would hold R_1B_1 percent of its net defensive position in excess reserves, and B_1C_1 percent in bills. With a federal funds market, banks holding excess reserves would be willing to substitute federal funds in amount F_1B_1, reducing the demand for cash reserves to R_1F_1, and other banks would willingly borrow federal funds of this amount to hold additional bills. The federal funds rate balances the borrowing and lending of federal funds at the position F_1.

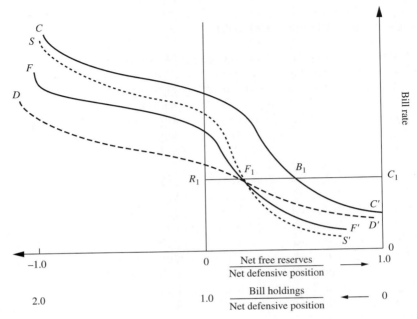

FIGURE 9.6
Change in banks' cash preference function due to federal funds market.

On the lending side, the degree to which banks are willing to substitute federal funds for excess reserves depends positively upon the funds interest rate. At a 0 percent federal funds rate, federal funds would have only disadvantages compared with reserve balances; none would be offered for sale, and F_1 would coincide with B_1. As the federal funds rate becomes higher, willing lenders appear and F_1 moves to the left.

On the borrowing side, the degree to which banks are willing to buy federal funds to finance higher inventories of bills depends negatively upon the federal funds rate. Above a certain rate the demand will normally be zero or negative; the potential borrowing banks will see no incentive to borrow in order to hold bills and indeed may substitute federal funds for bills. The critical rate at which borrowers' demand for federal funds becomes positive will normally be somewhat below the bill rate $0R_1$. With neutral expectations of the future of interest rates banks will require some premium on bills over federal funds to compensate them for the risk of capital loss on bills. However, expectations of a fall in the bill rate would raise the critical federal funds rate, providing a capital gains incentive to banks to borrow in order to hold bills. Below the critical rate, borrowing banks will place F_1 further to the left of B_1 the lower the federal funds rate.

The actual position of F_1 in Fig. 9.6 implies a federal funds rate, somewhere between zero and the bill rate $0R_1$, that equates the supply of funds by lending banks to the demand of borrowing banks.

How do the quantity of federal funds transactions and the federal funds rate vary with the bill rate? Through the position F_1 are drawn two curves, one to show the variation in demand for federal funds at a given federal funds rate as the bill rate varies, the other to show the variation in supply. The horizontal distance between DF_1D' and CC' represents at each bill rate the amount by which borrowers wish to expand their bill holdings on borrowed funds at the given federal funds rate. The demand increases with the bill rate.

The horizontal distance between SF_1S' and CC' shows the corresponding supply of federal funds from banks who would substitute them for excess reserves. This supply is smaller at higher bill rates because the gross holdings of excess reserves are smaller; for example, lending banks might be willing, so long as the federal funds rate is the same, to substitute federal funds for the same proportion of excess reserves. At the federal funds rate corresponding to F_1, demand will exceed supply at bill rates above OR_1, and supply will exceed demand at lower bill rates. In general, therefore, the equilibrium federal funds rate will be higher the higher the bill rate.

Does the discount rate set an upper limit to the federal funds rate? At the discount rate and above, there will be a demand for federal funds at bill rates high enough to induce borrowing. Some banks will prefer to borrow in the federal funds market rather than at the discount window, even if federal funds are somewhat more expensive. They will pay a premium to reduce the frequency of their use of the discount window. On the supply side, however, a premium of the federal funds rate over the discount rate gives some banks an incentive to borrow at the Federal Reserve in order to lend on the federal funds market. Such borrowings would supplement excess reserves as a source of federal funds. Among the lending banks would generally be some whose resort to the discount window has been so infrequent that they would not be deterred by fear of compromising their future access to Federal Reserve credit. These banks will borrow from the Federal Reserve to lend federal funds but not to buy bills; the reason is that they regard federal funds as a more adequate substitute for reserve balances. It is true that borrowing at the discount window to buy federal funds is contrary to Federal Reserve rules. But money is fungible, and it may be difficult to discern motivations.

The possibility of arbitrage between the discount window and the federal funds market means that the supply of federal funds will be elastic with respect to the federal funds rate, in the neighborhood of the discount rate. But it is by no means perfectly elastic. The supply of willing and eligible arbitrageurs is limited. To draw more banks into such arbitrage, moreover, a larger differential is needed to compensate for transactions costs and for the risks of Federal Reserve displeasure. A federal funds rate above the discount rate was rare in the 1950s and 1960s, at least as much because of Federal Reserve open market and discount rate policies as because of arbitrage. More recently the Fed usually tries to keep the federal funds rate above the discount rate, possibly to keep banks in its debt and easier to control.

The federal funds market is a mechanism by which the banking system can circumvent to some degree the limitations of Federal Reserve discount discipline. A bank can borrow indirectly more and more often than discount window administration would permit it to borrow directly. By borrowing federal funds that some other bank has borrowed from the Federal Reserve, a bank short of reserves can in effect substitute the untarnished discount window standing of the other bank for its own heavily used line of credit. Circumvention of Federal Reserve discount discipline is not the result of any deliberate conspiracy of the banks. Rather it is an unintended and impersonal consequence of the market. It is not even necessary to imagine that a bank borrows from the Federal Reserve with conscious and explicit intent to exploit a profit opportunity in federal funds. A bank in debt to the Federal Reserve would be more likely when the rate differential is favorable to lend an unexpected or transient accretion of funds on the federal funds market than to repay its debt. Anticipating this possibility, a bank will tend to borrow at the discount window larger amounts and more frequently than if the federal funds rate were low.

Figure 9.7 illustrates the determinants of the federal funds rate at given levels of the bill rate and discount rate. In comparison with Fig. 9.6, the roles of the bill rate and federal funds rate are reversed. The vertical axis in each part of Fig. 9.7 measures the federal funds rate, and the horizontal axis measures the same quantities as in Fig. 9.6, that is, from left to right the proportion of defensive position in net free reserves and from right to left the proportion in bills. The level of the bill rate is OR and the level of the discount rate $0d$. The vertical line BB' marks the division of the defensive position in the absence of a federal funds market. The demand for federal funds to finance increased bill holdings is the horizontal distance between DD' and BB'. The demand is greater the lower the federal funds rate. On the assumption of neutral expectations regarding the future of the bill rate, the demand is shown to vanish at a rate somewhat lower than the bill rate. The supply of federal funds to finance increased bill holdings is the horizontal distance between SS' and BB'. The supply vanishes at a rate somewhat above zero, on the assumption that some premium is

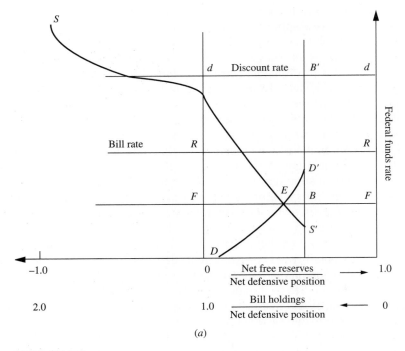

(a)

FIGURE 9.7
Determination of the federal funds rate: (a) bill rate low relative to discount rate;

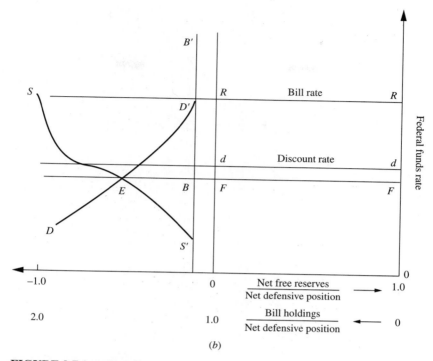

FIGURE 9.7 (continued)
(*b*) bill rate high relative to discount rate.

needed to induce a bank to go to the trouble of lending its excess reserves. The supply rises with the federal funds rate and becomes highly elastic in the neighborhood of the discount rate. The supply curve becomes steeply sloped again as the banking system stretches its credit at the Federal Reserve discount window.

The market-clearing federal funds rate is $0F$; the amount of extra bill holdings financed by federal funds is EB. There is a corresponding reduction in the net free reserves of the banking system. In Fig. 9.7*a* this reduction is entirely an economy of excess reserves, induced by the willingness of some banks to substitute federal funds lending for reserve balances proper. In Fig. 9.7*b* the reduction in net free reserves reflects also additional borrowing at the Federal Reserve.

The relationship of the equilibrium federal funds rate to the bill rate is illustrated in Fig. 9.8. For neutral expectations regarding the future of the bill rate the curve is NN'. The federal funds rate is always below the bill rate, and its elasticity with respect to the bill rate is very low when the federal funds rate is near the discount rate.

There is some indeterminacy at low rates where no transactions occur. Let $0B_1$ be the bill rate below which the demand for federal funds is zero at a federal funds rate $0F_1$. No transactions occur at rates lower than these; the relevant relationship begins at N. The curve B_0N shows for each federal funds rate the highest bill rate at which demand for federal funds is zero; for example, at a Federal Funds rate of zero the demand will be zero for any bill rate below $0B_0$, and positive above that rate.

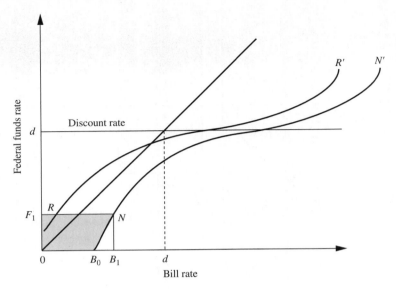

FIGURE 9.8
Relationship of bill rate and federal funds rate.

The shaded portion of the rectangle is the area of indeterminacy; at any pair of rates in this area both the demand and the supply are zero.

Expectations of a fall in the bill rate will shift the relationship to the left, for example to RR'; the prospect of capital gains on bills increases the demand for federal funds. With such expectations it is possible for the federal funds rate to exceed the bill rate. Expectations of capital loss on bills will of course cause the opposite shift in NN'.

Total federal funds transactions—the amount of bill holdings financed through the federal funds market—also rise with the bill rate. But, as depicted in Fig. 9.9, *transactions* are most elastic to the bill rate just in those ranges where the federal funds *rate* is least elastic, and vice versa. The quantity of federal funds lending and borrowing at each bill rate is also shown in Fig. 9.6, as the horizontal difference between FF' and CC'. As previously stated, the upshot of the federal funds market is to shift the banks' collective cash preference relationship from CC' to FF'.

The federal funds market permits the banking system to economize net free reserves, either by holding smaller excess reserves or by borrowing more freely from the Federal Reserve. This economy is a once-and-for-all phenomenon; the curve can shift further to the left only as the federal funds market becomes more nearly perfect. The establishment of an effective federal funds market since World War II did not mean that the banks had escaped the grasp of the Federal Reserve. It did mean that the Federal Reserve, to keep the bill rate at the same level, had to set a higher discount rate or provide a smaller supply of reserves. Once this adjustment was made, the Federal Reserve could operate along the banks' new cash preference curve, FF', as easily as it formerly operated along the old one, CC'.

The federal funds market is not the only mechanism by which the banking system economizes the aggregate supply of reserves by redistributing them to banks

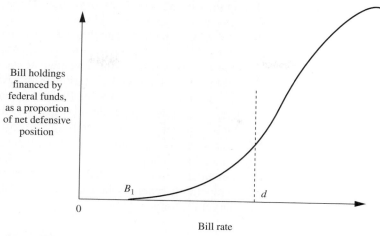

FIGURE 9.9
Relationship of federal funds rate to the bill rate.

that value them the most. Interbank deposits are a method of long standing. When a small country bank deposits money in its big-city correspondent, it makes an equivalent transfer of reserves. The country bank acquires a secondary reserve that, like federal funds, is an excellent substitute for primary reserves themselves. The country banker is remunerated by the services of the larger bank—foreign exchange dealings, securities transactions, investment advice, and perhaps not least, metropolitan entertainment, nowadays all that and interest too. These are services in which there are economies of scale and centralization. In return the city bank acquires reserves that it would otherwise obtain only by borrowing or selling earning assets. Having numerous correspondents with different patterns of seasonal and cyclical needs for funds, the city bank has the protection of large numbers against concentration of withdrawals at particular times. But in a period of general monetary tightness, the city bank's need for reserves is likely to be accentuated by the needs of its correspondents. Unlike explicit interest rates, the emoluments of correspondent balances are vaguely defined and cannot move up and down in concert with money market fluctuations.

Competition for the public's deposits, to the extent allowed by deposit rate regulation, is still another method of adjusting reserve positions. (See Chapter 7, Section 7.3.4, and Appendices A and B.) A bank short of reserves may be able to draw deposits from other banks, thus improving its net free reserve position by $\$(1-k)$, where k is the reserve requirement, for each dollar of deposits it attracts. If the bank must pay an interest rate r to obtain the deposit, the cost of a dollar increment in net free reserves is $r/(1-k)$. A bank with excess reserves will save a like amount for every dollar of reserves lost through transfer of deposits to another bank. (If deposits are not perfectly elastically supplied to an individual bank, a bank seeking new deposits may have to pay higher interest not only to new depositors but to all its depositors. Its marginal cost will exceed r. Likewise, the bank losing deposits may receive some consolation if it becomes cheaper to hold the remaining depositors.)

Marketable certificates of time deposit are an important money market instrument, and at present they require no reserves. Large metropolitan banks can control their deposit and reserve positions by varying both the rate they offer and the size of their outstanding CD liabilities. To the holder, or "depositor," a CD has most of the attributes of a Treasury bill of similar maturity. What is the advantage to the issuing bank, compared to borrowing federal funds? Major banks clearly see an advantage, for they frequently issue CDs at rates not only much above the Federal Reserve discount rate but also above the federal funds rate. A CD provides funds to the bank for a longer time—three or six months or even years. In the interim the cost of federal funds might rise. Even if federal funds were cheaper to begin with, a sequence of overnight borrowing for several months might prove more expensive. Banks can be expected to turn to the CDs to mobilize reserves when they expect increases in money market interest rates. By competition generally held expectations of money market rates will be reflected in market CD rates.

9.5
THE BANKING SYSTEM'S DEFENSIVE POSITION

Sections 9.3 and 9.4 were concerned with the composition of the banking system's defensive position. This section concerns its total size. The composition, it was argued, depends on the bill rate and the discount rate. Similarly, the aggregate defensive position may be taken to depend on the rate on commercial loans relative to the bill rate. Here the loan rate represents the additional earnings that a bank can obtain from investing another dollar in loans, while the bill rate represents the loss of earnings to a bank from reducing its defensive position by a dollar.

According to the argument of Chapter 7, the greater the marginal revenue from lending in relation to the marginal revenue from defensive holdings, the smaller the defensive position a bank will hold. The customer loan rate is not always literally the marginal revenue from commercial lending for an individual bank. As argued in Chapter 7, an individual bank does not face a perfectly elastic demand for loans. As a firm in monopolistic competition, with some ability to discriminate among customers, the bank has a lower marginal revenue the greater its volume of lending. But the loan rate and the marginal revenue from lending in individual banks will in general move together. A general increase in marginal revenue from lending in individual banks will be accompanied by a general increase in customer loan rates. A decline in demand for loans will mean a decline in both loan rates and marginal revenues. Similarly, as the argument of the previous sections indicates, the bill rate is not literally the marginal revenue of the defensive component of each bank's portfolio. If its defensive position were to be reduced by a dollar, a bank might choose not to reduce its bill holdings by a dollar, but to borrow from the Federal Reserve, buy federal funds, or reduce excess legal reserves, each for part or all of the dollar. Nevertheless for almost every bank each of these alternatives has to compete with a reduction of bill holdings.

Figure 9.10 shows a banking system's preference between the defensive and loan components of its portfolio, in relation to the loan rate. The vertical axis mea-

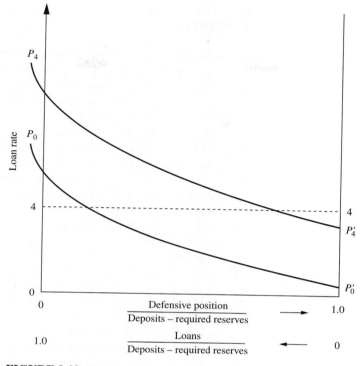

FIGURE 9.10
Relationship of banks' portfolio choice to loan rate.

sures the loan rate. The horizontal axis measures left to right the aggregate defensive position of the banks as a percentage of deposits in excess of required reserves. Thus it measures in the other direction the share of (deposits in excess of required reserves) invested in (loans in excess of capital funds). The basic balance sheet identity involved is

$$(\text{Defensive position}) + (\text{loans} - \text{capital accounts}) = (\text{deposits} - \text{required reserves}).$$

Each preference curve is drawn on the assumption of a given bill rate. For example, $P_4 P_4'$ might represent banks' portfolio choices at a bill rate of 4 percent, and $P_0 P_0'$ at a hypothetical bill rate of 0 percent. Each curve is negatively sloped, indicating that at a given bill rate a greater share of deposits will be invested in defensive assets, and a smaller share in loans, the lower the loan rate. Conceivably loan demand could be so great and so profitable that banks would have a negative defensive position: That is, the banking system's debt to the Federal Reserve would exceed its holdings of bills; in effect, some private paper would be discounted. In Fig. 9.10 the banking system is not pictured as shifting entirely into defensive assets even when the loan rate and, a fortiori, the marginal revenues of individual banks fall below the bill rate. Banks will continue to accommodate certain customers at a current loss, because of the profitability of maintaining long-run relations with them.

9.6
THE DEMAND FOR BANK DEPOSITS

The determinants of the demand for bank deposits have been discussed in general terms in Chapters 2 through 4 and in Chapter 7. For the present analysis the relevant factors are the bill rate, the loan rate, and deposit rates. With respect to banks' competition for deposits, there are, as explained in Chapter 7, two regimes to consider. In one regime, the rates of return on time and demand deposits can be taken as given. The rate on demand deposits is legally zero. The rates on time deposits are effectively set by ceilings imposed by the Federal Reserve. In the other regime, banks compete for deposits without the legal constraints of rate ceilings.

Other things equal, as rates rise on assets competitive with bank deposits, the public substitutes those assets for deposits. Clearly the demand for deposits will fall as the bill rate rises, inducing corporations and individuals to substitute bills for cash. Perhaps it is less obvious, though no less important, that the demand for deposits depends on the banks' own loan rate—the higher the rate of return on the banking system's assets, the lower will be the demand for its liabilities.

The reason is simply that a high loan rate is an incentive for the ultimate lenders of funds to bypass the banks in favor of direct lending to private borrowers. Savers lend directly to private borrowers by extending them book credit or buying their promissory notes, mortgages, bonds, and other obligations. The interest yields available on these investments have some influence on the willingness of these savers to lend to commercial banks at given rates on time and demand deposits.

In addition, savers have indirect ways of bypassing commercial banks, namely lending through nonbank financial intermediaries. These institutions compete with banks both for assets and for liabilities. Nonbank intermediaries have generally been free to adjust the rates they offer to their creditors. Before 1980, savings banks, savings and loan associations, and other thrift institutions were considered nonbanks to distinguish them from commercial banks, the only intermediaries subject to Federal Reserve rules. Clearly these nonbanks, paying interest on savings deposits or dividends on saving and loan shares, were important competitors for banks proper. They still are, but now they are subject to the same rules and are essentially banks. There are other nonbank intermediaries providing substitutes for banks' checkable deposits and time deposits: insurance companies, money market funds, bond funds, mortgage funds.

The indirect mechanism by which an increase in private loan rates lowers public demand for bank deposits, at given deposit rates, is as follows: The prospect of increased earnings from lending leads nonbank financial intermediaries to raise the rates they offer to their creditors. The liabilities of these intermediaries are substitutes, in several cases very close substitutes, for bank deposits. As the nonbank intermediaries gain funds, the banks lose them. For example, the result of an increase in returns on money market mutual funds is clearly a shift toward these institutions, away from bank deposits.

A simplified formal model of the first regime—deposit rates fixed—will contribute to understanding this important mechanism, by which the demand for bank deposits depends on, inter alia, the rates at which banks lend. Suppose that loans to private borrowers are homogeneous and that a perfect market determines a single loan rate (and associated with it a credit line parameter) prevailing for all borrowers and lenders. Banks are the only financial intermediary explicitly considered; lending through other intermediaries is not distinguished from direct public lending. The existing stock of private capital and its money value are taken as given. Together with the outstanding net debt of the central government, the value of the capital stock determines net private wealth. Government debt is assumed to take only two forms: demand debt and short-term debt. Under this assumption, all government debts are potential reserves, primary or secondary, for the banks.

As in Chapter 5, the population is divided into two groups: lenders, who have less than 100 percent of their net worth in equity in private capital; and borrowers, who have more than 100 percent of their net worth in such equity. The other assets available to lenders are four in number: direct loans, bank deposits, Treasury bills, currency. The yields of currency and bank deposits are institutionally fixed. Let the rates of return on equity and on bills be given. Consider how lenders apportion their wealth among the four assets, and how their apportionment depends on the loan rate. Their demand for direct loans will increase, and their holdings of each of the other three assets will fall, as the loan rate rises.

This is illustrated in the right-hand side of Fig. 9.11 corresponding to lenders' net worth. The vertical axis measures the loan rate. At loan rate A, for example, lenders

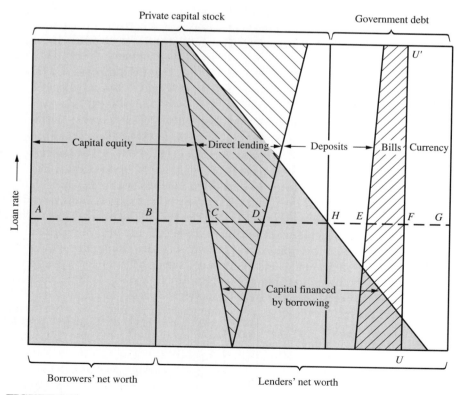

FIGURE 9.11
Public portfolio preferences and asset supplies.

will divide their wealth BG as follows: BC in capital, CD in direct loans, DE in bank deposits, EF in bills, and FG in currency. In similar fashion, the figure shows the lenders' portfolio at any other loan rate. As the curves are drawn, lenders diminish their holdings of each other asset (except currency, for which the demand is taken to be constant) and increase their direct lending as the loan rate rises.

The remainder of total private wealth is borrowers' net worth, AB in Fig. 9.11. Borrowers wish to hold capital in excess of their net worth, in an amount that depends inversely on the loan rate. At loan rate A, the amount of capital they wish to hold on borrowed funds is CH; in general their excess demand for capital is the horizontal difference between the curve through C and that through H. The total demand for capital at loan rate A is, therefore, AH; BC by lenders, and $AB + CH$ by borrowers. Borrowers are financed partly by lenders directly (CD) and partly by banks (DH).

If the existing stock of capital at current prices is AH, and net government debt is HG, loan rate A brings about portfolio balance for the public. At this rate, the demand for and supply of capital are equated. This is one condition of equilibrium, but not the only one. For the position in Fig. 9.11 corresponding to loan rate A to be a full equilibrium, not only the public but also the banks must be content. The public's holdings of government debt are EG. The remaining quantity of government debt HE is held by the commercial banks, either in the form of demand debt or in the form of bills; the division of the debt between these two categories is the decision of the central bank. For the banks to be content, the amount HE and its division between cash and bills must meet their demands for reserves and defensive position in view of their deposits DE and their loans DH. The equilibrium of the banks is the subject of the next section.

9.7
EQUILIBRIUM IN THE MONEY MARKET

Figure 9.12 reproduces the government debt segment of Fig. 9.11 and shows the disposition of the supply of government debt HG at various loan rates. A part, FG, is held by the public as currency; this quantity is taken to be insensitive to the loan rate. Another part is held by the public as Treasury bills; these holdings are smaller at higher loan rates. This was shown as EF in Fig. 9.11 for loan rate A, or in general as the horizontal distance between the curve through E and the vertical line UU' through F. In Fig. 9.12 it is convenient to show the same public demand for bills as EF' at rate A or in general as the horizontal distance between the curve through E and the curve through F'. A third part—between F' and F—is the legal reserve requirement of the banks, derived from the public's demand for deposits as shown in Fig. 9.11. If the required reserve ratio is one-tenth, for example, then the distance $F'F$ in Fig. 9.12 is one-tenth of the distance DE in Fig. 9.11. Deposits demanded by the public are smaller at higher loan rates. Therefore, required reserves are smaller at higher loan rates. Required reserves represent an indirect or derived demand of the public for government demand debt, just as public currency holdings are a direct requirement for such debt. In these two ways the public uses up a quantity of demand debt $F'G$. In addition the public holds EF' in bills, making a total demand

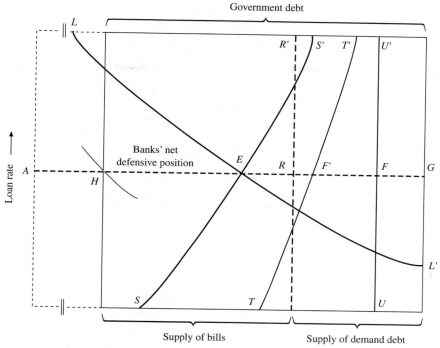

FIGURE 9.12
Bank portfolio preferences and asset supplies.

for government debt of EG. The remainder HE of the given supply of government debt is available for the net defensive position of the banks. The curve SS' through E, therefore, can be read as a supply curve, showing the supply of defensive assets to the banking system at different loan rates.

The banks' demand for defensive assets has been discussed in Section 9.5. There it was argued that, at a given bill rate, the banks' net defensive position will be a larger share of (deposits − required reserves) the lower the loan rate. Deposits are larger at lower loan rates; a fortiori the banks' dollar requirements for defensive position will be greater at low loan rates than at high. In Fig. 9.12 banks' demand for net defensive position is indicated by curve LL', drawn on the same assumptions regarding the bill rate and the level of the public demand for deposits as the other curves in the diagram. In Fig. 9.12 the supply and demand are equated at loan rate A; banks are content to hold the defensive position HE available to them at that rate. Since this rate, as Fig. 9.11 shows, is also the rate that equates the supply and demand for private capital, the situation depicted in the two diagrams is a complete equilibrium—for the banks as well as the nonbank public.

The banks' legal reserve account may also be shown in Fig. 9.12. Let the distance RG be the available quantity of demand debt; the determination of this quantity has been discussed in Chapter 8, Section 8.11. The remainder HR of the government debt is available to the public and the banks in the form of bills. The vertical line through R reflects an assumption that the composition of the debt is an autonomous decision of the authorities, independent of the loan rate. Central bank purchases of bills would move the line RR' to the left, leaving unchanged the total supply of debt. More of the debt would be monetized by open-market purchases, and banks would be enabled to hold more legal reserves. Open-market sales would by the same token move the vertical line through R to the right.

Since the horizontal distance to the right of TT', the curve through F', represents the public's direct and indirect requirements for demand debt, the supply of net free reserves to the banks is the distance from R to that curve. At loan rate A, for example, net free reserves of RF' are available to the banks. At low loan rates the curve lies to the left of R; the supply of net free reserves is negative.

Behind the scenes are two further implications of the equilibrium at loan rate A illustrated in the figures. The bill rate must stand at the particular level assumed in drawing the preference schedules of the banks and of the public. Suppose that level is I. Behind the scenes still further is the discount rate. It must be at such a level that a bill rate of I will induce the banks to hold exactly RF' in net free reserves. As argued in Sections 9.3 and 9.4, the fraction of their overall net defensive position that the banks will wish to hold as net free reserves depends on the relative levels of the bill rate and the discount rate. Here the fraction is RF'/HE; the rates must be such as to make the banks content with that fraction.

If deposit rates are variable—the second regime noted above—then equilibrium also requires that the rate and volume of deposits satisfy both the public and the banks. The public's demand curve for deposits in Fig. 9.11 must assume the equilibrium deposit rate, and for the banks this equilibrium deposit rate must be in line with the loan rate and the bill rate, as explained in Chapter 7. This observation tells nothing about the essential differences between the two regimes. These will be discussed in the next chapter, where a full equilibrium model will be displayed algebraically and displacements of equilibrium will be examined.

CHAPTER 10

Money and Government Debt in a General Equilibrium Framework

INTRODUCTION

The short-run equilibrium of the banking system and the economy, described in the previous chapter, is subject to changes of two major types. One source of change is government monetary and debt policy. By altering the variables under their control, the central bank and the Treasury can influence the money and credit markets and through them the real economy. The other source of disturbance is the economy itself—events outside the control of the monetary authorities. Business cycles, technological change, shifts of taste, nonmonetary policies of government, capital accumulation, population growth—all these things affect financial markets and institutions. Much of the activity of the monetary authorities is response or reaction to these external events, in an attempt to maintain stability in an economic system vulnerable to many powerful destabilizing forces. In spite of their efforts, it is probable that most of the historical variance of monetary and financial variables is a reflection of unsystematic and unpredicted external shocks rather than of deliberate government policy.

This chapter is concerned with sources of both monetary and economic change. If the modus operandi of policy actions attracts the major share of attention, it is because there is naturally more interest in mechanisms under control than in those that cannot be controlled.

In the equilibrium described in Chapter 9 the expected rate of return on physical capital is taken as given, equal to its anticipated marginal productivity in economic use. The equilibrium loan rate and other interest rates are such that the public would hold the existing stock of capital, at its cost of reproduction. The marginal productivity of capital is then the same as the rate of return on capital that equates its supply to the portfolio demands of the public, borrowers and diversifiers together. To use and adapt terms made famous by Wicksell, the natural rate of interest is equal to the market rate; and accordingly the reproduction price of capital is equal to the market valuation of equivalent existing capital; that is, the q ratio is equal to 1 (see Chapter 6, Section 6.2).

As analyzed in Chapter 6, these equalities can be disturbed either by events in the real economy or by financial events, including government policies. Technological and economic changes favorable to the investment outlook can raise the natural rate of interest; financial events and policies can lower the market rate. In either case, the discrepancy of the two rates will be associated with a rise in market valuation of capital relative to its reproduction cost. The resulting excess demand for capital will raise valuations of capital goods and stimulate investments that add to the stock of physical capital. Likewise, an increase in market rate relative to natural rate, with contractionary impact on the economy, may arise either from unfavorable economic events or from events that make financial assets more attractive relative to real capital.

More specifically, the market rate may change because of shifts in the expectations and liquidity preferences of the public and banks. Anything that diminishes their demands for defensive assets lowers the market rate. Alternatively the market rate may fall because of central bank measures—open-market purchases of bills, reduction of the discount rate, relaxation of reserve requirements. Indeed the possibility and purpose of monetary control arise mainly from the power of the central bank to move the market rate independently of the natural rate, either deliberately creating a discrepancy or averting a disequilibrium due to shifts either in nonpolicy influences on the market rate or in "real" factors determining the natural rate.

This Wicksellian, q ratio story applies strictly to a closed economy but also in its essentials to a large open economy with market rates that move, and can be moved, somewhat independently of interest rates elsewhere. In an open economy, for example, reductions of the domestic market rates relative to foreign interest rates and foreign rates of return on capital can raise the economy's foreign real investment, just as its reduction relative to the domestic natural rate stimulates home real investment. Foreign real investment is the country's current account surplus, exports net of imports. A link in the process by which expansionary monetary policy raises net exports may often be a decline in the exchange rate, a fall in the value of the home currency in terms of foreign currencies. This channel of transmission of monetary policy is further discussed later in this chapter.

This chapter combines the general equilibrium analysis of the monetary and banking system in Chapter 9 with the analysis of the market for capital in Chapters 5 and 6. Naturally the focus is on the ways in which changes in the size and composition of government debt affect money and capital markets. This story will be told in Sections 10.2 and 10.3. First, however, Section 10.1 considers recent theoretical claims that government financial policies have no macroeconomic consequences at all.

10.1
DOES GOVERNMENT FINANCIAL POLICY MATTER?[1]

The new classical economists have argued that government policies expected and understood have no real effects, because optimizing private agents will offset them to remain at their preferred positions.

10.1.1 Monetary Policy

Lucas (1977) and Sargent and Wallace (1976) have argued that rational agents simply scale up nominal prices proportionately to any anticipated monetary policy change, leaving the real money supply and relative prices unchanged. Monetary policy can have only real effects if it is unexpected. There are two fallacies in this argument, even if the new classical assumptions about rational expectations and market clearing are accepted. The first one concerns the effects of an anticipated step-up in the rate of growth of the money supply. Suppose that this does indeed carry with it expectations of commensurately higher inflation. That is a real change. The real rate of return on at least one asset (base money) is reduced, and this is bound to affect other real rates and through them relative prices and quantities. The second applies also to a one-shot injection of money and concerns the method by which it occurs. Suppose it is base money, printed to finance government purchases of goods or tax reductions or to repurchase or retire government bonds. Those uses all have real effects, as do the changes in private wealth and its composition resulting from the transaction. If it is bank money, the same observations apply to the transactions the central and private banks must make to create it. As explained in Chapter 3, Section 3.2.2.3, the only neutral way to engineer a change in the quantity of money, neutral whether anticipated or not, is trivial; it is to decree a scalar change in the monetary unit of account, making old francs into centimes and one hundred old francs into new francs. It is trivial and neutral because it applies not just to the currency but to all assets and debts denominated in the unit of account.

More generally, the neutrality of money and monetary policy depends on the joint assumptions of rational expectations and market clearing. Of the two, it is the second that is crucial to the far-reaching implications of the doctrine. When the assumption that prices clear markets completely, instantaneously, and continuously is relaxed, monetary policies will have real effects and it is rational for agents to expect that they will. The "new Keynesian macroeconomics" has responded to the new classical challenge by providing microfoundations for nominal "rigidities" and has integrated such rigidities into macroeconomic models with rational expectations. In those models, which combine rational expectations of prices and quantities with temporary excess demands and supplies in goods and labor markets, monetary policies—

---

[1]This section draws on Tobin (1980, Ch. 3).

anticipated as well as unanticipated—can influence aggregate demand, real as well as nominal.[2]

Moreover, while the new classical economists properly pointed out deficiencies of older literature in the modeling of expectations, their own remedies also leave much to be desired. In particular, they often neglect the intractable uncertainties generated by the unpredictability of the future expectations of other agents. In a famous parable, Keynes likened the stock market to a contest in which entrants strive not to identify the most beautiful baby portrait but to guess which portrait will be chosen by the most entrants. This and other grounds for skepticism on the efficiency of financial markets have been discussed elsewhere in this book (Chapter 2, Section 2.1, and Chapter 6, Section 6.5).

10.1.2 Deficit Finance

Barro (1974) and other new classical economists have argued that the method of financing government purchases of goods and services is inconsequential. The argument for the Ricardo-Barro equivalence theorem is simple. If government spending is not financed by contemporaneous taxes, it is financed either by selling interest-bearing time obligations or by issuing demand obligations, in effect printing money. If financed by selling nonmonetary debt, the public must know that taxes will be levied in future to pay the interest, perhaps the principal too. To provide for those future taxes, households will save more, precisely enough to purchase the new government securities. Aggregate household wealth net of the present value of tax liabilities is unchanged, and so therefore is aggregate consumption. Deferment of taxes accomplishes nothing, for good or evil. Since the present value of tax liabilities is computed at the same interest rate to be paid on government securities, the timing of the taxes makes no difference.[3]

But what if monetary issue is substituted for taxation? Central bank purchases of government securities extinguish both the stream of interest payments to the public and the associated future taxes. From the Ricardian viewpoint, the transaction increases household wealth by the full amount. It is no different in effect from

---

[2]For example, see Taylor (1980). The role of nominal rigidities is surveyed in Blanchard and Fischer (1989, Ch. 7). Blanchard (1981) analyzes the role of the q ratio in a model which combines rational expectations in financial markets with nominal rigidities in the output market.

The author of this book, in a series of articles including Tobin (1993), emphasizes that the new classical neutrality propositions require perfect flexibility of prices, so that excess supplies or demands at existing prices are eliminated in zero real time. Old Keynesian propositions do not depend on price "rigidity" in any commonsense meaning of the word. Following Keynes, he argues that fluctuations in aggregate real demand and output will not be eliminated by any practical approaches to perfect price flexibility. In his view, "new Keynesians" concede too much.

[3]James Buchanan (1976) calls this doctrine Ricardian, and it is true that Ricardo (1817, pp.146–149) presented the argument with characteristic clarity. However, he also added important practical qualifications—notably emigration to escape taxes—and concluded that deferment of taxes by internal borrowing is bad fiscal policy. Although somewhat misleading, Buchanan's term is convenient.

monetary creation to finance government outlays, or from that textbook favorite, "money rain." In either case, a monetarist Ricardian might believe that the price level would adjust to keep the real quantity of money unchanged. However, that belief is subject to the objections to monetary neutrality argued above. Note also that, from the same Ricardian viewpoint, a "bond rain" would have no effect. Thus the Ricardian equivalence theorem and monetarism are indispensable to each other.

A growing stock of zero-interest base money is in effect a source of revenue for the government, enabling it to get along with lower explicit tax revenues. This is *seignorage,* analogous to the charges imposed by sovereigns for coining precious metals. When inflation keeps pace with money growth, the seignorage is mirrored in a reduction in the real value of the outstanding demand debt, in effect a tax on its holders. Households and businesses may also feel the tax in efforts to economize their cash holdings for transactions. Sometimes inflation is called the cruelest tax; if this is true at all, it is true only of unexpected inflation. If people anticipate the inflation tax as a consequence of expected money growth to finance budget deficits, a Ricardian could say that it is the equivalent of current explicit taxes or nonmonetary debt issues. The public fisc might also reap seignorage from noninflationary growth of money in pace with growth of real national product. Here there is no corresponding hidden tax, except in the sense that holders of base money could have enjoyed real capital gains if the nominal money stock had been kept constant. In that case, higher explicit taxes would be needed at present or in the future.

The common sense of the Ricardian view is that society cannot enrich itself by blowing up the debts of some citizens to others. Neither can it impoverish itself by internal debt. We really do owe it to ourselves. Nevertheless this is by no means the whole story. The Keynesian view is that financing government purchases by borrowing or printing money has quite different macroeconomic consequences, especially in the short run, from financing them by contemporaneous taxation. This view downgrades the wealth and consumption effects attributable to expected changes in future tax liabilities, for several reasons.

1. *Life cycles and bequests.* In an ingenious contribution, Barro showed how mortal households can have effectively infinite horizons for consumption behavior. The condition is that each generation include in its utility function, along with consumption at various stages of its own lifetime, the *utility* of the next generation. A child's utility is a function, indirectly, of her personal endowment of earning power plus the gifts and bequests received from the parent. Within a given present value of taxation, a shift in the timing of payments from one generation to the next leaves the parent facing the same budget constraint as before. She will make up for the heavier taxation in store for the child by providing a larger bequest. The chain of overlapping generations behaving in this manner makes the horizon of each generation effectively infinite.

   Three considerations weaken the force of this argument.

   (*a*) As everybody knows, some households in each generation are childless, or indifferent to the lots of their children. Deficit spending enables these households to consume more at the expense of later generations. There are no incentives for the responsible households with children to consume less as a result of the substitution of borrowing for taxes.

(*b*) Parents' utility frequently depends to some degree on the size of their bequests to their children, independently of the utilities or personal endowments of the children. Giving is for the gratification of the giver, not just the welfare of the receiver.

(*c*) Many parents, even those who internalize their children's utility, will find utility optima at zero-bequest corners rather than at interior points. They would prefer negative bequests, but these are not within their options. These parents will, of course, bequeath no more but consume more if their taxes are reduced and those of their heirs correspondingly increased. This outcome is more likely if future generations are expected to benefit from technological progress.

2. *Liquidity constraints.* Even within the lifetime of one generation, households are generally not able to shift consumption at will from a later date to an earlier date. Earnings expected at age 50 usually cannot be spent at age 25. When such intertemporal substitution is possible, it generally entails borrowing at a higher rate of interest than can be earned on saving. Even in countries with sophisticated financial institutions and well-developed capital markets, opportunities for borrowing against future earnings from labor are limited. Compulsory or contractual saving, down-payment and collateral requirements, illiquidity of future retirement pensions—these and other market imperfections limit the intertemporal fungibility of lifetime resources, a fortiori intergenerational resources.

There are good reasons for all these departures from the theorist's presumptive norm of perfect capital markets. Chapter 5 introduced a common imperfection, quantitative collateral limits to loans. The implication of these facts of life is that a large fraction of households, even in affluent societies, are liquidity-constrained as well as wealth-constrained. Their horizons for consumption plans are shorter than their lifetimes, let alone the lifetimes of their lineal families. They will not be indifferent to the opportunity to defer tax payments. Even if they themselves must pay the taxes later, they will increase their consumption now. In effect the government lends to them at its borrowing rate of interest, an option not otherwise available in the credit market.

3. *Non-lump-sum taxes.* The Ricardian equivalence theorem in its pure form assumes lump-sum taxes. If real-world taxes are considered instead, the theorem is further weakened, for two reasons:

(*a*) Non-lump-sum levies generally induce tax-reducing behavior. Taxation of wealth or income from wealth makes a gaping hole in the Ricardian case, as Ricardo himself well knew. This is most obvious if current lump-sum transfer payments or per capita tax credits are financed by debt issues to be serviced, at least in part, by future wealth taxes. Few would doubt that the combination induces some substitution against saving and capital formation. This will be true even if consumers are immortal, or, through the Barro intergenerational linkage, have effectively infinite horizons.

What about wage taxes? To the extent that they tax proceeds of human capital investments, the above remarks apply. They may also induce substitution in favor of leisure and other uses of time that escape the scrutiny of tax collectors. Anticipating such substitutions by her heirs, a Barro model parent will know that to maintain her heirs' utilities it is unnecessary to maintain their endowments completely against expected increases in wage taxes. Substitutions will do part of the job, so the parent may in good conscience consume herself some of her tax cuts.

(b) Tax liabilities are rarely specified amounts levied on named individuals. They are almost always functions of individuals' circumstances—income, wealth, consumption, family size, and so forth. Consequently, anticipated taxes depend on expectations of those circumstances and of tax legislation. The Barro model parent is, of course, not really sure of her heir's income-earning capacity. The function of bequest is not just to raise the heir's expected utility. It is also to guard against disappointment or disaster in the heir's earning power. A parent so minded will provide a higher bequest the larger her estimate of the variance of the child's personal endowment. Taxation of income, wealth, or consumption lowers that variance. Suppose, then, that the expectation of higher taxes for debt service focuses on higher tax *rates*. The increase in the mean expected tax burden on the heir will tend to raise the parent's bequest; but given her uncertainty about the heir's other pretax endowments, reduction in the heir's after-tax variance tends to diminish bequests.

The discount rate for future taxes is the one appropriate for the streams of income on which the taxes are levied; given the uncertainties in those streams, that rate is higher than the discount for government obligations. The differential means that government bond issue does indeed raise net wealth even if taxpayers correctly expect that taxes will be increased to service the added debt.

In addition to its theoretical problems, the Barro-Ricardo thesis has weak empirical support [Tobin (1980) pp. 63–66, Haliassos and Tobin (1990)]. In particular, the United States experience in the 1980s provides a glaring counterexample. The large fiscal deficits during the Reagan administration were associated with a decline in private saving rather than the increase predicted by the debt-neutrality proposition. Moreover, this decrease in the private saving rate occurred despite fiscal incentives and higher real interest rates, which would normally be expected to increase saving.

In summary, the effects of government financial policies on private wealth and portfolio equilibrium cannot be dismissed by sweeping theorems of equivalence and neutrality. Rather they are to be sought in empirical studies of asset choice and saving behavior. The chapters of this book have attempted to offer some theoretical help in the formulation of those empirical studies.

10.2
GENERAL EQUILIBRIUM MODELS OF THE CAPITAL ACCOUNT

This section spells out a general equilibrium model of the financial system, which draws on and pulls together the analyses of the previous chapters. The approach focuses on the capital accounts of economic units, of sectors of the economy, and of the economy as a whole. A model of the capital accounts of the economy specifies a menu of the assets (and debts) that appear in portfolios and balance sheets, the factors that determine the demands for and supplies of the various assets, and the manner in which asset prices, interest rates, and other factors clear these interrelated markets. In this approach, monetary assets fall into place as a part, but not the whole, of the menu of assets. Likewise, the banking system is one sector whose balance sheet behavior must be specified, but not the only one. The characteristics of assets and of investors determine the substitutabilities or complementarities among assets. As discussed in Chapter 2, the relevant factors include costs of asset exchanges; predictability of real and money asset values at various future dates; correlations—positive, negative, or zero—among asset prospects; liquidity—the time it takes to realize full value of an asset; reversibility—possibility and cost of simultaneously buying and selling an asset; and the timing and predictability of investors' expected needs for wealth.

In a world of financial assets and well-developed capital markets, Keynes (1936, pp. 166, 168, 140–141) was right in perceiving the tactical advantage to the theorist of treating separately decisions determining total wealth and its rate of growth and decisions regarding the composition of wealth. A theory of the income account concerns what goods and services are produced and consumed, and how fast nonhuman wealth is accumulated. The decision variables are flows. A theory of the capital account concerns the proportions in which various assets and debts appear in portfolios and balance sheets. The decision variables are stocks. Income and capital accounts are linked by accounting identities—for example, increase in net worth equals saving plus capital appreciation—and by technological and financial stock-flow relations. Utilities and preference orderings attach to flows of goods and services; the values of stocks are entirely derivative from their ability to contribute to these flows. Some stock-flow relationships are so tight that this distinction is pedantic: The only way an art collector can obtain the flow of satisfactions from a chef d'oeuvre is to own that particular asset. But there is a vast menu of assets whose yields are generalized purchasing power, nothing more or less—investors do not have intrinsic preferences among engravings of security certificates.

Treatment of the capital account separately from the production and income account of the economy is only a first step, a simplification to be justified by convenience rather than realism. The strategy is to regard income-account variables as tentatively exogenous data for balance-sheet behavior and to find equilibrium in the markets for stocks of assets conditional upon assumed values of outputs, incomes, and other flows. Of course the linkages run both ways. Some of the variables determined in asset markets affect the flows of spending and income. In a complete equilibrium the two sides of the economy—one is tempted to call them financial and real—must be mutually consistent. That is, the financial inputs to the real side must reproduce the assumed values of the real inputs to the financial side.

The key behavioral assumption of this procedure is that spending decisions and portfolio decisions are independent—specifically that decisions about the accumulation of wealth are separable from decisions about its allocation. As savers, people decide how much to add to their wealth; as portfolio managers, they decide how to distribute among available assets and debts the net worth they already have. The propensity to consume may depend upon interest rates, but it does not depend *directly* on the existing mix of asset supplies or on the rates at which these supplies are growing.[4]

10.2.1 Two Interpretations of a Money-Capital Economy[5]

Monetary theory needs to specify explicitly what forms the nonmonetary parts of wealth can take. Many confusions and disagreements can be traced to ambiguities and differences in assumptions about the nature of wealth. A theory should state the menu of assets assumed available, specifying which are components of net private wealth (capital stock plus government debt) and which are intermediate assets (private debts). Moreover, the independent interest rates in an aggregative system have to be enumerated. An independent rate of return is one that is not tied to another rate of return yield by an invariant relationship determined outside the system, for example, by a constant risk differential.

The importance of the specification of asset menus can be brought out through a comparison of two special cases of a model with three assets—money, bonds, and capital. In the first model, bonds and capital are assumed to be perfect substitutes, while in the second model, money and bonds are perfect substitutes. Both cases therefore reduce to a two-asset, money-and-capital world, but they have different implications.

Keynes-Patinkin model. The assets of a formal model of Keynes's *General Theory* (1936) appear to be four or possibly five in number: (1) government demand debt, serving either as means of payment or as bank reserves, (2) bank deposits, (3) long-term government bonds, (4) physical capital, that is, stocks of the good produced on the income-account side of the model, and possibly (5) private debts, serving along with bonds (3) and demand debt (1) as assets held by the banking system against its monetary liabilities (2). Net private wealth is the sum of (1), (3), and (4).

Though there are four or five assets in this model, there are only two yields: the rate of return on money, whether demand debt or bank deposits, institutionally set at zero, and *the* rate of interest, common to the other two or three assets. For the nonmonetary assets of his system, Keynes simply followed the classical theory of portfolio selection in perfect markets; that is, he assumed that capital, bonds, and private debts are perfect substitutes in investors' portfolios. The marginal efficiency of capital must equal *the* rate of interest.

Keynes did not, of course, envisage literal equality of returns on consols, private debts, and equity capital. Indeed, he provides many perceptive observations on the sources and cyclical variations of the expectations and risk premiums that

---

[4]However, see Tobin and Buiter (1980), Tobin and Macedo (1980), and Tobin (1982a) for extensions of this framework that integrate saving and portfolio decisions.

[5]This section is based on Tobin (1961).

differentiate market yields. But in given circumstances these differentials are constants independent of the relative supplies of the assets and therefore inessential. Once one of the rates is set, the others must differ from it by appropriate allowances for risk and for expectations of price changes.

Thus Keynes had only one rate differential to explain within his theoretical model: the difference between the zero yield of money and *the* interest rate. This differential he explained in his theory of liquidity preference, which made the premium of bond yields above money depend on the stock of money relative to the volume of transactions and, presumably, aggregate wealth. Keynes departed from the classical model of portfolio choice and asset yields to explain money holdings, applying and developing an innovation borrowed from his own *Treatise* (1930, pp. 140–144, 248–257), a rate differential that depends systematically on relative asset supplies.

Most subsequent macroeconomists, whether disciples or opponents or just neutral fanciers of models, stuck pretty close to the Keynesian picture of the capital account. For example, Patinkin (1965) explicitly includes all the assets listed above, and no more, in his comprehensive model. Like Keynes, he has only one interest rate to determine. His difference from Keynes is his real balance effect.

As Hicks (1939), Kaldor (1939), and others pointed out, there are apparently no short-term obligations of fixed money value in this Keynesian scheme. Recognition of these near moneys would add one asset category and a second interest rate to the Keynesian model of the capital account. Transactions costs would be the major determinant of the money-short rate differential, and considerations of speculation and risk for investors of different types would determine the size and sign of the short-long differential.

An entirely different monetary tradition begins with a two-asset world of money and capital and ignores to begin with all closer money substitutes of whatever maturity. As mentioned in Chapter 3, Section 3.2.1.3, the authors of the Cambridge tradition (Lavington, 1941; Pigou, 1951) regarded direct capital investment as *the* alternative to money holdings. At the same time, they were content to regard the velocity of money as a constant. Why did they fail to carry into their monetary theory the clear inference that the demand for money depends not only on the volume of transactions but also on the return on capital? Perhaps the best guess is that for these economists the return on capital was in the short run a constant, explained by the classical duo, productivity and thrift. Money balances were adjusting to a rate already determined, not to a rate their adjustment might help to determine.

On its own logic, therefore, the constant-velocity approximation cannot apply in models where the rate of return on capital is variable. It is not applicable to cyclical fluctuations, in which variations of employment affect the productivity of the given capital stock. It is not applicable to secular growth, if capital deepening or technological change alters the return on capital.

Neither is the constant-velocity assumption applicable where money substitutes other than capital are available and have endogenously variable returns, for then the demand for money would depend on those returns. Paradoxically, the Cambridge tradition and its modern reincarnation in cash-in-advance models really have no room for monetary policy per se. In the two-asset, money-capital economy there are no assets which the central bank and the banking system can buy or sell to change the quantity of money (assuming they do not deal in capital itself).

What is the mechanism by which a change in the quantity of money brings about the proportional change in money income that constant-velocity theory predicts? Sometimes the mechanisms as described seems to assume a direct relationship between money holdings and spending on income account: When people have more money than they need, they spend it. It is as simple as that. Patinkin (1956, Ch. 8) rightly objects that spending on income account should be related to excess wealth, not excess money. If the mechanism is a real balance effect, then it works only when new money is also new private wealth, accumulated by the public as a result of government spending financed at the printing press or the mint.

A mechanism more in the spirit of the arguments of Lavington (1941), Pigou (1951), and Hicks (1939) is that owners of wealth with excess money holdings seek to restore the balance of their capital accounts. Trying to shift from money to capital, they bid up the prices of the existing capital stock, and since new capital goods and old must bear comparable prices, prices also rise in commodity markets. The process ends when, and only when, money incomes have risen enough to absorb the new money into transactions balances. The real rate of return on the capital stock remains unchanged. This process was described in Chapter 5, Section 5.1.

This mechanism can apply to increases in M due to expansion of bank lending—with private debts added to the menu of assets—as well as to increases associated with net saving. One aspect of the mechanism is then the process of which Wicksell (1935) gave the classical description, alluded to briefly at the beginning of this chapter. Banks expand the money supply by offering to lend at a rate, the market rate, lower than the return on capital, the natural rate. Excess demand for capital by new borrowers bids up capital values, with the repercussions already described. Whether this process has an end or not depends on whether the banks' incentive to expand is extinguished by proportionate increases of money supply, money income, and prices. For a pure credit economy, where all means of payment are based on monetization of private debts, this model produces no equilibrium. The end to the Wicksellian process depends on banks' needs for reserves, whether enforced by legislation or by their own transactions and precautionary motives.

An alternative money-capital model. An alternative two-asset model was presented in Chapter 5, Section 5.1.[6] Money and government debt are one and the same, and there are no private debts. The proportions in which owners of wealth desire to split their holdings between money and capital depend upon the volume of transactions and on the rate of return on capital. The return on capital is not a constant, as it seems to be in the Cambridge model, but depends on the capital intensity of current production. The differential between the return on capital and that on money depends on the relative supplies of the two basic assets; the liquidity preference mechanism is applied to a money-capital margin rather than a money-securities margin. This

---

[6]See also Tobin (1955), which includes a dynamic version of this model.

portfolio adjustment is like the mechanism of response to increase in the quantity of money described above for the constant-velocity model, but here it does not necessarily maintain the same velocity or the same return on capital. A real balance effect on consumption can be added.

A trivial extension of the money-capital model is to include other kinds of government securities, on the assumption that given certain constant rate differentials they are perfect portfolio substitutes for money proper. Then money in the model stands for the entire government debt, whether it takes the form of media of exchange or money substitutes. The differential between the return on capital and the return on any government debt instrument is determined by the relative supplies of total government debt and capital.

By a similar extension private debts could be added to the menu of assets, again with the proviso that they are perfect substitutes for government debt instruments but not for capital equity. This addition does not change the requirement of portfolio balance, that the net private position in assets of fixed money value stands in the appropriate relationship to the value of the capital stock.

Thus extended, the money-capital model winds up with the same asset menu as the Keynes-Patinkin model. Each has only one interest differential to be explained within the model. But there is a vast difference. The Keynes-Patinkin model assumes that all debt instruments are perfect substitutes for capital. The interest rate to be explained is the rate common, with the appropriate constant corrections, to all assets other than money itself. What explains this rate is the supply of money relative to transactions requirements and to total wealth. Monetary policy, altering the demand debt component of government debt, can affect the terms on which the community will hold the capital stock. Expansion of the real value of nonmonetized debt cannot do so, although in Patinkin's version it can influence the level of activity through the real balance effect on current consumption. The second money-capital model, in contrast, casts debt instruments on the side of money and focuses attention on the relationship between the total real value of government debt, monetized or nonmonetized, and the rate of return the community requires of the capital stock. It contains no role for monetary policy; only the aggregate net position of the public as borrowers and lenders is relevant, not its composition.

The two models give different answers to important questions. Does retirement of government long-term debt through taxation have expansionary or contractionary consequences? The question refers not to the temporary multiplier-like effects of the surplus that reduces the debt—these are of course contractionary—but to the enduring effects, through the capital account, of having a smaller debt. The instinctive answer of economists schooled in the Keynesian tradition is "expansionary." The supply of bonds is smaller relative to the supply of money; *the* rate of interest goes down, and investment is stimulated until the marginal efficiency comes down correspondingly. The answer of the money-capital model is, as indicated above, "deflationary." The assumed substitutability of bonds and money will keep the bond rate up. The decline in the government debt component of net private wealth means that investors will require a higher rate of return, or marginal efficiency, to hold the existing capital stock.

Granted that both models are oversimplified, which is the better guide to in-
stinct? Are long-term government debt instruments better substitutes for capital than
they are for short-term debt and money? Reflection on the characteristic properties
of these assets—in particular how they stand vis-à-vis risks of price-level changes—
may suggest that if government securities must be assimilated to capital or money,
one or the other, the better bet is money. However, emphasis on bond rates of interest
as costs or opportunity costs of direct investments or equity holdings could reverse
the verdict. Equities and real capital lose their capabilities as inflation hedges when
bond rates reflect inflation expectations and when those inflation expectations lead
wealth owners and portfolio managers to expect contractionary policies by inflation-
fighting central bankers.

Toward a synthesis. A synthesis of the two approaches must, of course, avoid
the arbitrary choices of either, sacrificing the convenience of assuming that all assets
but one are perfect substitutes. The price of this advance in realism and relevance
is the necessity to explain not just one market-determined rate of return but a whole
structure. The structure of rates may be pictured as strung between two poles, anchored at one end by the zero own-rate conventionally borne by currency (and by
the central bank discount rate) and at the other end by the marginal productivity
of the capital stock. Among assets that are not perfect substitutes, the structure of
rates will depend upon relative supplies. In general, an increase in the supply of an
asset—for example, long-term government bonds—will cause its rate to rise relative to other rates, but less in relation to assets for which it is directly or indirectly a
close substitute—in the example, short-term securities and money—than in relation
to other assets—in the example, capital.

In such a synthesis, monetary policy falls in proper perspective. The quantity
of money can affect the terms on which the community will hold capital, but it is
not the only asset supply that can do so. The net monetary position of the public is
important, but so is its composition.

One lesson of the simple money-capital models deserves to be retained. The
strategic variable—the ultimate gauge of expansion or contraction, of monetary
tightness or ease—is the rate of return that the community of wealth owners requires to absorb the existing capital stock (valued at current prices), no more, no
less, into their portfolios and balance sheets. The gap between the required rate of
return and the marginal product of capital—encapsulated in the q ratio—is a critical
determinant of the volume of new capital investment, as emphasized in Chapter 6
and again in the introduction to this chapter.

How far to go in disaggregation is, as always, a matter of taste and purpose; it
depends also on the possibilities of empirical implementation and testing. A minimal
program for a theory of capital account relevant to modern American institutions
would involve (1) five constituents of net private wealth: government demand debt,
government short debt, government long debt, foreign assets, and capital stock;
(2) two intermediate assets: bank deposits and private debts; (3) two institutionally
or administratively fixed interest rates: the zero rate on government demand debt
and the central bank discount rate; (4) six market-determined rates of return or asset
prices: the short-term interest rate, the long-term interest rate, the rate on private

debts, the bank deposit rate,[7] the market value of equity capital, and the expected return on foreign assets.[8] The following sections spell out a formal framework for this type of analysis.

10.2.2 Accounting Framework[9]

The general accounting framework for a theory of the capital account is indicated in Table 10.1, actually for a two-country world, America and Nippon (Japan). Rows represent assets or debts. A finer classification including items such as demand deposits or producers' durable equipment would be possible. Columns represent sectors of the two economies. Again, further disaggregation is possible. Entries in cells, in general, can be positive, negative, or zero. A negative entry means that the sector in question is a debtor in the kind of asset indicated by the row. All holdings must be valued in the same *numéraire,* for example, either in the monetary unit of account or in terms of purchasing power over consumer goods of either country. If dollars are chosen as the *numéraire,* yen-denominated assets are converted to dollars at the market exchange rate. For any asset, the sum across its row is the net exogenous supply of the asset to the world as a whole. For real property, this exogenous supply is each economy's inheritance from the past. For internally generated financial assets the net exogenous supply is, of course, zero. If from the country sums, the central government's holding of an asset is subtracted (or its debt added), the net holdings of the private economy result. The sum of a column represents the net worth of a sector. The sum of the final column for each country is national wealth. As indicated, private wealth differs from this total by the amount of the government's net worth. If the government is a net debtor, as will typically be the case, at least if publicly owned stocks of goods and properties are ignored, then private wealth exceeds national wealth. The capital-account relations with the rest of the world are also shown. Country A's net foreign assets can be calculated by subtracting N-owned A assets from A-owned N assets.

10.2.3 The Analytical Framework

The accounting framework of Table 10.1 can be brought to life as a framework for monetary analysis by (a) assigning to each asset a rate of return $r_i (i = 1, 2, \ldots, n)$,

---

[7]In reality, some deposit rates are market-determined and others may be administratively fixed. As reported in Chapter 3, Section 3.2.4, and in Chapter 8, regulation of U.S. deposit rates has been progressively relaxed in recent years, but some demand deposit rates are still fixed at zero. The implications of the specification of the deposit rate are discussed further below.

[8]The analysis of the market for foreign assets depends on whether the exchange rate is fixed or floating, and whether the home country is large enough to affect foreign interest rates. Even if the home country is small, however, the return on foreign assets is endogenous if the exchange rate is flexible. Under fixed rates, the endogenous variable is the level of international reserves held by the central bank. See Tobin and Macedo (1980) for a two-country financial model. The remainder of this discussion assumes that the exchange rate is flexible.

[9]The following two sections draw on Tobin (1969) and on Brainard and Tobin (1993).

TABLE 10.1

Asset/sector matrix for two countries

American assets	American portfolios					Japanese portfolios					World total
	House-holds	Business	Banks	Govern-ment	Total	House-holds	Business	Banks	Govern-ment	Total	
$ base money	+	+	+	−	0						0
$ deposits	+	+	−		−		+	+	+	+	0
$ treasury debt	+	+	+	−	−	+		+	+	+	0
$ household debt	−	+	+		0						0
$ business debt	+	−	+		−	+				+	0
Equity	+	−	−		−	+	+			+	+
Real property	+	+	−		+	+	+			+	+
¥ base money						+	+	+	−	0	0
¥ deposits	+	+	+	+	+	+	+	−	−	−	0
¥ treasury debt	+	+	+	+	+	+	+	+		−	0
¥ household debt						−	+	+		0	0
¥ business debt	+		+		+	+	−	+		+	0
Equity	+	+			+	+	+	+		+	+
Real property	+	+			+	+	+			+	+
Net worth	+	0	0	−	+	+	0	0	−	+	+
A-owned A assets	+	−	−	−	+						+
N-owned A assets						+	+	+	+	+	+
A-owned N assets	+	+	+	+	+						+
N-owned N assets						+	−	−	−	+	+

and (b) imagining each sector $j(j = 1, 2, \ldots, m)$ to have a net demand for each asset, f_{ij}, which is a function of the vector r_i and possibly of other variables as well. Of course, in practice many of the cells are empty; certain sectors are just not involved with certain assets, either as holders or as debtors.

Each sector is, at any moment of time, constrained by its own net worth. Its members are free to choose their balance sheets—the entries in the columns of Table 10.1—but not to choose their net worth—the sum of the column entries. Net worth is determined by past accumulations of assets and by current asset prices. An individual agent can neither change her legacy from the past nor, it is assumed, affect by her portfolio choices the current market valuations of her assets. Of course, as time passes the individual may save and may make capital gains or losses. A year later her net worth will be different, but it will be once again a constraint on her portfolio behavior.

This adding-up requirement has certain obvious and simple implications. For any sector, the sum over all assets of responses to a change in any rate of return r_k is zero:

$$\sum_{i=1}^{n} \frac{\partial f_{ij}}{\partial r_k} = 0. \tag{10.1}$$

This is also true for any other variable that enters the sector's asset demand functions. The exception is the sector's net worth itself; clearly the sum of asset changes due to a change in wealth is equal to 1:

$$\sum_{i=1}^{n} \frac{\partial f_{ij}}{\partial W_k} = 1. \tag{10.2}$$

The same properties will hold for demand functions aggregated over sectors, that is, for

$$f_i = \sum_{j=1}^{m} f_{ij}. \tag{10.3}$$

Each row of Table 10.1 corresponds to one market-clearing equation, by which the net demands of the m private sectors add up to the available supplies, whether issued by governments or otherwise exogenous. But these n equations are not independent. Whatever the values of the determining variables, the left-hand sides (net private demands) of these n asset equations sum to the same value as the right-hand sides (supplies), namely, to aggregate private wealth. Therefore, contrary to superficial first impression, the n equations will not determine n rates of return but only $n - 1$ at most.

The value of aggregate or sectoral wealth may depend on asset prices, which are themselves related to the r_i, the market rates of return, determined by the system of equations. This will be true of all assets whose life exceeds the length of the assumed period of portfolio choice. For example, the outstanding supplies of durable physical capital and of long-term government bonds change in value as their market rates of return change. Similarly, the domestic-currency value of foreign asset holdings rises when the domestic currency depreciates. Consequently, the $n - 1$ market-clearing equations actually include rates of return in two roles, as arguments in the asset demand functions and as determinants of the values of existing asset supplies and total wealth.

In some applications of the analysis there are fewer than $n - 1$ rates of return free to be determined. There are fewer endogenous rates of return than there are independent market-clearing equations. Some rates are institutionally or legally fixed—consider the conventional zero own-rate of interest on currency, the prohibition of interest on demand deposits, effective ceilings on interest paid on time and savings accounts. Some are constrained, at least in the long run, by real factors—for example, by the technological marginal productivity of physical capital assets. In these cases the capital account equations cannot be satisfied unless some asset supplies are not exogenous but adjust to clear the markets, or unless some relevant variables from the real side of the economy—income, price level, price expectations—assume appropriate values.

10.2.3.1 A money-securities-capital economy

First, consider an economy with only one private sector and three assets: money, government securities, and homogeneous physical capital goods, as in Section 10.2.1. The overall price level will be assumed constant at 1, so that nominal and real rates of return coincide.[10] The value of existing capital goods, or of titles to them, however, can diverge from their current reproduction cost, 1. Let q be the market price of existing capital goods. Let r_M, r_S, and r_K be the rates of return available from holding money, securities, and capital respectively (generally, the first of these is zero). Let R be the marginal efficiency of capital at its reproduction cost; let W be wealth and Y income. The vector of rates of return is denoted by $r = (r_K, r_M, r_S)$.

Wealth definition:

$$W = qK + M + S. \tag{10.4}$$

Balance equations:

$$f_1(r, Y/W)W = qK. \qquad \text{capital} \tag{10.5}$$

$$f_2(r, Y/W)W = M. \qquad \text{money} \tag{10.6}$$

$$f_3(r, Y/W)W = S. \qquad \text{government securities} \tag{10.7}$$

Equity market value:

$$r_K q = R. \tag{10.8}$$

Equation (10.8) expresses the inverse relation between the market valuation of capital equity and the market rate of return upon it. Suppose that the perpetual real return obtainable by purchasing a unit of capital at its cost of production p is R. If an investor must pay qp instead of p, then her rate of return is R/q. The consol formula

---

[10]See Tobin (1969) for an analysis of exogenous changes in price levels and expected rates of inflation in the model of this section.

Eq. (10.8) applies strictly only for perfectly durable capital. For depreciating capital, or physical assets of finite life, the relation of r_K and q will not be so simple or so pronounced.[11] But there will still be an inverse relation.

Here it is assumed for simplicity that securities are short-term, so that their market value is independent of their interest rate r_S. Otherwise, a relationship between the two could be introduced, like Eq. (10.8) for capital, and allowed for in the calculation of wealth.

The portfolio behavior functions have been written in a special form. They are homogeneous in wealth; the proportions held in the three assets are independent of the absolute scale of wealth. The adding-up requirement tells us that $f_1 + f_2 + f_3 = 1$; therefore, one of the three balance equations can be omitted. It is natural to assume that the own rate derivatives $\partial f_1/\partial r_K$, $\partial f_2/\partial r_M$, and $\partial f_3/\partial r_S$ are positive and that the cross-derivatives are negative. In other words, the assets are gross substitutes: The demand for each asset varies directly with its own rate and inversely with other rates. It will be remembered that $\sum_i \partial f_i/\partial x = 0$ for any x that appears as an argument in the functions f_i.

The ratio of income to wealth appears in all asset demand functions; if it appears in one, it must be in at least one of the other two also. The conventional assumption is that more money will be needed for transactions purposes at higher income levels. Whether income falls with wealth constant or wealth rises with income constant, a smaller fraction of wealth is needed to meet transactions requirements. The demand for money will fall relative to the combined demand for capital and securities. It is assumed that the partial elasticity of demand for money with respect to income is positive but does not exceed one. The reasoning is that transactions demand is, at most, proportional to income (elasticity equal to one), but transactions balances are only part of money holdings. It is also assumed, as a reasonable special case, that government securities, rather than capital, absorb changes in transactions requirements for money, that is, $\partial f_2/\partial(Y/W) = -\partial f_1/\partial(Y/W)$ and $\partial f_3/\partial(Y/W) = 0$.[12]

The exogenous variables in this short-run portfolio balance model are Y, M, S, K, R, and r_M, leaving q, W, r_K, r_S to be determined by the four independent equations. It is convenient to drop the capital equation (Eq. 10.5). Consolidation gives the following two equations, along with the definition of W, to determine q and r_S:

$$f_2(R/q, r_M, r_S, Y/W)W = M. \qquad (10.9)$$

$$f_3(R/q, r_M, r_S, Y/W)W = S. \qquad (10.10)$$

This setup leads to the conclusions presented in Table 10.2. The first two columns represent increases in government debt taking the form of money or securities. The third column represents monetary policy in the shape of open-market purchases. The fourth column represents monetary policy in the guise of an increase in the legally determined interest rate on money.

---

[11] See Chapter 6, Section 6.2 for further discussion of the relation of r_K and q.

[12] See Chapter 3 for a detailed discussion of the demand for money, which supports these assumptions.

TABLE 10.2
**Effects on endogenous variables of increase in
specified variables, with all others held constant**

Endogenous variables	Exogenous variables					
	M	S	M at expense of S	r_M	Y	R
q	+	?	+	−	−	+
r_S	−	+	−	+	+	?
r_K	−	?	−	+	+	+

What is the feature of money that leads to the results tabulated in the first three columns? That is, why does an increase in government debt in monetary form have a more expansionary effect on q than an increase in government debt in the form of securities? And why is substitution in private agents' portfolios of money for securities through central bank open-market purchases expansionary?

It is not because asset 1 has been called money and asset 2 securities. It is not because asset 1 is a means of payment or has any other intrinsic properties asset 2 lacks. It is not that asset 1 bears no interest—it may or may not. These properties have nowhere entered the analysis, except in the general sense that they explain why the assets are not perfect substitutes for each other. The essential characteristic—the only distinction of money from securities that matters for the results given above—is that the interest rate on money is exogenously fixed by law or convention, while the rate of return on securities is endogenous, market-determined.

When the supply of any asset is increased, the structure of rates of return and prices, on this and other assets, must change in a way that induces the public to hold the new supply. When the asset's own rate can rise, a large part of the necessary adjustment can occur in this way. But if the rate is fixed, the whole adjustment must take place through reductions in other rates or increases in prices of other assets. This is the secret of the special role of money; it is a secret that would be shared by any other asset with a fixed interest rate.

Note that a change in the supply of securities has ambiguous effects on the rate of return on capital and its market value. As discussed in Section 10.2.1, the direction of this effect will depend on the substitutability of securities with money and capital. If securities are close substitutes for money, then an increased supply of securities will be expansionary, that is, it will lower the required rate of return on capital and raise the market valuation. The rise in q does double duty in reducing the excess demand for capital: Given R, it lowers the rate of return of capital r_K, and it raises the share of capital in total wealth by raising the market value qK.

As observed above, an n-asset economy will provide no more than $n - 1$ independent market-clearing equations. The system will determine, therefore, no more than $n - 1$ rates of return. If the rate on one asset, money, is fixed, then the market rate of return on capital can, indeed must, be among the $n - 1$ rates to be determined. This enables the monetary authority to force the market return on physical capital to diverge from its technological marginal efficiency—or, what is the same thing, to force the market valuation of existing capital to diverge from its reproduction cost. By creating these divergences, the monetary authority can affect the current rate of production and accumulation of capital assets. This is the manner in which the monetary authority can affect aggregate demand in the short run.

If the interest rate on money, as well as the rates on all other financial assets, were flexible and endogenous, then they would all simply adjust to the marginal efficiency of capital. There would be no room for discrepancies between market and natural rates of return on capital, between market valuation and reproduction cost. There would be no room for monetary policy to affect aggregate demand. The real economy would call the tune for the financial sector, with no feedback in the other direction. Something like this occurs in the long run, where the influence of monetary policy is not on aggregate demand but on the relative supplies of monetary and real assets, to which all rates of return must adjust.

10.2.3.2 An extended model

Consider an open economy with a banking system as well as a general public sector that adds three new assets—foreign assets, deposits, and private loans—to the economy's menu of assets. There are also three new rates of return to be determined: r_F on foreign assets, r_D on deposits, and r_L on loans. A new interest rate relevant to the banks, the central bank discount rate d, can also be introduced; this is another instrument of monetary control.

Asset 2 is still the demand debt of the government, inclusive of the central bank. The size of this debt, net of the banks' borrowings from the central bank at the discount window, is the supply of currency and unborrowed reserves to the banks and the public. But of course M no longer corresponds to the quantity of money as conventionally defined (M1). Rather it represents high-powered money, the monetary base M0. As explained in Chapter 8, the stock of transactions money M1 would include the public's share of M0 plus bank deposits (or only demand deposits if, as is not done here, time deposits were distinguished). Thus, as in Chapter 9, M1 would be an endogenous quantity.

For simplicity, it will be assumed that transactions with the rest of the world occur exclusively in foreign-currency assets F, not in home-currency assets also, as in the more general accounting system above in Section 10.2.2. The assumption is unrealistic for the United States—foreigners do hold American assets. But it does not affect the conclusions and simplifies the exposition. Let the exchange rate be e, measured as domestic currency per unit of foreign currency. r_F is the expected rate of return on foreign assets measured in domestic currency, which is equal to the interest rate on foreign assets measured in foreign currency r_F^*, plus the expected rate of change of the exchange rate x. x may be a function of e if expectations of future exchange rates are affected by the current level of the exchange rate, as in Eq. 10.20. For example, if expectations are regressive, θ is positive and x is inversely related to e, that is, a spot depreciation entails an expected future appreciation. This would be true if market participants continued to expect a given future equilibrium exchange rate $\bar{e}$. The supply of foreign assets eF is determined by the past history of current account balances and central bank interventions in the foreign exchange market.

The central bank can increase the supply of foreign assets by selling F in exchange for either M or S. In the latter case, the central bank intervention is "sterilized," that is, it has no effect on the monetary base M. If the exchange rate is flexible, e adjusts to clear the balance of payments, whereas if the exchange rate is pegged, the supply of F must be adjusted by the central bank to offset any shocks to private sector supplies of and demands for foreign assets.

This model can be written as follows: Let r again be the vector of returns (r_K, r_S, r_M, r_F, r_D, r_L, d). For convenience, both bank and public portfolio choices will be written as functions of r. But it will be understood that the discount rate d is irrelevant to the public, and that the market rate on capital r_K is irrelevant to the banks, which are assumed not to hold such equity. The legally required ratio of bank reserves to deposits enters as k.

Wealth definition: $\qquad W = qK + M + S + eF.$ $\hfill$ (10.11)

Balance equations

Banks	Public		
	$f_{1P}(r, Y/W)W = qK$	(capital)	(10.12)
$kD + f_{2B}(r)D(1-k) + f_{2P}(r, Y/W)W = M$		(currency and reserves)	(10.13)
$f_{3B}(r)D(1-k)$	$+ f_{3P}(r, Y/W)W = S$	(government securities)	(10.14)
$f_{4B}(r)$		(deposits)	(10.15)
	$f_{4P}(r, Y/W)W = 0$		
	$f_{4P}(r, Y/W)W = D$	(definition of D)	(10.15a)
$f_{5B}(r)D(1-k)$	$+ f_{5P}(r, Y/W)W = 0$	(loans)	(10.16)
$f_{6B}(r)D(1-k)$	$+ f_{6P}(r, Y/W)W = eF$	(foreign assets)	(10.17)

Rate-of-return equations

$r_K q = R$	(capital)	(10.18)
$r_F = r_F^* + k$	(foreign assets)	(10.19)
$x = \theta(\bar{e} - e)/e$	(exchange-rate expectations)	(10.20)

The equity of bank shareholders is ignored, so that the items in the bank column sum to zero, just as the items in the public column sum to private net worth W.

There are eight independent equations. Y, M, S, K, R, F, r_M, d, and K may be taken as exogenous. The system may be solved for the relevant variables q, W, r_K, r_S, r_D, r_L, r_F, and e. In this interpretation, the interest rate paid on deposits is endogenous, market-determined. The banks' deposit supply function f_{4B} tells, for given values of other interest rates, the quantity of deposits banks wish to accept at any given deposit rate. In equilibrium this must be equal to the quantity of deposits the public wishes to hold at this same set of rates.

An alternative regime takes the deposit rate r_D as institutionally or legally fixed. Shifting this variable from the endogenous list to the exogenous category means that one equation must be deleted. The one to delete, of course, is Eq. 10.15. With an effective ceiling on the interest banks are allowed to pay, banks fall short of their supply curve $(-f_{4B})$. They accept all the deposits the public is willing to leave with them at the prevailing set of interest rates, and they would gladly accept more. Thus Eq. 10.15 becomes an inequality: $f_{4B} + f_{4P} < 0$. The remaining equations in the model still apply.

10.3
MONETARY POLICIES AND THE ECONOMY

The model of the previous section provides a framework for analysis of monetary policies, not only open market operations but also changes in required reserve ratios, the discount rate, and foreign-exchange market interventions.

10.3.1 Open-Market Operations

With the same assumptions about asset substitution, and about income elasticity of demand for high-powered money, the results of open-market operations in the extended model will be qualitatively similar to the simpler model of Section 10.2.3.1 as summarized in Table 10.2. They are likely to be quantitatively different, of course.

Consider the situation with fixed deposit rates. Fractional reserve banking means that bigger reshufflings of portfolios and larger changes in rates of return are needed to absorb a given increase in the supply of unborrowed high-powered money. Banks will seldom be induced to add much of the new supply to their net free reserves. So the public must be induced to hold some multiple of it as deposits. The change in rates of return necessary to accomplish this result may be very large in comparison with the 100 percent money regime of the simpler model.

The essential mechanism of deposit creation in a fractional reserve banking system was described in Chapter 9. In review, consider a $1 billion open-market purchase of T-bills by the Federal Reserve. Interest rates must adjust so that owners of wealth are content to shift from holding T-bills to demand debt, either directly or through banks and other intermediaries. Assume at first that public currency holdings are perfectly inelastic with respect to interest rates and transactions volume. Then the whole of the $1 billion is an increase in the supply of primary reserves, which must find its home with the banks either as required reserves or as net free reserves. Initially the deposits of the public in the banks will increase by $1 billion, and the free reserves of the banks will increase by a large fraction—nine-tenths if the required reserve ratio is 10 percent—of that amount. As banks try to convert these excessive holdings of free reserves into earning assets, they bid government and private debt away from the public. The nonbank holders of these assets are induced to sell them, and to hold bank deposits instead, by a fall in their returns. The bill rate must also decline as a result of reduction in supply resulting from the open-market purchase. Banks are willing to acquire bills in spite of their reduced rates of return because they are as a rule more profitable than free reserves.

How far this process of expansion of banks' deposits and assets goes depends on the banks' preferences for cash and for freedom from debt to the Federal Reserve, relative to the returns on less-liquid assets. If the banks' equilibrium demand for net free reserves were constant, deposits and earning assets would expand by the textbook multiples of the original accretion of reserves. For example, if the average required reserve ratio is one-tenth, deposits will expand by $10 billion and earning assets by $9 billion, from an increase in demand debt of $1 billion. However, as argued in Chapter 9, these classic multiples overstate the expansion, because some part of the new supply of reserves will serve to satisfy an enhanced appetite for net free reserves; not all of the new $1 billion will go into higher required reserves.

What is the adjustment of the public outside the banks? To absorb as required bank reserves most of the $1 billion increase in demand debt, the public must absorb a multibillion dollar increase in bank deposits, perhaps close to $10 billion. Here is the significance of fractional-reserve banking. A substantial change in rates of return is required to effect a drastic shift in portfolio composition. A part of the increase in public willingness to hold bank deposits will be induced by reduction in returns on interest-bearing government debt. Short debt, in particular, is regarded by many corporations and institutions as a close substitute for cash. But it is hardly likely that these rates can fall enough to make the public reduce its holdings of federal debt by anything like $10 billion. In the balance sheet of the public, most of the room for the multiple expansion of deposits must come from an increase in the debt of the public to the banks, in response to a reduction in interest rates on private loans. This adjustment is a shift by private lenders away from direct lending or from lending through nonbank intermediaries, which become less profitable, to bank deposits; the banks acquire the loan business given up. But at the prevailing expected rate of return on capital, the reduction in loan rates will stimulate new borrowing to finance new capital investment. Given that the supply of capital is fixed in the short run, to prevent the demand for capital from exceeding the existing stock, the market rate of return on capital must fall and its market valuation rise. Over time, investment will raise the stock of capital, as analyzed in Chapter 6, Section 6.1, but this process is gradual. The rise in the market valuation of capital also helps to restore short-run equilibrium by raising total financial wealth.

It is time to abandon the initial assumption that public currency demand is unresponsive. Increases in public holdings of currency could absorb much of the new supply of high-powered money M0, diminishing the needed expansion in bank deposits and bank assets. Currency demand could be stimulated by declines in interest rates. More important, it will increase significantly as the expansionary monetary policy raises the dollar value of transactions.

The above discussion has assumed a fixed interest rate on deposits. If some or all deposit interest rates are market-determined, they will fall along with other market rates. Banks will reduce rates on deposits as the profitability of employing deposits in purchases of public and private debt declines. This diminishes the public's incentive to acquire additional deposits, and therefore larger declines in interest rates, including the market rate of return on capital, are necessary to absorb the new high-powered money. More of the increment of demand debt is absorbed in free reserves than in the fixed-deposit-rate regime. The adjustment would be accomplished with the more moderate declines in rates the more the public absorbed some of the new demand debt in currency holdings.

Another feature of the extended model is that it introduces an international dimension to the transmission of monetary policy to aggregate demand. The decline in domestic interest rates accompanying an expansionary open-market operation now entails an excess demand for foreign assets and a depreciation of the domestic currency (a rise in e). Just as the rise in the market valuation of capital affects the equilibrium in the capital market through both rate-of-return and wealth effects, the currency depreciation reduces the excess demand for foreign assets through these two mechanisms. The expected rate of return on foreign assets measured in domestic currency decreases if exchange-rate expectations are regressive, as explained above. That is, a spot depreciation gives rise to an expected future appreciation of the home currency. The wealth effect of the depreciation is an increase in the share of foreign assets eF in total wealth.[13] Even if expectations are not regressive, the wealth effect may be sufficient to restore portfolio balance in the market for foreign assets. The impact of the currency depreciation on aggregate demand then depends on the price elasticities of exports and imports.[14]

10.3.2 Foreign Exchange Market Intervention

Open-market operations involve exchanges of demand debt and domestic securities. The central bank can also exchange foreign assets for domestic-currency debt, either demand or interest-bearing. If interest-bearing domestic debt and foreign assets are exchanged, the intervention is "sterilized," that is, it has no effect on the supply of high-powered money. A sterilized intervention is equivalent to an unsterilized intervention combined with an offsetting open-market operation in domestic assets. For example, consider a $1 billion purchase of foreign assets by the Federal Reserve, increasing the monetary base by $1 billion. To sterilize, the Fed sells $1 billion in Treasury securities, mopping up the increase in the base. The net effect is a $1 billion increase in Treasuries held by the public and a $1 billion reduc-

---

[13]This assumes that the net holdings of foreign-currency-denominated assets are positive. The wealth effect is perverse for negative net foreign asset holdings. However, this is unlikely in practice. When foreign holdings of domestic assets are allowed for (as they are in the accounting system in Section 10.2.2 but not in the extended model in Section 10.2.3.2), each country can hold positive amounts of the other's assets. If so, the wealth effects of exchange-rate revaluations are not perverse for either country. For further discussion and empirical evidence that gross foreign assets are positive for OECD countries, see Golub (1990). Note, however, that the currency denomination and legal nationality of an asset need not coincide (Golub, 1989).

[14]The current account balance, in turn, affects the exchange rate by redistributing wealth from the debtor to the creditor country. For analysis of the stock-flow relationships between the current account balance, the net foreign asset position, and the exchange rate, see Kouri (1976) and Tobin and Macedo (1980). A similar stock-flow analysis of investment, the capital stock and the q ratio, was sketched in Chapter 6, Section 6.1.3.

tion in the net supply of foreign assets to the public. Since the supply of high-powered money is unchanged, sterilized intervention will have lesser effects on aggregate demand than unsterilized intervention. In fact, the objective of sterilization is to affect the market for foreign assets and the exchange rate with minimal effects on domestic asset markets and rates of return. The effectiveness of sterilized intervention in achieving this objective depends on the substitutability of foreign and domestic securities.[15] If they are close substitutes, that is, the degree of international capital mobility is high, then changes in relative supplies will be ineffective in influencing the rate differential between foreign and domestic securities.

It is sometimes argued that sterilized intervention can affect financial markets simply as a signal of policy makers' intentions, as is often attributed to changes in the central bank discount rate (see Section 10.3.3 below). A number of studies have investigated these questions, with inconclusive findings.[16] Part of the problem is the difficulty of measuring the ex ante yield differential on foreign and domestic securities, because the return on foreign securities includes the expected exchange-rate change.[17]

The government can choose the currency composition of its debt, with effects similar to that of sterilized intervention by central banks. Many countries' public debts have a sizable foreign-currency component.[18] In the United States, however, the Treasury rarely issues foreign-currency denominated debt. The only exception was in 1978 when the Treasury issued $10 billion yen and deutsche mark "Carter bonds" in an attempt to bolster confidence in the dollar.

10.3.3 The Central Bank Discount Rate

In addition to its powers over the composition of the debt, the Federal Reserve has at its command certain control instruments that do not alter the structure of the debt. The most important are the power to set the discount rate at which banks can borrow reserves and the power to set required reserve ratios. Within broad limits, either or both of these tools may be substituted for open-market operations in government securities. Whatever degree of monetary restraint the authorities desire, there are a variety of combinations of instruments that can achieve it.

What are the monetary effects of lowering the discount rate, while the supplies of all categories of government debt remain unchanged? A word of caution is in order regarding interpretation of the phrase "lowering the discount rate." What is really to

---

[15] For a theoretical analysis of the effect of monetary and intervention policies in an open economy using a version of the model of Section 10.2.3, see Girton and Henderson (1977). In that model the menu of assets consists of money and securities in both the home and foreign countries, an abbreviated version of Table 10.1.

[16] For example, see Frankel and Dominguez (1993).

[17] For detailed discussion of the issues involved in measuring the extent of international financial integration, see Frankel (1991) and Obstfeld (1994).

[18] Golub (1989) provides empirical evidence on the magnitudes of foreign-currency government debts for OECD countries.

be analyzed is the difference it makes to equilibrium bank and public balance sheets and to the structure of interest rates whether the discount rate stands at one level rather than another, ceteris paribus. Among the other things to be taken as equal are the expectations of the market, its estimates of the future of the economy and of interest rates. The exercise is one of comparative statics. No attempt is made here to trace the process of change from one level of discount rate to another, in particular the alterations in expectation generated by the central bank's announcement of a new discount rate.

For many students of central bank policy the psychology of the announcement is the most important and perhaps the only important aspect of the discount rate. Unfortunately there is little of a systematic character that can be said about it. Will the public conclude from the announcement of a lowering of the discount rate that predictions of imminent recession are now confirmed by the expert economic intelligence of the central bank, and therefore regard the announcement as a contractionary portent? Or will the market judge that the authorities have thus indicated their resolute intention of preventing contraction, arresting or reversing a recession, and accordingly interpret the announcement as an expansionary sign? What do the authorities themselves regard as the likely psychological effects of their announcements? Clearly it is easy to become enmeshed in a game of infinite regress between the central bank and the market.

A conclusive justification for separating the analysis of discount policy from expectational effects is that the central bank can, if it chooses, separate them in practice. The authorities can and do make announcements, with calculated psychological impact, *without* changing the discount rate. The distinctive thing about lowering the discount rate is that it reduces the cost of advances to the banks.

Reduction of the discount rate gives banks incentive to reduce their net free reserves by increasing their debt to the Federal Reserve, substituting secondary reserve assets, in particular short government debt, for net free reserves, as described in Chapter 9, Section 9.3. As bank demand for bills increases, in response to the improved differential of the bill rate over the discount rate, the bill rate falls. The fall in the bill rate leads the public to supply bills to the banks, substituting deposits. The lower bill rate also stimulates banks to bid long debt and private debt away from the public; lower yields on these assets induce the public to shift further to deposits. All rates, including the market rate on capital, fall, although not in proportion to the initial fall in the discount rate. The new structure of rates provides banks incentive to decrease their net free reserves (increase their borrowing at the Fed) and at the same time provides the public inducement to expand their deposits by a multiple of the reduction in banks' net free reserves.

A rise in the discount rate has the opposite effects. Other rates rise, though not in proportion to the discount rate. Banks increase their free reserves, and the public diminishes its deposits by a multiple of the increase in banks' free reserves. The change in the rate structure must accomplish both of these portfolio shifts at the same time.

There are limits to discount policy at both ends. Banks may be so heavily indebted to the Federal Reserve that they will not respond to further incentive to borrow.

Or the bill rate may be so low that it would not compensate banks for the trouble and risk of borrowing to hold bills, even at a zero discount rate. At the other extreme, the discount rate may be so high as to be out of touch with the money market. That is, banks are already free of debt to the Fed, or substantially so, and increasing the bill rate cannot make them reduce indebtedness further. The relevant basic money rate is then the conventional zero rate paid on excess reserves and currency rather than the discount rate charged on borrowed reserves.

If deposit rates are free to fall along with other interest rates, the general decline in rates will be greater. But market rates will not fall as much as the discount rate. If they did, the banks would try to shift from bills into excess reserves, and the public might also shift from bills and bank deposits into currency. In this respect, the public might be particularly sensitive to interest rates on deposits, the immediate substitute for currency. To maintain equilibrium with the existing supplies of various assets, market rates must rise relative to the discount rate—essentially to compensate for the fact they are falling relative to the zero rate on currency or bank reserves.

10.3.4 Changes in Required Reserve Ratios

The second purely monetary instrument is prescription of required reserve ratios. This is an extremely powerful tool. Compare it, for example, with open-market operations in bills. The Federal Reserve can effect a given initial increase in free reserves, calculated against an unchanged volume of deposits, either by open-market purchases of bills from the banks or by a reduction in required reserve ratios. The first method does not alter the banks' overall defensive position; their holdings of free reserves plus bills amount to the same fraction of their disposable assets (total assets less required reserves) as before. The second method, reduction of required reserve ratios, improves the banks' overall defensive position at the same time that it augments their free reserves. Banks' free reserves plus bill holdings become a larger share of their disposable assets. The second method, therefore, gives the banks the greater incentive to expand loans. In the case of open-market operations, reduction of free reserves to desired levels entails a multiple-deposit expansion based on established reserve ratios. In the case of a lowering of required reserve ratios, reduction of free reserves to desired levels entails deposit expansion by a higher multiple, based on the new reserve ratios.

An implication of the foregoing comparison is that the Federal Reserve can have a net expansionary impact by simultaneously (a) reducing required reserve ratios so as to free reserves and (b) mopping up those freed reserves by open-market sales of bills. The immediate consequence of these two moves is that banks have the same free reserves as before but a larger supply of bills. As banks seek to swap bills with the public for more illiquid and risky assets, the bill rate will rise and the rates on less liquid and less safe assets will fall.

Once again, variability of deposit rates will accentuate the impact of the central bank's action. As bill and loan rates fall, banks will reduce the rates they offer for deposits, even though the reduction in reserve requirements lowers the cost of deposits to the banks. Flexibility of deposit rates makes necessary larger reduction in the constellation of interest rates to reabsorb the released reserves either in excess reserves or reserves required to back additional deposits.

The Federal Reserve always has a choice among various combinations of its instruments—reserve requirements, discount rate, open-market position—all of which would achieve the same impact on the economy through the banking system. In making this choice the Federal Reserve is in effect helping to determine how much interest federal taxpayers transfer to bank shareowners and others.

For example, the Fed could, within the limits of discretion allowed by Congress, increase reserve requirements and offset the restrictive effects of this action by open-market purchases of government securities. Even if the net result was that market interest rates were maintained, the government would save interest cost by the conversion of interest-bearing into non-interest-bearing debt. But the Federal Reserve would have to go even further, and reduce interest rates, either by additional open-market purchases or by lowering its discount rate. The reason lies in the *marginal* effect of the higher reserve ratio k, which consumes a fraction of the gain from attracting and lending an additional dollar of deposits.

10.4
SUMMARY

The models discussed in this chapter were meant to be illustrative and to give meaning to some general observations about monetary analysis. The basic framework is very flexible. It can be extended to encompass more sectors and more assets, depending on the topic under study. Other financial intermediaries can be introduced. More distinctions can be made among categories of government debts, types of private debts, and financial relations with other countries. Equally important, the assumption that physical capital is homogeneous can be dropped, and a number of markets, prices, and rates of return for stocks of goods introduced—distinguishing among houses, plant, equipment, consumers' durables, and so on.

According to this approach, there are two principal ways in which financial policies and events affect aggregate demand: (1) by changing the valuations of physical assets relative to their replacement costs, hence affecting the rate of capital investment and (2) by changing the rates of return on domestic assets relative to foreign assets, hence altering the exchange rate and international competitiveness. Monetary policies can accomplish such changes, but other exogenous events can too. Besides the exogenous variables explicitly listed in the illustrative models, changes can occur, and undoubtedly do, in the portfolio preferences—asset demand functions—of the public, the banks, and other sectors. These preferences are based on expectations, estimates of risk, attitudes toward risk, and a host of other factors. In this complex situation, it is not to be expected that the essential impact of monetary policies and other financial events will be easy to measure in the absence of direct observation of the relevant variables (in particular, the q ratio). There is no reason to think that the impact will be captured in any single exogenous or intermediate variable, whether it is a monetary stock or a market interest rate.[19]

---

[19]This point has been illustrated in simulation of a numerical model on the order of the extended model above. See Tobin and Brainard (1968). On the use of flow of funds statistics, as compiled by the Board of Governors of the Federal Reserve System, to implement empirically disaggregated models of financial systems, see Backus et al. (1980).

REFERENCES

Adler, Michael, and Bernard Dumas. "International Portfolio Choice and Corporation Finance: A Survey." *Journal of Finance* 38 (June 1983): 925–984.

Arrow, Kenneth J. *Aspects of the Theory of Risk-Bearing.* Helsinki: Yrjo Jahnsson Saatio, 1965.

Backus, David, William C. Brainard, Gary Smith, and James Tobin. "A Model of U.S. Financial and Nonfinancial Economic Behavior." *Journal of Money, Credit, and Banking* 12 (May 1980): 259–293.

Barro, Robert. "Are Government Bonds Net Wealth?" *Journal of Political Economy* (November/December 1974): 1095–1117.

Baumol, William J. "The Transactions Demand for Cash: An Inventory–Theoretic Approach." *Quarterly Journal of Economics* 66 (November 1952): 545–556.

Baumol, William J., and James Tobin. "The Optimal Cash Balance Proposition: Maurice Allais's Priority." *Journal of Economic Literature* 27 (September 1989): 1160–1162. *Essays 4*, Ch. 33.

Bischoff, Charles W. "Business Investment in the 1970s: A Comparison of Models." *Brookings Papers on Economic Activity* 1 (1971): 13–63.

Black, Fischer. "Noise." *Journal of Finance* 41 (July 1986): 529–541.

Blanchard, Olivier. "Output, the Stock Market and Interest Rates." *American Economic Review* 71 (1981): 132–143.

Blanchard, Olivier, and Stanley Fischer. *Lectures on Macroeconomics.* Cambridge, MA: The MIT Press, 1989.

Blanchard, Oliver, Changyong Rhee, and Lawrence Summers, "The Stock Market, Profit, and Investment." *Quarterly Journal of Economics* 108 (February 1993): 134–135.

Board of Governors of the Federal Reserve System. *The Federal Reserve System: Purposes and Functions.* Washington: Board of Governors, 1984.

Boskin, Michael J., Marc S. Robinson, and Alan M. Huber. "Government Saving, Capital Formation, and Wealth in the United States, 1947–85." In Robert E. Lipsey and Helen Stone Tice, eds., *The Measurement of Saving, Investment, and Wealth,* NBER Studies in Income and Wealth 52. Chicago: University of Chicago Press, 1989.

Brainard, William C., and F. T. Dolbear. "Social Risk and Financial Markets." *American Economic Review* 61 (May 1971): 360–370.

Brainard, William C., Mathew D. Shapiro, and John B. Shoven. "Fundamental Value and Market Value." In William C. Brainard et al., eds., *Money, Macroeconomics, and Economic Policy.* Cambridge, MA: MIT Press, 1991.

Brainard, William C., John B. Shoven, and Laurence Weiss. "The Financial Valuation of the Return to Capital." *Brookings Papers on Economic Activity* 2 (1980): 453–502.

Brainard, William C., and James Tobin. "Pitfalls in Financial Model Building." *American Economic Review* 58 (May 1968): 99–122.

———. "On the Internationalization of Portfolios." *Oxford Economic Papers* 44 (1992): 553–565.

Breeden, Douglas T. "An Intertemporal Asset Pricing Model with Stochastic Consumption and Investment Opportunities." *Journal of Financial Economics* 7 (1979): 265–296.

———. "Intertemporal Portfolio Theory and Asset Pricing." In John Eatwell et al., eds., *New Palgrave: Finance.* New York: Norton, 1989.

Brennan, M. J. "Capital Asset Pricing Model." In John Eatwell et al., eds., *New Palgrave: Finance.* New York: Norton, 1989.

Buchanan, James. "Barro on the Ricardian Equivalence Theorem." *Journal of Political Economy* (April 1976): 337–342.

Chan-Lee, James, and Raymond Torres. "*Q* de Tobin et Taux d'Accumulation en France." *Annales d'Economie et Statistique* 5 (1987): 37–48.

Chen, Nai–Fu, Richard Roll, and Stephen A. Ross. "Economic Forces and the Stock Market." *Journal of Business* 59 (July 1986): 383–403.

Ciccolo, John. "A Linkage Between Product and Financial Markets—Investment and *q*." Chapter 3 of *Four Essays on Monetary Policy,* unpublished Ph.D. dissertation, Yale University, 1975.

Clower, Robert W. "An Investigation into the Dynamics of Investment." *American Economic Review* 44 (March 1954): 64–81.

Crotty, James R. "Owner-Manager Conflict and Financial Theories of Investment Instability: A Critical Assessment." *Journal of Post Keynesian Economics* 12 (summer 1990): 519–542.

Cutler, David M., James M. Poterba, and Lawrence H. Summers. "Speculative Dynamics and the Role of Feedback Traders." *American Economic Review* 80 (May 1990): 63–68.

Delong, Bradford J., Andrei Shleifer, Lawrence Summers, and Robert Waldmann. "Noise Trader Risk in Financial Markets." *Journal of Political Economy* 98, (August 1990): 703–738.

Einzig, Paul. *Primitive Money.* Oxford: Pergamon Press, 1966.

Feldstein, Martin, and Charles Horioka. "Domestic Saving and International Capital Flows," *The Economic Journal* (June 1980): 314–329.

Fisher, Irving. *The Purchasing Power of Money.* New York: Macmillan, 1911.

———. *The Theory of Interest.* New York: Macmillan, 1930.

Frankel, Jeffrey A. "Quantifying International Capital Mobility in the 1980s." In D. Bernheim and J. Shoven, eds., *National Saving and Economic Performance.* Chicago: University of Chicago Press, 1991.

Frankel, Jeffrey A., and Kathryn Dominguez. "Does Foreign Exchange Intervention Matter? Disentangling the Portfolio and Expectations Effects for the Mark." *American Economic Review* 83 (December 1993): 1356–1359.

Frankel, Jeffrey A., and Kenneth A. Froot. "Chartists, Fundamentalists, and the Demand for Dollars." *Greek Economic Review* 10 (1988): 49–102.

Friedman, Milton. *Capitalism and Freedom.* Chicago: University of Chicago Press, 1962.

Friedman, Milton, and Anna Schwartz. *A Monetary History of the United States.* Princeton: Princeton University Press, 1963.

Friedman, Milton, and Leonard J. Savage. "The Utility of Choices Involving Risk." *Journal of Political Economy* 56 (August 1948): 279–304.

Froot, Kenneth A., and Maurice Obstfeld. "Intrinsic Bubbles: The Case of Stock Prices." *American Economic Review* 81 (December 1991): 1189–1214.

Garfinkel, Michelle R., and Daniel L. Thornton. "The Multiplier Approach to the Money Supply Process: A Precautionary Note." *Federal Reserve Bank of St. Louis Review* (July/August 1991): 47–64.

Gesell, Silvio. *The Natural Economic Order.* Berlin: Neo-Verlag, 1929.

Girton, Lance, and Dale Henderson. "Central Bank Operations in Foreign and Domestic Assets Under Fixed and Flexible Exchange Rates." In Peter B. Clark et al., eds., *The Effects of Exchange Rate Adjustments.* Washington: Government Printing Office, 1977.

Gleick, James. "Dead as a Dollar." *New York Times Magazine* (June 16, 1996): 26, column 1.

Goldfeld, Stephen M. "The Demand for Money Revisited." *Brookings Papers on Economic Activity*, 3 (1973): 577–638.

———. "The Case of the Missing Money." *Brookings Papers on Economic Activity* 3(1976): 683–730.

———. "Demand for Money: Empirical Studies." In John Eatwell et al., eds., *The New Palgrave: Money*. New York: Norton, 1989.

Goldsmith, Raymond W. *The National Wealth of the United States in the Postwar Period.* Princeton: Princeton University Press, 1962.

———. *The National Balance Sheet of the United States 1953–1975.* Chicago: University of Chicago Press, 1982.

———. *Comparative National Balance Sheets.* Chicago: University of Chicago Press, 1985.

Golub, Stephen S. *International Financial Markets, Oil Prices and Exchange Rates.* Unpublished Ph.D. dissertation, Yale University, 1983.

———. "Foreign-Currency Government Debt, Asset-Market Equilibrium and the Balance of Payments." *Journal of International Money and Finance* (June 1989): 285–294.

———. "International Capital Mobility: Net Versus Gross Stocks and Flows." *Journal of International Money and Finance* 9 (December 1990): 424–439.

———. "International Diversification of Social and Private Risk: The U.S. and Japan." *Japan and the World Economy* 6 (1994): 263–284.

Gordon, Robert J., and J. Veitch. "Fixed Investment in the American Business Cycle, 1919–1983." In Robert J. Gordon, ed., *The American Business Cycle: Continuity and Change.* Chicago: University of Chicago Press, 1986.

Gorton, Gary. "Banking Panics." In Peter Newman, Murray Milgate, and John Eatwell, eds., *The New Palgrave Dictionary of Money and Finance,* Vol. 1. London: Macmillan, 1992.

Graham, F. D., and C. R. Whittlesey. *The Golden Avalanche.* Princeton: Princeton University Press, 1939.

Gurley, J. G., and E. S. Shaw. "Financial Aspects of Economic Development." *American Economic Review* 45 (September 1955): 516–522.

Hakansson, Nils H. "Portfolio Analysis." In John Eatwell et al., eds., *The New Palgrave: Finance.* New York: Norton, 1989.

Haliassos, Michael, and James Tobin. "The Macroeconomics of Government Finance." In Benjamin Friedman and Frank Hahn, eds., *Handbook of Monetary Economics.* Amsterdam: North–Holland, 1990.

Hayashi, Fumio. "Tobin's Marginal q and Average q: A Neoclassical Interpretation." *Econometrica* 50 (January 1982): 215–224.

———. "Taxes and Corporate Investment in Japanese Manufacturing." NBER Working Paper 1753, 1985.

Hicks, John R. "A Suggestion for Simplifying the Theory of Money." *Economica* NS 2 (February 1935): 1–19.

———. *Value and Capital.* Oxford: Oxford University Press, 1939.

Ingersoll, Jonathan. *The Theory of Financial Decisionmaking.* Savage, Maryland: Rowman and Littlefield, 1987.

Jorgenson, Dale W., and Barbara M. Fraumeni. "The Accumulation of Human and Nonhuman Capital, 1948–84." In Robert E. Lipsey and Helen Stone Tice, eds., *The Measurement of Saving, Investment, and Wealth,* NBER Studies in Income and Wealth 52. Chicago: University of Chicago Press, 1989.

Kaldor, Nicholas. "Speculation and Economic Stability." *Review of Economic Studies* (1939–1940): 1–27.

Keynes, John Maynard. *A Treatise on Money.* 2 vols. London: Macmillan, 1930.

———. *The General Theory of Employment, Interest, and Money.* New York: Harcourt Brace, 1936.

———. "Alternative Theories of the Rate of Interest." *Economic Journal* 47 (June 1937): 241–252.

Kotlikoff, Laurence J. *Generational Accounting: Knowing Who Pays, and When, for What We Spend.* New York: The Free Press, 1992.

Kouri, Pentti J. K. "The Exchange Rate and the Balance of Payments in the Short Run and in the Long Run: A Monetary Approach." *Scandinavian Journal of Economics* (May 1976): 280–304.

Lavington, F. *The English Capital Market.* 3d ed. London: Methuen and Co., 1941.

Lerner, Abba. *The Economics of Control.* New York: MacMillan, 1940.

Levy, Haim, and Paul A. Samuelson. "The Capital Asset Pricing Model with Diverse Holding Periods." Unpublished manuscript, 1991.

Lintner, John. "The Valuation of Risky Assets and the Selection of Risky Investments in Stock Portfolios and Capital Budgets." *Review of Economics and Statistics* 47 (February 1965): 13–37.

Lipsey, Robert E., and Helen Stone Tice, eds. *The Measurement of Saving, Investment, and Wealth,* NBER Studies in Income and Wealth 52. Chicago: University of Chicago Press, 1989.

Lucas, Robert E. "Understanding Business Cycles." In Karl Brunner and Allen Meltzer, eds., *Stabilization of the Domestic and International Economy.* Amsterdam: North–Holland, 1977.

Lucas, Robert E., Jr. "Equilibrium in a Pure Currency Economy." In John H. Kareken and Neil Wallace, eds., *Models of Monetary Economies.* Minneapolis: Federal Reserve Bank of Minneapolis, 1980.

Luce, Duncan, and Howard Raiffa. *Games and Decisions.* New York: Wiley, 1966.

Machina, Mark J. "Choice under Uncertainty: Problems Solved and Unsolved." *Journal of Economic Perspectives* 1 (summer 1987): 121–154.

MaCurdy, Thomas E., and John B. Shoven. "Accumulating Pension Wealth with Stocks and Bonds." Unpublished manuscript, Center for Economic Policy Research, Stanford University, January 1992.

Markowitz, Harry M. "Portfolio Selection." *Journal of Finance* 7 (March 1952a): 77–91.

———. "The Utility of Wealth." *Journal of Political Economy* 60 (April 1952b): 151–158.

———. *Portfolio Selection: Efficient Diversification of Investments.* New Haven: Yale University Press, 1959.

———. "Mean-Variance Analysis." In John Eatwell et al., eds., *New Palgrave: Finance.* New York: Norton, 1989.

Marshall, Alfred. *Money, Credit, and Commerce.* London: Macmillan, 1923.

Meese, Richard E. "Currency Fluctuations in the Post Bretton Woods Era." *Journal of Economic Perspectives* 4 (winter 1990): 117–134.

Merton, Robert C. "Lifetime Portfolio Selection under Uncertainty: The Continuous-Time Case." *Review of Economics and Statistics* 51 (August 1969): 247–257.

———. "An Intertemporal Capital Asset Pricing Model." *Econometrica* 41 (September 1973): 867–887.

———. "Continuous-Time Stochastic Models." In John Eatwell et al., eds., *The New Palgrave: Finance.* New York: Norton, 1989.

Miller, Merton H., and Daniel Orr. "A Model of the Demand for Money by Firms." *Quarterly Journal of Economics* 80 (August 1966): 413–435.

Modigliani, Franco, and M. H. Miller. "The Cost of Capital, Corporation Finance, and the Theory of Investment." *American Economic Review* 48 (June 1958): 261–297.

Mossin, Jan. "Optimal Multiperiod Portfolio Policies." *Journal of Business* 41 (April 1968): 215–229.

Myrdal, Gunnar. "Om penningteoretisk jamvikt. En studie over den 'normala rantan' i Wicksells penninglara." [On money-theoretic equilibrium. A study of the 'normal interest rate' in Wicksell's monetary theory.] *Economisk Tidshrift* 33 (1931): 191–302.

———. "Der Gleichgewochtsbegriff als Instrument der geldtheoretischen Analyse." [The Equilibrium Concept as an Instrument of Monetary Analysis.] In F. A. von Hayek, ed., *Beiträge zur Geldtheorie*. Wien: J. Springer, 1993.

Obstfeld, Maurice. "International Capital Mobility in the 1990s." In Peter B. Kenen, ed., *Understanding Interdependence: The Macroeconomics of the Open Economy*. Princeton: Princeton University Press, 1994.

Oulton, N. "Aggregate Investment and Tobin's Q: the Evidence from Britain." *Oxford Economic Papers* 33 (1981): 177–202.

Patinkin, Don. *Money, Interest, and Prices*. 2nd ed. New York: Harper and Row, 1965.

Pigou, A. C. "The Value of Money." Ch. 10 of *Readings in Monetary Theory* (Irwin, 1951), reprinted from *Quarterly Journal of Economics* (1917–1918): 38–65.

Pratt, John W. "Risk Aversion in the Small and in the Large." *Econometrica* 32 (January/April 1964): 122–136.

Porter, Richard D., Thomas D. Simpson, and Eileen Mauskopf. "Financial Innovation and the Monetary Aggregates." *Brookings Papers on Economic Activity* 1(1979): 213–229.

Ramsey, Frank. "Truth and Probability." In *Foundations of Mathematics and Other Logical Essays*. London: Routledge & K. Paul, 1931.

Ricardo, David. "On the Principles of Political Economy and Taxation." In J. McCulloch, ed., *The Works of David Ricardo*. London: John Murray, 1817.

Robertson, D. H. *Money (Cambridge Economic Handbook)*. 4th ed. Chicago: University of Chicago Press (1st ed. 1922), 1959.

Robinson, Joan. "The Rate of Interest." In *Collected Economic Papers*. Vol. 2. Oxford: Basil Blackwell, 1964.

Roll, Richard. "A Critique of the Asset Pricing Theory's Tests: Part I." *Journal of Financial Economics* 4 (March 1977): 129–176.

Ross, Stephen A. "The Arbitrage Theory of Capital Asset Pricing." *Journal of Economic Theory* 3 (December 1976): 341–360.

Samuelson, Paul A. "Lifetime Portfolio Selection by Dynamic Stochastic Programming." *Review of Economics and Statistics* 51 (August 1969): 239–246.

Sargent, Thomas, and Neil Wallace. "Rational Expectations and the Theory of Economic Policy." *Journal of Monetary Economics* (April 1976): 169–183.

Schmidt, Klaus J. W. "Tobins q? Myrdals Q! Ein Fallbeispiel für den Wert von Fremdsprachenkenntnissen." [Tobin's q? Myrdal's Q! An example of the value of knowing foreign languages.] *Kredit und Kapital* 28 (1995): 175–200.

Schuler, K., and L. H. White. "Free Banking: History." In Peter Newman, Murray Milgate, and John Eatwell, eds., *The New Palgrave Dictionary of Money and Finance*. Vol. 2, 198–199. London: Macmillan, 1992.

Sensenbrenner, Gabriel. "Aggregate Investment, the Stock Market, and the Q-Model: Robust Results for Six OECD Countries." *European Economic Review* 35 (May 1991): 769–825.

"Seymour Harris: Tribute." *Essays in Economics.* Vol. 4. Cambridge: MIT Press, 1996, 787–790.

Sharpe, William F. "Capital Asset Prices: A Theory of Equilibrium under Conditions of Risk." *Journal of Finance* 19 (September 1964): 425–442.

Shiller, Robert J. *Market Volatility.* Cambridge: MIT Press, 1989.

———. *Macro Markets: Creating Institutions for Managing Society's Largest Economic Risks.* Oxford: Oxford University Press, 1994.

Sprenkle, Case M. "The Case of the Missing Currency." *Journal of Economic Perspectives* 7 (Fall 1993): 185–193.

Stevens, Guy V. G. "On Tobin's Multiperiod Portfolio Theorem." *Review of Economic Studies* 34 (October 1972): 461–468.

Stiglitz, Joseph E., and Andrew Weiss. "Credit Rationing in Markets with Imperfect Information." *American Economic Review* 71 (June 1981): 393–410.

Summers, Lawrence. "Taxation and Corporate Investment: A *Q*-Approach." *Brookings Papers on Economic Activity* 1 (1981): 67–127.

Taylor, John. "Aggregate Dynamics and Staggered Contracts." *Journal of Political Economy* 88 (1980): 1–24.

"The Theory of Portfolio Selection." In F. Hahn and F. Brechling, eds., *The Theory of Interest Rates,* Macmillan & Co., 1965, 3–51.

Tobin, James. "Asset Holdings and Spending Decisions." *American Economic Review* (May 1952): 109–123.

———. "A Dynamic Aggregative Model." *Journal of Political Economy* (1955): 103–115.

———. "The Interest Elasticity of the Transactions Demand for Cash." *Review of Economics and Statistics* 38 (August 1956): 241–247. *Essays 1,* Ch. 14.

———. "Liquidity Preference as Behavior towards Risk." *Review of Economic Studies* 25 (February 1958): 65–86.

———. "Money, Capital and Other Stores of Value." *American Economic Review* 51 (May 1961): 26–37.

———. "The Theory of Portfolio Selection." In F. H. Hahn and F. P. R. Brechling, eds., *The Theory of Interest Rates.* London: Macmillan, 1965.

———. "A General Equilibrium Approach to Monetary Theory." *Journal of Money, Credit, and Banking* 1 (February 1969): 15–29.

———. "A Proposal for International Monetary Reform." *Eastern Economic Journal* 4 (1978): 153–159.

———. *Asset Accumulation and Economic Activity.* Chicago: University of Chicago Press, 1980.

———. "Money and Finance in the Macroeconomic Process." *Journal of Money, Credit, and Banking* 14 (May 1982a): 171–204.

———. "The Commercial Banking Firm: A Simple Model," *Scandinavian Journal of Economics,* 84:4 (1982b): 495–530.

———. "Financial Structure and Monetary Rules." *Credit und Kapital* 16 (1983): 155–171. *Essays 4,* Ch. 19.

———. "A Mean-Variance Approach to Fundamental Valuations." *Journal of Portfolio Management* (fall 1984a): 26–32.

———. "On the Efficiency of the Financial System." *Lloyds Bank Review* (July 1984b): 1–15.

———. "Money." In John Eatwell et al., eds., *The New Palgrave Dictionary of Money and Finance.* Vol. 2, *Essays 4,* Ch. 5. London: Macmillan, 1992.

———. "Price Flexibility and Output Stability: An Old Keynesian View." *Journal of Economic Perspectives* 7 (winter 1993): 45–65. Republished with appendix added in Willi

Semmler, ed., *Business Cycle Theory and Empirical Methods.* Norwell, MA: Kluwer Academic Publishers, 1994.

Tobin, James, and Jorge A. Braga de Macedo. "The Short-Run Macroeconomics of Flexible Exchange Rates: An Exposition." In John S. Chipman and Charles P. Kindleberger, eds., *Flexible Exchange Rates and the Balance of Payments.* Amsterdam, North–Holland, 1980.

Tobin, James, and Willem H. Buiter. "Fiscal and Monetary Policies, Capital Formation, and Economic Activity." In George M. von Furstenberg, ed., *The Government and Capital Formation.* Cambridge, MA: Ballinger, 1980.

U.S. Department of Commerce. *Statistical Abstract of the United States 1994.* Table #776.1994.

von Furstenberg, George M. "Corporate Investment: Does Market Valuation Matter in the Aggregate?" *Brookings Papers on Economic Activity* 2 (1977): 347–397.

von Hayek, Friedrich A., ed. *Beiträge zur Geldtheorie.* Wien: J. Springer, 1993.

von Neumann, John, and Oskar Morgenstern. *Theory of Games and Economic Behavior.* Princeton: Princeton University Press, 1947.

Wicksell, K. *Lectures on Political Economy, vol. II,* 190–201. New York: Macmillan, 1935.

Witte, James G., Jr. "The Microfoundations of the Social Investment Function." *The Journal of Political Economy* 71 (October 1963): 451–456.

Name Index

Adler, Michael, 83
Allais, Maurice, 46
Ames, Glena, xxiv
Arrow, Kenneth, 67, 68
Axilrod, Stephen, xxiv

Backus, David, 291
Barone, Emilio, xxiv
Barro, Robert, 4, 266–269
Baumol, William, 46
Bernoulli, Daniel, 63–64
Bischoff, Charles, 153
Black, Fischer, 11
Blanchard, Olivier, 152, 153, 266
Boskin, Michael, 3, 24
Boyer, Joseph, 134
Brainard, William, 86, 106
Breeden, Douglas, 34, 97, 157
Brennan, M. J., 167
Buchanan, James, 266
Buiter, Willem, 271

Chamberlin, Edward, 171
Chan-Lee, James, 153
Chen, Nai–Fu, 9
Ciccolo, John, 153
Clower, Robert, 153
Crotty, James, 151
Cutler, David, 11, 162

de Gaulle, Charles, 54
Deliveli, Emre, xxiv
Delong, Bradford, 11, 162
de Macedo, Jorge Braga, 271, 276, 286
Dolbear, F. Trenery, 167
Dominguez, Kathryn, 287
Douglas, Paul, 230
Dumas, Bernard, 83

Eccles, Marriner, 211
Einzig, Paul, 27

Feldstein, Martin, 6
Fischer, Stanley, 266
Fisher, Irving, 26, 45, 53
Frankel, Jeffrey, 162, 287
Fraumeni, Barbara, 3
Friedman, Milton, 53, 65, 164, 212, 217
Froot, Kenneth, 161, 162

Garfinkel, Michelle, 234
Gesell, Silvio, 17, 59
Girton, Lance, 287
Gleick, James, 208
Goldfeld, Stephen, 50, 58
Goldsmith, Raymond, 1, 3
Golub, Stephen, 83, 86, 161, 286, 287
Gordon, Robert, 153

Gorton, Gary, 209
Graham, E. D., 215
Grawe, Roger, xxiv
Gurley, J. G., 5

Hakansson, Nils, 34
Haliassos, Michael, 4, 269
Hamilton, Alexander, 206–207, 214
Harris, Seymour, xxiii–xxiv
Harrison, Laura, xxiv
Hayashi, Fumio, 151, 153
Henderson, Dale, 287
Hester, Donald, xxiv
Hicks, John, 53, 57, 272, 273
Horioka, Charles, 6
Huber, Alan, 3
Hume, David, 53

Ingersoll, Jonathan, 70, 97

Jackson, Andrew, 207
Jevons, William Stanley, 63
Johnson, Karen, xxiv
Jorgenson, Dale, 3

Kaldor, Nicholas, 57, 272
Keynes, John Maynard, 11, 41, 45, 56,
       57, 148, 150, 152, 162–164, 165,
       197, 247, 265, 266, 267, 270,
       271–273, 274
Kotlikoff, Lawrence, 219
Kouri, Pentti, 154, 286

Lavington, F., 45, 272, 273
Lerner, Abba, 153
Levy, Haim, 96
Lintner, John, 156
Lipsey, Robert, 1
Lucas, Robert, 45, 265
Luce, Duncan, 64

Machina, Mark, 64, 71
MaCurdy, Thomas, 93
Markowitz, Harry, 64, 69, 70, 79–80
Marshall, Alfred, 55
Marx, Karl, 63
Mauskopf, Eileen, 58
Meese, Richard, 162
Menger, Karl, 63
Merton, Robert, 34, 97, 157
Miller, Merton, 52, 148, 158

Modigliani, Franco, 148, 158
Morgenstern, Oskar, 64
Mossin, Jan, 96, 97
Myrdal, Gunnar, 150

Obstfeld, Maurice, 161, 287
Okun, Arthur, xxiv
Orr, Daniel, 52
Oulton, N., 153

Patinkin, Don, 271–272, 273, 274
Pigou, A. C., 45, 272, 273
Porter, Richard, 58
Poterba, James, 11
Pratt, John, 67, 68

Raiffa, Howard, 64
Ramsey, Frank, 64
Rhee, Changyong, 152
Ricardo, David, 4, 266–269
Robertson, D. H., 54
Robinson, Joan, 97
Robinson, Marc, 3
Roll, Richard, 9, 158
Ross, Stephen, 9, 157

Samuelson, Paul, 96, 97
Sargent, Thomas, 265
Savage, Leonard, 65
Schmidt, Klaus, 150
Schuler, K., 207
Schwartz, Anna, 212, 217
Sensenbrenner, Gabriel, 153
Sharpe, William, 156
Shaw, E. S., 5
Shiller, Robert, 11, 26, 161
Shleifer, Andrei, 11
Shoven, John, 93
Simpson, Thomas, 58
Smith, Gary, xxiv
Sprenkle, Case, 233
Stein, Jerome, xxiv
Stevens, Guy, 95
Stiglitz, Joseph, 119
Strauss, Althea, xxiv
Summers, Lawrence, 11, 152, 153, 162
Suryatmodo, Koen, xxiv

Taylor, John, 266
Thornton, Daniel, 234

Tice, Helen Stone, 1
Tobin, James, 4, 27, 46, 59, 69, 70, 86, 89,
        94–95, 106, 147, 148, 151, 152, 157,
        158, 159–160, 161, 163, 167, 170,
        265, 266, 269, 271, 273, 276, 279,
        286, 291
Torres, Raymond, 153

Veitch, J., 153
von Furstenberg, George, 153
von Neumann, John, 64

Waldmann, Robert, 11
Wallace, Neil, 265
Wallich, Henry, xxiv
Walras, Leon, 63, 114
Wehrle, Leroy S., xxiv
Weiss, Andrew, 119
White, L. H., 207
Whitehead, Alfred North, 57
Whittlesey, C. R., 215
Wicksell, K., 150, 264, 273
Witte, James, Jr., 153
Wolfgang, Johann, 150

Young, Ralph, xxiv

Index

Acceptability in payments, 26
Accounts
  bank reserves, 224–225
  banking system, 222–229
  banks, individual, 172–173
  Federal government, 217–222, 276
  national, 1–8, 129–130, 134–140, 276
  private, 1–8, 276
  (*See also* Balance sheet)
Accumulation
  objectives, 33–38
  of wealth, 6–7
Adjustment credits, 226
Aggregate consumption, 157
Aggregate demand, effects on, 290
All-cash sequences, 93
Appreciation, 21–22, 28
Arbitrage pricing theory (APT), 81, 157, 158,
    160
Arrow-Pratt risk aversion, 67, 68
Asset-market equilibrium, 146, 269–284
Asset menus, 164–165, 170–171
Asset pricing, 9–11, 146–169, 2A
  bubbles, 10, 30, 162, 216
  (*See also* Capital asset pricing model)
Asset values
  fundamentals approach, 11, 159–161
  theory of, 10
Assets
  banks, 171–172, 174–181, 249–257,
    276–284
  capital, 147–155, 264

defensive, 171–172, 181, 193
durable, 5–6
foreign, 2, 6
inside, 108
in Keynes's *General Theory,* 271–273
means of payment, 27–28
monetary, 134–141
national compared with private,
    5–6, 276
outside, 108
paper, 3
preferences, 9–11
properties of, 9–11
  divisibility, 11, 15
  liquidity, 11–14
  predictability, 11, 16–20
  return, 11, 21–26, 28
  reversibility, 11, 13–15
  value, 11–14
  yield, 11, 20–24, 28
rate of return, 21, 156
  risk premiums, 156–157
real values of, 23–24
reproducible / nonreproducible, 2
risk-weighted, 244
riskless, 89–90
risky, 89
safe, 89
saving, 7
speculative, 10–11, 30
tangible, 1–2, 5–6
Asymmetry of gains and losses, 43

Automatic teller machine (ATM), 46, 58
  and demand for money, 50, 233–234
Automatic transfers, 58

Balance sheet, 276
  bank, 171–172
  banking system, 217–229
  Federal, 218–219
  national, 217–229
  national and international, 276
  (*See also* Accounts, Assets)
Bank notes, 207, 209, 212
Bank of Canada, 229
Bank of England, 206, 209, 211
Banking Act (1935), 213
Banking panics, 208–210, 211, 214
Banking systems, 135, 137
  branches, 174
  Canada, 178–179
  defensive position, 174–181, 256–257
  monetary policy and, 170
  reserve requirements, 178–179
  United Kingdom, 178–179
  United States, 206–208 (*see also* United
    States monetary and banking system)
    reforms, 212–213
Bankruptcy, 227
Banks
  accounts (*see* Accounts)
  agricultural, 227
  capital of, 208
  chartering, 207, 209, 213
  commercial, 155, 170–171
    compared with savings, 206
  defensive assets, 171–172, 181, 193
  defensive position (*see* Defensive position)
  deposits (*see* Deposits)
  failure of, 181–182, 208–212, 227
  Federal Reserve credit to, 226–227
  holdings of government debt, 137
  investments, 171, 182–184, 189
  loans (*see* Loans)
  maximization of profit, 182–184
  model of banking firm, 170–204
  monopolies, 174
  national, compared with state, 207
  portfolio decisions, 172, 197–198 (*see also*
    Portfolio selection)
  profits, 174–181
  regulations (*see* Regulations)
  reserve tests, 223–224
  reserves (*see* Reserves)
  service charges, 50–51
  wildcat, 207

(*See also* Federal Reserve System; United
    States monetary and banking system)
Barter, 26
Bequests, economic influences of, 267–269
Bernoulli's solution to paradox, 63, 64
Bills (*see* United States Treasury bills)
Board of Governors of the Federal Reserve
    System, 171, 210, 213
Bonds, 29, 161
  "Carter Bonds," 287
  predictability of, 16
  purchasing power bonds, 26
  savings, 217
  zero-coupon, 217
Borrowed reserves, 224–225
Borrowers, 122–123, 172–174, 259–260
Borrowing
  behavior, 108, 109–113, 115
  discount window, 210, 226–227,
    251–253
  Federal Reserve Banks, 226–227
  float, 227–228
Branch banking, 174
Bretton Woods, 216–217
British Commonwealth, 17
Bryan, William Jennings, 214
Bubbles, 10, 30, 162
  gold, 216
Bureau of Labor Statistics, 23
Businesses
  and banks, 195–196
  corporate investment, 147–152
  unincorporated, 147
  valuation of, 147

Cambridge school, 45, 272
Canada
  Bank of Canada, 229
  branch banking, 174
  reserve requirements, 178–179
  secondary reserves, 243
Capital
  of banks, 182, 208
  human, 2–3
  marginal physical product of, 103
  market, 1–8, 101–145, 164, 264
  market value of, 106–107, 128, 147–154,
    159–161, 168–169, 279–282
  monetization of, 129, 135–137
  monetized, 134–140
  in national wealth, 1–8
  ownership of, 3
  private (PC), 1-8, 134–135
  rent of, 102–103, 104

replacement cost of, 107, 128, 147–154, 159–161, 168–169
valuation of assets, 147–155
Capital accounts, 270
accounting framework for, 276
analytical framework for, 276–279
general equilibrium models, 269–271
transactions, 40
Capital asset pricing model (CAPM), 156–157
arbitrage pricing theory, 157
assessment of, 157–159
consumption capital asset pricing model (CCAPM), 157–159
extensions of, 157
fundamental approach, 159–161
intertemporal capital asset pricing model (ICAPM), 157
market-clearing and, 168–169
Capital gains, 7–8
Capital goods, 103–104
assured homogeneous, 102
depreciation of, 102
heterogeneity of, 149
Capital market equilibrium, 105–107, 126, 269–284
Capital markets, 1–8, 101–145, 164, 264
Capital ratio requirements on banks, 208
Capitalism, 3
Cardinal utility schedule, 63–64
Carrying costs, currency and deposits, 51
"Carter bonds," 287
Cash, 44–45
all-cash sequences, 93
assets
perfect liquid, 12–13
unpredictability of real return, 24
compared with time deposits, 46–50
Cash concentration accounts, 58
Cash-in-advance models, 45
Cash-management technologies, 58
Cash preference behavior of banks, 246, 248
CD (see Certificates of deposit)
Ceilings, 172, 258
deposit rate, 180
interest rate, 58, 180, 212
Central banks
discount rates, 287–289
foreign exchange market interventions, 286–287
monetary policies, 284–290
open market operations, 284–286
required reserve ratios, 289–290
(See also Federal Reserve System)
Certificates of deposit, 256
Chartered banks, 207, 209, 213
Checking accounts, 50–51, 58–59

China, 3
Civil War, 209, 215
Cleveland, Grover, 214
Coins
copper, 213
full-bodied, 213
gold, 27
Susan Anthony dollar, 229
token, 213, 214
Collateral, 109
Commercial banks, 155, 170–171, 205–206
compared with savings banks, 206
Consol, 17, 18, 29, 217
Constant money multiplier, 232–239
Constant-velocity approximation, 233, 272–273
Consumer goods, 1, 147
Consumer theory and portfolio selection, 71
Consumers' Price Index (CPI), 23–24, 165
Consumption
aggregate, 157
behavior, 267–269
multiperiod, 97–98
of wealth, 5–6, 270
Consumption capital asset pricing model (CCAPM), 157–159
Contingent sequences, 92
Contingent strategies, 92
Copper coins, 213
Corporate investment
neoclassical theory of, 149, 151–152
stock-flow model of, 153–156
Corporate securities, 148–149
Corporations, 147–153
Costs of portfolio management
asymmetry in, 43
expected, 187–188
shifts and decisions, 32–34
CPI (see Consumers' Price Index)
Credit, Federal Reserve Bank, 226–227
adjustment, 226
discount window, 226–227
extended, 227
Credit cards, 50, 233, 234
Credit limits, 118–119
Credit lines, 124
Currency, 102
bank notes and bank reserves, 217–224
and capital, 102–106, 117–129
vs. deposits, 50, 233–234
early, 207
electronic, 208
European, and the Treaty of Maastricht, 216
Federal Reserve notes, 211, 215
gold and silver, 213–215

greenbacks, 209, 215
history of, 205, 213–215, 216
holdings, 50–51
international transfer tax, 163
and panics, 208, 211
public demand for, 228–229
real value of, 24

De Gaulle, 54
Debt
    bank loans, 171–204
    collateral, 109
    composition changes of, 221
    default, 109
    government (*see* Government debt)
    inside/outside, 108
    loans, 101–145
    short-term compared with demand, 244
    valuation, 28–30
Debt management, 221–222
Decision-making costs, 33
Default, 109
Default risk, 118–119
Defensive assets, 171–172, 181
    yield of, 193
Defensive position, 172, 175–176, 188
    banking system, 256–257
    composition of
        federal funds market, 248–256
        no federal funds market, 244–248
    increase in, 182–183, 184
    loss of, 182–183
    marginal revenue from, 175–176, 195
    negative, 176–179, 188–189, 197
        penalties for, 193–194
    size of, 256–257
    zero, 177, 180
Deficit finance, 266–269
Deficits, 2, 4, 219
    Reagan years, 269
Deflation, 7
Demand debt, 244
Demand deposits, 170, 222, 233–234
    bank's uncertainty about, 182
    vs. currency, 50, 233–234
    interest on, 50, 172
    rates of return, 258
    vs. time deposits, 182
    vs. Treasury bills, 222
    (*See also* Deposits)
Deposit insurance, 197, 212
Depository institutions (*see* Banks)
Depository Institutions Deregulation and
        Monetary Control Act of 1980, 58

Deposits, 50–51, 207
    bank, 172–174
    bank's control over, 172–174, 190–191
    ceilings on interest on, 172, 179, 180, 189,
        200
    certainty about, 198–202
    competition for, 172–174, 180–181, 255,
        258
    vs. currency, 50, 233–234
    demand deposits, 170, 222, 233–234
        bank's uncertainty about, 182
        interest on, 50, 172
        rates of return, 258
    demand for, 172, 182, 258–260
    effects of increases in, 176, 179–180
    endogenous, 200–202
    exogenous
        and costless, 198–200
        and costly, 200
        and stochastic, 203–204
        but random, 202–203
    expected, 189–191, 195
        disposable, 194
        exogenous changes in, 189, 191–193
    interbank, 255
    interest on, 50, 172, 234
    loss of, 173–174, 182–183
    rate of return on, 258
    relation to reserves, 228–239, 234–239
    reserve requirements on, 194, 221–222,
        234–239
    retention of, 195–196
    vs. time deposits, 182 (*see also* Time
        deposits)
    and transactions, 180
    vs. Treasury bills, 222
    uncertainty about, 181–191, 202–204
    value/cost of, 179–180, 189–191
    withdrawal of, 172, 181–182, 228–229
Depreciation, 22, 102
Depression, 210
    Great Depression, 129, 210, 211–212,
        238
Deregulation of finance, 206
Discount rates, 149, 210, 235, 246–248,
        251–253
    and asset values, 29–30
    central banks, 287–289
    reduction/rise in, 287–288
Discount window, 210, 226–227,
        251–253
Diversification, 34, 60
    economy of risk from, 73–76
Diversifiers, 108
Divisibility, of assets, 11, 15

Division of labor, 6
Dollars
    coins, 229
    defined, 26–27
    history of, 213–215, 216
    silver dollar of Spanish America, 213
    Susan Anthony, 229
Douglas, Paul, 230
Durable assets, 5–6
Dynamic programming approach, 97–98

Eccles, Marriner, 211
Economies of scale, 43, 49, 233
Efficient frontier, 80–81
Electronic currency, 208
Endogenous deposits, 200–202
England
    Bank of England, 206, 209, 211
    branch banking, 174
    pounds sterling, 209, 213
    reserve requirements, 178–179
    secondary reserves, 243
Equilibrium, 101, 116–117, 180, 188
    asset-market, 146
    capital market, 105–107
    changes in, 263–264
    general, models of, 269–271
    loans/investments, increase in volume of,
        189
    market, return on capital as equilibrator,
        114–116
    market, financial market value of capital as
        equilibrator, 116–117
    money market, 260–262
Equity, 193
    purchasing power of, 25–26
    value/cost of, 179
Equity stock, 29
Europe, early currency of, 213
European Union, 216
Excess reserves, 225
Exchange costs, 15, 21
Exchange rates, 161, 282–284, 286–287
Exchange Stabilization Fund, 226
Exogenous deposits, 198–200, 202–204
Expected costs of deposits, 184
    marginal, 188
    opportunity, 187
Expected defensive position, 186, 189
Expected deposits, 189–191, 195
    disposable, 194
    exogenous changes, 191–193
    increase in, 189
Expected profit, 182–184

Expected utility maximization, 62–66, 69
Extended credits, 227

Failures, bank, 129, 181–182, 208–212, 227
Fallacy of misplaced concreteness, 57
Fat-tailed distributions, 71
Federal debt (see Government debt)
Federal Deposit Insurance Corporation (FDIC),
    212
Federal Reserve System
    Banking Act of 1935, 213
    Board of Governors of, 171, 210, 213
    establishment of, 209
    failure of, in Depression, 211–212
    Federal Reserve Act of 1913, 210–211
    Federal Open Market Committee (FOMC),
        211, 213, 229–231, 237
        control of supply of reserves, 222–225
        open-market operations, 228, 235–238
        federal funds, 224
        federal funds market, 249–257
        net free reserves, 225, 235–239
        sterilized intervention, 286–287
    Federal Reserve Banks, 171, 210–211
        assets, 171, 178, 219
        balance sheets, 219
        credit to banks, 226–227
        currency, 227, 228–229
        discount rates, 149, 210, 235, 246–248,
            251–253
        discount window, 210, 226–227,
            251–252
        Federal Reserve notes, 211, 215
        float, 227–228
        gold reserves, 225–226
        international reserves, 225–226
        liabilities, 219
        security holdings, 228
    membership of, 210
Financial innovation
    automatic teller machines, 46, 50, 58,
        233–234
    automatic transfers, 58
    credit cards, 50, 233, 234
    debit cards, 59
    electronic currency, 208
Financial markets, 103, 161–165
    asset prices, 146–169
    effects on, 263
    monetization of capital, 129,
        135–137
    sterilized intervention, 286–287
First Bank of the United States, 206–207
Fisher effect, 25–26

Fisher, Irving, 45, 53
Fixed costs, 46
Fixed penalties, 192–193
Float, 227–228
Forecast errors, 58
Foreign assets, 2, 6
Foreign exchange market intervention,
    286–287
Foreign exchange rates, 263–291
Foreign real investment, 264
Former Soviet Union, 3
Fractional reserve banking, 284
Fractional shares, 15
Free banking, 207, 208
Full-bodied coins, 213
Fundamental valuation, 159–161, 165–166
Fundamental values, 161–164
Fundamentals approach, 11, 159–161, 165
Futures markets, 164

G-7, 163
Games of chance, 62, 63
Garn-St. Germain Depository Institutions Act
    (1982), 58
General Theory, (Keynes), 148, 150, 165,
    271–273
Gesell, Silvio, 17
Glass-Steagall, 212–213
Gold, 209, 210, 211
    certificates, 226
    coins, 27
    history of, 213–217
    paper gold, 226
    reserves, 215–217, 225–226
    speculative bubble, 216
Golden Avalanche, The, 215, 238
Goldsmiths, 205
Goods and services
    new/used, 147
    payment for, 27
    purchase of, 26
    valuations of, 147
Government debt, 2, 4, 17, 101, 102,
    259–260
    bank holdings of, 135–141
    composition of, 217
    federal short-term, 222, 244
    interest-bearing, 135–141
    in money-capital models, 273–275
    Treasury vs. Federal Reserve, 219–221
Government deficit, 2, 4, 219, 269
Great Depression, 129, 210, 211–212,
    238
Greenbacks, 209, 215

Gresham's law, 214
Gross monetary assets (GMA), 135–141

Half-dollars, 229
Hamilton, Alexander, 206–207, 214
High-powered money, 223, 228, 232–233
Holding companies, 206
Homogeneous capital goods, 102
Human capital, 2–3
Hunt brothers, 215

Imperfect asset markets, and portfolio
    selection, 32–38
Imperfect liquidity, 13, 14
Imperfectly predictable assets, 16
Implicit qs, 151–152
Incentive effect, 88
Income accounts, 270
    transactions on, 39–40, 44
Income effect, 88–89
Income-velocity theory (see Velocity of money)
Independent Treasury System, 209
Indifference curves, 71–73, 86
Individual wealth (see Private wealth)
Inflation, 7, 23, 83, 165, 264, 267
Inside assets, 108
Inside debts, 108
Inside-money model, 108, 118
Interbank deposits, 255
Interest
    on checkable deposits, 234
    on demand deposits, 50, 172
    negative, 16–17
    payments, 58–59, 178–179
    on reserves, 178–179
Interest-bearing debt, 135–137
    exchanged with foreign assets, 286
Interest rates, 230
    ceilings on, 58, 172, 180, 212, 258
    on checkable accounts, 58–59
    and inflation, 165, 264
    loans, 109
Intermediate monetary aggregates, 230–231
    M2, 137
International Monetary Fund, 2, 163, 219, 226
    gold deposits, 216
    paper gold, 226
International capital-ratio requirements, 208
International reserves, 225–226
International transfer tax, 163
Interstate banking, 207
Intertemporal capital asset pricing model
    (ICAPM), 157
Inventory model, 49–50

Investment motive, 39, 56–57
Investment portfolio (*see* Portfolio selection)
Investments, 171
    compared with working balance, 41–43
    increase/decrease in banks, 182–184, 189
    multiperiod, 91–98
    preferences, 61, 86
    stock-flow model, 153–154, 270
    and uncertainty, 188–189
    (*See also* Portfolio selection)
Irreversible assets, 13, 15

Jackson, Andrew, 207
Japan, 6, 276

Keynes, John Maynard, 11, 41, 45, 56, 270
    finance motive, 54–56
    General Theory, 148, 150, 165, 271–273
    investment motive, 56–57
    precautionary motive, 57, 197
    speculative motive, 57
    stock markets, 162–164, 266
Keynes-Patinkin model, 271–273, 274
Keynesian liquidity preference curves, 247
Keynesian macroeconomics, 265, 267

Labor theory of value, 63
Legal ceilings (*see* Ceilings)
Lenders, 119–122, 259–260
Lending behavior, 108, 113–114, 119–122
Leptokurtic distributions, 71
Liabilities
    bank, 170
    business, 107–128
    Federal Reserve Bank, 219
    government, 207, 209
    household, 277
    national, 1–8, 263–291
Life cycles, 267–268
Liquidity
    of assets, 11–14
    economic effects of, 268
    imperfect, 13, 14
    perfect, 12–13
    in portfolio selection
        imperfect asset markets, 32–38
        perfect asset markets, 31–32
Loan market, 107–108
    models of, 109–117
    introduction/improvement, 115–116, 118
    no-currency model, 117–118

Loans, 115, 171–174
    collateral, 109
    credit lines, 124
    default, 109
    Federal Reserve, to banks
        adjustment credits, 226
        extended credits, 227
        seasonal credits, 227
    interest rate, 109
    margin requirement, 109
    rates, 256–259
    retention as deposits, 194
    uncertainty of returns on, 188–189
Lock boxes, 58
Long maturities, 217
Long-term securities, 217

Maastricht treaty, 216
Margin requirement, 109
Marginal expected costs, 188
Marginal physical product, 103
Marginal revenue, 175–176, 195, 256
Marginal risk, 52
Market-clearing, 168–169, 265
Market equilibrium
    financial market value of capital as
        equilibrator, 116–117
    return on capital as equilibrator, 114–116
    with currency, loans, and capital, 126–129
    with no currency, 123–126
Marketable securities, 217
Marx, Karl, 63
Mathematical expectation of return, 62
Maturities, 217
Mean-variance analysis, 69–71
Media of exchange, 27–28, 205
    competing, 233–234
Mexico, loan to, 226
Miller-Orr model of precautionary demand,
    52
Modeling, 94–95
Modigliani-Miller theorem, 148, 158
Monetarism, 105, 267
Monetary assets, 134–141
Monetary base, 223
    unborrowed, 232
    zero-interest, 267
Monetary Control Act (1980), 171
Monetary policy, 265–266, 284–290
    and banking systems, 170
    controlling money supply and debt, 221–229
    equilibrium, 263–264
    foreign exchange market intervention,
        286–287

open-market operations, 284–286
targets, 229–230
(*See also* Discount rates; Reserve
    requirements; Federal Open Market
    Committee)
Monetary theory, objectives of, 4, 5, 8, 57
(*See also* Velocity of money)
Monetized capital, 135–139
financial markets and, 129
Money, 57
acceptable means of payment, 26–28
demand for, 46
    automatic teller machines, 50, 233–234
    credit cards, 50
    changes of, 58
    finance, 39, 54–56 (*see also* Investment
      motive)
    high-powered, 223, 228, 232–233
    investment motive, 39
    money value compared to real value,
      24–25
    precautionary, 41–43, 57, 197
    speculative, 57
    stock and flow, 40–43
    transactions motive, 39–40
    transactions velocity, 39–40
    velocity of, 44–45, 49–50
Monetary aggregate, 232
M2, 137
Money-capital economy
alternative money-capital model, 273–275
Keynes-Patinkin model, 271–273
synthesis of models, 257–276
Money-demand equation (Goldfeld), 50
Money markets, 234, 236, 239
certificate of deposit (CD), 256
equilibrium in, 260–262
federal funds, 224
Money multiplier, 135, 141, 232–233, 234
Money rain, 267
Money-securities-capital economy, 279–282
Monopolies, 174
Mortgages, 164
Multiperiod investment, 91–98
consumption and portfolio choice, 97–98
portfolio choice, modeling, 94–95
Multiple-deposit expansion, 238
Mutual funds, 234

National assets (*see* National wealth)
National bank notes, 209, 212
National Banking Act, 207
National banks, 207, 210
National debt (*see* Government debt)

National Income Product Accounts (NIPA),
    219
National saving, 6–7
National wealth
accumulation of, 6–7
compared with private wealth, 5–6
consumption of, 5, 6
United States, 1–3
Negative defensive position, 176–179, 197
Negative interest, 16–17
Neoclassical theory of corporate investment,
    149, 151–152
Net free reserves, 225, 235–239
defensive position, 244–248
and rates to banks, 245
variation in, 239
Net monetary assets (NMA), 134–137
Net worth, 3–5
Neutral risks, 62
New classical economists, 265–266
New Deal, 213
New York Federal Reserve Bank, 211, 213
Newton, Isaac, 214
Noise traders, 162
Non-interest-bearing demand obligations,
    219
Non-lump-sum taxes, 268–269
Nonbanks, 258
Nonmarketable securities, 217
Normally distributed returns, 69, 70–71

Open economies, 264
Open-market operations, 228, 229, 235–238,
    284–286
Operating targets, 229–230
Opportunity costs, 185
expected, 187
Ordinal utility, 63
Organization for Economic Cooperation and
    Development (OECD), 163
Outside debts, 108
Outside-money model, 108, 118, 126

Panic, 208–210, 211–212, 214
Paper assets, 3
Paper gold, 226
Partially predictable assets, 16
Patinkin (*see* Keynes-Patinkin model)
Pecuniary costs, 197
Penalties for illiquidity, 223
fixed and proportional, 192–193
for negative defense position, 176–179,
    193–194

Perfect asset markets, and portfolio selection, 31–32
Perfect liquidity, 12
Perfect negative correlation, 78–79
Perfect positive correlation, 78–79
Perfectly predictable assets, 16, 17
Permanent wealth, 40–41
Personal checks, 27, 233, 234
Portfolio balance, 101–105
Portfolio choice (*see* Portfolio, selection)
Portfolio decisions, 270
    sequential, 96–97
Portfolio selection
    accumulation objectives, 33–38
    of banks, 171–172, 174–181, 244
    imperfect asset markets, 32–38
    modeling, 94–95
    multiperiod consumption and, 97–98
    optimal, 86–89, 96
    perfect asset markets, 31–32
    ranking, 61–63
    single future consumption date, 92–94, 96
    uncertainty, 61–68
Portfolio sequences, 32–33, 91–92
    all-cash, 93
    contingent, 92
    stationary, 94–95
    variable, 94
Portfolio shifts, 32–33
Portfolios
    expectation of return/risks, 73–86
    maximization of expected profit, 182–184
    more than two assets, 79–81
    profit, 174–181
    with safe asset, 90
    without safe asset, 90
    two-asset, 76–79
    and working balances, 54–55
Pounds sterling, British, 209, 213
"Power to tax is the power to destroy," 207
Precautionary demand, 43
    Miller-Orr model, 52
    and uncertainty, 51–53
        for banks' defensive position, 181–191
Precautionary portfolio behavior, 43
Precautionary motive, 41–43, 171, 197
Predictability of assets, 11, 16–20
    bands, 19–20
    differences in, 17
    real value, 24
    and uncertainty, 19–20
    yields, 20–21, 24
President of the United States, 213
Price-indexed instruments, 165
Prices, of assets, 9–11, 146

Primary reserves, 171
    increase of, 227
    (*See also* Reserves)
Principle of expected utility maximization, 64, 69
Private assets (*see* Private wealth)
Private capital (PC), 101, 134–135
Private net worth, 3–5
Private wealth (PW), 3–4, 137
    accumulation of, 7–8
    compared with national wealth, 5–6
    consumption of, 5–6
    decline in, 269
    effects of monetary policies on, 265–269
Privately held U.S. government interest-bearing debt (PHGD), 135–137
Privatization, 3
Psychological costs, 197
Purchasing power, 25–26
    measurement of, 23–24
Purchasing power bonds, 26

q ratio, 106, 116, 148, 149, 264
    saving-investment nexus, 155–156
    stock-flow model, 153–154
    stock market compared with implicit, 151–152
    Tobin's q, 151–152
q theory of investment, 150–151
Quadratic utility, 69–70
Quantity theory of money, 53–54

Ranking of portfolio, 61–63
    and expectation of utility, 62–66
    and mathematical expectation of return, 62
    and neutral risk, 62
    and risk averters, 62
    and risk lovers, 62
Rate of depreciation, 102
Rate of return, 21, 156, 258
    zero, 16–17
Ratio of market value to replacement cost (*see* q ratio)
Ratio of reserves to deposits (*see* Reserve requirements)
Real return, 24
Real values, 23–24
Recession, 209–210
Regulations, 206, 207
    of banks, 182
    chartering banks, 172, 209, 213
    of deposit interest rates, 212

Rent of capital, 102–103
Rental market, 103
Replacement costs, 148
Repos, 222
Reproducible assets, 2
Required reserve ratios (*see* Reserve
    requirements)
Reserve balances, 224
Reserve base, 234–239
Reserve requirements, 172, 216–217, 222–224,
    235–239
  Canada, 178–179
  ratios, 194–195, 208, 229
    changes in, 289–290
  risk-based, 244
  United Kingdom, 178–179
Reserve tests, 223–224
Reserve-to-deposit ratio, 229
Reserves, 171–172, 229–230
  accounting for, 224–225
  adjustment of
    competition for deposits, 255
    federal funds market, 249–254
    interbank deposits, 255
  borrowed, 224–225
  changes in supply of, 225–229
  effects on, 228–229
  excess, 225
  interest on, 178–179
  primary, 171, 227
  purpose of, 181, 182
  required (*see* Reserve requirements)
  secondary, 171, 222, 239, 243–244
  supply of, 222–225
  total, 224–229
  unborrowed, 224–225, 228, 229, 234–238
Returns
  on assets, 11, 21–23, 28, 156
  normally distributed, 69, 70–71
  real and nominal, 24
Reversibility, of assets, 11, 13–15
Ricardo-Barro equivalence theorem,
    266–269
Risk, 62
  averters, 62
  and diversification, 73–76
  expectations of return and, 73–76
  lovers, 62, 67–68
  measurement of as standard deviation of
    return, 69–71
  neutrality, 67, 196–197
  systematic, 157
  undiversifiable, 156–158
Risk-averse behavior, 68, 98–99
Risk-averse borrowers, 132

Risk aversion, 196–197
  absolute, 68, 99–100
  characterizations of, 67–68
  relative, 68, 99
Risk-based capital requirements, 244
Risk-expectation, indifference curves, 71–73
Risk-loving behavior, 67–68
Risk premium on asset returns, 156–157
Risk ranking (*see* Ranking)
Risk-seeking borrowers, 131–132
Risk-weighted assets, 244
Riskless assets, 89–90
Risky assets, 89
Robertson, D. H., 54
Roosevelt, Franklin D., 54, 211, 215
Royal Mint, 214
Rural banks, 206–208, 227

Safety margin, 208
Saving, 7
  decrease in, 269
Saving-consumption decision, 98
Saving-investment nexus, 155–156
Savings and loan associations (S & Ls)
  failures of, 182
  history of, 206
Savings banks, compared with commercial
    banks, 206
Savings bonds, 217
Savings deposits, 12
Schumpeterian phenomena, 149
Seasonal credits, 227
Second Bank of the United States, 207
  demise of, 209
Secondary reserves, 171, 222
  defensive position, 244–248
  need for, 239, 243–244
  Treasury bills, 243
  (*See also* Reserves)
Securities, 217
  corporate, 148–149
  Federal Reserve, 228
  market abuses, 212–213
  nonmarketable, 217
  transactions, 155
  Treasury, 217
Seignorage, 267
Separation theorem, 89–90, 126,
    166–167
Service charges, 50–51
Shareowners, 206
Shifting costs, 32–33
Short maturities, 217
Short-term debt, 243–244

Short-term securities, 217
Silver, 213–215
Silver dollar of Spanish America, 213
Single-period portfolios, 96
Smart cards, 208
Soviet Union (*see* Former Soviet Union)
Speculations, 162–63
    gold, 216
Speculative assets, 10–11, 30
Speculative motive, 57
Speculators, 11
Square root rule, 49–50
St. Petersburg paradox, 63
    Bernoulli's solution, 63, 64
Stamped money, 17
Standard deviation, 69–71
State bank notes, 209
State banks, 207, 210
Stationary discount rates, 29–30
Stationary sequence, 94–95
Steady-state equilibrium, 154
Sterilized intervention, 286–287
Stock-flow model of investment, 153–154,
    270
Stock market
    crashes, 162
    qs, 151–52
Strong, Benjamin, 211, 212
Substitution effect, 88, 89
Susan Anthony coin, 229
Sweden, branch banking, 174
Synchronization of outlays and receipts, 44
Systematic risk, 157

Takeovers, 162
Tangible assets, 5–6
    inventory of, 1–2
Tax liabilities, 269
Taxes, 266–268
    bank notes, 207
    inflation, 267
    international transfer tax, 163
    non-lump-sum, 268–269
Theorems
    equivalence (Ricardo-Barro), 266–269
    separation, 89–90, 126, 166–167
    Modigliani-Miller, 148, 158
Theory of asset values, 10
Theory of corporate investment, neoclassical,
    149, 151–152
Theory of efficient financial markets, 10–11
Theory of inventories, 49–50
Theory of investment, q theory, 150–151
Theory of value, 63

Time deposits, 46–50, 56, 180, 182, 193
    marketable certificates of, 256
    rates of return, 258
Timing, and accumulation objectives,
    33–34
Tobin's q, 151–152
Token coins, 213, 214
Total reserves, 224
    changes in, 225–229
Transactions
    costs, 51
    and demand for money, 46–50, 233–234
    deposits, 180
    federal funds, 254
    income account vs. capital account, 39–40,
        44
    international transfer tax, 163
    security, 155
Transactions motive, 39–40, 54–56
Transactions velocity, 39–40, 234
Transferable demand obligations, 217
Treasury (*see* United States Treasury)
Treasury bills (*see* United States Treasury
    bills)
Treaty of Maastricht, 216
Two-asset economics
    capital market equilibrium, 105–107
    money-capital models, 271–273
    portfolio balance, 102–105
    portfolios, 76–79
Two-parameter distributions, 70, 71

Unborrowed monetary base, 232
Unborrowed reserves, 224–225, 228, 229,
    234–238
Uncertainty, 19–20, 61–62
    capital, 103–104
    deposits, 181–191, 202–204
    effects of, 185–189
    loans/investments, 188
    portfolio selection, 61–68
    and precautionary demand, 51–53
Undiversifiable risk, 156–158
United Kingdom (*see* England)
United States Congress, reserve requirements,
    216–217
United States Federal Reserve System (*see*
    Federal Reserve System)
United States monetary and banking system
    branch banking, 174
    central banking, 178, 207
    debt (*see* Government debt)
    deregulation, 206
    federal balance sheet, 218–219

316   Index

free banking, 207, 208
history, 205–208
  Banking Act (1935), 213
  Bretton Woods, 216–217
  currency, 213–215
  Federal Reserve Act (1913), 210–211
  gold and silver, 213–217
  Great Depression, 210, 211–212, 226
  interest rates, 230
  panics, 208–210, 211–212, 214
  reforms, 212–213
interstate banking, 207
national wealth, 1–3
privately held government interest-bearing debt (PHGD), 135–137
regulations, 206, 207
reserve requirements (*see* Reserve requirements)
United States Treasury, 27
  control of currency, 227
  debt (*see* Government debt)
  Exchange Stabilization Fund, 226
  gold (*see* Gold)
  liabilities, 170, 207, 209
  securities, 217
    indexed, 26
United States Treasury bills, 28, 29, 217, 222
  bill rate, 236–238, 247–254, 256–258
  as secondary reserves, 243
Used-good markets, 147
Utility
  concept of, 63
  expected, maximization of, 62–66
    and mean-variance analysis, 69
  household, 267–269
  schedules, 62–63, 91
    cardinal, 63–64
    examples of, 64–69
    ordinal, 63
  theorists, 63

Valuation, 158–159
  of assets, 11–14
  businesses, 147–152
  capital assets, 147–155, 264
  corporate capital, 147–153
  earning assets, 148–149
  fundamental, 159–161, 165–166

new and used goods, 147
present value of future returns, 28–30
securities market, 148–149
(*See also* q ratio)
Value
  money, 57
    compared to real value, 24–25
  real, 23–24
  of yields, 20–23
Variable portfolio sequence, 94
Velocity of money, 49–50
  income, 40
  traditional explanation of, 44–45
  transactions, 39–40
Velocity theorists, 45

Walras's law, 114
Wealth
  accumulation of, 6–7
  consumption of, 5–6, 270
  national (*see* National wealth)
  net worth, 3–5
  permanent wealth, 40–41
  private (*see* Private wealth)
  valuation (*see* Valuation)
Whitehead, Alfred, 57
Wicksell, K., 264
Wicksellian process, 264, 273
Wildcat banks, 207
Withdrawals, 172, 181–182
  effect on reserves, 228–229
Working balance, 39, 40–43, 46
  compared with investment balance, 41–43
  definition of, 43–44
  demand for, 43–45
  penalties for too high/low, 43
  in portfolios, 54–55
World War I, 135
World War II, 130, 135–137, 217, 230

Yield, 11, 20–23, 28
  and appreciation, 21–22, 28
  real value of, 23–24
  and return, 20–23

Zero defensive position, 177, 180
Zero-coupon bonds, 217
Zero rate of return, 16–17